⸙ Thinking Europe ⸙

MAKING SENSE OF HISTORY
Studies in Historical Cultures
General Editor: Stefan Berger
Founding Editor: Jörn Rüsen

Bridging the gap between historical theory and the study of historical memory, this series crosses the boundaries between both academic disciplines and cultural, social, political and historical contexts. In an age of rapid globalisation, which tends to manifest itself on an economic and political level, locating the cultural practices involved in generating its underlying historical sense is an increasingly urgent task.

Recent volumes:

Volume 46
Thinking Europe: A History of the European Idea since 1800
Mats Andrén

Volume 45
Borders in East and West: Transnational and Comparative Perspectives
Edited by Stefan Berger and Nobuya Hashimoto

Volume 44
Historical Reenactment: New Ways of Experiencing History
Edited by Mario Carretero, Brady Wagoner and Everardo Perez-Manjarrez

Volume 43
Dynamics of Emigration: Émigré Scholars and the Production of Historical Knowledge in the 20th Century
Edited by Stefan Berger and Philipp Müller

Volume 42
Transcending the Nostalgic: Landscapes of Postindustrial Europe beyond Representation
Edited by George S. Jaramillo and Juliane Tomann

Volume 41
Territory, State and Nation: The Geopolitics of Rudolf Kjellén
Edited by Ragnar Björk and Thomas Lundén

Volume 40
Analysing Historical Narratives: On Academic, Popular and Educational Framings of the Past
Edited by Stefan Berger, Nicola Brauch and Chris Lorenz

Volume 39
Postwar Soldiers: Historical Controversies and West German Democratization, 1945–1955
Jörg Echternkamp

Volume 38
Constructing Industrial Pasts: Heritage, Historical Culture and Identity in Regions Undergoing Structural Economic Transformation
Edited by Stefan Berger

Volume 37
The Engaged Historian: Perspectives on the Intersections of Politics, Activism and the Historical Profession
Edited by Stefan Berger

For a full volume listing, please see the series page on our website:
http://www.berghahnbooks.com/series/making-sense-of-history

THINKING EUROPE

A History of the European Idea since 1800

Mats Andrén

berghahn
NEW YORK · OXFORD
www.berghahnbooks.com

First published in 2023 by
Berghahn Books
www.berghahnbooks.com

© 2023, 2025 Mats Andren
First paperback edition published in 2025

All rights reserved. Except for the quotation of short passages
for the purposes of criticism and review, no part of this book
may be reproduced in any form or by any means, electronic or
mechanical, including photocopying, recording, or any information
storage and retrieval system now known or to be invented,
without written permission of the publisher.

Library of Congress Cataloging-in-Publication Data

Names: Andrén, Mats, author.
Title: Thinking Europe : a history of the European idea since 1800 / Mats Andrén.
Description: [New York] : Berghahn Books, 2023. | Series: Making sense of
  history, volume 46 | Includes bibliographical references and index.
Identifiers: LCCN 2022019395 (print) | LCCN 2022019396 (ebook) | ISBN
  9781800735699 (hardback) | ISBN 9781800735712 (open access ebook)
Subjects: LCSH: Europe--History--Philosophy. | Europe--Politics and
  government. | European federation. | Europe--Boundaries--History. | Europe-
  -Economic integration. | European cooperation. | National characteristics,
  European.
Classification: LCC D299 .A515 2023 (print) | LCC D299 (ebook) | DDC
  940.2/7--dc23/eng/20220518
LC record available at https://lccn.loc.gov/2022019395
LC ebook record available at https://lccn.loc.gov/2022019396

British Library Cataloguing in Publication Data

A catalogue record for this book is available from the British Library

The electronic open access publication of *Thinking Europe: A History of the European
Idea since 1800* has been made possible through the generous financial support of
the University of Gothenburg.

This work is published subject to a Creative Commons
Attribution Noncommercial No Derivatives 4.0 License.
The terms of the license can be found at http://
creativecommons.org/licenses/by-nc-nd/4.0/. For uses
beyond those covered in the license contact Berghahn Books.

ISBN 978-1-80073-569-9 hardback
ISBN 978-1-80539-726-7 paperback
ISBN 978-1-80073-570-5 epub
ISBN 978-1-80073-571-2 web pdf

https://doi.org/10.3167/9781800735699

Contents

Preface	vii
Acknowledgements	ix
Introduction	1

Part I. Unity and Borders (1800–1914)

Chapter 1. Dreaming of Unity	17
Chapter 2. Longing for Borders	46
Chapter 3. Looking for Common Ground	78
Chapter 4. Performing Communality	104

Part II. Crisis and Decline (1914–1945)

Chapter 5. Passage to a New Europe: The First World War	133
Chapter 6. Fearing Crisis	166
Chapter 7. Organising for Europe	189

Part III. Integration and Identity (1945–)

Chapter 8. Claiming European Unity and a Europe of Nations	227
Chapter 9. Elevating European Awareness	268

Conclusion	298
Bibliography	309
Index	343

Preface

As is typical for someone of my generation, the gradual dissolution of communism in the 1980s and its sudden collapse in 1989–91 changed my outlook in that I began to recognise the importance of issues related to Europe, nations and nationalism, in both the past and present. This was not least because the threat of oppression and violence was lurking beneath Europe's national revivals, reminding us of nationalism's troubling history. Following the completion of my thesis on the history of ideas at the University of Gothenburg in 1990, I engaged as a teacher and researcher in the emerging field of European studies, enthralled by the entanglements of Europe and its internal borders. At the Centre for European Studies at Gothenburg University (CERGU), we began to explore the issue of cultural borders more deeply, observing the paradox of the increasing impact of cultural borders that developed despite ongoing economic, legal and political integration. We hosted a conference in 2007 and published the proceedings in *Cultural Identities and National Borders* (2009). In the period 2009–13, our international network held some remarkable workshops, which resulted in the Berghahn anthology *Cultural Borders of Europe*. In the wake of these experiences, I saw the possibility of writing a book on the subject.

In addition, inspiration for this book came from travelling in Europe. I have always loved visiting bookshops when abroad, as they reveal something about their cities, and offer a glimpse into the national mind. Starting in the early 2010s, I began to observe a growing number of books about European crises, conveying warnings and predictions of the imminent collapse of the European Union. No matter whether I was in Oslo or Porto, in Florence, Munich or Cambridge, they were always on the bookstore shelves. Local authors – Austrian, Czech, Dutch, Irish, Spanish, etc. – wrote about the topic. I asked myself whether this growing interest might be indicating the end of European integration or, conversely, stronger Europeanisation. Moreover, I observed that the literature was unconsciously reiterating themes from the intellectual history of Europe.

Work on this book began with a short draft written in the final weeks of 2013 when public attention was largely directed towards the Euro crisis, which was threatening to destroy the European Union. As I continued writing drafts of short chapters of what I believed would be a quickly written, minor book, 2014 and 2015 brought the migration and refugee crisis, and a worrisome rise in nationalistic mindsets, extending far beyond the traditional nationalist groups and parties. I arrived in Cambridge in 2016 on the day after the Brexiteers had won the referendum. Clearly, nationalist sentiments were strong. From 2017 onwards, I have been fortunate to be able to dedicate a substantial amount of time to the research and writing of this book. Since then, additional events regarding Europe and its borders have occurred, including the Covid-19 pandemic that started in 2020 and Russia's invasion of Ukraine in 2022. One blessing of writing an intellectual history of the idea of Europe is its contemporary relevance, bringing energy to my work and offering new conundrums on which to reflect.

Acknowledgements

My academic home, the Department of Literature, History of Ideas, and Religion, and its directors – currently Katarina Leppänen and before her Cecilia Rosengren – have frequently encouraged me to write this book. I am grateful to Riksbanken Jubileumsfond for granting me a sabbatical year, which proved to be most valuable for completing the project.

I owe a great deal to everyone with whom I have discussed aspects of the concept of Europe. I have been privileged to have ongoing discussions when supervising doctoral students in the history of ideas, and when reviewing contributions to special issues with colleagues from my department Literature, History of Ideas, and Religion (LIR) as well as from the Center for European Studies at Gothenburg University (CERGU), and from other universities in Europe: Linda Berg (GU), Ettore Costa (GU), Ben Dorfman (Aalborg University), Hjalmar Falk (GU), Klas Grinell (GU), Ann Ighe (GU), Anton Jansson (GU), Karolina Enquist Källgren (Stockholm University), Katarina Leppänen (GU), Rebecka Lettevall (Malmö University), Julia Nordblad (Uppsala University), Jens Norrby (GU), Jacopo Perazzoli (Università degli Studi di Milano), Sune Bechmann Pedersen (Lund University), Brian Shaev (Leiden University) and Jon Wittrock (Malmö University). I am lucky to have colleagues who make valuable comments at seminar presentations, give feedback on drafts, engage in individual exchanges and remark on possible paths to explore. All their input has been invaluable, as has their encouragement to pursue and complete the project. For this help, I wish to thank Lisbeth Aggestam (GU), Claes Alvstam (GU), Tove Andersson (GU), Michael Azar (GU), Björn Billing (GU), Henrik Björck (GU), Alexandra Bousiou (GU), Joris van Eijnatten (Universiteit Utrecht), Marius Hentea (GU), Gustav Holmberg (GU), Adrian Hyde-Price (GU), Pasi Ihalainen (University of Jyväskylä), Johan Järlehed (GU), Pavol Jacubec

(GU), Werner Jeanrond (University of Oslo), Maria Johansen (GU), Johan Kärnfeldt (GU), Alma Nordenstam (Karolinska Institutet), Axel Nordenstam (University of Stockholm), Anna Nordenstam (GU), Olof Larsson (GU), Bo Lindberg (GU), Rutger Lindahl (GU), Fredrik Portin (GU), Christine Quarfood (GU), Arne Rasmusson (GU), Cecilia Rosengren (GU), Ola Sigurdson (GU), Urban Strandberg (GU), Ingmar Söhrman (GU), Katharina Vajta (GU), Michael Wintle (University of Amsterdam), Martin Wiklund (University of Stockholm) and Karin Zelano (GU).

CERGU has long provided a focal point for European research in Gothenburg. The lively exchanges at breakfast, working seminars, guest seminars, and conferences create a perfect environment for research and reflection on European issues that by necessity need a multidisciplinary setting. Importantly, for the last few years, this has been made possible by CERGU's directors and coordinators: Linda Berg, Klas Grinell, Ann-Kristin Jonasson, Birgitta Jännebring, Rutger Lindahl, Andreas Moberg and Angie Sohlman.

The final manuscript benefited from three anonymous reviewers' constructive and helpful reports, from Angie Sohlberg's careful language editing, and from the exactitude and great understanding of history writing of the anonymous copyeditor at Proper English AB. I also wish to thank the whole editorial staff at Berghahn Books for guiding the manuscript into a published volume, especially senior editor Chris Chappell for being willing to take my proposal further, editorial associate Sulaiman Ahmad for help with a range of practical issues, production editor Caroline Kuhtz, and Nigel Smith for the sharp eye during the final editing of the chapters. Any remaining shortcomings of the work are my sole responsibility.

The material for the two sections on Central Europe and 'Mitteleuropa' in chapters 2 and 5 was presented extensively in my Swedish book *Att frambringa det uthärdliga: Studier kring, gränser, nationalism och individualism i Centraleuropa*. Some material in the sections on citizenship and local self-government in chapter 4 appeared in my Swedish book on local self-government in Sweden, *Den europeiska blicken och det lokala självstyrets värden*. Some of the material in chapter 8 appeared in 'Europe of Nations, Europe without Nationalism', in the journal *History of European Ideas* 46(1) (2020), 13–24. Some of the material for chapters 8 and 9 emerged in the chapter I co-authored with Joris van Ejnatten, 'Nationhood between European Unity and the Nation State', in Pasi Ihalainen and Antero Holmila (eds), *Nationalism and Internationalism Intertwined: A European History of Concepts beyond Nation States* (New York: Berghahn Books, 2022), 223–46, as well as in my chapter, 'The Controversial Concept of European Identity', in the 2017 volume *Cultural Borders of Europe: Narratives, Concepts and Practices in the Present and the Past*, edited by Mats Andrén, Thomas Lindkvist, Ingmar Söhrman and Katharina Vajta (New York: Berghahn Books, 2017), 159–69.

Introduction

Like most Europeans in the early 1900s, my grandmother lived in a multinational empire. She grew up, as many others did, in an area with more than one language. To communicate with people on the Baltic island of Hiumaa, one would need to know Estonian, which was spoken by most of the farmers, Russian, to communicate with the administration, and German, to talk to the estate owners – and there were also some Swedish-speaking farmers. By the time she married, she was a citizen of the Republic of Estonia, one of many new states that had emerged in Europe after the First World War. She lived in a proclaimed nation state that comprised several ethnic minorities. During the Second World War, my grandmother, like many Europeans, experienced her country's loss of independence, and she fled with her husband and children. She settled in Sweden and died only months before the re-emergence of Estonia as a sovereign state in 1991. Her life not only spanned national borders but the shifting of the international border between Eastern and Western Europe.

The nineteenth and twentieth centuries saw a range of upheavals that changed people's lives in Europe, during which notions of a new Europe were present: for Napoleon as well as for the victors in Vienna in 1815; in the revolutionary year of 1848; during the two world wars and their aftermaths; and, finally, after the fall of communism in 1991. A 'new Europe' connoted unity, peace and fairness, but could also insinuate the dominance of one or more powers. Often, it became associated with European superiority – more for some, less for others. Students of European history are well aware that these periods also encompassed surges of nations and nationalism: 'the spring

---

Notes for this section begin on page 13.

of nations' in 1848; an avalanche of declarations of national independence marking the final year of the First World War; and nationalism emerging after the dismantling of communism in Central Europe. Evidently, the visions of a new Europe and the ventures to establish borders came in pairs.

This leads to the central argument of my book, which is that the concept of Europe is intrinsically associated with unity and borders within Europe. For well over two centuries, calls for unification have met arguments for national borders, triggering entanglements and contestations. In the early 1800s, not only were the dreams of Europe becoming 'one large nation', as it was put by August Wilhelm Schlegel,[1] of interest, but so were hopes voiced by Germaine de Staël 'to give birth to those great existences of mankind, which we call nations'.[2] In the late 1910s and early 1920s, Tomáš Masaryk's call for a 'New Europe' of democratic and independent nation states and H.G. Wells's talk of the dawning age of nationalities met with critical discussions concerning Europe's many borders, e.g. by Julien Benda and José Ortega y Gasset.[3]

The first objective of this book is to examine and recount the intellectual paths that feed into the concept of Europe. The book offers a comprehensive approach, beginning with the emergence of a more visionary concept of Europe in the political turmoil and intellectual crossroads of the early nineteenth century, and continuing to the present. I illustrate these conflicting political visions and diverging interests, as well as distinctions between perceptions emerging from different parts of Europe. The second objective is to explain the post-war concept of Europe and its contemporary meanings. This is only possible if we view the historical understanding of Europe that takes into account not only unity, but borders. A grasp of the relevant intellectual history is essential to understanding the processes that took place before the 1950s, and how they shaped the mind of the post-war period, as well as to assessing how historical perceptions and representations define contemporary Europe and affect current issues. A longer historical perspective is also necessary for considering the public discourse, illuminating the civic debate and supporting the effectiveness of decision making to avoid past mistakes and assimilate past achievements.

Currently, although Europe is considered a unity, it is simultaneously comprehended in terms of its borders and divisions – a potentially explosive combination, if not carefully managed. In fact, Europe is unifying and dividing at the same time. The twentieth century saw a doubling of the number of sovereign European nation states. Add to this the territories with extensive self-governance, such as the former Danish colony of Greenland, as well as regional self-rule in Belgium, Great Britain and Spain, and it is difficult to avoid acknowledging a genuine state-making tendency related to national sentiments. In other contributions, I have emphasised that previous decades have seen an increasing emphasis on cultural borders.[4] This is also a question of quantity when we consider the upswing in Europe's minority languages and cultures such as Gaelic and Sápmi, the substantial numbers of Europeans who belong to non-Christian religions, and those who speak languages of non-European origin. Contemporary European states face a variety of cultural borders within existing political borders. On the other hand, while the number of members of the European Economic Community (EEC)/European Community (EC)/European Union (EU) has risen from six in 1958 to twenty-seven at the beginning of the 2020s, we may acknowledge the integration tendency, as well. Moreover, the deepening of integration further indicates a tendency towards unity, apart from the recognition of nation states and national sentiments.

The EU addresses this duality concerning European integration with its slogan 'Unity in Diversity'. Clearly, although European unity and nations may seem contradictory, these are the conditions necessary for integration. European integration, which would not be needed if not for the existence of nation states and borders (be they cultural or territorial), takes place under the guise of a conceived community. To understand the implications of this, we have to find the reasons for this way of thinking in history. Indeed, long before the EU, European integration occurred through transnational ideas, associations, and even movements, as well as exchanges and learning from each other across both territorial and administrative borders.

Attempting to explain nationalism and integration as different phases of European history would be a mistake. In such a narrative, nationalism came first, followed by integration and an evolution towards unification. To present integration as only parenthetical would also be a mistake. Both perspectives are incorrect. The first fails to acknowledge the long intersection of European integration and nation building, of Europeanness and national identity. It represents what Ariane Chebel D'Appollonia calls 'a false sacralization of Europe'. Bo Stråth rejects it as a 'teleological understanding of Europe as a self-propelling project on a steady advance towards a predetermined goal'. The second narrative fails to pay homage to the advances achieved through integration, and evokes a fear of new wars on the continent. For D'Appollonia, it is another 'false sacralization', this time of the nation. Thus, Bo Stråth underscores 'a need for a new narrative about Europe'. By offering a thorough examination of the intellectual history of the concept of Europe, my book provides the necessary input for a new narrative.

This intellectual history can explain our present hopes, fears and concerns regarding Europe. Recently, we have seen much confusion and discontent, with the ideal of European unification clashing with the interests of some nation states. In the 2010s, this was demonstrated by a seemingly unending list of divergences, mostly regarding issues of immigration and financial regulations connected with the Euro. In the public debate, calls for a stronger union stand against the protection of national sovereignty, and the drive towards a European super state is encountering emerging nationalisms. Importantly, historical perceptions and representations of Europe are of the utmost importance in order to understand the mindset that paved the way for contemporary Europe. Robert M. Dainotto gives a timely argument for this: 'It is what has been said and written for around three centuries about and around Europe that still determines what we think and do about it; what our dailies report; and what our policy makers decide'.[5] It is striking – and rather uncomfortable – that, with very few exceptions, the vast majority of literary publications on EU crises over the last decade have hardly taken note of the historical legacy of the ideas that are in use.

Thinking Europe: The History of a Concept

Since around 1800, the notion of Europe has posed as a new attraction for Europeans – or, to put it more bluntly, it has occupied our minds and framed how we conceive the world. For many centuries before, the concept of Europe connoted a geographical continent and was only occasionally invoked in political contexts. Since 1800, the concept has become crucial to political thinking in Europe, spreading widely and becoming affixed to other concepts, such as civilisation and individualism, thereby redefining previous contexts. Not only was there a civilisation but there was a European civilisation; not only individualism but a European individualism. The magnetism of the concept was felt far and wide, with implications for both culture and politics. Europe became associated with claims to preserve existing society as well as to transform it, with national ambitions and with ideas regarding relationships between European neighbours and the rest of the world. Yet, Europe has never been easy to define: does it exist, is it lost, or is Europe something that ought to be built? Is it characterised by shared traits or by dividing borders? By history or by values? By Christianity or by thriving trade and innovative individuals? By success and victories or by threats from the outside? By progress or by steady decline and acute crisis?

No doubt, Europe is not only a historical but also a political concept. Europe may appear to be a geographical description, but when seeking its exact connotation, an essentially normative concept emerges. Even in terms of geographical definition, it is impossible to separate ideological meanings from the concept of Europe. Is Russia a European country or not? What about Turkey? In the present, Europe often signifies the EU, which highlights the association with normative values. In a similar vein, key contemporary contestations concern the issue of European values, what they imply, and whether member states adopt them. Hence, the linguistic classification of the word 'Europe' as a noun is insufficient. Europe is also seen as a verb, indicating the contestations surrounding normative values in combination with performative claims of how to manage disputes and diverging interests.

Previous research has typically paid special attention to common traits of the idea of European unity, such as peace, prosperity and cooperation against common enemies. Often, this research traces a certain logic through the centuries, which is similar to that of post-war European integration: a certain degree of national sovereignty must be ceded to common institutions in exchange for peace, welfare and the common good.[6] Research has reflected the new interest in the idea of Europe since 1990, citing the proximity of the European integration political project to 'the idea of Europe', 'the idea of European unity', 'the European idea', and 'European identity'. A contribution often referred to is Gerard Delanty's *Inventing Europe*, which typically interprets the idea of Europe as 'a universalising idea under the perpetual threat of fragmentation within European society', and 'a unifying theme in a cultural framework of values as opposed to a mere political norm or name for a geo-political region'. He connects the European idea with common 'cultural frames of reference', and associates it with post-war integration.[7] In the anthology *The Idea of Europe*, Anthony Pagden makes a similar connection in defining the idea of Europe as 'determining features of . . . a political and cultural domain', relating it to the contemporary hope and possibility of developing a European identity and a sense of belonging to a shared community.[8] In the same volume, Ariane Chebel D'Appollonia contends that 'the European Union must become a visual and compelling identity'.[9] These partisan approaches share the variability of and continuous ongoing debate about the meaning of the idea of Europe. Recently, we have found more attention to the association of the concept of Europe with division, and some research stresses the history of manifold borders within Europe, noting that recent decades have presented us with both unification and an increased emphasis on borders, especially cultural ones.[10] However, much recent research keeps a focus on Europe as a unifying idea, but engages with it through new perspectives, forgotten voices, and neglected materials. These contributors are well aware of the risk that comes with formulating a linear history of an idea that is growing into maturity. To escape such a trap, they criticise Eurocentric ideas and include views that previous histories tended to omit. For instance, Patrick Pasture's *Imagining European Unity*, which concentrates on the idea of peace and on ideas concerning the institutional organisation of Europe, extends the historical list of plans of unification.[11] Consequently, we need to take precautions to avoid presenting

European unity and European integration as old notions that finally broke through in the 1950s, and since then have been further refined and won the recognition of most European nations, or as representations of society's natural development into ever greater units.

When we look at the history of the concept of Europe, the focus is not on the EU, its institutions, policies or treaties. Certainly, it is vital to note that the EU is an existing institution that has central functions to fulfil for contemporary European society. It is the main framework for shared legal, economic and political actions. As such, it is also an arena for political struggles, legal disputes and economic competition. European integration redefines key societal concepts such as state and sovereignty, it struggles to find legitimacy by addressing democracy and citizenship, and it aims to encompass the diversity of national identities. Still, since around the 2010s we have seen divisions that fuel a legacy of hierarchies within the EU – between north and south, and east and west. As of the early 2020s, illiberalism and right-wing extremism have established themselves all around Europe. Britain, one of Europe's major countries, has left the EU, initially bringing the member states together but leaving the question of whether others will follow. The Covid-19 pandemic has effectively highlighted the temptation to maintain national borders. Accordingly, the EU has become an arena and an object for ideological struggles. In these, the concept of Europe plays an essential role, and today it is often represented in terms of European integration and European identity. Implemented in phases, we have no definite answer as to what integration will look like in the future. At stake are questions about Europe's past and future, its structure and place in the world, and the various meanings of Europe. My approach is to critically examine the different meanings of the concept of Europe, with respect to how it has changed over time, how it has been controversial, and how it has been the object of different opinions.

In presenting a historical narrative of the concept of Europe, this book also addresses the idea of European unification in the post-war period. Historians have long discussed whether European integration began as a scheme to overcome the nation state and establish a federal European system, or as a measure to strengthen the nation state. After thirty years, Alan Milward's groundbreaking historical study continues to be inspirational, revealing the national interests in the making of the European Community. The supranational institutions were seen as paving the way for strengthening the nation state: when sovereignty was transferred to the European Commission, it was because the national benefits were deemed rather significant. Not only the legislators but also the citizens of the member states accepted in practice or passively, with enthusiasm or in silence, that the construction of the nation state and the creation of the EEC/EC went hand in hand. Some 'national policies aiming at national reassertions had to be internationalised in order to make them viable'; consequentially, 'the reinvigorated nation-state had to choose the surrender of a degree of national sovereignty to sustain its reassertion'.[12] Still, Milward leaves a question without a convincing answer: How could this combination meet with such approval? Milward's answer is the Second World War, and my study confirms that changes did indeed take place in the concept of Europe that facilitated post-war integration. However, he does not take into account the long-term causes. His thesis of the collapse of the nation state in the 1940s omits that the mindset was already somewhat prepared, and that the concept of Europe had contrasting aspects long before the post-war period began. New states that favoured the ideal of national sovereignty emerged during the interbellum period. Yet, this same period saw an increase in the discourse on European cooperation and unification, as recently demonstrated by researchers. However, we should also take the long-term history into account. Concepts, narratives, practices of cooperation, and even integration were at hand throughout the nineteenth century.

My book aims to shed light on post-war European integration by interrogating the intellectual history of the discourse on Europe. In sharp opposition to Andrew Moravcsik, whose famous book, *Choice for Europe*, explicitly downgrades the impact of ideas, I say we cannot understand the history of Europe without taking into account how people were thinking about Europe.[13] For institutional arrangements of European integration to be possible, and to define much of post-war political history, the integration must be in accordance with overall thinking about how we can accommodate Europe and all of its components.

We need to be cautious when examining the concept of Europe, and its traditional associations with progress and a higher standard of European development. Seminal works on European history demonstrate the existence of authoritarian models of governance and political thinking throughout the previous two centuries – besides exclusionary nationalism, which has sometimes veered towards racism and notions of ethnic cleansing. These works reinforce the fact that post-Enlightenment European history should not be recounted as a simple progression towards freedom and democracy.[14] In addition, Luisa Passerini has forcefully stressed the need to examine the cultural legacy of Europe: 'We can no longer share the type of Europeanism that existed in the past. Eurocentric and male-centred, we must find new forms of Europeanness that allow the full respect of differences. This means we cannot avoid passing through a critique of Europe's cultural legacy'.[15] In recognising differences, Passerini urges us to acknowledge and criticise the fact that 'European identity has long included hierarchies and exclusions – a "Europe-Europe" and a "lesser Europe"'.[16]

Thinking Europe: An Intellectual History

To present a new history of the concept of Europe, I make use of crucial advances in intellectual history. First, in reading the ideas in the context of each period, I have unearthed disputed meanings and values with respect to changing opinions. Second, in conceiving the concept as essentially open to competing definitions marked by different spaces of experience and horizons of expectation, I understand the concept of Europe as situated between remembrances of the past and anticipations of the future. Third, I frame and interpret the case as a transnational piece of history. Together, I rely on the three main advances utilised within intellectual history: the contextual, the conceptual, and transnational turns.[17]

To a significant extent, my book applies the lessons of transnational history. Gerard Delanty recently inquired into a transnational approach to the idea of Europe, saying 'that a more explicitly developed transnational approach to the European heritage might reveal a different and more compelling account of the past that would give substance to the European cultural heritage as a unity in diversity'.[18] I consider my book to offer such an account from the field of intellectual history. Beginning with Europe as a distinct theme in the nineteenth and twentieth centuries, the book examines debates and discourses that transcend borders. It combines Europeanising procedures with the history of mutual learning processes.[19] European history reveals an exchange of shared values that has helped to guide European countries in the construction of their societies. Europeanisation took place long before it was institutionalised through the EU, and can be seen in both the similarity of common institutional settings and how European countries mirror each other. They largely imitate each other in an overarching quest for modernisation, and a more distinct quest for approximation, which begins with increased trade and new means of communication.[20] For intellectual history, the learning processes concern the dissemination of key concepts (e.g. Europe), theories, ways of thinking, and values (e.g. nationalism), as well as the comprehension of them all as European. This is a Europeanisation that concerns common intellectual inspirations to argue for changes in particular communities. It entails adopting similar values, learning from others, and taking the same direction. Moreover, it is about imposing on others: it justifies European supremacy abroad and defends the dominance of the main powers within Europe. Consequently, the international turn in history and, more specifically, its transnational approaches within intellectual history, influence my research.[21] I recognise the many academic articles in recent years that have drawn on transnational history and accompanying concepts, not least concerning the interwar period.

There is an obvious risk that studies of the concept of Europe may offer homogenising interpretations, especially when the object is European unity. Therefore, it is of certain interest to expose hierarchical orders in the comprehension of Europe. In this, I am inspired by Robert Dainotto's demonstration of eighteenth- and nineteenth-century Europeanism in *Europe (in Theory)*, which contrasts some well-known French philosophers with less recognised Spanish and Italian ones, emphasising historical sources that question 'Eurocentrism not from the outside but from the marginal inside of Europe itself'.[22] His approach presents a lesson from the historiography of Dipesh Chakrabarty, Walter Mignolo, Edward Said, and others. Recently, subaltern and postcolonial theory has been applied in studies of the idea of European unity, with ambivalent results. On the upside, we are presented with materials previously less considered or freshly examined in new ways, stressing the effects and legacies of Eurocentrism and the need to stay cautious about partisan EU narratives. On the downside, such studies risk interpreting the idea of European unity as mainly the confirmation of a colonial mindset, without giving other motives much consideration.[23] These studies leave much of the complexity of the concept of Europe behind, as they disguise differences and hierarchies within Europe. Dainotto warns of another risk. Referring to the concept of Eurocentrism, he remarks that applying it tends to contrast Europe to the rest of the world, especially former colonies, petrifying Europe's outer borders. He writes that the 'homogenizing assumptions of the term, in fact, run the perpetual risk of obliterating the interior borders and fractures of European hegemony; they hide from view Europe's own subaltern areas'.[24] This brings us back to the margins within Europe. Dainotto's cases are from the south of Europe, but his thought is certainly relevant to the other European margins as well. Hence, Dainotto's approach inspires my examinations in the following chapters of the concept of Europe, in recognising how the concept of Europe addresses the centre and margin within Europe, and how it creates divisions within Europe.

Consequentially, another precaution is to desist from reiterating a common master narrative that focuses solely on the British, French and German discourses on Europe. For a historian of Europe, it is tempting to follow the paths of the core West European countries. Certainly, these countries are of great importance, and this book offers a thorough demonstration of the concept of Europe among British, French and German intellectuals. However, to uncover differences, hierarchies and divisions in the comprehension of Europe, this book includes a variety of voices and perspectives from Southern Europe, Central Europe, and Scandinavia, from large, small and middle-sized countries, recognising similarities and dissimilarities between various parts of the continent.

This is a study of Europe as perceived by intellectuals. Narratives of intellectual history typically focus on one field, such as the history of philosophy or the history of political ideas or historiography, often depending on the academic locating of intellectual history in the historical, political or philosophical disciplines. Coming from the history of ideas in Sweden, long a discipline in its own right, it comes naturally to keep the study's focus on the idea and concept of Europe, rather than on Europe's colonial, diplomatic, economic, legal, political or social history. Recently, there have been several valuable publications in this field.[25] However, in my approach, I look for intellectuals operating in several fields – as writers and public intellectuals; as scholars of, for example, law, history and philosophy; and sometimes as politicians. I am interested in those who have been considerably quoted and translated, who represent different political ideas, and, most importantly, who have demonstrated significant and developed views of Europe and its future. Coming from different parts of Europe and being of different nationalities, they illustrate a transnational discourse on the concept of Europe that also includes exchanges, meetings, and mutual actions. Generally, they have published books, often many, but they have also written for newspapers and given public lectures, helping them to become well known. My research examines concepts, intellectual changes, and performances. It is based on a number of cases and engages in discussion with the research in this broad field, offering a fresh historical narrative. The material comprises written documents, primarily books, but also articles, targeted journals, and proceedings of Europeanist conferences. Expanding Internet archives provide new materials that enrich the picture, bringing out a deeper complexity. This means that I operate with an exceptionally wide-ranging selection of primary sources. I balance reading large bodies of material against the careful analysis of key texts. This book examines a varied array of examples from well-known figures such as Friedrich von Hardenberg (Novalis), Germaine de Staël, José Ortega y Gasset, Tomáš Masaryk, Julien Benda, Richard Nikolaus Coudenhove, Salvador de Madariaga, Regis de Rougemont, Edgar Morin, José Saramago, Agnes Heller, and many more. My working model also enables the acknowledgement of largely forgotten contributions to the historiography of the European idea. These include the calls made around 1820 by the Danish official, George von Schmidt-Phiseldeck, for a 'European Union' and a 'European citizenship' to respond to the debate about decolonising the Americas, and the plan drafted by Hilde Meisel in 1942 for a socialist European unity to avoid subjugation to the United States and the Soviet Union. In addition, assessment of the concept of Europe makes it possible to recognise well-known intellectuals who are rarely included in this research field. These include the Austrian Nobel Peace Prize winner Bertha Suttner, the Italian writer and historian Ferrero Guglielmo, the Swedish suffragist and peace activist Elin Wägner, the British poet and essayist Stephen Spender, and the Czech philosopher and dissident Jan Patocka, to mention but a few.

As a final note regarding my approach, I do not find it meaningful to distinguish between the idea and the concept of Europe, and therefore use both terms synonymously. Both signify references to Europe, whatever their associated meanings. Today we often hear about European identity and awareness; accordingly, my approach is to examine what meanings intellectuals are attributing to them.

Thinking Europe: The Book

The following chapters do not ask what directly led up to and resulted in the treaties forming the EC; they do not scour the archives of the 1950s, which economic, diplomatic, legal and political historians have already examined using a fine-tooth comb, nor do they accept the 1950s as the beginning of European integration.[26] The chapters acknowledge the importance of changing moments, presenting explorations of specific upheavals, events and debates that triggered discourses on Europe, while insisting upon the long-term effects these have had on intellectual history.

The book is divided into three parts and nine chapters. Each chapter introduces a main theme and associated sub-themes that relate to the concept of Europe during a specific period, and tend to remain associated with the concept in later periods. The reader will find relevant theoretical considerations embedded in the chapters. The first part addresses the themes of unity and borders in the 1800–1914 period. Its four chapters examine the main aspects of unity and borders: (1) the idea of European unity, (2) the understanding of borders, (3) definitions of Europe, and (4) the adoption of shared concepts, values and standards. Chapter 1 examines visions of unity concerned with international relations, trade, constitutional rule, peace, and federation design, and how these visions emerged together with many of the political ideas of the nineteenth century. European unity was seen as related to monarchical rule, but also to the voicing of anti-autocratic opposition, illustrating hierarchies within European societies. Next, to examine how unity and borders are entangled, Chapter 2 focuses on the emerging calls for cultural and political borders between nations, and on the many statements of cultural, political and religious divisions between Northern and Southern, and Eastern and Western Europe. Nationalists legitimised exceptionalism to confer essential features not only on their own nations but also on Europe. The concepts of Southern, Northern, and Eastern Europe were associated with political divisions and cultural hierarchies, whereas Central Europe connoted national strivings and imperial interests that were often in conflict with each other. In Chapter 3, we turn to definitions of European exceptionalism, which concerns distinctions between Europe and, primarily, Asia and America. Examining the concept of European unity of culture and civilisation, the chapter reveals how Europe became associated with religious divides between Catholicism, Lutheranism and Orthodoxy, and with political divides between the competing main powers of Europe. Definitions of Europe as one culture or civilisation were entangled with a master story of England, France and Germany as the primary nations while the others lagged behind. Chapter 4 looks at the exchange and dissemination of ideas and values, with citizenship, local self-government, and individualism cited as examples often subject to adaptation and translation. Quests for modernisation and the approximation of standards illustrate the interplay between centre and margins, and how intellectuals have urged their countries to follow the models of England, France, and later Germany.

The three chapters in the second part treat the themes of crisis and decline, revealing how the mindset of crisis accelerated the dynamic of unity and divisions from 1914 to 1945. These chapters highlight: (5) how the concept of the nation state advanced because of the First World War; (6) the concepts of European crisis and decline; and (7) the manifold plans and initiatives for unifying Europe during the interbellum, and the idea of European unity during the Second World War. The theme of Chapter 5 is how the Great War affected the concept of Europe. Certainly, divisions were high on the agenda, but calls for European unity retained some attraction, and the conception of a large German-led 'Mitteleuropa' spread widely in Germanic countries. Significantly, the idea of independent nation states in Europe seriously challenged the trust in ever-growing empires. Intellectuals, primarily from the margins of Central European empires, launched visions of a new Europe based on the nationality principle, which finally achieved a political breakthrough and marked the passing to the interwar period. The chapter acknowledges this as a profound change of view that fundamentally redefined the concept of Europe. Chapter 6 emphasises the impact of the redefined concept of Europe that focused on its many national borders. The main theme is the multiple conceptions of crisis in the cultural language of European unity, with their references to hard factors such as the new national borders after the downfall of continental empires and the economic consequences of the war, and to soft factors such as moral and ethical decline, nihilism, and a lack of self-confidence among Europeans. The examinations illustrate divisions and arguments for moral and cultural unity, besides the conception of European exceptionalism. An astonishing aspect of the concept of Europe from the beginning of the interwar period up to the end of the Second World War was the many attempts to organise for the sake of creating political cooperation and a European federation. Chapter 7 highlights the many organisations put forward in a context of sharp tensions, not only struggling to overcome divides but also reflecting divides and hierarchical views of Europe.

The two chapters in the third part – on integration and identity – explore the concept of Europe during the era of integration. Chapter 8 treats the crucial decade following the Second World War, and Chapter 9 examines the notions of European awareness and European identity, bringing the story up to the present. Chapter 8 presents a post-war concept of Europe that includes criticism of nationalism and war technology but continues to be associated with unity and borders. The early post-war mindset favouring European unification included adherence to nations and nation states, but it drew a red line against communism, stressing the post-war divide of the Iron Curtain. Europeanists retained a sentiment of exceptionalism and of having a world mission, even when they recognised that the United States was now the world leader. From the outset, the EEC/EC/EU understood their task as representing Europe, even 'being' Europe. Chapter 9 outlines the thematic awareness of Europe among historians in the 1950s and 1960s, Central European dissidents in 1970s and 1980s, and finally the many intellectuals discussing European identity well into the 2010s. Calls for stronger European identity have met with criticism concerning the divisions and makings of hierarchies within Europe. During the 2010s, discussions of Europe, what it was and what it should be, its divisions and hierarchies, were sparked by a series of crises. The conclusion underlines the discourse as a sign of continuing and growing interest in advancing European awareness.

Notes

1. Schlegel, 'Ueber Litteratur', 77.
2. De Staël, Germany, 18.
3. Masaryk, *Das neue Europa*; Wells, *What Is Coming?*, 192; Benda, *Discours à la nation Européenne*; Ortega y Gasset, *The Revolt of the Masses*.
4. Andrén and Söhrman, 'Introduction', 9–10 (2009); Andrén and Söhrman, 'Introduction' (2017); Andrén, 'Controversial Concept', 159–70; Andrén, 'Entanglements'.
5. Dainotto, *Europe (in Theory)*, 8.
6. E.g. Heater, *The Idea of European Unity*, 181–82.
7. Delanty, *Inventing Europe*, 3–4.
8. Pagden, 'Introduction', 1, 23.
9. D'Appollonia, 'European Nationalism', 190.
10. Andrén et al., *Cultural Borders of Europe*; Delanty, *European Heritage*.
11. See, e.g., Dainotto, *Europe (in Theory)*; Gosewinkel, *Anti-liberal Europe*; Hansen and Jonsson, *Eurafrica*; Pasture, *Imagining European Unity*, viii–xi; Wintle, *The Image of Europe*.
12. Milward, *The Rescue*, 45.
13. Moravcsik, *Choice of Europe*, 477, 488.

14. Evans, *The Pursuit of Power*; Mazower, *Dark Continent*; Stråth, *Europe's Utopias of Peace*.

15. Passerini, *Love and the Idea of Europe*, 19.

16. Passerini, 'Ironies of Identity', 205.

17. Connolly, *Political Discourse*; McMahon, 'Return of the History of Ideas?'; Müller, 'On Conceptual History'; Koselleck, *Zeitschichten*; Armitage, 'The International Turn'.

18. Delanty, 'Legacies, Histories, Ideas'.

19. Berger and Tekin, '"Europeanized" European History'; Schlögel, 'Europe and the Culture of Borders'.

20. Thorough studies include Högselius, Kaijser and Vleuten, *Europe's Infrastructure Transition*; Kaiser and Schot, *Writing the Rules*.

21. Armitage, *Foundations*; Armitage, 'The International Turn'; Lacqua, *Internationalism Reconfigured*; Leonhard, 'Conceptual History'; Marjanen, 'Transnational Conceptual History': Reijnen and Rensen, 'European Encounters'.

22. Dainotto, *Europe (in Theory)*, 4–5.

23. We can see this, for instance, in Hansen and Jonsson, *Eurafrica*.

24. Dainotto, *Europe (in Theory)*, 4–5.

25. Buettner, *Europe after Empire*; Evans, *The Pursuit of Power*; Stråth, *Europe's Utopias of Peace*.

26. A well-read and recent example of a narrative of post-war integration is Middelaar's *The Passage to Europe*.

Part I

UNITY AND BORDERS (1800–1914)

CHAPTER 1

Dreaming of Unity

Time for Europe

> Those were fine, magnificent times when Europe was a Christian country, when one Christendom inhabited this civilized continent and one great common interest linked the most distant provinces of this vast spiritual empire.
> —Novalis, 'Die Christenheit oder Europa'[1]

The beginning of the nineteenth century saw the emergence of a more visionary concept of Europe.[2] It was time to talk about Europe. Throughout the nineteenth and twentieth centuries, the idea of European unity existed in many variations remarkable in their mutability and how they were bound to the situation in which they were formulated. Still, some main themes recurred, and this is where we begin. We will ask what the dreams of European unity consisted of in the context of an order with continued monarchical rule and in which the strength of the major empires was defended. At the same time, Europe was evoked in opposing visions of constitutional rule and the people ruling through parliament. Ideas of European unification thus reflected the hierarchical order of society and its contestations. This first chapter examines Europe as a unifying idea in political discourses between 1800 and 1914. It mainly examines how the concept of Europe was entangled with various political ideas, representing different visions, while Chapter 2 will shift focus to examine how Europe's internal borders are an indispensable component of the concept of Europe.

Notes for this section begin on page 42.

Previous philosophical and scholarly discussion during the Enlightenment had enhanced the concept of Europe. The Enlightenment was associated with an impressive expansion of trade and knowledge, with the cultivation of humanism and science that spread reason and rational thinking. It represented both increased wealth and the liberation of the individual. Europe was seen as a place for democracy and tolerance, which also included a substantial amount of public discussion. Europe was modern and, as such, it represented an era superior to previous periods of European history, even better than ancient Greece and Rome. 'Progress, teleology, and manifest destinies – these are the key terms of the history of universalised Europe that only begins in the eighteenth century', rightly laid down by Roberto Dainotto in his genealogy of early Eurocentrism.[3]

The epigraph of this chapter is from the beginning of *Die Christenheit oder Europa* by Friedrich von Hardenberg, the author commonly known as 'Novalis'. It was written in 1799 but not published until 1826, long after his death.[4] It is no coincidence that Novalis mentions European unity, as the idea, which was first established in the late seventeenth century, achieved widespread currency soon after. He shared the notion of a common medieval idea of a European nation with other contemporary German romantic writers such as August Wilhelm Schlegel: 'Europe was destined to be one large nation, and the prerequisites existed during the Middle Ages'.[5] Although Christianity was to a steadily lessening degree viewed as defining the European during this period, it was still referred to as a basic value, though not the only unifying characteristic. In truth, Novalis had revived an older and medieval usage of the word 'Europe'. For many centuries, and throughout the Middle Ages, the word Europe was seldom used, but when it did occur it connoted Christianity or the 'Christian community'.[6] Starting from the late fifteenth century, however, it gradually became more common and was used more regularly, as by Erasmus.[7] This coincided with the economic and commercial centre of gravity moving north from the Mediterranean to England, France and Germany.[8] In the age of the great discoveries and the imposition of strengthening European power on the world, the ancient myth of Europe as a Phoenician princess violated by Zeus was revived. Moreover, Europe was frequently portrayed on maps and paintings as the world's queen.[9] Europe could be characterised by industry, arts, government, and the activity of scholars. Some have suggested that the context for the emergence of the concept of Europe may have been the threat from the Turks and overseas expansion, as well as contact with both new territories and new peoples.[10] Besides this, there were also internal strides: when the ambitions of France, the Habsburg Empire and Spain were expanding, threatened rulers took to the idea of a European order of peace and freedom from foreign powers. At the beginning in the sixteenth century, the concept of Europe was already spelled out in the canonical literature, be it by Cervantes, Rabelais or Shakespeare, or by John Donne, Erasmus of Rotterdam, or Ludivico Ariosto.[11] Starting from the seventeenth century, Europe began to be used as a noun and an adjective encountered in the titles of books, journals, and even a ballet, in political circles and in ballads sung in the streets, as well as in political and satirical pamphlets. It is worth noting that the British historian Peter Burke mentions that this does not indicate a common European consciousness, as people in all parts of society still mainly described themselves as belonging to particular local sites or regions.[12]

When Novalis refers to Europe as the community of Christendom, it is one of the advocates of German Romanticism who is speaking, and here he is at odds with counter-revolutionary thinkers in both France and Britain.[13] Yet, some of the Enlightenment heritage was kept in mind, because he mentioned both scientific progress and the burgeoning European trade. Yet, the author's statement is a rejection of Enlightenment ideals and a lamentation that love has been eliminated from trade and business – no longer do greedy people have time for 'the soul slowly collected'. Novalis is talking about the spiritual, the conscience of human beings, and argues that knowledge should be reunited with faith.[14]

Thus Novalis's concept of Europe differs from that formulated in the circles around the new French regime in the same era. When Napoleon returned from the Egyptian campaign in 1799, he stated his belief that Europe was a civilisation that had developed into being vastly superior to others. He considered the European ability to organise societies the key factor, and he talked about the need to have an armed Europe in case of Eastern attacks. In his Europe, Paris was obviously the capital, France was the most important nation, and other countries were either allies or future conquests. In the years that followed, the notion of establishing a continent-wide empire grew in Napoleon's mind, and he cultivated the myth of himself as the successor to Charlemagne. He argued that the differences between European countries were not significant: the European peoples really constituted one people and one single nation with one religion and tradition, and the only thing missing was a strong power to unite them in one system.[15] Still, that power was France and his Europe was very much a French one, just as it had been for the French Enlightenment philosophers – Montesquieu, for example, considered France the leading power of Europe.[16]

Napoleon's thoughts were supported not only by his French audience but also by many in other parts of Europe. Those who supported the view of France and its revolution as a role model against the previous autocracies often acknowledged Napoleon's armies as liberators. Publishers and authors in the south-western parts of the German states often expressed similar thoughts with regard to the creation of a new Europe owing to Napoleon. France was seen by many as the most mature country in Europe. During the revolution, the French had rejected previous prejudices and the old order of society, so it was natural that they should be the leaders of the new Europe that was to be built.[17]

In addition, Novalis's Europe differed from the concept of a European republic, a concept very much current at the turn of the eighteenth century. Both Napoleon's advocates and his opponents claimed that the European states had much in common. The former said that Napoleon wanted to establish a French republic within a European republic consisting of sovereign states.[18] The British and German critics claimed that the European republic should not be dominated by one power, but should rather find a balance that would protect one state from being conquered by another, as was the intent of the Westphalian Peace Treaty.[19]

In the Napoleonic Wars, both French and British fought for a better Europe. Before the Battle of Trafalgar, Nelson invoked the blessing of the Lord for his country, but he also included Europe in his prayer: 'May the great God, whom I worship, grant to my country, and for the benefit of Europe in general, a great and glorious victory'.[20]

It has been suggested that the 1806–13 British continental blockade of France and her allies was important in establishing a more focused perception of Europe as a unity, as the continental powers were fenced off from their colonies and economically and politically forced to integrate.[21] It was at this time that modern perceptions of a new Europe were definitively established. The word 'Europe' was now widespread, as it had become a highly attractive concept. This is an important explanation as to why Napoleon and others promoted France as the country that represented Europe. This is a recurring feature of the concept of Europe that can be characterised in terms of particularism and universalism, with some parts of Europe being commonly seen as more European than others. At the same time, Novalis was able to point out that specific European traits had developed in Germany. Other Germans had described their country as the heart of Europe, and the Germans as its blood. According to them, Germany was the site of the most revolutionary European achievements, such as the invention of the European system of balances between the main powers, printing, and the Reformation, and thereby it had had an immense political and cultural impact on Europe.[22]

Although the introductory phrases in Novalis's writings seem to express nostalgia for a bygone era, he was not reactionary in wishing for the re-establishment of an older order of society. When he considered previous eras, it was to establish standards for future development, referring to history to find arguments and using them as legitimising sources. Novalis's general thesis was that both Christianity and the Catholic Church had played a vital role in the Middle Ages, while the German and French varieties of Protestantism and the Enlightenment could be seen as representative of new eras. His hope was that religion would create comprehensive and continent-wide mutual interests. This was no trivial past idea being inserted in place of the new. He viewed both medieval Catholicism and later Protestantism as 'indestructible forces in the heart of humans'. The old strength was depicted in terms of respect for the old, including faith in the absolute hierarchical order. The new strength could be seen as delightful freedom, new opportunities, and general human rights that allowed people to socialise freely. Religion became a third force, making the old and new walk together in harmonious unity, and it was only by combining these strengths that Europe could be rejuvenated.[23] This was a plea for Europe to be a Christian continent, for a Christianity going beyond the divide between Catholics and Protestants, and for a new church of unity. It is a vision moving towards universalism and beyond the particularism of European divisions.[24]

Europe of the Monarchs or Europe of the People

The European dream of Novalis was set against the political struggles of his time. He criticised the existing state systems and their deficiencies and paucities. In the place of strife, he saw the possibility of closer contact and cooperation between European states, and even indicated that a common super state could be created, but that for this to happen, unity would have to be aroused from its slumber.[25] For Novalis this was nothing that worldly powers could achieve. Only a Christianity that transcended national borders and embraced the nations, making them realise the need to end bloodshed and conclude peace, could bring rebirth to Europe.

When Novalis invoked the dream of European unity, he was adopting a well-used theme. The idea of European political cooperation was already quite old. A few examples show Europe as an organised association. After the Turkish conquest of Constantinople in 1453, Spanish and Italian humanists raised their voices to call for a Europe united against the Turkish threat. Pope Pius II aimed to unite Western Christendom and the Europeans under his flag. European leaders drafted a plan to achieve peace among the European states so that they could fight the common enemy. The King of Bohemia, George von Podebrad, tried to create a union within Christendom in which the Pope's role was secondary, but the aim was nevertheless to overcome the Turks.[26] Dreams and sometimes plans of European unity have repeatedly been launched during the nearly half a millennium that has elapsed since then.

The word 'unity' is partly misleading as the aim has never been to create a completely homogenised Europe; beginning with the early pleading, it was instead cooperation among princes that was called for. The idea was that their diplomats would hold a congress and negotiate a treaty, which the princes would then sign. From then on, they would form a shared leadership. They would all benefit from avoiding expensive and devastating wars, instead gaining the opportunity to enrich their countries. The most famous of these schemes was the Grand Design of the French minister the Duke of Sully, who worked closely with Henry IV. It was published in his memoirs in 1640 and was a political dream of a reorganised Europe consisting of Christian countries (but excluding the Orthodox ones), with a balance between states and supra-state institutions, and with a senate that wielded the ultimate power and safeguarded peace and security.[27] It was inspirational for the English Quaker William Penn, who published a widely read pamphlet in 1693 asserting the need for a shared parliament of the European princes, which would institute a common law. It would strengthen Christianity and facilitate protection against the Turks, save blood and money, and improve security as well as friendship between the peoples and their rulers.[28] The pleas for a treaty were revived in the next century by the French political philosopher Abbé de Saint Pierre, who included Russia but not Turkey. He called for a federation in which the states and monarchs could guarantee one another mutual security, ruling through a common senate with a rotating presidency.[29]

What was called for was unity in the sense of a federation consisting of a number of states, each of which should continue to exist, but within a larger framework. However, to be taken seriously, something still needed to be added. Jean-Jacques Rousseau had high regard for the confederations of the Helvetic League and the German Reich, and saw them as models for building a European confederation. However, he had great doubts about such an order for Europe, believing it would be naive to think that monarchs would voluntarily give up any of their power, as they were mostly interested in extending their territories. Monarchs' pleas for a European federation in the name of peace easily gave rise to the repression of other nationalities, such as when Austria, Prussia and Russia suppressed Polish aspirations for independence, a suppression of which he had been highly critical.[30] Frederick the Great of Prussia wrote ironically when he commented upon Saint-Pierre's proposal, that it was a fine piece on the method to obtain perpetual peace, very useful indeed, 'if not only for the lack of acceptance of the European Monarchs and some other small things of the same kind'. These early proposals depended on the good will of the princes and did not garner mainstream support.[31]

The evolution of the idea of European unity also mirrored the pervasive changes in political thought that took place during the Enlightenment, especially after the American and French revolutions, in favour of the people and the *demos* as principles of governance. From then on, modern perceptions of legitimacy and citizenship became central to political theory. To be considered legitimate, governance needed to be based on a legal constitution and legal representation.[32]

Although the concept of political unity had been launched by Novalis's contemporaries, their focus had shifted and they often sided with demands for constitutional rule, which continued to be controversial in many European countries.[33] For example, the Comte de Saint-Simon pleaded for a federal Europe with a common constitution and parliament, which would represent the people rather than the emperors and the states. Simultaneously as Novalis was writing his pamphlet, and once again when it was time to set the terms for peace after the Napoleonic Wars, Saint-Simon demanded a new organisation of the political system of Europe: parliaments should rule the countries with a supreme European parliament reigning above them all. Rule by the people would lead to European unification, and when the peoples of Europe had established parliamentary regimes, the establishment of a European parliament would follow.[34] This sounds like modern democracy, but the electorate he had in mind was still delimited by income and literacy to only a thin layer of the population.[35] Still, Saint-Simon trusted that a new society was emerging, with a new and larger scale of production, much more international trade, and new modes of communication and transport. These were forces that he expected would bring about the unification not only of European economies and societies, but also of the political order.

Another example is that of philosopher Karl Krause, who in 1814 presented a plan for a federation of states that would unite the peoples of Europe in an alliance of free and independent states and avoid despotic rulers. Change was in the air in terms of political thought. As a Kantian philosopher, he argued that any European federation should be based upon law, and that the grounds for legality should not be sought in history, but in reason. He stated that the federation should be headed by a Bundesrat consisting of one leader from each state, and that all treaties, laws and decisions should be ratified in all the languages of the federation.[36]

It says something of the new importance of the idea of Europe that, when Napoleon's hope for a new continent-wide order was dashed in 1814 and, once again, at Waterloo in 1815, his defeats were taken as an incentive to proclaim a new European order that kept to the idea of unity. While exiled on Saint Helena, Napoleon claimed that his ambition was to introduce a European association for overall prosperity, with the same laws and one European court of appeal, with one currency and one system for weights and measures;[37] his opponents, the men of the Holy Alliance, also pleaded for a new Europe. The tsar proposed a federation of Christian peoples acting as one nation, signifying a new Pax Europaea. The Russian party shared the sentiment of Novalis, whom they had not read, with the addition of Christian morals as the antidote to the horrors of the French Revolution. Austrians, Prussians and the British did not share these sentiments, but nevertheless joined the movement to organise Europe anew. Metternich aimed to reconstruct the balance of power when he proposed the conservative vision of the unity of the thrones.[38]

An altered mindset was in place when the victors convened in Vienna. In 1714, when the signers of the Treaty of Utrecht discussed a Christian Republic of which the states were part, the change in terms of diplomacy was already underway. Then phrases like the 'principal powers of Europe', 'the general well-being of Europe', and 'the balance of Europe' entered the vernacular.[39] In Vienna in 1814, the notion of Europe was definitely taking hold. The hosts in Vienna presented the Congress as the very moment for the making of European unity. A cantata composed for the opening of the Congress by Ludwig van Beethoven, commissioned by the Austrian emperor to brighten the festivities, expressed much of the excitement. The text was written by Alois Weissenbach, a poet and professor of medicine at Salzburg University, who was rewarded with titles and a new position in the Habsburg capital. *Der Glorreiche Augenblick* (The glorious moment) begins with the chorus emphasising the historical moment that was about to take place:

> **Chorus**
> Europe stands!
> And the times
> that ever move forward,
> the chorus of peoples
> and the old centuries
> look on in wonder.

For several months, Vienna was seen as the very centre of diplomacy and the heart of negotiations. The six emperors present included the tsar of Russia, the Prussian king, and other German princes, as well as high-ranking delegates from all European states, including the victor of Waterloo, the Duke of Wellington. The city became Europe:

> **Chorus**
> Vienna!
> Adorned with crowns,
> favoured by gods,
> the city whose citizens serve monarchs,
> accepts the greetings
> of all peoples from all times
> who may pass your way,

for now you are the queen of cities.
Vienna! Vienna!
Vienna
Oh heaven! What delight!
What drama I see before my eyes!
What only Earth has, lofty and sublime,
is gathered together within my walls.
My breast throbs! My tongue stutters!
I am Europe – no more a mere city.

Nothing less than the creation of unity by establishing eternal ties was to be accomplished in Vienna. What was once divided should be joined together, just as Europe would create a union and build itself anew:

Vienna
The highest event I see happening
and my people will bear witness,
when a shattered continent
comes together in a circle again,
and brothers at peace together
embrace mankind set free.
Chorus
World! Your glorious moment!
Vienna
And to my Emperor's right hand
all the sovereign hands reach out,
to bind together an eternal union.
And on my shattered walls
Europe is rebuilding itself.[40]

Indeed, the victors of the Napoleonic Wars initiated a system of summit meetings in Vienna that were designed to deal with common issues in order to reach compromises and avoid further war. This system did not rest on international law but was essentially a device put in place for the allies to dominate the continent, and an indication of the reaction to liberal reforms. The allied political leaders had 'adopted the practice of acting in the name of "Europe" rather than simply for themselves', according to historian Mark Jarret. The Congress System was a novel way of organising Europe that relied on diplomacy but lacked a foundation in international law, and was a method of continuing monarchical rule.[41] The alliance issued a widely read announcement:

> The intimate union established among the monarchs, who are joint parties to this system, by their own principles, no less than by the interests of the people, offers to Europe the most sacred pledge of its future tranquillity . . . The Sovereigns, in forming this august union, have regarded as its fundamental basis their invariable resolution never to depart, either among themselves, or in relations with other states, from the strictest observation of the principles of the right of nations; principles, which, in their application to a state of permanent peace,

can alone effectually guarantee the independence of each government, and the stability of the general association. . .[42]

This system of European cooperation was to achieve some initial success. The new way of organising Germany as a federation of states was considered instrumental in establishing peaceful relations. It was stated that they were giving up the right to go to war with one another, without giving up their sovereignty.[43] When the Elbe Navigation Act of 1821 allowed all ten countries along the banks of Elbe to utilise the waterway, connecting south-eastern Europe with the Atlantic Ocean and the Baltic Sea through the German ports of Hamburg and Lübeck, this was seen as an important development for international trade.[44]

In any case, while the original Congress System lasted only a few years, it was followed by several proposals for a Europe ruled by one government during the nineteenth century. Although some hailed the Holy Alliance as successful in the aftermath of the Congress, in time, it would lose much of its lustre and symbolic importance. Pleas for a European Union or a United States of Europe offered the possibility to voice democratic ideas, when these were gaining new force. In the revolts of 1848, critiques of the old regimes often criticised the Vienna Agreement, dismissing it as a Holy Alliance of the princes that left little space for nationalistic or democratic movements, instead propagating 'the holy alliance of the people' as expressed by Giuseppe Mazzini. The buzzword 'nationalities' implied a new order with a democratic basis. Through nationalities, the people's voice was heard, breaking with empires and the reign of the aristocracy. Revolutionaries added the social question of eliminating poverty and bringing progress to millions of people.[45] In the aftermath of the revolts and the failure of attempts at democratic reform, the Italian nationalist leader Mazzini campaigned continuously for a Europe with free and democratic nations that represented the people and not its monarchs. Still, this would not be enough: 'We do not simply strive to create Europe; our goal is to create the United States of Europe'.[46] To cite just two more examples, the exiled German liberal democrat Julius Fröbel claimed that a federation between the West European states was the sole way of solving Europe's problems.[47] The French revolutionary Victor Constant did the same from his American exile, denouncing the existing political system as outdated. The development of social forces and the economy were beginning to bypass monarchical control, and it was only a matter of time until the modern world would set limits on the power of kings. The United States of Europe and its republican institutions would, according to Constant, eventually replace them.[48]

Europa in the World

Following the Congress of Vienna, it became possible to discern the main dimensions of the idea of European unity in the nineteenth century. This was expressed in detail in the writings of a largely forgotten Danish official who was widely read for a period. Konrad George von Schmidt-Phiseldeck, who held doctorates in both theology and philosophy, developed his views of a European federation in a retrospective view of the Holy Alliance, which he held in high regard, seeing the accomplishments of the monarchs as providing a new principle for managing internal conflicts and new prerequisites for Europe. However, even though Schmidt-Phiseldeck saluted the Vienna Agreement, we may not reduce his claim for European unity to the actions of the princes and their diplomats; it also included the people, whose spirit was to permeate the governance. This remained a key theme in the idea of European unity in the nineteenth century. For Schmidt-Phiseldeck, the best way to accomplish the well-established governance of states was through representative constitutions and a balance between monarchy and democracy. The European federation should include a permanent congress with representatives of the states. The acts of the federation should have a legal basis in a European court that oversees compliance with treaties. Moreover, he shared the view of the declarations from Vienna as well as many previous tracts that European unity was the way to ensure peace and security for the states that would allow them to reduce the large costs of keeping troops and making war with their neighbours. As he was writing shortly after the end of the Napoleonic Wars, he was mindful of discussing the great debts of the European states, which had begun to limit their resources. Even Great Britain, which had led the coalition against France and enlarged its power, had started to suffer the economic consequences of the war.[49] Giving up the right to wage war against one another was also of the utmost importance for future welfare, he wrote, and added that a European federation would not be easily established, as the legacy of mutual antipathy among states was persistent. Regardless, this quest for peace stood out as one of the key themes in the discussion of European unity in the decades that followed.

Schmidt-Phiseldeck became known among his contemporaries for his 1820 book *Europa und Amerika*. Its popularity spread quickly, and it was published in both English and French within the same year, as well as in the more minor languages Dutch and Swedish. The next year he wrote a new book focusing on the importance of creating a European federation, *Der europäische Bund*.

Defining Europe by comparing it with something else was nothing new; in fact, this had been done from the very beginning. The Europe of ancient Greek culture – the word 'Europa' was used as a synonym for Hellas – possessed an excellence of geography, governance, and the quality of its population.[50] For Charlemagne, Europe was a Christian Empire threatened by Muslims making their way through the Pyrenees. During the Siege of Vienna, Europe was Christianity challenged by Turks. However, Schmidt-Phiseldeck was the first to look at European unity from the perspective of global politics and economic relations.[51] For him Europe had to face changes outside the continent with new tools in view of the independence of the United States and the striving of the Spanish and Portuguese colonies in Latin America for freedom. Some of them were already free states; others had recently declared their independence and he anticipated that the rest would follow. A spirit of independence had taken hold of the American continents, and that had consequences for the world economy. A new era had begun, he explained, on 4 July 1776 when 'independence was declared by the United States of America'.[52] The liberated America became a new hub in the world economy that challenged earlier European trade routes. Europe had a new and strong rival on the other side of the Atlantic, one that would grow even more powerful when it could connect its trade routes to other independent states in America and with a population growing from the influx of European immigrants. This was a new era with a new dynamic, wrote Schmidt-Phiseldeck, with the United States in a central position, which would change the basic conditions for Europe, a region that would now become poorer after its loss of people and possessions to America. He raised the question of whether Europe should resign from being the 'king of the world'.[53]

The consequences of the decrease in trade could be grave, with resignation throughout the continent and a decline in social order.[54] One possibility would be to expand existing links with those colonies that remained, and to conquer new ones. However, Schmidt-Phiseldeck feared that the essential tools for doing this were not available, contending that the European states would be incapable of maintaining their monopolies on trade – Europe would have to look for another path. This implied a turn inwards for Europe, with a focus on the development of internal trade and economic life on our continent proper, in order to replace what was lacking in external trade. There was need for concerted action within the frame of a federation: like the United States of America, Europe would have to view itself as a federation of states reaching from the Urals to the Atlantic, from Lapland to the southernmost points of Sicily and Crete.[55]

This led to the creation of the name 'the European Union', perhaps in a work he presented in Copenhagen in 1821.[56] A European Union would be 'a hope of rescue for Europe', a continent that is amply supplied with the riches of nature and an 'ennobled humankind'. However, trade and industry were hampered by privileges and monopolies, tariffs and proscription, when Europe's borders should have instead 'been open and inviting' as they were in the American confederation.[57] Schmidt-Phiseldeck underscored common interests regarding trade both within the continent and overseas, and explained the need for a common European monetary standard and credit funds. Overall, this was also an endorsement of free trade (within the borders of Europe) in the tradition of Adam Smith and in opposition to mercantilist economic doctrines.[58] Free trade, it would turn out, was also one of the themes that appeared in the calls for European unity during the nineteenth century.

Schmidt-Phiseldeck concluded that there were obvious internal benefits of constructing a European federation, although these were not enough to make it a reality. For the European states to overcome internal conflicts and antipathies, a pressure or even a threat from the outside would be needed. He found this in the new world order of broken European dominance, in which the discord of Europe worked to the advantage of its competitors. Europe's war increased the other side's trade and brought it new territories. The conclusion was that 'a bit at a time we will lose what could only be saved by the greatest efforts of the combined forces of the whole of Europe, which could at least obtain useful conditions for trade, . . . even more could be saved if they were guided by the joint draft of a foresighted wisdom'. According to Schmidt-Phiseldeck, only when Europe stood united would it be possible to withstand the external pressure. Challenged by another continent, Europe would have to act as one continent.[59]

In those days, the changing relations of the world were not only a concern to Europe and America, but were also instrumental in deciding the fate of the Ottoman Empire. Once the mightiest power in the world, it had besieged Vienna as recently as 1683. Austria had afterwards conquered Hungary, but in the south-east the Ottoman Empire was still powerful, and Sarajevo still one of its strongholds. It was not yet 'the sick man of Europe', but for many it was obvious that the Ottomans were losing strength and even declining. If Europe had once been threatened by an expanding Turkish Empire, while conquering new territories on the Iberian Peninsula and across the Atlantic, it now was the other way around. In the west, it had a new rival, but in the east, the possibility of expansion arose. Well aware of this decay, Schmidt-Phiseldeck looked towards the south-east to replace the loss of colonies overseas by expanding Europe in that direction. Europe would have to gather itself against Turkey as the common enemy with the aim of expanding civilisation and Christianity. After conquering new lands, this would be a new opportunity for immigrants to move to the south-east, meaning that Europe could avoid losing great swaths of its population to the Americas.[60]

Over only a few years, Schmidt-Phiseldeck wrote three books that explored how to create a united Europe with its many virtues. His works illustrate how the idea of European unity of that time created a dynamic that inspired some authors to develop rich and various plans for how future societies could be created, often including statements about living in society and explorations of the human preconditions for peaceful coexistence.[61] Schmidt-Phiseldeck presented vivid descriptions of Europe, its challenges and potentials. Among other things, he emphasised the significance of education, the place of the church, and the importance of public sentiment. He indicated that, to bring about enough consistency and momentum for Europe to assert itself within the new world order, it would be insufficient to create a federation of the states and take all sorts of political measures, or to institute various legal and economic reforms. It would be necessary to harness the spirit and consciousness that Europe's people belonged to a community that went beyond the individual nation states. Schmidt-Phiseldeck understood the differences between the nationalities as inextinguishable, as they were rooted in tradition and historical circumstances. They could, however, be transcended by human reason and willpower. It would be necessary to suppress the egotism of the states in favour of the common good. Knowledge would have to be disseminated about the European family and Christian nation, with its shared morals and civilisation. A greater understanding of the common ground between the familiar and the foreign would have to be promulgated. Knowledge of European geography and history would be important, as well as the establishment of European associations. Foremost, travel throughout the continent would need to be facilitated to create the desired spirit of familiarity and affinity, so more 'wandering years' would be needed for apprentices, as well as more scholarly journeys. In short, the exchange of ideas, knowledge and resources would forge a stronger European political unity.[62]

Schmidt-Phiseldeck stands out as an early promoter of a concept of European unity, using America as a template, along with Harriet Martineau's *Society in America* of 1837, and Alexis de Tocqueville's *Democracy in America*, also published in the late 1830s. The United States was considered the future of Europe, both as something positive to imitate and as something negative to avoid. Not least did this genre emphasise the development of the North American states as a case from which Europe could learn. Fascination came together with fear. America was expanding in all respects: its growing population was taking new lands under its command all the way across the continent to the Pacific, driven by a broad economy based on both agrarian and industrial livelihoods. Europe, on the other hand, had reached its borders, lacked the same dynamic, and was challenged by its own offspring. Europe needed to stand strong in order to face the competition from North America.[63]

As the nineteenth century continued, Schmidt-Phiseldeck's vision of Europe's future turned out to be both right and wrong. The competition for trade routes remained an issue.[64] However, he badly misjudged the opportunities for further development of European trade and interests in Africa and Asia. African colonisation featured largely on the agenda throughout the century that followed and, together with further expansion in Asia, European strength continued to increase. He was correct, however, in his belief that America would grow more powerful: the rising star of America was indeed a challenge for the old world, he cautioned repeatedly.

By the end of the nineteenth century, this challenge was more apparent than ever, recognised by large parts of Europe's populations. Migrants wrote home to parents and siblings left behind, boasting of their new wealth and privileges. Wealthy Americans took long trips to Europe. The very richest Americans – such as the Carnegies and the Rockefellers – spent large sums in Europe buying art and antiquities.[65] The American view of the changing balance of power between Europe and America was quite frank: Europe was divided by internal competition, while the United States was growing in population and capacity, destined to be a leading global power. As stated by a member of the House of Representatives in 1870: 'The mighty republic of the United States, which sprang into existence less than a century ago, will be the acknowledged law-giver and arbiter of the world'.[66]

The growing economic strength of the United States challenged European trade and industry, which in turn furthered the dream of a European federation. Proposals soon followed that copied some of America's economic arrangements, including a customs barrier around Europe and the reduction of internal customs duties in order to withstand American competition. More suggestions of that kind were heard in France and Germany than in Great Britain, where worries about losing industrial supremacy were considerable but were less often followed by a plea for European unity.[67]

Design of the Federation and Its Bodies

The need for a federal political order in connection with an international legal order was often brought up. For instance, the draft of a European federation by Krause contained a plan to form a federation in accordance with international law, the prospect being to establish lasting peace and order for Europe.[68] Schmidt-Phiseldeck considered the voluntary agreements within the frame of the Congress System a step in this direction, the next of which would be to establish European law.[69]

Not every plea was as concrete regarding just how to achieve a federation. Strong faith in historical development together with a strong command of rhetoric could be as persuasive, as one can see in the following lines by Saint-Simon:

> There will undoubtedly come a time when all the people of Europe will feel that questions of common interest must be dealt with before coming down to national interests. Then evils will begin to lessen, troubles abate, wars die out. That is the goal towards which we are ceaselessly moving, towards which the advance of the human mind is carrying us![70]

Mazzini also had a strong belief in progress that would inevitably lead towards the reconstitution of Europe into nations forming democratic states. Up to then, he proclaimed, they had been divided and hostile to one another, because each was represented by a caste or dynasty. Democracy would change this and associate the nations with one another, amicably. They would then view one another as sisters, and 'gradually unite in a common faith and a common pact, in every way that regarded their international life. The Europe of the people would be one, avoiding alike the anarchy of absolute independence and the centralisation of conquest'.[71]

We should remember that the idea of a United States of Europe or a European federation permeated political thinking throughout Europe. It popped up in all kinds of political camps, and leftists, liberals and conservatives alike adopted it. Mazzini considered it important to form an alliance of the people as an alternative to the Holy Alliance of the emperors. On the other hand, those who wished to retain the European order of the Congress System wanted a central European body with legal authority and military force in order to be able to intervene in case of any revolutions among the states.[72] Propagandists of the federal state promoted the European federation in prolonging their efforts to convince the public of the good of federalism.[73] The idea of a European Union or federation was upheld by many regardless of political ideology, without much notice or further exploration. However, some issues were repetitive, and there were a fair number of examples of more thorough analysis, to which we now turn.

Different aspects of precisely how such a federation could be implemented and how it could function circulated throughout Europe. The decisive initiative would come when two of the main republican countries ruled by the people decided to form a federation. Saint-Simon singled out England and France, while Considerant hoped for France and Germany. If two began, others would join, said Charles Lemonnier, who steered one of the peace movements half a century later.[74] A French philanthropist said that, to avoid further military rivalry or new wars, a permanent congress representing all the states of Europe should be established to preside over cases of conflict that might arise between them. The possibility of instituting free communication and exchange of goods would lead to further cooperation, he added.[75] Ernest Renan, the French historian and republican publicist who, after the Franco–Prussian War of 1870, pleaded for a European community, upheld the need for a higher authority to coordinate the nations. Europe should intervene when two nations could not agree on their relations. The United States of Europe ought to have a congress that could judge nations, 'imposing justice on them, and correcting the principle of nationalities in the light of the principle of federation'.[76]

Experts on international law outlined detailed proposals for constitutional arrangements. James Lorimer, an Edinburgh professor, was in favour of a union like the one in the United States. Johann Caspar Bluntschli, a professor in Heidelberg, wanted to safeguard the sovereignty of the states within a federation, saying that the cultural differences and historical legacies were of much greater importance in Europe than in North America: an American people existed, but a European people did not. In addition, history had shown that a universal monarchy would fail, just as the ambitions of the Habsburgs and Napoleon had been dashed when they attempted to assert their power over Europe. Therefore, the federation should monitor the legal systems of its members as much as possible; the members should maintain their own governments and armies, and not be governed by one universal monarch or one European parliament – thus cooperating, but not forming a unified state. The tasks of the federation would be limited to international law, keeping the peace, international administration, and the administration of justice. Bluntschli's proposal was a modest one, in which a federal council would not threaten the sovereignty of the individual states if it kept to the management of issues that concerned them, such as the organisation of cross-border transportation, communications, and trade treaties. Hence, the cooperating states would be less inclined to have large military forces and could gradually achieve disarmament.[77]

Both Lorimer and Bluntschli touched on one issue that had so far received little attention, but that would eventually be on the agenda of the organisation of European bodies. William Penn had already mentioned the language issue: 'I will say little of the *Language* in which the *Session of the Sovereign Estates should be held*, but to be sure it must be held in *Latin* or *French*; the first would be very well for *Civilians*, but the last most easie for *Men* of Quality'.[78] His conclusion aligned with a world where these languages were the lingua francas of the elite. One hundred years later, Schmidt-Phiseldeck was still confident in the role of French, but Karl Krause believed a new awareness of the people had emerged, when he called for all treaties, laws and decisions to be ratified in all the federation's languages.[79]

Lorimer's idea was to keep to one language, just as the United States kept to English. It had to be a living and relevant language, which disqualified Latin. The best option was French, with the benefits of 'clearness and perspicacity' and the fact that it was already well established in the diplomatic corps.[80] To make it possible for the delegates of the federal council to communicate, Bluntschli's advice was to adopt a multilingual model. He proposed to make English, French and German the official languages, in addition to making all the documents further available by translating them into the other languages of the federation.[81]

Calls for a 'United States of Europe' first peaked in 1870 when France lost a short war against Germany. Open letters distributed on the streets of Paris and sent to both the French and German governments pleaded for France and Germany to melt down their cannons and unite. However, the many French demands for a united Europe were partly an attempt to curb the new Reich of Bismarck, and one open letter begged the German soldiers to bring back home fresh ideas of republican rule.[82] Victor Hugo made the case for imposing French in the European parliament: 'The United States of Europe speaking German would mean a delay of three hundred years. A delay, that is to say, a step backwards'.[83] Some British observers of the American continent also believed that a federation of European states would be the best means of avoiding further war. A representative of The Peace Society recalled the European congresses that gathered after the Napoleonic Wars to establish a peace treaty as 'the germ of a common authority', adding dryly that it would have been better if they could have taken place before the wars had broken out.[84]

The last decade of the nineteenth century saw much agitation for a European federation and the United States of Europe. Writers from several countries showed interest in the ideas being discussed. Sociologists, historians and economists supported this interest, and politicians and royalty of the highest rank, such as the prime ministers of Britain, Germany and Italy, were heard from, as was the foreign minister of Austria-Hungary, the German emperor, and the Russian tsar.[85] Moreover, it was argued that the Concert of Europe was an embryonic federation, or even that the federation was already in existence, although only as a loose concept.[86]

Among those pleading for European unification there were some like Bluntschli, who took a modest stand, claiming that it would take time to establish a federation like the United States of America. Nevertheless, a federation brought new hope and, according to a French voice, there was 'a slow development of the federative idea. Unfortunately, we are only at the beginning of this development; the fruit of federation is not yet ripe, but it exists and grows unnoticed each day'.[87] The novelist and peace activist Bertha von Suttner recognised tendencies towards a federation beginning at the time of the Concert of Europe, with the formation of a European code of law and a European tribunal. The necessity of having only one army was obvious, 'but the development into a strong, healthy, living thing is yet to be'.[88]

One goal was to create better political and economic relations, so it was suggested that the European federation should set up a customs union, which would lead to other forms of future cooperation.[89] Such a suggestion was complemented by the French historian Anatole Leroy-Beaulieu with one that left out Russia, Turkey and Great Britain, as they were seen as lacking a common European history and thus the prerequisites to develop a sense of European solidarity. Leroy-Beaulieu's European federation was not one of an expansive empire or huge maritime forces. His recipe for success was to include fewer states, be less ambitious, call it a European federation, and definitely avoid using the United States of America as a blueprint. This would respect the nationalities and the independence of the member states. The realisation of the federation was to take place over the course of a series of minor steps in both political and economic matters, including meetings and conferences, conventions regarding sanitary matters and monetary issues, and treaties on trade and jurisdiction. This would encourage the growth of a European sentiment. The top priority, however, would be to set up a customs union.[90]

Typical of the more cautious Bluntschli and Leroy-Beaulieu was their preoccupation with the design of the institutions of the federation, which entailed not only detailing exactly what states were to join, but designing the federal bodies and their responsibilities. The plan offered by the French lawyer Gaston Isambert included no more and no fewer than nineteen states, including among them both Great Britain and Russia. Notably, none of the plans took account of Turkey. Isambert proposed four bodies – a legislative council, a high court, a congress and an executive directory – each with an exact number of representatives, and a note on how and by whom they were to be nominated.[91]

Progressing in a conservative manner was also kept in mind when the pan-American movement was paid attention for its attempt to draft a federation framework. Pan-Americanism represented a future in which states would be connected by moral power and common interests, said the Austrian Nobel Peace Prize laureate Alfred Fried. While Europe battled with cannons and diplomatic intrigues, America could focus on the production of necessities and trade. In addition, when Fried stated that Europe should aim for a similar kind of expansion of internal relations instead of mustering for war, he already sounded like a proponent of post-war European integration:

> [T]he states of Europe must go ahead balancing their bodies, facilitating their transport, internationalising their management, and establishing security through mutual protection agreements. By adaptation and order in their living conditions, they will change the spiteful outlines of their political relations and achieve a policy of understanding and mutual compensation. With all the greater chance of success will they then be able to stand up to global competition.[92]

The pleas for unity concerned the arguments that Europe needed cooperation to hold on to its top position and to avoid new wars, as was discussed at the international conferences in Berlin in 1892 and in The Hague in 1899 and 1907. Although the confrontations between the main powers of Europe were minor during the nineteenth century, at least compared with those of the previous years and those that followed, there was much concern about the increasing arms build-up.

Unite for Peace

> How many wars must be waged, how many covenants must be tied, torn and tied again, in order to finally bring Europe to the principle of peace, which alone is of benefit for the states and citizens, to focus their attention on themselves, and to gather their forces for a sensible purpose![93]

In 1789, Friedrich Schiller asked for peace between the states in order to direct all energy towards more reasonable goals. It should be strongly emphasised that dreams of European unity are often presented as peace projects and against the background of warfare on the continent. Saint-Pierre and Saint-Simon, Penn and Krause, all promised that their designs would give Europe enduring peace. Schiller was in good company; a few years later Immanuel Kant presented his famous booklet *Zum ewigen Frieden*, a title that acknowledged a pub in the Netherlands. With a satirical wink, he argued that no perpetual peace would come from mere toasting. It was not enough to dream of peace, as the philosophers had done, as heads of state would never tire of war. Kant's idea was that a lasting peace for Europe could only be achieved under two conditions: a legally founded federation would have to be established to change the conditions for international relations; and the federation would have to be created between states that are not considered their rulers' personal property, but rather constitute republican societies.[94] Still, the requests of Schiller and Kant were followed by a new wave of unrest and the Napoleonic Wars, ending only with the Vienna Congress.

In the mid-nineteenth century, Victor Hugo stepped forward as a populariser of the concept of a United States of Europe that would do away with borders throughout the continent.[95] He actively supported the series of peace congresses held in Brussels, Frankfurt, Paris, London, and other British cities between 1848 and 1853, which had been assembled on behalf of various groups that together formed a peace movement.[96] In an often-cited inaugural speech, he announced that 'a day will come' when the nation states will merge and we will see a European brotherhood, 'when the bullets and the bombs will be replaced by votes, by the universal suffrage by the people'.[97]

One might ask whether Schiller, Kant and Hugo were heeded. New wars were waged in Europe during the nineteenth century, but they were fewer and more limited than they had been before. The period between 1815 and 1914 was comparatively peaceful. However, colonial military forces ruled with an oppressive power outside the continent, and inside its borders, military force upheld authoritarian power.[98] Once again, we can see that monarchs claimed to be fostering European cooperation when they intervened to help one another to suppress rebellions, while insurgents simultaneously rallied support from citizens of other states, and for a future European Union governed by the people.[99] When one considers the combined armies marching through the continent, and all the military force and threats of war, it is not very surprising that calls for European unity became connected to pleas for peace. The declaration of the Vienna Congress and the calls for a United States of Europe all indicated that peace would be vital to the future of Europe.

Moreover, the unity appeals were fuelled by peace proposals that sought closer cooperation between the European states to limit the increasing expenses of post-war reconstruction and prevent the eruption of new wars. Lord Salisbury, the British prime minister and for many years leader of the Conservatives, voiced grave worries about the accumulation of new weapons, of numerous instruments of death that improved with each passing year, and of the arms race that each nation had to take part in for its own safety. He declared in the House of Lords that a federation with a common government was the way to avoid a large-scale war in Europe and 'the only hope we have'.[100]

The peace movement and the peace congresses continued to propose the notion of a federation with a pan-European parliament. Tracts and manifestos were presented, and an initiative was undertaken to publish a bilingual monthly entitled *Les Etats Unis d'Europe – Die Vereinigten Staaten von Europa*. The European federation was a frequent theme and at times treated extensively by representatives of the various peace groups.[101] The businessman and sociologist Jacques Novicow lived much of his life in France and wrote in French, but was also seen as influential in both the German and British peace movements.[102] The main problem facing Europe, according to his diagnosis, was the right of each state to its sovereignty, which the states saw largely as their right to rob and invade their neighbours through the means of war. The federation would guarantee peace, freedom and security for the member states, and it would make it possible for them to reduce military production.[103] Leading peace activists Alfred Fried and Bertha von Suttner, both winners of the Nobel Peace Prize, agreed that a united Europe was the only possible option to avoid a devastating war. Von Suttner supported pan-Europeanism as opposed to the militant movements that were marching through Europe, mentioning the pan-Slavism of Russia, the pan-Germans, and the Camelots in France.[104] In addition, they pleaded for a Europe distinct from the one of the Congress System of the monarchs. In Suttner's words:

> It is the might of the mighty, not the rights of the weak, that they want to support. Much stress is laid on the consideration that is due the will represented by the great powers, not on the consideration that should be given the cause of the weak. Compassion, righteousness, and liberty; that is the triad that must lie at the basis of a genuine peace concert![105]

Peace activists turned to the concept of Europe when searching for ways to avoid war. The most commonly cited path to unification was the one proposed by Saint-Simon and Monnier: to begin with a federation between the main powers, especially between France and Germany, which would ease the tensions from the previous war and the issue over Alsace-Lorraine.[106] Additionally, the notion of a customs union had been in place from the very beginning.[107] Others believed that it was more important to install a universal monarchy on the continent. Even though many expected the federation to be realised shortly, such suggestions did not lead to tangible measures apart from explicit wishes and statements at conferences. One might ask – as Monika Grucza did in a recent dissertation – whether the proposals were really taken seriously by the statesmen, or whether they were only of interest as means to strengthen the positions of their own countries.[108] This was obviously the case when Russian tsar Nicholas II initiated the peace conference in The Hague in 1899 with a call for disarmament, evoking joy and cheering but also strong doubts. The call was considered the beginning of a new historical era as well as unrealistic, utopian and fraudulent. In fact, the proposal originated from his minister of war, who realised that Russia would not be able to afford an arms race with Western countries. Strong public opinion and a range of internal factors led to the realisation of the conferences, which ultimately produced some conventions, even though certain groups disliked the ventures and were pessimistic about the prospects. In fact, it was not only peace on the agenda, but also the conduct of warfare.[109]

In addition, the notion of peace through the establishment of a United States of Europe had begun to gain ground in popular culture. Bertha von Suttner mentioned the idea in her international bestselling novel *Die Waffen Nieder* (from 1889), in which she noted that the reasons for militarism and warfare are found on the European rather than national scale. Ideas about a European federation are presented, if not yet really elaborated upon in the way she would after the peace congresses in the 1890s. In a later novel, she wrote of her desire to establish various friendly alliances that would ultimately result in a European Union.[110]

The French astronomer and novelist Camille Flammarion borrowed the idea of the United States of Europe, and applied it to early science fiction in 1894. In his vision of the future of humankind, the only reasonable course for Europeans was to stop engaging in new wars and ongoing nationalist conflicts. Nation states had lost their relevance, and in due time had ceased to exist altogether. This future vision indeed showed a distinct interest in the idea that reached beyond political discussions. However, Flammarion placed the unification in the twenty-fourth century, adding extra centuries for the nation states to finally give up. In other words, he placed the United States of Europe in the far distant and utopian future, leaving little hope for an immediate breakthrough.[111]

In a notable 1907 novel by Robert Hugh Benson, which is set in England at the end of the twentieth century, Europe has indeed united but is threatened by an Eastern Empire that stretches throughout Asia and Australia. This story is far from utopian, describing the downfall of Christian culture and the reign of the anti-Christ.[112] Another novel by Otto Lehmann-Russbüldt from 1907 placed the United States of Europe even closer in time. After growing awareness that peace was the only way to ensure prosperity and continuing progress, following the German invention of a master weapon used in a short war against Russia and after a generous peace offer from the Germans, a treaty was signed in London in 1938. This vision was called a fantasy by its author, understanding its plot as distant from reality. The German author ended his utopian contemplation with the inauguration of a common parliament of the European states that had some degree of supra-national power to uphold peace. It was labelled a 'cultural parliament', with the task of making decisions regarding joint cultural tasks. This was apparently not a narrow concept of culture, but rather one that took into account broad aspects of life in society.[113]

In 1913, a contemporary observer – Suttner – wrote that the unifying of Europe was an old postulate of the peace movement that now more than ever had become its key argument. The movement's main representatives pleaded for it in Italy, France and Germany; they presented articles on the issue and even entitled one of their journals *Les Etats Unis d'Europe*. For Suttner, Europe had evolved from being something merely geographical, to the embodiment of peace. The idea of Europe calls for disarmament, incarnates all efforts to avoid war, acts in this one direction – only it does not exist, she sadly concluded.[114]

In the arguments for peace there were few indications of nostalgia or anything that would recall a former European unity; instead, they were forward-looking. 'The golden age of the human race is not behind us; it lies before us, in the perfection of the social order. Our fathers did not see it; our children will arrive there one day; it is up to us to clear the way', Saint-Simon wrote.[115] The seminal Kantian suggestion is echoed, that there is no peaceful state of nature to look back to and restore. Instead, peace should be achieved by looking forward and using human reason: it has to be installed, and that can only take place through cooperation between republican states within the frame of a federation.[116]

Visions of Europe

Looking back on the period from the late eighteenth century to the First World War, we can learn a great deal from the different political visions connected to the idea of European unity. From early on, it is possible to discern a market-oriented liberal vision guided by the desire to install a free trade bloc, beginning with Schmidt-Phiseldeck and Richard Cobden. Perry Anderson suggests three others: the conservative vision, which pays particular attention to the balance of power and distinguishes Europe as a specific unit; the leftist vision, which connects European unity to revolutionary objectives of changing the social order; and the technocratic vision, which begins with the recognition of the role of experts and later suggests the use of technical measures regarding economic and legal institutions, focusing on an 'inter-governmental, as distinct from federal, conception of European unity'. Of the adherents to the conservative vision mentioned by Anderson, we have already met Novalis, Schlegel, and the upholders of the Vienna Treaty and the Congress System. Anderson also mentions other representatives of the Romantic Period, besides the historians Leopold von Ranke and Jacob Burckhardt's marrying of unity and variety, harmony and self-development, into a narrative of European uniqueness. In terms of the leftist vision, we have seen, among others, the utopian socialist Henri Saint-Simon. The energetic insurgent Guiseppe Mazzini is not easy to label, but his insistence on women's emancipation, workers' rights, and social justice makes it reasonable to place him within a general leftist vision.[117] Anderson also includes in this camp the politician and journalist Pierre-Joseph Proudhon, whose ideas of reorganising society led to his being designated the father of anarchism, his follower Mikhail Bakunin, and the leaders of the pre-war social democracy. In the technocratic camp, Anderson includes the authors of moderate but detailed proposals for the European federation: the long-time editor of the peace journal *Le États Unis d'Europe* Charles Lemonnier, the Kantian-inspired jurist Johann Caspar Bluntschli, the historian Anatole Leroy-Beaulieu, and the lawyer Gaston Isambert, all from the late decades of the nineteenth century.[118]

It is definitely appropriate to distinguish the different visions of European unity that emerged from different political ideologies, highlighting that the concept of Europe is both contested and central to political thinking of the period. However, apart from the liberal, conservative and leftist visions, the technocratic vision also deserves acknowledgement. Anderson cites examples from both sides of the Rhine that share a drive to investigate and clarify in detailed, concrete terms a potential federal system, with its institutional arrangements and necessary institutions of constitutional law. These texts intend neither to rally the people to rebel against the princes nor to make them accept the existing order. They have nothing of the vigour or inciting power found in many of the demands for peace. Instead, they are rather dry presentations of technicalities, implying that a federation would be possible if the experts were equipped to deal with the required procedures.[119] Bluntschli, who comes from the tradition of Sully and Saint-Pierre in his calls for constitutional law of a European federation with both a parliament and commission, is an example of this vision, emphasising the need for arrangements for cross-border transportation, communications, and trade treaties as the sole way to unify. He claimed that unity would not erode national sovereignty, but that it would help states to disarm and thereby make them wealthier.[120]

Despite how these authors' visions of Europe differ, many of them have two things in common: they see threats to Europe's wealth, and they see risks arising from European military conflict. Therefore, they turn to other fields of human action and exchange to evoke the dream of European unity. Peace and welfare are recurring objectives that have motivated appeals to European unity.

In fact, dreams and visions have always seen Europe in temporal terms. In the Romantic vision of Novalis, there was once a unity when Europe consisted of a single Christian doctrine. This nostalgic view implied that it was possible to revive spiritual unity, which could pave the way for political unification. This was a characteristic conservative vision, which hearkened back to an imagined memory of more harmonious times to envision the idea of a shared future. Liberals and leftists were instead forward looking, concentrating on establishing a new legal and political order. In their vision, time's imperative demanded unification. One can look to Schmidt-Phiseldeck, who understood the growing importance of trade and industry, the need for markets, and the competition from America. Still, leftists were also sometimes guilty of nostalgic, Romantic thought. Mazzini, who was anxious to create a new order in Europe, exemplifies this. On celebrating the beauty, dignity, and historical importance of the city of Rome, he presented the city as the temple of humanity, from which 'will one day spring the religious transformation destined for the third time to bestow moral unity'.[121]

Notes

1. Quotation from Drace-Francis, *European Identity*, 90.
2. Thompson, 'Ideas of Europe', 57–58.
3. Dainotto, *Europe (in Theory)*, 50–51.
4. For the reasons for the postponement, see O'Brien, *Novalis*, 227.
5. Schlegel, 'Ueber Litteratur', 77: 'Europa, bestimmt nur eine einzige grosse Nation auszumachen, wozu auch die Anlage im Mittelalter da war'.
6. Leyser, 'Concepts of Europe'.
7. Erasmus, *Praise of Folly*, 78, 101.
8. Dainotto, *Europe (in Theory)*, 34–41.
9. Wintle, *Image of Europe*, 219–81.
10. Yapp, 'Construction of Europe'.
11. Dainotto, *Europe (in Theory)*, 42–45.
12. Burke, 'Did Europe Exist before 1700?'.
13. In England with Edmund Burke, in France with Joseph de Maistre and Louis de Bonald, and later in Spain with Juan Donoso Cortéz; see Perkins, *Christendom and European Identity*, 24–28.
14. Novalis, 'Die Christenheit oder Europa'.
15. Thompson, 'Ideas of Europe'.
16. Verga, 'European Civilization'; Dainotto, *Europe (in Theory)*, 67.
17. Gollwitzer, *Europabild und Europagedanke*; Thompson, 'Ideas of Europe'.
18. Périer, *A Speculative Sketch*, 11, 14, 26, 119. Du Périer also talks of a 'European Union' and a 'European society', further indicating the strong idea of unity, in spite of the war between the European states; see 18, 23.
19. Andrews, *The Present Relations*, 157–58; Heber, *Lines on the Present War*; Vogt, *System des Gleichgewichts*, vi.
20. Quoted from Barrow, *Auto-Biographical Memoir*, 283.
21. Woolf, 'European World-View'.
22. Krause, 'Entwurf'; Vogt, *System des Gleichgewichts*, vi.
23. Novalis, 'Die Christenheit oder Europa'.
24. Svennungsson, 'Christian Europe', 121–27.
25. Novalis, 'Die Christenheit oder Europa'.
26. Heater, *European Unity*, 13–14; Mikkeli, *Europe as an Idea*, 33ff.
27. Sully, *Grand Design of Henry IV*.
28. Penn, *Present and Future Peace*; Heater, *European Unity*, 32–33, 66–76.
29. Heater, *European Unity*, 70–84.
30. Dainotto, *Europe (in Theory)*, 134–37.
31. Bluntschli, 'Die Organisation', 288: 'wenn nur nicht die Zustimmung der europäischen Fürsten und noch einige ähnliche Kleinigkeiten dazu fehlen würden'. Lorimer, *The Institutions*, 223–26.
32. See, e.g., Heater, *Citizenship*, and Württemberg, 'Legitimität, Legalität', 712–15.
33. Heater, *European Unity*, 111.
34. Saint-Simon, *Selected Writings*, 135. See also Heater, *European Unity*, 103–4.
35. Woytinsky, *Tatsachen und Zahlen*, 7–10.
36. Krause, 'Entwurf', 195–208.
37. Thompson, 'Ideas of Europe'.
38. Jarret, *Congress of Vienna*, 174–76.
39. Yapp, 'Construction of Europe', 142–45.
40. Beethoven and Weissenbach, 'The Glorious Moment'.
41. Jarret, *Congress of Vienna*, 70, 359.

42. Ibid., 194.
43. Schmidt-Phiseldeck, *Der europäische Bund*, 85.
44. Hinsch, 'The River Elbe'.
45. Mazzini, 'Europe: Its Condition', 277–80.
46. Mazzini, *Cosmopolitanism of Nations*, 135; the quotation is from an article of 1850.
47. Fröbel, 'Die europäischen Ereignisse', 56.
48. Beecher, *Victor Considerant*, 374–77, 388.
49. Schmidt-Phiseldeck, *Europa und Amerika*; Schmidt-Phiseldeck, *Der europäische Bund*; Schmidt-Phiseldeck, *Die politik*.
50. Pagden, 'Conceptualizing a Continent', 36–37.
51. Schulze and Helm, 'Schmidt-Phiseldeck'.
52. Schmidt-Phiseldeck, *Europa und Amerika*, 15.
53. Ibid., 127, 227.
54. Schmidt-Phiseldeck, *Der europäische Bund*, 79–85.
55. Ibid., 154–60.
56. Ibid., 279.
57. Schmidt-Phiseldeck, *Europa und Amerika*, 154–60.
58. Schmidt-Phiseldeck, *Der europäische Bund*, 177–80, 269.
59. Ibid., 106–9, 14–17, 153–54. Original quote from 148: 'Stück vor Stück werden wir verlieren, was nur die höchste Anstrengung der vereinten Kräfte der gesammten Europa, wenn diese nach gemeinsamen Entwürfen einer vorschauenden Klugheit geleitet würden, noch zu retten, oder wenigstens, . . . in einem für die Zwecke des gesellschaftlichen Verkehres Erspriesslichen Verhältnisse zu erahlten vermöchte'.
60. Schmidt-Phiseldeck, *Europa und Amerika*, 166–69.
61. See, e.g., Schmidt-Phiseldeck, *Der europäische Bund*, 110–12.
62. Schmidt-Phiseldeck, *Politiken*, 41–72, 111–12.
63. See also Fröbel, 'Die Zukunft Europa'.
64. Britain also made concerted efforts to find the Northwest Passage above the North American mainland; see Beattie and Geiger, *Frozen in Time*.
65. Rietbergen, *Europe*, 377–86.
66. Appleton, *Europe and America*, 22.
67. See, e.g., the Austrian Julius Wolf, *Das Deutsche Reich*, 31–37, 47–48, and *Materialien*, VII.
68. Krause, 'Entwurf', 194–208.
69. Schmidt-Phiseldeck, *Der europäische Bund*, 39–42.
70. Saint-Simon, *Selected Writings*, 135.
71. Mazzini, 'The Holy Alliances', 275.
72. E.g., Adler, *Der Krieg, die Congressidee*, 46–48.
73. E.g., Carlo Cattaneo, Joseph Proudhon and Constantin Franz.
74. Lemonnier, *Les Etats Unis d'Europe*, 189–90; Beecher, *Victor Considerant*, 403–4.
75. Jean-Baptiste André Godin, who is cited in Herriot, *Europe*, 36–40.
76. Renan, 'Open Letter to David Strauss', 141–42.
77. Bluntschli, 'Die Organisation', 291–312.
78. Penn, *Present and Future Peace*. Emphasis in original.
79. Krause, 'Entwurf', 195–208.
80. Lorimer, *The Institutions*, 223–25.
81. Bluntschli, 'Die Organisation', 291–312.
82. Beecher, *Victor Considerant*, 400–407.
83. Hugo, 'Letter to M. D'Alton Shee'.
84. Amberley, 'Can War Be Avoided?', 618.
85. Grucza, 'Bedrohtes Europa', 103–17.

86. Salisbury, 'Europeisk Federation'.

87. Novicow, *Die Föderation Europas*, 639; in the German original: 'die langsame Entwicklung der Föderalistischen Idee. Leider sind wir noch am Beginn dieser Entwicklung; die föderative Frucht ist noch nicht reif, aber sie besteht und wächst unbemerkt alle Tage'.

88. Suttner, *Memoirs*, 154.

89. See, e.g., Leroy-Beaulieu, 'Les États-Unis D'Europé', 455; Waechter, 'For United Europe'.

90. Leroy-Beaulieu, 'Report General', 9: 'L'union de peuples européennes ne doit donc pas être l'oeuvre d'un internationalisme niveleur, supprimaut l'existence ou l'independence profit d'une unite plus vaste qui les absorberoit et les engloutirait dans son sein'.

91. Isambert, 'Projet d'organisation politique'.

92. Fried, *Pan-Amerika*, 292–97; quotation from 296–97: 'müssen die Staaten Europas daran gehen, ihre Einrichtungen auszugleichen, ihren verkehr zu erleichtern, ihre Verwaltung zu internationalisieren und die Sicherheit durch auf Gegenseitigkeit errichtete Schutzverträge herzustellen. Durch eine Anpassung und Ordnung ihrer Lebensverhältnisse werden sie die gehässigen Grundzüge ihrer politischen Verhältnisse ändern und zu einer Politik der Verständigung und des gegenseitigen Ausgleiches gelangen. Mit um so grösserer Aussicht auf Erfolg werden sie alsdann in den mondialen Wettbewerb eintreten können'.

93. Schiller, 'Was heisst Universalgeschichte', 250: 'Wie viele Kriege mussten geführt, wie viele Bündnisse geknüpft, zerrissen und aufs neue geknüpft werden, um endlich Europa zu dem Friedensgrundsatz zu bringen, welcher allein den Staaten wie den Bürgern vergönnt, ihre aufmerksamkeit auf sich selbst zu richten, und ihre Kräfte zu einen verständigen Zwecke zu versammeln!'

94. Kant, 'Zum ewigen Frieden'.

95. Heater, *European Unity*, 114.

96. Tyrrell, 'Making the Millennium', 75; Nicholls, 'Richard Cobden', 362.

97. Recently cited by Laqueur, *After the Fall*, 10. See also Metzidakis, *Victor Hugo and the Idea*.

98. This period was not as peaceful as some have claimed, with 14 wars between states on the European continent, 58 wars outside of Europe, and 540 'violent domestic social and interstate military conflicts'; see Stråth, *Europe's Utopias of Peace*, 21, who refers to Halperin, *War and Social Change*.

99. See, e.g., the report 'Politiska nyheter' in *Dagens Nyheter*.

100. Grucza, 'Bedrohtes Europa', 103–17; for other examples, see Palmstierna, 'Europas förenta stater', and Fried, *Der Kaiser*, 1–41. On Salisbury, see https://en.wikiquote.org/wiki/Robert_Gascoyne-Cecil,_3rd_Marquess_of_Salisbury, retrieved 5 November 2020.

101. Grucza, 'Bedrohtes Europa', 103–17.

102. Crook, *Darwinism, War and History*, 116.

103. Novicow, *Die Föderation Europas*, 20–38.

104. Hamann, *Bertha von Suttner*, 255–56.

105. Suttner, *Memoirs*, 154.

106. E.g., Stein, *Vereinigten Staaten von Europa*, 17.

107. E.g., Réveillère, *L'europe Uni*; Suttner, *Memoirs*, 62–65.

108. Grucza, 'Bedrohtes Europa', 103–17.

109. Tuchman, *The Proud Tower*, 229–88, especially 229–37.

110. Suttner in Vegeseck, 'Der Frieden in 100 Jahren', 68–69.

111. Flammarion, *Omega*.

112. Benson, *Lord of the World*.

113. Lehmann-Russbüldt, *Die Schöpfung*.

114. Suttner in Vegeseck, *Vermeidung des Weltkrieges*, 481–82, 518.

115. Saint-Simon, *Selected Writings*, 135.

116. Kant, 'Zum ewigen Frieden', 197.
117. Falchi, 'Democracy, Women, Mazzini', 15–30; Urbinati, 'Mazzini and Republican Ideology', 183–204.
118. Anderson, *The New Old World*, 475–504.
119. Ibid.
120. Bluntschli, 'Die Organisation', 291–312.
121. Mazzini, *Joseph Mazzini*, 316.

CHAPTER 2

Longing for Borders

The question we will now turn to concerns the prerequisites for, and historical understanding of, the association of the concept of Europe with cultural and political borders within Europe. What are the basic tenets of how we think about European borders, of Europe as divided by national borders and with regional hierarchies? This chapter will consider borders within Europe by turning to the concepts of nation, and of macro regions such as Central, Eastern and Southern Europe.

The significance of borders had a solid cultural foundation. Ezra Talmor has regarded it as 'a great irony that, side by side with the emergence of the idea of Europe – say around the end of the seventeenth century – many decisive factors had already led to the idea of a divided Europe'.[1] The European system of states was well underway, Christianity was further divided, and Latin had decreased in importance in favour of vernacular languages, which all implied borders. Nevertheless, the modern European concept of border emerged from the tension between cultural dividing lines and an all-embracing idea of unity, raising questions about how the drawing of borders fits with the idea of European unity. In subsequent research, the interest in territorial borders expanded together with an awareness of their complexity and a realisation that it is necessary to look at the cultural aspects of borders. Philosopher Étienne Balibar states that a territorial notion of borders in Europe only provides 'dead ends'.[2] The conclusion from previous research is that the cultural dimensions of border making are of great significance.[3]

We can make two observations at this point: first, if unity is seen as the fundamental concept, borders should not exist and ought to be eradicated;

Notes for this section begin on page 73.

second, if cultural and political borders are regarded as a given, how to manage them becomes the issue. The hypothesis of the clash of civilisations advanced by Samuel P. Huntington, who argues that future conflicts will arise from cultural and religious differences, is based on such an assumption.[4] However, there are also those who defend notions of tolerance and multi-culturalism,[5] so it is not universally accepted that cultural divisions must end in clashes and conflicts.

The Border Paradox

At first, maps depicting Europe did not show many of today's European borders, with some showing no borders at all. The 1569 map by the famous Flemish cartographer Mercator shows roughly the borders of the then emerging states, which leaves the continent with only a dozen or so countries altogether. Renaissance maps that viewed Europe from a continental perspective lacked clearly defined borders for countries; rather, the images they presented suppressed division.[6] This was not because there were no boundaries. In reality, Europe in the early modern age had some five hundred political units, so even if the cartographers had wished to include them all in one map, it would simply have been too difficult.[7] Of course, some states existed, but they coexisted with a myriad of individual territories having jurisdictional independence.[8] The cartographers were simply keener on indicating regions than political borders,[9] not being that interested in the latter. Not only were there numerous independent or semi-independent units, but allegiances and loyalties were constantly changing, causing enclaves to shift from one prince to another. This situation eventually changed, and in the eighteenth century, Johann Matthias Hase, a cartographer from Wittenberg, made a remarkable rendering of European borders, displaying not only state borders, but also those between regions, provinces, duchies and principalities. He depicted Italy as one country, though divided into smaller parts in the same way that he divided France, Germany and Sweden.[10] Clearly, these maps reflected the political reality, with most states having weak administrative and political centres. Much of the centralisation of European states was accomplished by Napoleonic reformers and by those inspired by their example. Cartographers reflected public interest in another development: just as the Enlightenment was an era when the ideas of Europe and European unity proliferated, so did it also usher in growing interest in borders.

The maps of the nineteenth century give us an indication of how European borders were conceived. Several maps produced in Germany bring a new level of complexity to the notion of political borders. The Ottoman

Empire was always included as a European state, though with a division between Turkish Europe and Asia Minor. One map differentiates among imperial states, kingdoms, duchies/principalities, and republics.[11] The cartographers attached a certain complexity to the borders of Germany and Italy, not least because they included several political actors. Different kinds of political borders demarcated the Habsburg Empire, as it encompassed Italian provinces as well as Bohemia and the Austrian provinces that belonged to the German Federation.[12] Ironically, when Europe as a whole is viewed from far away in an American school atlas, probably from around 1827, slightly more than a dozen states are shown: Italy is represented as one state, Prussia as another, and the other German states outside the Habsburg Empire are tidily bundled into an additional single state.[13]

Strikingly, the number of countries included in the maps remained stable at around sixteen or seventeen throughout much of the century. Germany was represented at times as one country, and when both Germany and Italy finally became nation states, the number became even smaller. It was reasonable to view the European system of states as stable with its homogenisation of laws, economic relations, and administration. When the 1878 Congress of Berlin granted independence to new states in the Balkans, it also brought more states to the maps, adding a degree of stability to the region even as the Ottoman Empire was disintegrating. Furthermore, the maps show increased exchange between the states due to the new means of communication by telegraph, rail, and steamship lines.[14]

Maps of Europe from the final decades of the nineteenth century also testify to religious and national divides. A German map that proudly depicts the unified German Empire includes a supplement with one minor map dividing Europe into Protestant, Catholic, Orthodox and Islamic regions, and another dividing the continent according to twenty-five different nationalities.[15] These kinds of observations bring us closer to a true paradox: the dreams of unity in the nineteenth century were accompanied by accentuated differences, by an impulse to stress borders not only between Europe and other continents but also within Europe – for example, between states, nations and regions. These borders were both political and cultural in character. The differences between regions such as Eastern and Western Europe were highlighted as cultural markers. The national languages, customs, and cultural expressions were highlighted among nations large and small, either with or without their own state. More nations began to demand political and legal rights, and so the cultural dimensions evolved hand in hand with political ambitions and demands for institutional arrangements. When European unity, whether political or cultural, was evoked, it began to be framed by the increasing importance of borders throughout Europe. This can be deemed the border paradox of Europe.

Time for Nations

> Germany may be considered, from its geographical situation, as the heart of Europe, and the great association of the continent can never recover its independence but by the independence of this country. Difference of language, natural boundaries, the recollections of a common history, contribute all together to give birth to those great existences of mankind, which we call nations; certain proportions are necessary to their existence, certain qualities distinguish them; and, if Germany were united to France, the consequence would be, that France would also be united to Germany . . . the vanquished would in time modify the victor, and in the end both would be losers.[16]

These words are from the preface to *Germany* – originally published in French as *De l'Allemagne* – by the French-Swiss writer Anne Louise Germaine de Staël. In pleading for the value of nations she is a leading proponent of the nationalistic ideas that were to exert considerable influence on Europe. The book was originally published in 1810 when the German states were under French dominion. The author had already moved to Switzerland, was firmly anchored in the Enlightenment culture of pre-revolutionary Paris, and was especially influenced by her reading of Montesquieu. Later, she had a longer stay in Germany, during which she met representatives of the early Romantic movement, and made friends with August Wilhelm Schlegel. She belonged to a group of writers who were initially positively disposed towards, and took part in, the French Revolution, but who soon distanced themselves from it as it radicalised. She had previously been a republican, but later defended monarchist rule and wanted it to be deemed constitutional.

De Staël maintained that the Germans were not yet forming a nation. As long as Germans were still raising weapons against each other, they were still a nation only 'in the mind'. However, being a nation in the mind was an indispensable start from which national independence could eventually be born. To begin with, the Germans could claim the self-confidence that was part of the characters of the English, French and Spanish, a self-confidence that all of these citizens had thanks to their histories within empires. Germans would be able to see that they were, 'generally speaking, both sincere and faithful; they seldom forfeited their word, and deceit was foreign to them'; moreover, they had 'good sense and goodness of heart' and the 'power of labor and reflection'. However, it was 'imagination more than understanding that characterises the Germans', and she quotes a writer who wrote 'that the empire of the seas belonged to the English, that of the land to the French, and that of the air to the Germans'. The Germans were seen as impractical, slow, and somewhat committed to inertia, but they were also keen on music and had a good sense of poetry.[17]

It was in no way a novelty to present peculiarities of certain nationalities. In 1697, it was reported that the ballet *L'Europe galante* conceived of the French as 'fickle, impulsive, dandified', the Spaniards as 'true-hearted and sentimental', and the Italians as 'jealous, subtle, hot-tempered'.[18] However, describing the diversity of Europe could sometimes come across more crassly, and Daniel Defoe's satiric rhymes were much more stirring:

> Pride, the first peer, and president of Hell,
> To his share Spain, the largest province fell. . . .
> Never was nation in the world before,
> So very rich, and yet so very poor.
>
> Lust chose the torrid zone of Italy,
> Where Blood ferments in rapes and sodomy. . . .
> Here, undisterb'd, in floods of scalding lust,
> Th' infernal king reigns with infernal gust.
>
> Drunk'nness, the darling favourite of Hell,
> Chose Germany to rule, and rules so well. . . .
> Whether by Luther, Calvin or by Rome,
> They sail for Heav'n, by wine he steers them home.
>
> Ungovern'd Passion settled first in France,
> Where mankind lives in haste and thrives by chance.
> A dancing nation, fickle and untrue.
> Have oft undone themselves, and others too:
> Prompt the infernal dictates to obey,
> And in Hell's favour, none more great then they.
>
> . . .
>
> By Zeal the Irish; and the Russ by folly;
> Fury the Dane; the Swede by Melancholy;
> By stupid Ignorance the Muscovite:
> The Chinese by a child of Hell, call'd Witt;
> Wealth makes the Persian too effeminate:
> And poverty the Tartars desperate:
> The Turks and Moors by Mah'met he subdues;
> And God has giv'n him leave to rule the Jews;
> Rage rules the Portuguese, and Fraud the Scotch;
> Revenge the Poles; and Avarice the Dutch.[19]

Even though Europeans were considered to have a great deal in common, defining their national characteristics was an established pastime. Establishing a collective European consciousness had to take into account that Europe was a continent of differences composed of various parts. The French intellectual historian Paul Hazard underscores how the European mind had changed by 1700, by which time national divisions had become part of the mental mapping. He stated that Europe was nothing but 'a jig-saw of barriers' that 'are rigidly defined' yet changing all the time.[20]

In works by Enlightenment philosophers and historians we can see that the concept of Europe was often professed in terms of both unity and diversity. These writers elaborated on the glories of the state system. The success of Europe, argued Adam Ferguson in Edinburgh, coincided with emulation between its states: division went hand in hand with success.[21] His colleague William Robertson commended the progress in which 'the powers of Europe had formed into one great political system', creating a united system of various kingdoms.[22] Edward Gibbons conceived of Europe as a large republic, with widespread cultivation and general happiness among its inhabitants, that stands 'above the rest of mankind' thanks to 'the system of arts and laws and manners'. In France, Antoine de Rivarol described it as 'one immense republic . . . composed of empires and kingdoms, the most formidable that has ever existed'.[23]

Madame de Staël went further than this when she indicated the need to encourage certain qualities in each particular nation. This had been done before, but her standpoint hinted at proto-Romantic thinking when she gave 'language, natural boundaries, the recollections of a common history' a central place in defining and making a nation, as well as when she turned to literature, philosophy, and religion to show the national character. We should not forget that this was written when French armies had flooded Europe and that de Staël was offering an alternative view of Europe. Her conclusion was that nations had to develop their distinctiveness if they were to be independent. If unified, she said, the nations would not make progress, but would adapt to each other and end up losing their identities. Therefore, she explicitly rejected the ideal of a common European nation.[24]

Still, de Staël's pleading for German independence did not make her an advocate of independence for every nation. Even if Europe was not considered a united entity, but rather seen as comprising multiple states, it was necessary for a nation to have 'certain proportions' and 'certain qualities' to be sovereign. This was later to become one of the more contested issues of nationalism, but throughout the century of *De l'Allemagne*, the idea that a state and a nation state had to be of ample size and contain large resources remained fundamental. Such nations would be able to accomplish greatness; they would not be victims of destiny and they could change history. Baroness de Staël considered the German nation to be fully adequate, and if it was not possible to unite all Germans, then one could at least begin with Prussia and its neighbours.[25]

Europe was not excluded from this concept of a nation. De Staël indicated that Germany was the heart of Europe: geographically it is located in a central area of the continent, and in other ways it had always been and would continue to be decisive for the rest of Europe. She claimed that the early German universities were the first of their kind, 'open to the rich and the poor, to the knight, the clerk, the citizen'.[26] Among other examples, she hinted that Germans had introduced the concept of freedom to Europe, as well as the idea of showing respect for women, which was not yet common elsewhere.[27]

The Parts of the Whole

Lorenz von Stein, an ardent Hegelian pupil writing in Vienna during the mid-nineteenth century, believed that Europe was to be considered a whole consisting of states and specific regions. As a whole it was entrusted with a specific civilisational task. Its strength was the interdependence among its constituent states. In a Hegelian manner, he argued that history would now be driven by Europe, this 'wonderful continent'. In the same way as the Enlightenment philosophers before him, he defined Europe as a place of multifaceted connections among states, which had become more peaceful, with improved economic laws that allowed for greater freedom of trade. Outside Europe, there was no such mutual exchange between states, which led to stagnation, while Europe was forward thinking and full of exchange, creating mutual dependence without threatening the independence of the constituent states.[28]

Stein talked mainly about states, rather than making any real distinction between states and nations, as this was of no interest to him. One should also consider that the concept of the nation was becoming controversial in his day, especially as there were no homogeneous nations, and the states were still mostly multinational. In those years, the new national affiliations were rarely presented as being opposed to a European affiliation, as they encapsulated both universalism and particularism. As European nations, they were supposed to represent something universal as well as something particular. It was essential for progressives discussing nations that they were parts of a whole. This was true for many of the revolutionaries of 1848, such as Mazzini, who considered the demand for nationality 'not as a mere tribute to local pride or local rights, but as a question of European division of labour'.[29] This was also true for Stein who, as a spokesperson for the government of Vienna, was one of Mazzini's opponents; even so, he argued that Europe, on the one hand, was a shared organism with a common future, but on the other, it consisted of independent bodies. He believed that Europe had accomplished a long-lasting period of peace thanks to the congress system, and that it had a common cause in protecting itself from external challenges and attacks, citing threats from Russia and the Ottoman Empire. Stein claimed that Europe was becoming more united; this did not hinder each nation's individual development, as it was important for the nations and various parts of Europe to develop in their own ways, to contribute to the good of Europe as a whole.[30]

The concept of Europe was increasingly associated not only with multiple states but also with multiple nations. It has never been easy to establish the exact meaning of 'nation'. In the legacy of the French Revolution and Enlightenment philosophers such as Jean-Jacques Rousseau, a nation was recognised as a community of citizens with constitutional rights given by the state, the sovereignty of the people being based on political democracy. From German Romanticism, the idea spread that a nation had something to do with language, common cultural traditions, and shared origins, emphasising its most basic characteristics. The Romantics often turned to Johann Gottfried Herder, who stands out as a major philosopher of the concept of national borders in symbiosis with culture. Herder's idea was that national borders originated from autochthonous cultures – for example, German culture, which was the product of history – strengthened by the creation of national languages.[31] National cultures were to be preserved. Herder mainly focused on German culture, but his ideas were interpreted as vital for promoting national identity among other peoples as well, especially those who did not have their own states, such as Poles, Hungarians, Czechs, Slovaks and Italians.[32]

Current historical research on nations and nationalism has gone in two directions. Researchers who see nationalism as an outcome of modern society look mainly to the Enlightenment and the French Revolution for its origin, focusing on the connections between the modern state, industrial society, and the creation of national identities. They argue that a common language and solidarity within a shared community facilitate both the expanding state administration and the mobility of the workforce for industrial needs. A keyword in this research stream is 'invention', the concepts of nation and nationalism being regarded as deliberate constructions with political, economic and social interests behind them.[33] Others have sought the ways in which ethnic communities can be connected to modern nationalism, studying how myths, symbols, memories and values are passed down from past communities, creating historical continuity. Likewise, they also recognise significant and obvious differences between older ethnic communities and modern nations.[34]

The parallel histories of nationalism and the concept of Europe are striking, confirming how deeply embedded they are in each other. In other words, it is hard to think about Europe without discussing nations, nationalism or nation states. The concepts of nationalism and Europe both have their beginnings in the early modern age, when European unity was first proposed. This was also a period when humanists struggled to unify the national languages, and the concept of the nation began to encompass the people of a specific territory. This can be considered a kind of premodern nationalism distinct from later and more advanced concepts.[35] Early notions of the nation and Europe catered to the ruling elites, the former confirming that the nobles should decide who should be included in a nation, and the latter giving the task of creating a European federation to the monarchs. A further parallel is that both came into general use during the Enlightenment, after which they became institutionalised, with European conferences settling issues between the main European powers, and the nationalistic ambitions of the states growing through the twentieth century. A political–democratic notion of the nation began to emerge, as a community where the people possessed sovereignty through constitutional and democratic governance. The same went for the notion of a Europe of the people, as Saint-Simon and others had advocated. It was also during this time that the romantic idea of the nation became popular, which, in the aftermath of Herder, emphasised shared tradition and language. From this perspective, the nation was associated with moral greatness, and with the mission of preserving and sometimes expanding itself. At the same time, an idea of Europe began to circulate that underlined the heritage of a shared religious community and its moral magnitude. As early as the post-Napoleonic period, notions of both Europe and nation had begun to accentuate the role of a shared economy in building the community, and it was through a shared economy that a nation or Europe could emerge. Moreover, both nationalism and the concept of Europe had been the subject of institutionalisation. The institutionalisation of nationalism began to take off before the First World War, earlier than the institutionalisation of Europe as a concept; on the other hand, it can be argued that the nation states, as such, only emerged after the dismantling of Europe's colonial empires, which took place following post-war integration. To all this is added the impact of intellectuals and academically trained elites in the construction of both Europe and nations – and in the previous chapter we met an array of such philosophers, historians and novelists who wanted to link their work to politics.

It is worth noting that 'the chief architects of nations throughout European history have been scholars or scholars-cum-politicians'.[36] However, we should also pay attention to how these 'chief architects' combined pleas for their nations with the concept of Europe. There is a basic pattern in which each nation has one or more significant features that are of importance in themselves, while also adding essential aspects to Europe as a whole. In Spain, for example, religion and the monarchy were highlighted together with references to reconquering the Iberian Peninsula and the expulsion of Islam, a battle lasting many centuries in which Catholicism and the monarchs liberated Europe.[37] In Germany, Johann Gottlieb Fichte emphasised that the German nation had been historically crucial to establishing European societies, and was indispensable to attaining a peaceful order.[38] Mme de Staël claimed that Germany was the native land of thought, and its writers were 'the best-informed and most reflective men in Europe'.[39] Germany was the upholder of the Reformation, which she considered the solid basis of all progress in Europe. The progress of the German nation was thus good for Europe as well.[40]

The notions of the nation and Europe are closely connected. For instance, nations can be considered parts of a single European family just as citizens of one country are considered parts of a family within a nation. The nation and Europe are also seen as complementary opposites, as when a nation is depicted in all its splendour, cultural brilliance and victorious glory, whereas Europe is respectfully described in more rational terms. European clarity and national devotion rely on each other, as do sense and sensibility.[41] An excellent illustration of this is provided by Tomáš Masaryk, a major Czech nationalist leader. On the one hand, he recalled the Enlightenment and the French Revolution as groundbreaking for Europe, as the turn to reason and the approval of human rights were central to the Czech national revival; on the other hand, the Enlightenment and the French Revolution were contrasted to Czech national tradition. Philosophical rationalism was contrasted to humanism, revolution to reform, shallow lustre to human depth, care of the soul, morality and religion: 'Those who want to think and feel Czech should be aware of the difference'.[42]

The Europe of nations could be recognised as peaceful, as by Herder who dismissed warfare as outdated, because the European future lay in trade and diligence, but it could also be recognised as an aggressive space. For example, Napoleon had stated that Europe was in need of a superior power that should dominate in order to bring more uniformity to the nations.[43] Another example is that of some German nationalists of the late nineteenth century who gladly invoked expansion towards the Black Sea. The Pan-German League proudly declared: 'An deutschen Wesen soll die Welt genesen'.[44] By then, German nationalists were continually referring to threats from neighbours. Articles in widely read family journals homed in on threats to the German language in Belgium, the Netherlands and France, and especially on intimidations of German culture in Alsace. Another article from the same year cited the feelings of hatred among the Danish people towards Germans, and the lack of respect for German culture in Denmark.[45] The idea of threats from other nations mounted after the unification of Germany, in the boom years of economic and military strength of the late nineteenth century. According to an obituary from 1876 of the Czech historian František Palacký, often called the 'father of the Czech nation', Palacký himself hated everything German, and the Czech national movement was linked to Russian interests.[46]

At that time, the concept of nation could entail liberation from other powers as well as the ability to demonstrate both strength and domination over others. With such national ideas, Europe was a place of internal hostilities, strife and military conflict.

Contemporary historians are careful to distinguish between states and nations. According to Charles Tilly, the actions of the former are of a military kind, while the latter present an alluring opportunity to erect more centralised states by making them more homogeneous. The great efforts made to implement unified administration and public service, law and economy, language and culture have helped to strengthen nationalism,[47] partly by shaping nations out of existing states and partly by provoking nationalism among minority cultures.

In the early twentieth century, the nation challenged the state as the basic model for organising society. This can be observed by the variety of people of differing backgrounds and contrasting political programmes who paid tribute to the advantages of adhering to a nation instead of a state. While contrasting nation and state, the German conservative Paul Lagarde criticised Bismarck's new state for being a lifeless machine that acted mechanically: its representatives lacked personality and only acted in accordance with laws, fulfilling their legal obligations with a kind of chemical purity. The nation, on the other hand, he considered a living organism with a soul of its own, having the personality and religious atmosphere of the country. He said that the nation had grown through history, and with it one could find shared values, moral well-being, and a soul.[48] As a representative of a small nation without a state of its own, Tomáš Masaryk instead depicted states as relics of an older era of autocratic rule, while nations, with their shared language and democratic governance, belonged to modern times. The message was clear: behind each and every state there should be a nation.[49] He explicitly rejected the notion that contemporary Czech nationalism needed a long history, citing a contemporary German textbook on the issue, which said 'the best one can do is to completely exclude the words "nation" and "national" from history writing as misleading' as they instead had to do 'with contemporary tendencies'.[50] Indeed, these controversies regarding the concept of nation had much in common with the two main branches of modern research on nations and nationalism. One branch recalls Masaryk in insisting that nationalism was a modern construction and even an invention not found before the eighteenth century; the other echoes Lagarde's notion of continuity from older ethnic communities to modern nationalism.[51] Indeed, the concepts of nation and nationalism were still seen as controversial in those days, just as they are in the multicultural Europe of the twenty-first century, with its increasing number of borders and bickering over the definition of each and every nationality.

This well-established connection between nationalism and the concept of Europe had some surprising consequences. Regarding the division between Catholicism and Protestantism, one could see the former as more often in favour of European unification thanks to the long tradition of a common Roman Catholic Church. One would assume that the Protestants, on the other hand, might be more in favour of independent states, thanks to the tradition of separate national churches. However, this was only sometimes true. One reason was that there was a strong affinity between the concepts of European unity and progress, as well as between progress and Protestantism, while Catholicism was regarded as an obstacle to development and thereby to the creation of a European federation, as noted by French historian Henri Martin in 1866.[52] Another reason was that European unity was usually not seen as an alternative to the European system of states, but rather as an extension and improvement of state cooperation. This view was upheld by the Swiss-German law professor Johann Caspar Bluntschli, who was a Protestant nationalist but argued for a European federation.[53] The more important division was the one between Eastern and Western Christianity, as the definition of Europe as a Christian civilisation did not necessarily include Russia or the Orthodox Church, and often excluded it, though it did include both Protestants and Catholics.[54]

Ways of Defining Uniqueness and Supremacy: North and South, East and West

Indeed, European borders have a bearing on nations and states outside of Europe as well. Another aspect of great importance is how regions are demarcated. In fact, in the intellectual history of Europe we find a strong inclination to divide the continent into different parts, an inclination that grew in importance in the Enlightenment. The East–West divide emerged in the early eighteenth century, and reached a first pinnacle one hundred years later. The cultural divide between North and South is older, and has been documented at least since the Renaissance. After the Reformation, the Catholic South regarded the North as saturated with the evil writings of Luther and the horrible armies of the Swedish king, while northerners viewed the South as stunted and in decay.[55]

Going back to Montesquieu, we can see a clear demonstration of the separation between regions when he defines the peoples and societies of Southern and Northern Europe as being differently shaped by the climate. Passions, for instance, are livelier and idleness more common in the people of the South, who are strongly impressed by honour, while in the North, thrift and liberty are found.[56]

Herder perceived the North–South divide as the most important division when he characterised the peoples of Europe. The Alps represented a fundamental dividing line and, like Montesquieu, he identified climate-driven differences. He recognised communality between the inhabitants of Northern Asia and Northern Europe, as well as an affinity between South West Asians and Southern Europeans.[57] Schlegel identified a common mode of thinking in this statement in his short-lived journal *Europa*: '[S]cientific aspirations moved to the North, while art and poetry stayed in the South'.[58] Other writers reiterated the divide, while identifying the German states as a border zone. The Northern states then included Scandinavia, Poland and Russia, while the others belonged to the South.[59] Mme de Staël found among the French, Italian, Spanish and Portuguese 'less inclination to abstract thinking than among the German nations; they are more addicted to the pleasures and the interests of the earth'.[60]

The bordering of Europe is not only about geography and space, but also about time. While geographical borders are often mentioned upfront, the temporal distinction between old and new is also significant. When Montesquieu drew the border between a thriving North and a lazy South at the Apennine Mountains, it was not only or primarily recognised as a spatial boundary, but essentially as separating the southern countries from the present. It was historical progress that gave the northern countries their prerogatives of constitutional freedoms, constitutional forms of government, and private property. When Montesquieu went to Rome, he saw its social life as underdeveloped – in the eyes of a tourist or an archaeologist, the city belonged to the past; by contrast, Europe – that is, Northern Europe – represented progress and the future. This was established and underlined by de Staël and the Romantics when they transferred the heart of progress from France to Germany.[61]

However, cultural differences between the North and the South were highlighted throughout the following decades. The people in the North continued to be considered more rational and organised, and were therefore seen as more successful and healthier, while those in the South were regarded as more relaxed and leisure-minded. Southern Europe was depicted as awash in creativity, in contrast to the barren North. Differences between the North and the South were often incorporated into national identities, as well. France, Italy and Germany are obvious examples where the southern parts of the countries were considered more backward and conservative in lifestyle and morals, while the northern parts, home to Paris, Milan and Berlin, were portrayed as vibrant and modern.

Writing in the middle of the nineteenth century, Lorenz von Stein clearly acknowledged the impact of dividing Europe into different states with different roles to play. Stein sorted these states into three groups, also recognising larger regions of Europe. In Western Europe he included Spain, England and France, countries with interests that spanned the Atlantic, to the west and to the south. Great Britain dominated the European connection to the west, at the cost of the interests of Spain and France. Eastern Europe consisted of only one state, the immensely large Russia, with its mission to civilise Asia. In between was Central Europe, dividing East and West from each other yet also holding them together. Stein demanded a balance between the three parts, seen as necessary in order to secure peace and the continuation of Europe's mission to civilise the world.[62]

By the middle of the nineteenth century, people had begun to identify areas that were clearly located between the West and the East, such as Central or Middle Europe and the Baltic. A contemporary of Stein, the Riga-based writer and journalist Julius Eckardt, claimed that the Baltic provinces owed their culture to many different influences: Russian, Swedish, German, Polish and Lithuanian. Baltic culture was supposed to be a framework safeguarding against the East, established in contrast to the German, Roman and Slavic.[63]

Not until the eighteenth century was the Eastern border of Europe placed at the Ural Mountains. An early attempt – possibly the first – is mentioned in *Das nord- und ostliche Theil von Europa und Asien* (published 1730) by the Swede Philipp Johann von Strahlenberg. Returning home after thirteen years in prison, he presented what he had learnt about Russia's geography and history, its warfare, trade, and natural resources. The book is remembered for Strahlenberg's rejection of previous attempts to draw a boundary between Europe and Asia in accordance with the rivers Don, Volga and Ob. Citing climatic and geographical considerations, demonstrating differences in geology, animals and vegetation, Strahlenberg moved the border farther east, claiming that the Ural Mountains represent 'Terminus inter Europam et Asiam'. In doing this, he also extended the eastern reaches of Europe.[64]

An early mental division of Europe into East and West can be seen in travel reports describing a border that had not previously been emphasised: between Austria and Hungary, between Prussia and Russia, and between the countries west and east of the Baltic Sea. French Enlightenment authors spoke intermittently of the existence of eastern areas that were obviously European but where people lived in the most pitiful and unenlightened conditions. Voltaire, who travelled through these parts, regarded them as another Europe that was unknown to the leading European countries.[65] In Germany, Herder talked about Eastern Europe, claiming it had Oriental characteristics but was also the region of the Slavs. He posited that the Slavs would awaken from their oppression and be liberated, while he also maintained the general mental division of Europe. Eastern Europe and especially Russia had failed to introduce elements that were fundamental to the civilised parts of Europe, such as a strong civil society, a substantial bourgeoisie, and an independent nobility to counteract the power of the state. To put it bluntly, the essential elements of Western development and advancement were simply lacking. This way of depicting Russia and this particular definition of Eastern Europe were introduced to a larger public as the unity between the victors from the Congress of Vienna eroded, especially in the 1830s, 1840s and 1850s when Russia was considered a more serious threat.[66] Then, the European part of Russia had often been depicted as Eastern Europe,[67] which had at that time included Finland, the Baltic countries, and a large part of Poland. M. D'Erbigny believed Russia to be 'superior to Asia and inferior to Europe', having resources and might but nevertheless 'always vanquished by the civilisation of Europe'.[68] Richard Cobden underlined the difference between the peoples of Russia and Western Europe, the former being uneducated, without ambition, and mostly interested in religion, and the latter wanting to take civilisation to further heights. Russia, he wrote, lagged behind and its people were mainly peace loving, though its autocrats looked for opportunities to expand and therefore threatened Western Europe.[69] Henri Martin was repulsed by Russia. Not only was it the main enemy striving for world power and hoping to crush the nations of Western Europe, but it was also quite a different society: Western and Eastern Europe 'have hardly any resemblance with each other and make up two very different regions – Eastern Europe, which is Russia, has much more of Asian than of European character. . .'. Here, in the West, ruled principles of individual freedom, family rights, and private property; there, in the East, was a governed despotism over individual rights, family and property. Western Europe was considered a family of nations of Aryan origins, while Eastern Europe was a society lost to the Tatars and a long tradition that spanned Attila, Genghis Khan and Timur Lenk; Peter the Great and his heirs ruled behind a mask of Europeanness in Eastern Europe. In Western Europe, one found law and order, whereas in Eastern Europe, one found uncertainty.[70]

This was a far cry from the ambitions of the Russian elite to establish Russia as a civilised, European country. Their idea was to exploit the Ural Mountains as a cultural barrier between European Russia and Asia, claiming that the western part of the empire represented European civilisation, which had obtained large colonies in the East.[71] Support for the view of Russian Europeanness was expressed by Finnish nationalists who found themselves under Russian rule. It was obvious to Zacharias Topelius that Russia, and thus also Finland, belonged to Europe. A complication was that their language was not one of the Indo-Germanic languages of Europe due to immigration by their ancestors. Topelius had no problem with finding the origin of Finnish in Russian territory. Moreover, he claimed that it was obviously not a common language that unified the Finnish and Swedish inhabitants of his country.[72] However, in Russia this view could be flipped, as Nikolaj Danilevsky did in *Russia and Europe*, published in 1869, which was probably the only work that attempted a systematic presentation of the theories of pan-Slavism. As far as Danilevsky was concerned, the Slavs were separate from Europe and would only create a civilisation that was radically different. This was expressed in a historical–philosophical theory of how civilisations replaced themselves. European civilisation was the tenth and the most advanced civilisation, but it was also on the way out; Russia was to be the eleventh. Danilevsky claimed that a future Slav civilisation could develop a universal humanity hitherto unknown. While Greek civilisation had been political, Roman cultural, and European both, Slav civilisation was to encompass these spheres, but add to them religion. Danilevsky's book represented a movement that favoured tsarist rule and religious orthodoxy: the first pan-Slavic committee was founded in Moscow in 1858, followed by other Russian cities, and supported by the Ministry of Foreign Affairs and the Orthodox Church. For the pan-Slavists, the enemies were always the Turks and sometimes the Germans. They expected backing among Czech, Polish and Baltic Slavs for the Russian liberation of these areas. They turned to the Balkans and sought support from their Orthodox Slavs, offering Russian support for their liberation from the Turks. Consequently, they objected to the definition of Eastern Europe as half-barbaric or uncivilised.[73]

As Eastern Europe rose to prominence, the notion of Western Europe became more popular. It has been argued that the perception of 'East' was long of greater importance than that of 'West'. For example, when works by Orientalists and fiction writers were published in the nineteenth century, a distinction between the East and Europe was often seen as essential. At least from the beginning of the twentieth century, the idea of the West had become more prominent and had begun to be seen as essential. This was because the idea of the West had gained several associations that had previously been reserved for a more general European idea. The Western parts of Europe were thereafter increasingly seen as parts of a culture shared with North America.[74] However, the use of the concept in a binary way was established from the very beginning, even though the usage differed slightly depending on the context. Early on, geographers used the terms Eastern and Western Europe, and this binary was well established by the middle of the nineteenth century.[75] Starting from the 1850s, we can already find evidence that these notions had been set in motion. When discussing the German question, Gustav Diezel spoke of 'die Westen' and 'die westeuropäische Civilisation' in contrast to Russia, but without using the words 'Eastern Europe'.[76] In writing of the consequences of the Crimean War, Richard Cobden frequently mentioned Western Europe. Interestingly, he spoke of an eastern question but did not use the concept of Eastern Europe.[77]

Oswald Spengler took this to a new level when he claimed that one could no longer use the word 'Europe'. He declared that, although it could be used as a geographical term, it was not applicable when considering historical or political matters. For instance, ancient Greece could not be divided into a European and an Asian part, as that would make Homer and Pythagoras Asian, and Russia could not be culturally defined as European, although that was geographically correct. Therefore, it was not viable to create a historical content for the concept of Europe; it was more relevant to speak of East and West.[78]

What They Talk About, When They Talk About Central Europe

Demarcations between regions became popular and turned out to be useful, not only when describing and defining areas, but also when making statements about social conditions and what policy was desirable, or when envisioning potential new regimes. By the middle of the nineteenth century, the region south of the Finnish Sea had been named the Baltic, and Baltic languages were recognised. Scandinavists were advocating the unification of the Danish, Norwegian and Swedish peoples. Geographers had recognised the Balkan Peninsula, and the Balkans would soon be considered a region. The Mediterranean meant both the sea as well as the surrounding region.[79] A close reading of texts mentioning the notion of Central Europe – or 'Mitteleuropa' as it was mainly called in the Austrian and German discourses – reveals how such a concept can be used to describe much more than a simple geographical region, and should be regarded as a social act aimed at achieving specific goals. The concept of Central Europe demarcates an area shared by Eastern and Western Europe, and defined as exhibiting both distinct features and ones viewed as essentially European. The concept of Central Europe differs in one fundamental way from that of Eastern Europe: the former is rooted mainly in that area, and it does not imply that the region is less European than the neighbouring Western Europe.[80]

The discourse of Central Europe began amidst the events of the fateful year of 1848. There are earlier geographical works distinguishing Central Europe as a region in addition to Northern and Southern or Eastern and Western Europe.[81] This was well clarified in previous research, while the impact of the events of 1848 has been largely forgotten.[82] However, the first evidence of the noun 'Mitteleuropa' used as a political concept is from discussions in the Frankfurt Parliament on 24 July 1848. As such, it had almost never been used before, and this occasion was its true birthplace and origin. It was first launched in order to describe the emerging empire of Germany, supplemented with western Slavs and Hungarians in order to gather a population and resources large enough to match, on the one hand, Russia, and on the other, the Romance peoples.[83] By tracing the development of this concept, it is possible to see it becoming a viable and useful notion for examining different groups and separate interests.

'Mitteleuropa' was used regularly in the 1850s. The notion outlined an area that spanned several states, and was characterised by progressive civilisation and a high level of culture and knowledge. It mediated the different parts of Europe and connected its western parts with the Orient. 'Mitteleuropa' brought together and set up an 'imagined community' (cf. Benedict Anderson) to which a common language was not fundamental, as in the contemporary nationalism, but that was marked by a quest for military strength to withstand the expanding Russian Empire and a free trade area that would make it possible to compete with the growing economies of Britain and France. 'Mitteleuropa' was less a legacy of Herder's national cultures and more a mode of economic thinking and an outcome of the model established in the Congress of Vienna regarding balance in international relations. The best-known of those members of the Frankfurt Parliament who spread the concept was Carl von Bruck, who soon became the Austrian minister of trade, and later of finance. It was during his period in office that trade tariffs were abolished within the Habsburg Empire, to increase trade and lead to various sorts of progress. He appointed counsellors with similar economic views, positive towards Central Europe.[84] One of them wrote that 'the customs union is a forerunner of another mightier, self-conscious, active and living unit'.[85] In addition to this, the chancellors Ludwig von Pfordten of Bavaria and Julius Fröbel of Saxony pleaded for a recognised 'Mitteleuropa', demanding a federation of the German states and Austria that would include Hungary and the Slavic parts of the Habsburg Empire. We can observe a decisive launching of the notion.[86]

This 'Mitteleuropa' would both unite the Germans and welcome the different nationalities within the Habsburg Empire. Fröbel had great hopes, making two trips to Vienna where he met influential people and gained support from government representatives. In September 1848 he wrote the following in a pamphlet:

> I regard our history to be so closely connected with the western Slavs, southern Slavs, Magyars and Vlachs, that we should not wish to dissolve this connection. A large democratic federation, where we unify with said peoples, and whose capital is Vienna, seems to me to be the only reasonable plan for the political configuration of 'Mitteleuropa'.[87]

An eagerness for political modernisation permeates the proposals. Bruck wanted constitutional governance, proving the close connection between these proposals and the liberals. Another Austrian minister, Gustav Höfken, dreamed of a democratic and republican federation, as it would further 'all spiritual flowering, material wealth, humanity and civilisation in general'.[88]

'Mitteleuropa' not only conjured up new divisions within Europe, but it also played a part in Austrian efforts to withstand Prussia, giving Austria an upper hand in the question of Germany. At the same time, it promised economic wealth to all of the German states. Both politically and economically, it represented a modern project. Nation states were sometimes seen as passé and limited, while multinational states belonged to the future.[89] All of the states would benefit from improved finances if only one army was necessary. Austria could take advantage of skilled labour from the other German states, which, in turn, could make use of Austria's vast natural resources. Austria would have better access to markets and, together with the German states, could help to spread German culture and civilise the countries farther east.[90]

The discourse on 'Mitteleuropa' often addressed the German question. Höfken wrote that the establishment of Mitteleuropa could help Germany to overcome its divisions and once more become a mighty power. The ultimate objective behind the union was to raise the German nation to a 'higher existence'.[91]

Even though the Austrian government's use of 'Mitteleuropa' included the Slavic peoples of the Habsburg Empire, it was not in the minds of Bruck, Höfken or the others to limit the dominance of the Austro-Germans within the Habsburg Empire. However, the discourse also included attempts to define a 'Mitteleuropa with a stronger position for the non-German nations of the Habsburg Empire. After the Hungarian revolt was defeated, Lajos Kossuth introduced the idea of a Donau Federation, where the Hungarians were united with the Romanians and Austro-Slavs.[92] Other uses of 'Mitteleuropa' maintained Czech nationalism against the German-dominated Austrian state and German nationalism in Bohemia. These were not prominent issues but of minor importance. They consisted of ill-conceived plans with no government backing. However, they were presented by leaders of the nationalist movement and, as such, became significant. They further illustrated the manifold and partly conflicting implications of addressing a larger part of Europe that encompassed several nations. They stood out as examples of the contestability of the meanings assigned to the concepts defining the divides through Europe.

In 1849, František Palacký used the Czech expression 'střední Europy' (Central Europe) to define an area where language had become the main characteristic of nationalism, claiming Herderian views so typical of nationalists in Central Europe. For communities, Palacký continued, language was as important as religion had been previously, and the divides between the Austrian nationalities threatened war if the principle of equality of nations and languages failed to be accepted in the empire.⁹³ In an article published in December 1849, Karel Havlíček criticises 'Mitteleuropa' as built upon the political interests of German nationalism. He presents an alternative for a new Austria ('Novo-Rakouska'), constitutionally governed on the basis of Slavic nations and fully separate from Germany.⁹⁴ Six months later he himself recognised a 'Mitteleuropa' that comprised the Slavic nations of the Austrian Empire in addition to the Austro-Germans and the Hungarians. He reasoned that the Slavic nations of Austria were weak and needed to be united – the empire needed a more solid foundation. Havlíček saw 'Střední Europy' or 'Mitteleuropa' as a new Austria where Slavic nations would have freedom and national rights equal to those of the Germans. He foresaw a future inside Austria with its firm protection against tsarist autocrats and Russian expansionism.⁹⁵

This way of redefining the concept was never established as an alternative to the Austro-German 'Mitteleuropa'. It was too strongly associated with the 'Mitteleuropa' visions of the Austrian government to be reconciled with Austro-Slavic notions. In Prussia, 'Mitteleuropa' was also intertwined with the interests of the Austrian government and considered an economic threat to the Northern German states, which, with their underdeveloped industry, would suffer in the common market.⁹⁶ The notion was further considered a political threat. When Bismarck was envoy of the German Bundestag in the 1850s, he wrote reports to the Prussian chancellor in which he frequently expressed his suspicions of Austria and its efforts to connect with the southern German states by setting up a Central European empire.⁹⁷ Constantin Franz, a Prussian writer with conservative beliefs, posited that 'Mitteleuropa' was only a guise for Austrian aspirations to take leadership in all German lands: 'Mitteleuropa' was nothing but an extended Habsburg Empire, a federation led by Austria, which entailed nothing but a Greater Austria.⁹⁸

Visions of a common market and economic union of both empires were kept alive, partly by Austrian politicians, and as late as 1879, a proposal was discussed by both the Austrian and Hungarian governments. It was mainly Austrian and Hungarian economists who conveyed the idea to new generations, and the notion regained prominence starting in the 1880s. Several chambers of commerce in Austro-Hungarian (as the empire was often called after autonomy was granted to Hungary in 1866) cities spoke in favour of a union resembling 'Mitteleuropa'. It was called for in a German economic journal, and addressed by the scientific society for Austrian economists at a meeting in 1900. In the new century, societies were founded to advance economic cooperation in 'Mitteleuropa'. Some wanted cooperation to be confined to promoting economic interests, while others wanted a common market and some even a political union.⁹⁹

In addition, there were hopes for a 'Mitteleuropa' among some Germans, though they were mostly conservative thinkers opposed to the Germany that Bismarck had created in 1871 and continued to lead for many years. Paul Lagarde picked up the theme in his reflections on the state of art from the 1880s, and Ottomar Schuchardt returned to it in his main work two decades later. They pleaded for a nationalism that recognised a need for Germans to colonise Hungary and the western Slavic lands, believing that the agrarian sectors were of primary and industry of secondary importance, and that the German nation was under threat. Lagarde warned against the Russians, and Schuchardt against the Czechs, Hungarians and Italians in Austria who hated German culture and were forcing back the Germans. Bismarck was criticised for having excluded Austria and having created an overly Prussian bureaucracy and a state that only promoted egoism and materialism.[100]

Lagarde wanted Germany and Austria to form a shared state called 'Mitteleuropa'. This would open up new territories for German settlers who wished to cultivate land, and it would impede the spiritual depletion characterising Bismarck's Germany.[101] Schuchard wanted a federal 'Mitteleuropa' comprising states and nations that upheld German culture; it would include both the Baltic countries with their German populations, as well as Switzerland, the Netherlands and the Scandinavian countries. He also believed that Finland should be liberated from the grip of the Russians. He referred to a favourite quotation of the Swedish King Oscar II, who said: 'My heart is French, but my reason is German'.[102] The federation, he stipulated, should be organised with one army, one common spoken language, and one single economic market. The leaders of the states should form an assembly in charge of foreign policy, administration, finances, the army, the navy and the colonies. It would be complemented with a people's assembly possessing limited power.[103]

The notion of 'Mitteleuropa' spread farther as cartographers, geographers and historians made use of it. The first maps that presented 'Mitteleuropa' were published in the smaller German states after the uprisings of 1848: in Baden a geographical map, in Würtenberg a travel map, and in Frankfurt am Main a railway map. All were published in the period when these states were cultivating closer relationships with Austria and opposing Prussian dominance with intermittent hostility. Maps were published in both Austria and Prussia with variations on 'Mitteleuropa', such as 'Zentral Europa' and 'Zwischen-Europa' (Central and Middle Europe). Up to 1871, maps published in Vienna emphasised the Habsburg Empire, depicting only its territories or including some of the neighbouring states such as the Netherlands and Belgium. Prussian-made maps gave the impression that German-speaking lands were located in the middle of Europe, implying that Germany was of special importance in Europe. After the 1871 unification, when relations were beginning to improve between Austria and Germany, a map made in Vienna equated 'Mitteleuropa' with 'the German sea', including all parts of Central Europe with German-speaking populations.[104]

Around 1900, the notion of 'Mitteleuropa' gained a firmer foothold among geographers, who were eager to take on the task of settling its geographical scope. In determining its characteristics and defining its borders, these geographers were making decisions touching on the contemporary question of whether Germans and Austrians belonged to the same culture. One example is the German and Austrian Alpine Club, which had several geographers as members and a name that indicated a shared culture. Geographers gained support from the German government, which prioritised the study and teaching of geography; after 1871, geography quickly became a university discipline with its own professors, and in 1881 it was even introduced in Prussian gymnasiums.[105] The textbooks, the most extensive of which had 650 pages, presented 'Mitteleuropa' as a geographical entity and professed the basic idea of German and Austrian fellowship.[106]

A whole range of arguments were marshalled. One textbook included Switzerland, Belgium and the Netherlands in 'Mitteleuropa' because of their similar physical geography. Another added the western Slavic and the Baltic peoples, because they all belonged to the German cultural sphere.[107] There were nuanced differences among the geographers as to how to define the borders of 'Mitteleuropa', as well as other significant borders. One belief was that a nation was ultimately tied to nature. A nation's lands may vary through history, but its existence should always be directly connected to the territory it possessed at the moment.[108] For some, it was possible to include cultural aspects, even though the physical prerequisites remained of greatest importance. In examining the conditions of 'Mitteleuropa', it seemed that its physical geography was manifold and rich in a variety of ways, which was not true of Eastern Europe; consequently, the political geography was characterised by a few large kingdoms in the east, while there were many smaller kingdoms in the west. Physically, 'Mitteleuropa' mostly resembled Western Europe, but it also had elements of the lowlands typical of Eastern Europe. The advantages of 'Mitteleuropa' were identified: it had the most favourable climate, with abundant rainfall, mild winters and cool summers.[109]

To sum up, different visions intensely related to different national and imperial interests obviously contributed to the concept of Central Europe. The strength of these essentially politically motivated rationales became evident in their impact on the geographical mapping of Europe.

Entangled Ideas: Reconciling Borders with Unity

The first chapter of this book presented material about European dreams of unity, and this chapter has outlined aspects of the borders of Europe. Now it is germane to move on to the issue of how to reconcile borders with unity. We can see that European unity is a concept complicated by its relationship to nations, states and regions, and that several ideas of unity must coexist.

To begin with, there is the unity of multinational states, empires and federations. All European states comprised populations with different languages and various historical legacies. Minorities in some states were making persistent claims for recognition. Most states in Europe had overseas colonies – Russia, for example, had expanded far into the east, and other states had expanded in one direction or another. The mightiest states – Austria, France, Great Britain and Russia – claimed to be empires. As we have already touched upon, the rising power of the United States stood out as a model of how to marry the longing for independence with the advantages of a larger federal state. In Great Britain, people discussed whether it was time to reshape British colonial rule into an imperial federation, meaning that those colonies with a high percentage of British citizens would be given self-rule.[110]

An illustrative example is that of the Habsburg Empire before its collapse at the end of the First World War. In the discourse on the Austrian idea versus the different nationalities, one can see that dreams of unity and the proposed advantages of a suprastate permeate the different nationalities, despite the nationalists' pleas. Ideas of unity were not necessarily tied up with linguistic homogeneity, as one common state can speak several languages. The linguistic map of the Habsburg dominion looks like a hastily stitched patchwork quilt. German was the most spoken language, but it was still only spoken by less than a quarter of the population, while the rest spoke Czech, Slovak, Polish, Ukrainian, Slovene, Italian, Hungarian, Romanian, Ruthenian, and so on. Faced with growing nationalisms, many people had to choose nationhood. This could be seen as a choice between different nationalities, but it could also be seen as one between the existing state and the idea of a distinct nation based on linguistic communality. The alternative was to call for an all-Austrian identity not based on a common language, but originating in a distinct idea or feeling that everybody could adapt to, that would be supranational in its character. Such an idea could be viewed as progress; the goal of the Austrian state, it was argued, should be to encourage progress with the help of a constitution and citizenship rights.[111] Or the idea could be seen as a gesture of tolerance between nationalities, classes, beliefs, and ways of thinking.[112]

The most distinguished text conveying a supranational idea was the 1841 pamphlet *Austria and its Future* by the official and nobleman Victor von Andrian-Werburg. His designation of freedom as the foundation of Austrian nationality included a dismissal of Slavic, Hungarian, Italian and German nationalisms, as well as a rejection of the centralist role of Austria – understandably, the author took the precaution of publishing anonymously. A spirit of freedom would spur on the quest for a common civic nationality, giving the rulers a more united and more easily governed state. The people would feel a new sense of solidarity and a respect for their fatherland, as well as a 'love of the shared freedom'. Andrian-Werburg emphasised the need for a leading idea or principle to present to the people, but saw no such idea among the officials, nor indeed in the Austrian state. He took the idea of freedom as a founding principle from Alexis de Tocqueville, whose newly published book on democracy in America cautioned as to the drawbacks of centralist rule and how it restricted individual freedom. The pamphlet's thesis on freedom of the press and judicial independence was appreciated and repeated, as was the overall notion of decentralisation.[113]

Others kept to the more common European idea of nationalities being distinguished by their languages, and rejected the existence of Austrian nationalism. Even then it was rational to advocate a common Austrian state, which, it was believed, would guarantee places for the nationalities within its borders. This line of thinking was expressed in extremely blunt terms by Czech nationalist František Palacký: if this state did not already exist, then it would have to be created.[114] The argument was that Austria existed in the interest of its nationalities. To protect itself from outside forces such as Russia and Asia, it would need to cultivate mutual respect with, and safeguard, its peoples. The argument followed Herder precisely, underlining the importance of language, as each people had a mission to develop their own distinguishing features and contribute to the development of humankind. For example, the Bohemian German Leo Thun maintained that the Czech language should not be forgotten and replaced with German, as was otherwise a common view.[115]

When the included nationalities began to see that unification would benefit them in some way, the idea of gathering multiple nationalities within the frame of one state started to gain strength. In 1907, a wide-ranging pamphlet was written by a representative of the Romanian national party who was acquainted with the heir of the Habsburg throne, Archduke Franz Ferdinand. He presented a plan for a federal organisation of the empire based on ethnographic guidelines, with fifteen countries making up the Austrian federation. All would emerge as independent states, just as homogeneous as the Western European states, in hopes that this would solve many of the previous national conflicts. The plan was given some consideration in Austria, not least because it was reported that Franz Ferdinand himself wanted to federalise the Habsburg lands.[116] During the last years of the Habsburg Empire, several factors favouring a multinational state were identified: the advantages of a borderless economic community (proposed by the economist Gustav Stolper); the thousand-year-old cultural unity of the Central European nations, which shared historical experiences and a regional home to a mix of nationalities (proposed by the social democratic leader Karl Renner); the interdependence of the nationalities meant that they could not develop separately, so the multinational state would be the best form of political organisation for them (proposed by the Christian socialist leader Ignaz Seipel); and only within the multinational state would it be possible to safeguard peace (proposed by Stolper and Seipel).[117]

Obviously, much support for the multinational state came from Austria itself. However, Austria-Hungary's Dual Monarchy was much admired in other countries for the way it safeguarded peace and stability within its borders by using both constitutional principles and decentralisation policies. Austria-Hungary, it was reported to the British public by a journalist in 1899, 'bears testimony to the possibility of creating an organic entity out of the most heterogeneous conglomerate of nationalities'.[118]

Apart from ideas of a multinational state, the notions of progress and modernity motivated the struggle for unity, backed by the claim that civilisation is an essential unifying force and that modern history is marked by a progression from smaller units to larger ones. The young Lord Salisbury objected to 'the splitting up of mankind into a multitude of infinitesimal governments, in accordance with their actual differences of dialect or their presumed differences of race', as it would only 'undo the work of civilisation and renounce all the benefits which the slow and painful process of consolidation has procured for mankind'. His conclusion was that 'it is the agglomeration and not the comminution of states to which civilisation is constantly tending'.[119]

At times, the uniting of Europe was seen as part of a process leading towards a higher civilisation, because it meant a 'widening of the area within which no sword shall be drawn and no shot fired saved by command of the central authority'. The state building of Germany was deemed an example for Europe to follow: many centuries of war between the different German states had come to an end; Germany was governed by a parliament that represented its entire empire; and peace reigned in all its lands between the borders of France and Russia.[120] The idea that larger units should be created at the expense of minor states was popular during the nineteenth century. Although not explicitly stated, one can infer that the relatively small states were the problem, and the larger entities were the solution. Occasionally, this position was expressed in radical terms. For instance, in

1846 it was predicted by a German economist and reformist that, within a hundred years, there would be only three or four states left in Europe.[121] We see the same belief expressed by the historian Heinrich Treitschke, who in 1897 concluded that there was no future for smaller states in Central Europe. In the long run, second-rate states such as Switzerland and Sweden would fade into the background; small states would not survive and the great powers of Europe would ultimately decide upon the future of the continent.[122]

Others did not hesitate to accept the legitimacy of smaller states such as Belgium, but also saw the need for cooperation and strategic action. The proposal that followed was for European states to take on federalism. For instance, a Scottish traveller wrote about 'the superiority of small independent states federally united', and claimed federalism to be a more efficient alternative than forced centralisation.[123] In the early twentieth century, the peace activist Jacques Novicow was convinced that a European federation would one day be in place, either through the deeds of statesmen or through growing consciousness among the masses of its necessity, something that should already have been apparent in the peace movement. Inspired by the ideas of Herbert Spencer and other social Darwinists, he described this federation as a progressive step towards a further association of humankind in the ongoing evolution of societies.[124] Bertha von Suttner also found support for a historical movement towards cooperation by reading Spencer and Darwin, but her favourite was Henry Thomas Buckle, who discerned a shared European civilisation, despite the differences and cleavages among the states. The progress of history was meant to inspire, wrote Suttner, as peace would necessarily follow from the development of culture.[125] In these examples, we can see 'a teleological understanding of modernity' that would become, and still remains, instrumental to the integration project of the EU.[126]

The idea of political integration was originally embedded in a context of historical philosophical concepts of drift towards larger political units. The concept of integration can be traced to late seventeenth-century mathematicians such as Sir Isaac Newton and Gottfried Leibniz, who wrote of the compilation of different parts into a larger and more complex unity. In the late nineteenth century, both the noun 'integration' and verb 'to integrate' spread to other fields of knowledge, from science to the humanities, from metallurgy to philosophy. The famous British philosopher Herbert Spencer, whose books sold a million copies during his lifetime, contributed to the popularity of integration by introducing it as one of the basic natural principles of both biology and psychology, and of the formation of society and ethics. He saw an overarching evolution that brought further integration to both nature and society. 'Political integration' was his label for the specific evolution of political institutions, a concept that quickly became known in France and Germany thanks to translations and to being passed on by his disciples.[127]

In this context, integration can connote the long process unfolding over the last millennium or even the history following the break-up of the Roman Empire, during which small units were first combined to make larger ones, and later emerging European states embraced ever larger territories. Wordsworth Donisthorpe highlighted the history of the British Isles, beginning with the unification of some of the small units into the first kingdom called England in 829, continuing with the conquest of Wales, and concluding with the inclusion of Scotland and Ireland. Then he mentioned the more recent unifications of Italy and Germany, and predicted the imminent disappearance of Belgium, the Netherlands and Denmark from the list of independent states. His key concept to describe this process was political integration, a process stimulated by the 'wonderful applications of steam and of electricity to the satisfaction of man's wants', by the progress of science and the spread of education to the lower classes.[128]

Spencer and his followers tended to think about society in terms of biology, even talking about it as a social organism. Donisthorpe defined the size limits of a state or political body that could be compared to a living organism, and the ability of its different parts to cooperate. Just as a human body has limits set by the ability of internal organs to work together, so it was with society. The trend towards larger states could be related to the growing ability to communicate, increasing knowledge, more widespread information, and greater concentrations of people living in urban areas: 'Hence, there has resulted a constant tendency towards increasing integration'. However, this also meant that political integration would be limited, depending on how well nations fit together: being separated by great distances, different stages of development, and diverging expectations of government could tear artificial units apart.[129] We can conclude that, from its beginning, the concept of integration was also a concept that dealt with limits and borders.

The Border Paradox of Europe: The Diversity of Unity

Europe is not only about unity; it is also about finding and constructing borders. Since the Enlightenment, there has been a far-reaching interest in defining borders, an interest that also concerns the concept of Europe. The concept of Europe is indeed embedded in discourses of divisions. These divisions are so commonly remarked upon that they seem to be autochthonous entities to which further claims and meanings are added. Contemporary discussions and arguments are borrowed from history, which indicates the interconnectedness between differences and borders in the making and presentation of European unity, constituting an important part of its meaning. Borders are often presented as absolute and engraved in stone, even before further claims or doubts are weighed.

However, we should bear in mind that sometimes the concepts that define the community of a nation or region tend to hide and/or overcome potentially controversial issues. Regarding nations, class interests can be subordinated to national solidarity. Cohesion is created by avoiding the cultural boundaries of religions and languages, or by not minimising and suppressing minorities. Narratives are elaborated upon and implemented in order to forge the communal history of a nation. The concept of the region can be used to subordinate the ambitions of individual states in order to find common, supranational interests. Cultural borders can either be glossed over or made into positive features. Religious factions are hidden or, when possible, used to define the region ('Eastern Europe is Orthodox'). Linguistic borders are relegated to the back seat. Possible conflicts over borders can be suppressed, and even completely hidden.

Notes

1. Talmor, 'Reflections', 63.
2. Balibar, 'World Borders, Political Borders'; Balibar, 'Europe as Borderland'.
3. The rich research on borders includes that of geographer Henk van Houtum, who stresses the ongoing significance of cultural borders, political sociologist Chris Rumford, who emphasises the differentiating function of borders, and a wide range of research within the humanities that discusses borders in connection with identity. For an overview of earlier research on cultural borders, see Andrén and Söhrman, 'Introduction'; for a recent discussion, see Allmendinger et al., *Soft Spaces in Europe*.
4. Huntington, 'The Clash of Civilizations?'.
5. E.g., Benhabib, *The Claims of Culture*.
6. Hale, *The Civilization of Europe*, 36.
7. Tilly, *Coercion, Capital, and European States*.
8. Elliott, 'Europe of Composite Monarchies', 51.
9. Hale, *The Civilization of Europe*, 34–35.
10. Hase, *Evropa*.
11. *Neue Wandkarte von Europa*.
12. Weiland, *Europa*.
13. Woodbridge, *School Atlas*, 289.
14. Stülpnagen and Bär, *Karte von Europa*.
15. Ibid.
16. De Staël, *Germany*, 18.
17. Ibid., 18–21, 33–36.
18. Quotation from Hazard, *Crisis of the European Mind*, 54.
19. Defoe, *The True-Born Englishman*, 11–12, partly cited in Hazard, *Crisis of the European Mind*, 54.

20. Hazard, *Crisis of the European Mind*, 437.
21. Verga, 'European Civilization'.
22. Robertson, *Reign of Charles V*, x.
23. Quotation from Gossman, 'The Idea of Europe', 207.
24. De Staël, *Germany*, 18–23.
25. Ibid., 18–23.
26. Ibid., 393.
27. Dainotto, *Europe (in Theory)*, 153–57.
28. Stein, *Oesterreich und der Frieden*, 2–17.
29. Mazzini, *Selected Writings*, 118.
30. Stein, *Oesterreich und der Frieden*, 1–11.
31. Herder, *Ideen* II, 259–60, 272–73, 385–92, 484–85.
32. Andrén, *Att frambringa det uthärdliga*, 85–87.
33. In this stream, seminal works by historians include: Gellner, *Nations and Nationalism*; Gellner, *Encounters with Nationalism*; Anderson, *Imagined Communities*; and Hobsbawn, *Nations and Nationalism*. Central texts are compiled in Hutchinson and Smith, *Nationalism*. An important contribution in the social sciences is Billig, *Banal Nationalism*.
34. Groundbreaking works in this stream include Hutchinson, *Modern Nationalism*; Smith, *Ethnic Origins of Nationalism*; and Smith, *Nations and Nationalism*.
35. Cf. Hirschi, *Origins of Nationalism*, 9, 14, 44–46.
36. Ibid., 15.
37. Ferrer y Suberana, 'La nacionalidad', 71.
38. Fichte, *Reden an die deutsche Nation*, 211–15; Thompson, 'Ideas of Europe', 38.
39. De Staël, *Germany*, 23–24.
40. Ibid., 298–307.
41. The thesis of European clarity and national devotedness is ingeniously developed in Dahlstedt and Dahlstedt, *Nationell hängivenhet*.
42. Masaryk, *Česka Otázka*, 11–12; Masaryk, *Jan Hus*, 11–14, 42–43; quotation from *Jan Hus*, 14: 'Kdo myslit a cítit chce česky, tohoto rozdíly musí si být vědom'.
43. Thompson, 'Ideas of Europe', 38–39.
44. Also cited by Emperor Wilhelm II in 1907; see Ernst, *Reden des Kaisers*, 120–22.
45. 'Anonymous article' in *Illustriertes Familien-journal*, 88–91.
46. Schütz, 'Franz Palacky', 828–30. The article ended with the quotation: 'Er hat umsonst gelebt – umsonst gewirkt' (He lived in vain – worked in vain).
47. Tilly, *Coercion, Capital, and European States*.
48. Lagarde, *Deutsche Schriften*, 98–138.
49. Masaryk, 'Independent Bohemia', 117–19; Masaryk, 'The Problem of Small Nations', 135–38.
50. Masaryk, *Jan Hus*, 97–121. The work Masaryk cites is Lindner, *Geschichtsphilosophie*.
51. See, e.g., Hobsbawn and Ranger, *The Invention of Tradition*; Anderson, *Imagined Communities*; Smith, *Ethnic Origins of Nationalism*; Hutchinson, *Modern Nationalism*.
52. Martin, *Russland und Europe*, 289.
53. Bluntschli, 'Die Organisation'.
54. See, e.g., De Gurowski, *Russland und die Civilisation*, 2.
55. Davidson, *The Idea of North*, 38.
56. Montesquieu, *Spirit of the Laws*, 238, 355, 484.
57. Gollwitzer, *Europabild und Europagedanke*, 93–94.
58. Schlegel, 'Ueber Literatur', 77: 'das wissenschaftliche Streben zog sich nach Norden, die Kunst und Poesie blieb im Süden'.
59. Gollwitzer, *Europabild und Europagedanke*, 86–87.
60. De Staël, *Germany*, 21–22.

61. Dainotto, *Europe (in Theory)*, 70–80, 148–51.
62. Stein, *Oesterreich und der Frieden*, 1–11.
63. Eckardt, *Die baltischen Provinzen Russlands*, ix–x, 1–2.
64. Strahlenberg, *Das nord- und ostliche*, 10–23, 92–3, 105–9, 173–6.
65. Wolf, *Inventing Eastern Europe*. Wolf claims that Voltaire and others used the perception of a backward Eastern Europe to create their own ideas and theories about the Enlightenment. By creating an Eastern Europe, borders between civilisation and barbarism were clarified. In Eastern Europe, features of civilisation were found, more so than in Asia, but it was also partly stuck in barbarism. However, this has been questioned by later research that sees a discourse on Eastern Europe beginning in the nineteenth century. For a compilation of the critique, see Drace-Francis, 'A Provincial Imperialist'.
66. Adamovsky, 'Euro-Orientalism'.
67. E.g., von Reden, *Ost-Europa*.
68. D'Erbigny, *Future Destinies of Europe*, 136. Originally published in Brussels, it has reportedly been translated into Italian as well; see Section V.
69. Cobden, *What Next and Next?*, 19–21.
70. Martin, *Russland und Europa*, xi, xxviiff, 2, 19, 108, quotation from 19: 'haben fast keine Aehnlichkeit mit einander und bilden zwei sehr verschiedene Regionen – Ost-Europa, das heisst Russland, hat viel mehr von asiatischem als von Europäischem Character...'. Similar views are presented in Talbot, *Europa den Europäern*, xvi: there ruled nihilism, 'der Leugnung jedes Grundsatzes, worauf die Kultur Europas beruht' (the denial of every principle on which the culture of Europe is based).
71. Woolf, 'European World-View', 91–92.
72. Topelius, *Boken om vårt land*, 110–11 and 131–32.
73. Seton-Watson, *Decline of Imperial Russia*, 90–93; Danilevsky, *Russland und Europa*, 275–9; Topelius, *Boken om vårt land*, 110–11, 131–32.
74. GoGwilt, 'True West', 38–42.
75. E.g., Rotteck, *Europe: Vorlesungen*; Pütz, *Manual of Modern Geography*.
76. Diezel, *Frage der deutschen Zukunft*.
77. Cobden, *What Next and Next?*
78. Spengler, *Der Untergang des Abendlandes*, 21–22.
79. Mishkova and Trencsényi, *European Regions and Boundaries*.
80. This section draws on my extensive study in Swedish of the history of the idea of Central Europe: *Att frambringa det uthärdliga: Studier kring gränser, nationalism och individualism i Centraleuropa* [To make it bearable: Studies on borders, nationalism, and individualism in Central Europe]. Previous research on the German concept of Mitteleuropa in general includes Meyer, *Mitteleuropa in German Thought*; Droz, *L'Europe Centrale*; Agnelli, *Idea di Mitteleuropa*; and Brechtefeld, *Mitteleuropa and German Politics*.
81. E.g., Hoffmann, *Europa und seine Bewohner*. See also Adamovsky, 'Euro-Orientalism'; Schultz and Natter, 'Imagining Mitteleuropa'.
82. See, e.g., the overview in Bugge, 'The Use of the Middle'; and Rider, 'Mitteleuropa, Zentraleuropa, Mittelosteuropa'.
83. *Stenographischer Bericht*, 1113–14.
84. The most expressive of these was Gustav Höfken; see, e.g., his *Deutschlands Zoll- und Handelseinigung*, 110–15.
85. Ibid., 291: 'Der Zollverein ist Vorläufer und Vorarbeiter einer andern mächtigern, selbstgewissen, thatkräftigen und lebendigen Einheit'.
86. Fröbel, *Wien, Deutschland und Europa*, 5–13: Pfordten, 'Denkschrift', 62–63.
87. Fröbel, *Wiener Oktober-Revolution*, 7–8: 'Ich finde unsere Geschichte mit denen der Westslaven, Südslaven, Magyaren und Wallachen so eng verbunden, dass wir uns aus der Verbindung nicht sollten lösen wollen. Ein grosser demokratischer Staatenbund, in welchem

wir uns mit den genannten Völkern vereinen, und dessen Hauptstadt Wien ist, scheint mir der einzige vernünftige Plan für die politische Gestaltung von Mitteleuropa zu sein'.

88. Bruck, *Die Aufgabe Österreichs*, 5–6, 32–45, 61; Moering, *Entweder – oder*, 3–10, quotation from 8: 'aller geistigen Blüthen, des materiellen Wohlstandes, der Humanität und civilisation im Allgemeinen'.

89. Höfken, *Deutschlands Zoll- und Handelseinigung*, 104–11, 129–30, 280–84.

90. Bruck, *Die Aufgabe Österreichs*, 51–58, 63f, 84; Moering, *Entweder – oder*.

91. Höfken, *Deutschlands Zoll- und Handelseinigung*, 104–11, 129–30, 280–84.

92. Kühl, *Föderationspläne im Donauraum*, 18–22.

93. Palacký, *Radhost III*, 59–64.

94. Havlíček, *Politické Spisy II*, 805–10.

95. Ibid., 169–78, 187–98.

96. Hübner, *Die zolleinigung Oesterreichs*, 5–7.

97. Poschinger, *Preussen im Bundestag*, vol. I, 45–46, 103–6, and vol. III, 499.

98. Frantz, *Unsere Politik*, 14–18, 61–64.

99. Rumpler and Niedrekorn, *Der Zweibund 1879*. See also Bosc, *Zollalliancen und Zollunionen*, 237–41, 256–81, as well as Matlekovitz, *Die Zollpolitik der Monarchie*.

100. Lagarde, *Deutsche Schriften*, 98–118; Schuchardt, *Deutsche Politik der Zukunft*, 98–100, 276–88, 303, 324–30.

101. Lagarde, *Deutsche Schriften*, 90–93, 121–22, 127.

102. Schuchardt, *Deutsche Politik der Zukunft*, 374: 'Mein Herz ist farnzösisch, mein Verstand aber ist deutsch'; see also 356–80.

103. Schuchardt, *Umrisse einer Staatsverfassung*.

104. I used twenty-two maps; for full references, see Andrén, *Att frambringa*, 47–51.

105. Andrén, *Att frambringa det uthärdliga*, 51–61.

106. Schulz, 'Entwicklungsgeschichte der Pflanzdecke Mitteleuropas', 229–447; Schulz, 'Verbreitung Phanerogamen in Mitteleuropa', 269–360; Ule, 'Niederschlag in Mitteleuropa', 435–516.

107. Kirchhoff, *Schulgeographie*, 157–60; Kretschmer, *Historische Geographie von Mitteleuropa*, chapter I.

108. Kirchhoff, *Mensch und Erde*, 80–82.

109. Kretschmer, *Historische Geographie von Mitteleuropa*; see chapter I-I, and about the climate, see 131.

110. I have learnt much about British federalism from Jens Norrby – see his doctoral thesis upcoming in 2022; see Burgess, *British Tradition of Federalism*; Bosco, *The Federal Idea*.

111. Moering, *Sibyllinische Bücher*, 21–35.

112. Fröbel, 'Die Österreichische Politik', 410.

113. Andrian-Werburg, *Österreich und dessen Zukunft*, 36, 147–48, 189–205.

114. Palacký, 'O poměru Čech', 11–13.

115. Thun, *Über den gegenwärtigen Stand der*, 40–85.

116. Popovici, *Gross-Österreich*, 307–10.

117. Renner, *Oesterreichs Erneuerung*; Seipel, *Nation und Staat*; Stolper, *Das Mitteleuropäische Wirtschaftsproblem*; Stolper, *Wir und Deutschland*.

118. Stead, *United States of Europe*, 37.

119. Salisbury, 'English Politics and Parties', 22.

120. Stead, *United States of Europe*, 54–58, quotation from 56.

121. List, *Gesammelte Schriften II*, 433.

122. Treitschke, *Politics*, 32–34.

123. Laing, *Notes of a Traveller*, 56–57.

124. Novicow, *Die Föderation Europas*, 659–80.

125. Hamann, *Bertha von Suttner*, 71, 79–85.
126. Marquand, *The End of the West*, 53.
127. Spencer, 'The Development of Political Institutions'.
128. Donisthorpe, *Individualism*, 11.
129. Ibid., 11–15, quotation from 11.

CHAPTER 3

Looking for Common Ground

Calls for European unity came from more than one direction, as appeals for political unity were bolstered by appeals invoking cultural and civilisational unity. This chapter expands on the ways in which Europe was defined as a unity beyond politics, while being divided by certain hierarchies. One was an act of demarcation, contrasting Europe with other parts of the world by emphasising its differences. Another defined Europe as a unified culture and civilisation, and entailed looking beyond its internal political and cultural borders. Civilisation was a crucial concept here because it unambiguously represented the tendency to consider Europe a universal model. Even so, it was defined as a unity with internal borders between states and nations, as well as with religious and linguistic divides. The ideas of both European culture and civilisation included what Dipesh Chakrabarty has called 'the stagist theory of history, on which the European ideas of modernity were based'. For Chakrabarty, this 'historicism' was a means to enable Europe's domination of other parts of the world. This was an important aspect. However, we should also be aware of how this historicism enabled a mindset within Europe that saw England and France as the first nations, followed by Germany, to be sites 'of the first occurrence of capitalism, modernity, or Enlightenment'.[1] In the master story of European progress, other nations lagged behind. The concepts of European culture and civilisation also indicated hierarchies within Europe.

Notes for this section begin on page 100.

Defining Europe by Contrasts

When looking for Europe, it is crucial to draw lines that define other parts of the world. Consequently, Europe is contrasted with the outside world. This definitional act, resting on what philosophers call binary opposition, has changed through history and various contexts but has always remained, defining Europe and giving it meaning.[2] Let us begin by taking a very broad perspective, and look back to the Frankish leaders and their quests for power. They understood the concept of Europe in the context of their struggle with the Roman popes. For the latter, Europe was nothing more than a geographical continent, like Africa or Asia, whereas the Frankish Europe comprised either provinces of the emperor's dominion or the Christian lands.[3] In both cases, it was something to guard and, if necessary, defend. As such, the concept of Europe could be used as propaganda. An eighth-century Frankish chronicler applied the term 'Europeenses' to Charles Martel's forces fighting the Saracens, and the court of Charlemagne established an imagination of him as the king of Europe, naming Christianity the religion of the European empire, which was under foreign threat from the Muslims. The people around Charlemagne often spoke of Islamic incursions as dangerous foreign threats to the cohesion of the Frankish kingdom. His grandfather had defeated the Muslims at the Battle of Tours in 732, which was an enormous achievement according to the official historiography. Regarding the battle, the truth is more likely to be found in the historiography of the other side, which hardly mentions it. Obviously, the external threats from the Muslims were real, but they were also evoked to create unity and legitimise a certain form of governance in the kingdom.[4]

A second essential period for defining Europe is the passage from medieval to early modern times, from the Fall of Constantinople in 1453 to the conquests of the Inca and Aztec empires in the newly discovered Americas. From the outside, Europeans were viewed in a negative light. The Byzantines looked upon the European crusaders' ravages and barbaric customs with disgust. The Aztecs condemned the conquistadors' hunger for wealth, which made them act more like apes than human beings: their chattering and their insensitivity to traditional rites and social customs were intolerable. But the Europeans possessed a military strength that gave them authority and self-esteem. The Byzantines were hoping to call on the Western rulers' military strength during their last decades of declining power. The Aztecs were astonished by the God-like men on horses and amazed by their metallic skin, but they were also terrified by their weapons.

During this period, the term 'Europe' began to be used more frequently than before. Byzantine historians mentioned a Europe that included the Latin kingdoms, England and Iceland, as well as northern cities such as Bergen and

Stockholm, countries populated with Livonians, Lithuanians, Poles and Bohemians, and a Russia described as the largest kingdom in Europe. It is with this Europe that these scholars hoped the remaining parts of the Byzantine Empire would be associated.[5]

When Pope Pius II acted to close the ranks of Christendom in 1460 and mount a joint campaign against the Muslims, he spoke of Europe and the Europeans. This occurred several years after the Fall of Constantinople and in conjunction with the Turkish conquests of the last remaining Christian areas in Greece.

The third period, which is critical for defining Europe in sharp contrast to something else, is the Enlightenment. Charles Louis Montesquieu emphasised that Asians were not rational, but controlled by their emotions rather than logic. In Asia, the states were ruled by despots, characterised by inertia and a lack of initiative. In contrast to Europe, Asia was completely uncivilised. Montesquieu's explanation of Europe's superiority invoked a kind of balance that was simply unknown in Asia. The various populations in Europe were more or less equally strong, while those in Asia were either strong or weak. According to Montesquieu's climate theory, the temperate zones were widespread and extended in Europe, whereas in Asia, there were substantial borders between zones of coldness and warmth.[6] Johann Gottfried Herder illustrated a new self-confidence when he claimed that Europe was a 'wonderful continent', in contrast to the isolated Asian states that did not compare themselves with others but instead concentrated their energies on keeping out anything foreign. Their politics were despotic and their inhabitants resigned and unwilling to change the order. It was habit that ruled these kingdoms. At the same time, he noted, there was competition between the states in Europe, which constantly gave them the experience of either peaceful trade or military action. The continuous contact among the European states had been a breeding ground for science. Scholars therefore had a certain degree of independence vis-à-vis the state, and formed an association that transcended borders. In Europe the states exploited scientific knowledge but did not possess it. Herder did not find these essential incentives among Asian scholars who, if they could be found at all, acquiesced to their rulers.[7]

This Eurocentrism was often used as a framework and was included in the theory of world history, which emphasised that the leading powers and peoples had previously been Asian, but were now European. This approach can also be found in Herder's works, but it was Hegel who refined it, declaring that world history began in Asia and would end in Europe. As far as Hegel was concerned, history through the ages revolved around the development of freedom and reason. In its early stages, society was best developed in the Orient, in kingdoms characterised by obedience and fidelity towards the ruler. The free will of individuals developed only in Europe – namely, in the Greek world and the Roman Empire. For Hegel, it was with the arrival of Christian culture that Europe started to lead the world, and world history reached its full potential. This was especially true of the Prussian kingdom of Hegel's days, where he saw reconciliation and unity between the individual and the state, fulfilling the goal of history to realise a generally prevailing freedom of reason.[8] Although the view of a special historical mission for the Prussian state should be seen in light of his position in Berlin, Hegel's concept of Europe as a place where the free will of individuals evolved, in contrast to the Orient, was widely upheld.[9]

With his work *Orientalism*, which had an enormous impact after its publication over four decades ago, Edward Said brought awareness to how European concepts may have very little to do with the people and societies they purport to describe.[10] His perspective has been groundbreaking for postcolonial studies, and reaffirmed by other studies.[11] Yet, it has also been demonstrated that the European image of Islam and Arabic cultures cannot be assessed as one-dimensionally negative. The picture of Islam and Islamic culture that developed in the early modern age was less negative than it became after 1800, when the differences became exaggerated. The Arabic language was always highly esteemed, and the comparative study of languages was based on familiarity with both the Indo-European and Semitic languages, and among the latter Arabic was defined as closely related to both Hebrew and Aramaic – both essential Biblical languages.[12] Arabic culture could even be thanked for the progress and superiority of Europe well into the nineteenth century. A few examples include Europe's culture of knighthood, tournament games, poetry, architecture, the technical uses of chemistry, mathematics, medicine and economics – and even the introduction of artichokes, saffron, coffee and sugar.[13]

In geographical presentations of a more popular kind, European advantages were underscored. Humankind had 'made the most decisive advancements' in Europe, 'in science, in useful and ornamental arts, and in general civilization', as claimed by Mary-Ann Venning in the 1820s. Her book was intended for youths, who read that the 'European is generally strong, active and intelligent'. The success of the continent was greatly contrasted with the lack of success of its neighbours. Although maps showed a partly Turkish Europe, and Istanbul was said to be located on the European shore of the Bosporus, Venning wrote that 'the chief employment of the Turk is smoking and drinking coffee'.[14] The ineptitude of the Ottoman Empire was a popular theme among Europeans who hailed their own modernity. The liberal free-trade propagandist, Richard Cobden, railed against an empire that had been in contact with Europe for hundreds of years without learning from its modern discoveries and technical improvements. If one could find a printing press in the land it would surely be run by a foreigner, and the 'steam engine, gas, the mariner's compass, paper money, vaccination, canals, the spinning jenny, and rail-roads, are mysteries not yet dreamed about by Ottoman philosophers'. He believed that neither science nor literature would take hold among the Turkish people.[15] The Europeans were simply more advanced, and their individual free will was more evolved. Their ability to reach perfection was pre-eminent, and they constituted a refined part of humanity. In the eyes of Schmidt-Phiseldeck, Europe was nothing less than the role model for the rest of the Earth.[16]

In comparing itself with other continents, Europe did not necessarily always understand itself as superior, and certain Enlightenment opinions testified to another point of view. Herder said that the people of Europe did not rise to culture by themselves, but thanks to eastern influences and foreign religions. Asia and Egypt were innovators of crafts, trade and science.[17] Among Romantic philosophers, an idea of Europe developed that also included negative aspects; sometimes it was even claimed that Asia and America served as correctives for Europe. The mechanical knowledge of Native Americans, which they used to develop roads and vehicles, was deemed inferior, but their crafts were seen as superior. The Native Americans were lacking in some virtues but superior to Europeans in others, possessing overpowering strength, passion and courage that could be likened to those of the ancient Greeks. In Asia and among the Native Americans, the individual person had not been as emancipated as in Europe, but a more primeval humanity remained – something essential that Europe lacked. Often this understanding was prompted by a profound nostalgia for religious sentiment and the wisdom lost in a Europe ruled by reason.[18]

In the nineteenth and twentieth centuries, comparisons between Europe, Asia and America – mainly the United States – were common. Even in the last instance, positive and negative views were presented. Regarding freedom, democracy and equality, the United States was mostly viewed with admiration. This large country to the West was regarded as a better and more modern Europe, and was often cited as a role model. It was considered a society based on freedom of speech and thought. Instead of feudal oppression and autocratic monarchies, there were civil rights and a democratic representative system of governance. America was also seen as a role model because it had been created by Europeans acting as free men, so it was implicitly or explicitly argued that the example of the New World should be followed by the old.[19] There were exceptions to this positive view of America, however: as long as the slave trade existed, it was condemned as a token of incomplete development, and it had a lack of empathy, compared with Europe. The British author Harriet Martineau applauded the principles of equality evident in American society, but was quick to say that the country did not live up to its own high ideals: 'the civilisation and morals of the Americans fall far below their own principles'. She wrote that although five states had abolished slavery, it was still practised by many others. She also wrote that the 'principle of the equal rights of both halves of the human race' was obligatory for a functional democratic society, and that that principle regarding women's political and economic freedoms was lacking in American society of the 1830s.[20] Moreover, it was claimed that some forms of progress had gone too far in America, as illustrated by its perfectly straight streets, precise sense of purpose, and overly intense modernity. Europe was seen as the opposite, with its traditions and slowness. This contrast was assessed in both positive and negative terms.

The arts of music, theatre and literature reflected these contrasts. Alexandre Dumas, son of the novelist of the same name, wrote a play about a disgraceful and unpolished stranger who came from America.[21] In a novel by the American writer Henry James, who actually lived mostly in England, an American businessman finds art, knowledge and honesty, but also ugliness, evil and passivity when visiting Europe, and France in particular. He detests Europe but ultimately realises that it has made him question his more utilitarian American way of life. Another of James's novels inverts this notion, contrasting the European guests with their hosts and siblings in New England. The former have had cosmopolitan lives, living in various countries and cities around Europe, being accustomed to a formal daily life. They realise that, in America, individual freedom is more evident; for example, women are less dependent on their fathers or husbands than they are in Europe. Americans are less formal and more spontaneous, looking for practical and effective ways of doing things; their feelings are more outspoken, while their respect for morals and tradition is stronger.[22]

As a consequence of contrasting Europe and the Europeans with other continents and peoples, the perception of the superiority of the white race began to expand. The idea of race became popular during the Enlightenment, and was fully fledged by the nineteenth century, serving as a template for most Eurocentrism of the age. It was often said that Europe conquered the world due to the emergence of the white race. The Europeans were long considered to belong to a single white race. For one author, it differed from other races in its ability to adapt and build civilisations, and though divided into Slavic, Germanic and Romance peoples, these main groups were still to be considered one and the same race.[23] A popular textbook said that the 'European race, to which we belong, is distinguished from all the rest by a natural complexion of white, mingled with red. . . . They usually have straight hair, an oval face, an expanded forehead, a rounded full chin, and generally the most regular and beautiful features'. Almost all of the peoples living in Europe were included, but also some others: 'It also embraces the nations of Western Asia, as far as the river Oby, the Belur Tag, and the Himmaleh Mountains, with the people of Barbary, Egypt and Abyssinia, and the Moors of Northern Africa'. Obviously, these were former civilisations and high cultures, connected by the same white race.[24]

The notion of a dominant European white race changed, especially when it became common to highlight the diversity of Europe's races at the end of the nineteenth century. By then the Romance, Germanic and Slavic peoples were considered the three European, or Aryan, races. Moreover, some groups of people were distinguished as non-Aryan: Magyars, Turks, Jews, Finns and Lapps, Latvians, Albanians and Romani.[25] In this period, eugenics had become institutionalised as a science. Charles Darwin's cousin Francis Galton presented the English term 'eugenics' in 1883. The German term '*Rassenhygiene*' was introduced several years later to refer to the doctrine of preventing the degeneration of the population.[26] Because of the popularity of the notion of race, it was not surprising that it was occasionally brought into the discourse of a United States of Europe. By this token, unity was not something that only concerned political relations between France, Germany, Great Britain, and the other states; it was not limited to the cultural dimension, but could also imply that the white race should be brought together into one community to resist the threat of the yellow race.[27]

The notion of the 'scientific' superiority of the white race was most apparent in the theories of the racial hygienists. At universities and dedicated institutions, research on racial hygiene was supported, and groups were founded to spread its teachings. Moreover, Eurocentrism made its mark on theories in other sciences. With the first publication of *Black Athena* in 1987, Martin Bernal challenged the dominant historiography of the European heritage of antiquity. He claimed that an 'Aryan model' of history had been established by a large number of German philosophers in the nineteenth century in order to cast ancient Greek culture as more European than it actually was. The Aryan model claimed that Greek culture was the result of Indo-Germanic tribes conquering the Greek peninsula; this model replaced an older model that emphasised connections between different cultures around the Mediterranean. Bernal himself has shown great interest in the value of the latter theory, and has noted that ancient Greek culture did not have exclusively European roots, but was multicultural, with Egypt playing a significant role.[28]

A temporal difference underpinned many of the contrasts established during the Enlightenment between Europe and white Europeans, on the one hand, and non-Western lands, cultures and peoples on the other. The more developed and progressive Western cultures were considered temporally ahead of the others: they were more advanced and the others were lagging behind. In some cases, these non-Western lands had reached only the very early stages of development, while others were on their way, but had not yet advanced as far as the cultures of Europe. The Europeans, therefore, assumed 'the white man's burden', as Rudyard Kipling famously put it, to guide the others out of their backwardness, lifting them up to higher culture and better standards. Making contrasts by propounding differences in temporality bestowed legitimacy on Eurocentric worldviews and colonial dominance.[29]

Towards a Notion of European Civilisation

Johann Gottfried Herder warned that a united Europe would soon become a despotic state that deprived its constituent nations of their individuality. Nevertheless, he described Europe as an enlightened continent with a shared specific culture characterised by diligence, invention, science, and joint efforts.[30] Jean-Jacques Rousseau rejected the idea of European political unity as well as existing centralised and absolutist states in favour of smaller political units and looser confederations. He presented a kind of unity that was not formally ratified in a confederation but silently brought together the politically divided Europe by means of other ties, such as common interests, common principles, and a certain 'conformity of habits and customs'. The different states of Europe were united, whether or not they strove to be, and they 'constituted a kind of whole, united by identity of religion, of moral standard, of international law: by letters, by commerce and finally by a species of balance which is the inevitable result of all these ties'.[31] There were similar elements of thinking, for instance, in the writings of Edmund Burke, the conservative advocate of the English Enlightenment, and harsh critic of the French Revolution. He claimed that there were shared customs and traditions in Europe that originated from common sources. They had evolved over the centuries and were recurrent in religion, political economy, science, and educational institutions.[32]

The pleas for political unity all considered the formal and legal aspects of a possible European union or federation. They were of a practical nature, aiming at overcoming the physical warfare among European states by establishing another institutional and political level. However, the dreams of Europe were also about other kinds of unity that did not necessarily imply economic, legal or political unification. Europe was also about looking for common ground that would go beyond both political and mental borders.

The idea of an existing European unity was planted in the soil of Enlightenment philosophy. One might wonder about the extent to which the kind of unity that Herder, Rousseau and Burke posited was already in existence. Apparently, Novalis did not see it this way, as he emphasised the many religious divides and political conflicts. Today we know that some degree of unity existed among the elites in terms of customs, morals, and ability to communicate with one another (mostly in French). In the seventeenth and eighteenth centuries, the integration of high culture took place, and the 'Republic of Letters' was established among the intellectual elites.[33] On the other hand, there was linguistic heterogeneity among the lower classes, and Europe was a conflict-ridden continent with a multitude of contradictory interests, not least regarding religion. Although Rousseau and others were in search of a common European culture or civilisation, this was almost non-existent, and where it did exist, it was overshadowed by internal strife and warfare.

The search for common ground was evident in texts from the first half of the nineteenth century that defined various features regarded as typically European. There were mentions of such things as European states, countries, nations, peoples, and even a European world. These features were responsible for giving rise to European industry, commerce, communication and education, which in turn produced European goods and wealth. The inhabitants of Europe had European manners, customs, ideas, governments and religions; they also had European art, literature, schools and universities. All of these existed thanks to European thought and the European mind. There was a European spirit of enterprise and a European spirit of experimental research. There was a movement to establish the idea of common ground within the area that, more than anything else, defined the cultural distinctiveness of Europe; comparative studies of linguistics even contended that European languages had a shared origin. Early on, the Edinburgh professor Alexander Murray distinguished five groups of Europeans – the Celts, Teutones (Germans), Slavs, Greeks and Romans, and Finns (including Hungarians) – and declared that he could 'ascertain the general affinities of the European nations by examining the origin and progress of their languages'.[34] The theory was that the main European languages had shared the same beginnings.[35] Not only were there European languages, but also a European (that is, Latin) alphabet. The importance of this was emphasised with Eurocentric overtones: civilised languages had established writing, and the world under European dominion would benefit if it adopted its alphabet. How simple it would be if the British rulers of India could impose their own language and writing. How advantageous it would be if the European alphabet could be implemented in China, supplanting the use of Chinese characters.[36]

In the search for common ground going beyond political borders, we can identify two concepts that were especially important and much relied upon: culture and civilisation. Others were invoked, but not nearly as often.

Take, for instance, 'European spirit'. This was occasionally referred to in English, but was not developed as a theme or stressed as a specific feature, as opposed to the way both culture and civilisation were mentioned, and hardly any books from that period refer to the notion of a European spirit in their titles. A search of digital libraries gives a tentative measure of the impact of these notions. Looking at the frequency of mentions in titles between 1800 and 1914, the English term 'European civilisation' is used twenty-eight times more often than is 'European spirit'. The difference is even greater in French, in which 'civilisation européenne' results in forty-eight times more hits than does 'esprit européenne', while in Spanish 'civilisacion europea' is fourteen times more frequent than 'espiritu europeo' and in German 'Europäische Civilisation' is seven times more common than 'Europäische Geist'. We can also compare the relative frequencies of mentions of 'European culture' and 'European civilisation' by searching in digital libraries. Searching for 'European civilisation' results in about three times more hits than for 'European culture'. In Spanish and French, the ratios are 4:1 and 6:1 respectively, whereas in German the relationship is reversed, such that 'European culture' gives slightly more than twice as many hits.[37]

'European culture' was a catchphrase used by German writers in the nineteenth century to relate a shared history and refer to common cultural features. These writers discussed how European culture influenced the peripheries, and how it should be imposed on newly conquered territories, such as Bosnia after the Habsburgs took control of it from the Ottomans. Textbooks proclaimed the advanced state of European culture: 'The state of Culture has in most of the European states reached a height, which we have previously not seen in any other parts of the world'.[38] In the English-speaking world, the concept of European culture was used more rarely and mainly with reference to intellectual life – for example, belles-lettres and philosophy, the world of learning, progress in science, and technological improvements.[39]

The notion of culture could refer to Europe and to common experiences, ways of life, and traditions, regardless of whether they were Danish, Swiss or Greek. This was more common in Germany than in other countries. However, deciding what constituted Europe's distinguishing traits was no simple task, so culture was not on the mark when it came to defining the common basis of Europe.

Culture was, however, equipped to deal with the divisions of Europe, because already by the late Enlightenment the concept was useful in capturing the distinct differences and unique qualities of the various European nations. Compared with other countries, Germany encountered more of this, at least in part thanks to the influence of Herder, who was one of its main propagators, inspiring many to look at national cultures in a positive light. Yes, the notion of a European culture was in place, but so was that of a German, French and British culture, and soon of a Czech, Finnish and Estonian culture, and so on. Drawing upon the history of ideas, we can conclude that culture has been strongly associated with nationalism. In fact, there was another way to express the dream of continent-wide unity that went beyond political borders.[40] The concept of civilisation differs from that of culture because it can more readily connote a unity that goes beyond a single nation. When the term civilisation was used in nationalism and national ventures, it was to indicate that one nation had or should take the leading role in European civilisation.

The idea of a shared European civilisation became increasingly common in the early nineteenth century. It is well worth looking further into how it is defined. To address a shared community across borders, the attraction of referring to civilisation starts from the assumption of a community of the mind with shared experiences, prerequisites and objectives. This was done from an early stage, without any implication of creating a single political entity.

'Civilisation' was a new word that had entered the European consciousness in the late eighteenth century, preceding 'European civilisation' by only a few decades. We know that 'civilisation' was used in English in the second half of the eighteenth century in the context of assimilating the barbaric Scottish Highlanders to civil manners, civil law, and the demands of the economy.[41] In an authoritative account of the word in French, the historian Lucien Febvre dates its first use to 1766. The noun 'civilisation' was constructed and originally used in the vocabulary of political economy and soon spread among the well-educated. It was constructed from the much older verb 'civiliser' (to civilise) and from the participle 'civilisé' (civilised). It soon became a landmark of the great aspirations of progress that we can detect in the urge to investigate humanity and nature, in the trust in scientific knowledge, and in the hopes of being able to design a better society. Civilisation was initially a universalist idea, an ideal that society should strive for. With such great hopes attached to the word, one would perhaps not be surprised that the daughter of a deputy to the National Assembly in Paris was reportedly baptised 'Civilisation' in 1792. However, only a few decades later, it was considered to be the existing reality of Europe.[42]

In nineteenth-century literature on European civilisation, 'civilisation' was often used synonymously with 'culture', indicating an ever-closer union between the concepts of Europe and progress.[43] Civilisation could simply mean the distinction between living in a society versus life as a savage. In this instance, civilisation was not seen as the result of a specific kind of government, but rather how one could become a social being through education: 'civilisation is the present product of that education'.[44] Added to this was the increase in knowledge, the production of goods, and the enjoyment of conveniences.[45] As civilisation implied that Europeans were more educated and their riches were greater, it also established a starker contrast and superiority to other continents.

Civilisation could invoke a shared monarchical system, resemblances in public life, a basically shared Christian religion, a common lifestyle, and shared cultural practices.[46] Others professed that civilisation was a modern and liberal society as opposed to authoritarian rule and conservative norms – if not yet in place, it was in the making.[47] One could also say that civilisation described all of Europe because there was some understanding of science and knowledge in all of them, including in countries still considered barbaric, such as Russia and Portugal. As a consequence, some parts of Europe were said to have enlightened nations

> in which knowledge is more general, and sciences and arts are found in the greatest perfection . . . All the branches of art and manufacture are carried on in a more skilful, productive and useful manner, with the aid of machinery, and minute division of labour. Commerce is extended to every quarter of the globe. The political institutions are also such as to give greater liberty and more safety than in other countries.[48]

In all its varieties, the concept of a 'European civilisation' was intended to inculcate a feeling of unity. This is obvious in how historians addressed the concept. European nations were defined by particular histories, by being predominantly Catholic or Protestant, and often by one shared language, whereas the history of European civilisation was defined by Christianity, a communal history, and forgotten language issues. François Guizot, whose *The History of Civilization in Europe* of 1828 became greatly influential throughout Europe, took up the tradition from certain Enlightenment historians of writing a general European history, giving the genre a new vigour by taking country-level differences into account.[49] He wrote

> that a certain unity pervades the civilization of the European states; that, notwithstanding infinite diversities of time, place, and circumstance, this civilization takes its first rise in facts almost wholly similar, proceeds everywhere upon the same principles, and tends to produce well nigh everywhere analogous results. There is, then, an European civilization.[50]

His main argument is that diversity is what distinguishes Europe from earlier civilisations, in which one single principle dominated and led to monotony in all aspects of social life. Be it Greek, Roman, Indian or Jewish civilisation, all lacked the endless variety of modern Europeans, who did not accept any limitations or artificial standards but were free to grow and shape their own lives. Guizot found progress to be central to civilisation, and the peoples of Europe were advancing and improving their conditions. Social relations were becoming better organised. Not only was each nation's prosperity improving but wealth was becoming more equally distributed. In addition, individual progress was occurring. The human mind was developing, which affected intellectual life, intelligence and morals. Guizot argued that both social and moral development were needed: 'they reciprocally produce one another' such that civilisation is not possible with only one or the other, and can only move forward with the cooperation of both society and its individual members. Societies advance with the help of rational refinement, and individuals strive for perfection as rational beings. Guizot hoped to prove this by looking to history, by better understanding how civilisation had progressed in times of both success and crisis.[51]

Although Guizot's view of Europe was generally accepted, he considered France its centre and leader, stressing its sociability and greatness, arguing that he did not find a single idea that was not of French origin.[52] Thus, his very exposition of European civilisation included borders within Europe as well as a view of France as the most civilised country. Guizot had widespread influence, not least in Great Britain,[53] where, however, there was less willingness to view France as the centre of civilisation – there it was rather that England was in the lead.[54]

A major voice in the British discussion of a European civilisation was that of historian Henry Thomas Buckle. He believed that a European civilisation was one in which humankind's might would elevate it above nature, transcending non-European civilisations. It had a spirit that was secular and sceptical, based on proven abilities and radical scientific discoveries, freeing political subjects and bringing more tolerance to religion. Europe was created using the power of the human mind and the progress of human knowledge, which had already civilised a number of European countries: 'the growth of European civilization is solely due to the progress of knowledge'. According to Buckle, European civilisation would bring progress and liberty, and like Guizot, he also believed that it would go hand in hand with division: 'The national progress, in connection with popular liberty, could have originated in no other part of the world except in Europe; where, therefore the rise of real civilization . . . [is] alone to be studied'.[55] England, America, Germany, France and Spain were proudly held up as the most prized examples of European civilisation. Europe was one, yet also divided.

Buckle and Guizot were the prime exponents of a new theory of history that emphasised Europe and had its roots in the Enlightenment. It was understood that history should no longer be confined to themes and ideas from antiquity, as Europe was superior to the Greeks and Romans. This was a theory that focused on what made Europe European, both by definition and in contrast to others.[56]

Shared versus Divided Christianity

Throughout the nineteenth century, the shared civilisation of Europe was repeatedly mentioned as a fact, but with an understanding of the political and religious divides of the continent. Christianity's role as a common foundation was emphasised, as was its support for the progress of civilisation, the ultimate proof being the advance of Europe into a leading position.[57] On the other hand, much attention was paid to the impact of the Reformation and the divide between Catholicism and Protestantism.[58] Guizot mentioned, for instance, the special importance of Christianity to European civilisation in the development of the human intellect, noting the significance of the Reformation when the Church of Rome had become static, and he upheld the importance of advancing the principles of 'justice, legality, publicity, liberty'.[59]

The criticisms of Catholicism, especially the inquisition, were based on the social restrictions imposed by the church. A visceral indictment from Dutch-ruled Brussels in 1828 attacked Catholicism and the Catholic monarchs of Austria, France, Italy and Spain for opposing civilisation. Only Protestant countries with rulers who were in touch with the progress of civilisation could save Europe; earlier it was Prussia that had defended it, but now it was primarily England and secondarily the Netherlands.[60] Others settled for a more modest argument about the importance of the Reformation for European progress, and might have conceded that some reforms of the Catholic Church were also important in this respect.[61] The division between the North moving quickly forward and the South moving at a slower pace became clear when progress was presented as a prerogative of Protestantism. Christianity thus became essential for European civilisation, with the Protestant spirit of the North as its powerful engine.[62]

The Spanish theologian Jaime Luciano Balmes earned a reputation around Europe for his defence of Catholicism as establishing the foundations of European civilisation. Lutheranism brought incredulity, religious indifference, and an incapacity for morality and happiness to the people, whereas Europe under the influence of Catholicism went from disorder to order, such that 'civilisation advanced at a firm and steady pace'.[63] Protestantism did not favour civilisation, but was instead an obstacle and destroyer that further divided sixteenth-century Europe. Quite opposite to Guizot's view is a telling passage by Balmes, insisting that certain evils were because of Protestantism: 'There is no middle path: either civilised nations must remain Catholic, or they must run through all the forms of error'.[64] However, he found a general trend of increasingly close relationships in modern Europe: it had been three hundred years since anything had been 'isolated, everything is general and acquires by expansion a terrible force', and all 'nations are connected, objects are assimilated, relations increase'.[65] Protestantism had spread as a consequence of this, but had not caused the general trend. Only Catholicism could claim to have played the principal part and to have the most intimate relationship with civilisation, whereas 'Protestantism has prevented civilization from becoming homogeneous, in spite of a strong tendency urging all the nations of Europe to homogeneity'.[66]

Balmes differed from Guizot in the privileged position given to Catholicism, but also in downgrading diversity to an obstacle to European civilisation: through commerce, printing and the arts, a perfect state of homogeneity could have been created were it not for Protestantism, which divided the European community into two parts and sowed 'mortal hatred' between them. This understanding of the Reformation was vital to Balmes, as he expounded on how the division spread. In the absence of spiritual unity based on religion, a schism had become present in all parts of societal life:

> Civil and political institutions, and all the branches of learning, had appeared and prospered in Europe under the influence of religion; the schism was religious; it affected even the root, and extended to the branches. Thus arose among the various nations those brazen walls which kept them separate; the spirit of suspicions and mistrust was everywhere spread, things which before would have been innocent and without importance, from that time were looked upon as eminently dangerous.[67]

Some did not see the difference between Catholicism and Protestantism as essential to the progress of civilisation. Gustav Diezel, a radical revolutionary in 1848 and later a journalist, argued that individual economic freedoms were the source of European civilisation, and said that some Catholic states defended them while they were not allowed in others. Referring to England and France as the two most civilised states, and noting one to be Catholic and the other Protestant, he attempted to downplay the religious disputes. However, he recognised England as having greater success in industry and trade, but this he attributed to its economic freedom, as opposed to the absolute state-imposed economy of France, insisting that it had nothing to do with religion.[68]

This is how the notion of a common European civilisation was born, with a shared destiny beyond the conflicts between Catholics and Protestants, who had a culture in common and were citizens of a community of states. The Protestant jurist Johann Caspar Bluntschli mentioned a feeling of shared belonging and kinship that united the European states, in spite of the divides caused by the Reformation. Demarcated from Asia, a unique European civilisation existed. A system of states and community rights was built upon this, as was the foundation for both past and future cooperation: 'The Holy Alliance, that was joined by almost all European states, was . . . a religiously motivated expression of the same basic idea, that the Christian European states should be continuously connected to one another in an organised community of rights'. From these starting points, he expounded his proposal for a European federation.[69]

Civilisation on Everybody's Lips

By the mid-nineteenth century, civilisation was on everybody's lips: 'Civilisation! Surely has no era talked more about civilisation than ours; it is also certain that no other spoken word is more futile and hypocritical'.[70] These words capture the popularity of the concept, which had split and begun to point in two directions: it was used both in a general and abstract sense, and it was applied more narrowly and concretely to policy issues. Apart from European civilisation, other civilisations had also begun to be represented. A work published in Madrid portrayed the Incas not only as people who ruled an empire, but also as a civilisation.[71] An English Quaker called for the recognition of the Native Americans of North America as a civilisation.[72] There were discussions of a Muhammadan civilisation, and of a Central African civilisation.[73] All of these civilisations, however, were left behind by the forward progress of Europe. Accordingly, the notion of civilisation served the purpose of putting Europe in a binary position – Europe was a modern civilisation versus an ancient one, an occidental civilisation versus an Arabic one – and ageing civilisations were compared with newer ones, with some civilisations being better or worse, and some being in between.[74] Europe was a Western civilisation, set against the backwardness of Russia.[75] Civilisation was the opposite of barbarism, the former being active and energetic with members who could mobilise endless resources.[76]

One would expect that in the mightier states of Europe, with their empires that stretched across the oceans, there would be suggestions that these states might represent their own specific civilisations. It was definitely so in Spain, where it was as common to refer to a specific Spanish civilisation as to a shared European one.[77] The idea of an English civilisation had taken root both in Britain and across the Atlantic, although it was not as pervasive as in the case of Spain.[78] Guizot used the notion 'la civilization française' very rarely in his book, and only slightly more 'la civilization romaine'. Buckle rarely referred to an 'English civilisation', and never wrote about a 'British civilisation'. Overall, both French and British authors seemed more prone to talk about the civilisation *in* Britain/England and *in* France than about specific civilisations of their own. In doing so, they claimed that their country was at the centre of European civilisation and at the zenith of its achievements.[79]

It was possible to imagine the existence of a national civilisation, just as it was possible to imagine the existence of a common European nation that included the English, German, Italian and Swedish. These were, however, exceptions that failed to change the general configuration. In the same way that nations signified a community that was separate from other nations and seen as unique, so did its civilisation distinguish Europe as separate from Africa and Asia, with common features shared by its people. The concepts of nation and civilisation form a binary in that they are opposites that are dependent upon each other when their meanings are defined; for example, European civilisation includes several nations, while these nations are separate entities that at the same time are part of the larger civilisation.

There was more to it than that, however, as the strong connection to Europe was also a commitment. A country that was truly civilised and mighty would have a responsibility to spread this civilisation to new lands. Hence, when the Crimean War ended and some parts of the Ottoman Empire were transferred to the Habsburg Empire, a government adviser said that Austria should undertake a 'mission, to be the bearer of civilisation in the lands newly won for Europe'.[80]

It says something about the peculiar intersection of nations and European civilisation that this civilisation's origin was a matter of opinion. European civilisation was often believed to be three thousand five hundred years old, beginning in Ancient Hellas, with classical culture playing an important role.[81] Others saw the beginning in Christianity, and still others turned to the modern world and stressed the importance of the British, French or German nation. It was common to regard the current civilisation as predated by others. Guizot mentioned Greek, Roman, Indian and Jewish civilisations, and other historians further elaborated upon the theme. All of them took care to discuss the supremacy of the civilisation of Europe: although the Greek and Roman civilisations had accomplished great things, neither of them could be compared to the contemporary one, and although there were other civilisations one could set against Europe's, it was the European civilisation that reigned supreme.

Moreover, the beginning of European civilisation was an issue that involved the status of European states relative to one another. Writing during the era of Italian unification, Bertrando Spaventa discussed modern philosophy as shared between the European people, just as European nations had a shared life and civilisation. At the same time, he explicitly attested to an Italian philosophy that underpinned the efforts to define the idea of Italian nationality. This blending of European unity and nationality was done using 'Italian intellect' – the value of bringing all parts of European thinking into a harmonious unity. 'Italy opened the door to modern civilisation', he concluded, referring to a range of philosophers – among them Bruno, Campanella and Vico.[82]

There were those who clung to the idea of a European civilisation, although arguing about its origins in either classical Greece or Rome, and disagreeing as to whether Britain, France or Germany was the key country influencing its development. The Spanish Jesuit Juan Andrés, who had been expelled from his homeland together with his order, presented a remarkable Arabic theory of the origin of civilisation. He was not alone in discussing Arabic influences. In England, France and Italy, representatives of the well-educated world discussed Arabic influences on poetry. Frederick II and his court were acknowledged as a hub of Arabic learning in the thirteenth century. However, Andrés had a farther-reaching interpretation of this, saying that Europe should pay tribute to Arabic teachings for many of its traditions, including literature, medicine, jurisprudence, astronomy and mathematics. In these areas, Europe had learned quite a lot from Arabic culture, and it was only thanks to this that Europe had eventually become culturally and intellectually superior. It was from this perspective – which has recently been emphasised by Roberto M. Dainotto – that Andrés placed the origin of European civilisation in Southern Europe. He especially emphasised the way European culture had learned from Spain and not from France. Following a similar line of thought, the Italian Orientalist Michele Amari stated that the Mediterranean – in particular, Sicily – was the origin of European civilisation, as it was where freedom, solidarity and equality had first taken hold on the continent, long before the French Revolution and even before the Enlightenment. With a radical turn of historical perspective, Amari argued that Europe was living in darkness when the Muslims introduced such ideals in Sicily.[83]

Here, we should consider a historically significant genre: travel tales published as books or in popular journals, in which Europeans are confronted with natives on other continents. Here exoticism plays a part, and fascination with the unknown goes hand in hand with the blessings of European civilisation, its organisation of society, level of learning, ways of life, and prosperity. Locations where Europeans were operating were emphasised, be it a trade station, church, or small colonial setting. Aspects of this can also be seen in travel tales from provincial parts of Europe – in the Balkans, for example, some behaviours are seen as European while others are not, and some institutions as influenced by European civilisation and others as not.[84]

However, we can also observe that referring to the concept of civilisation can be a means to gain legitimacy for actual policies. In the decades around the mid-eighteenth century, we can find examples of authors examining the policies of economic free trade, education, and external relations towards Russia. Richard Cobden, among the most ardent apostles of free trade in Britain, argued that it was a blessing for Europe. It was for the good of its people and for the good of its civilisation, because it extended European trade to new areas and cities – for example, Odessa on the Black Sea. Commerce greatly benefited civilisation, which 'is the grand panacea which, like a beneficent medical discovery, will serve to inoculate with the healthy and saving taste for civilization all the nations of the world'.[85]

Professor Karl Hermann Scheidler claimed that a deficiency in educational institutions threatened not only the healthy development of the state and the democratic principle that all classes of society needed good education, but also the continued progress of European civilisation. He argued especially for the preservation of the agricultural institute of Hofwyhl, and referred to notable figures from many European states who had visited or mentioned it, making it a role model for other institutions in Europe: royalty, professors, and representatives of higher bureaucracies were mentioned, most notably Tsar Alexander, who not only paid a visit but even made sure that sons of the leading Russian aristocratic families were educated there. Scheidler emphasised that education was the main factor in cultivating civilisation, because human beings attained a human life only by interacting with others, learning from others, and using reason. Consciousness and intellectual life were developed by learning, so good institutions for education were necessary. Existing civilisations were seen as resulting from societal education. As Europe was the leading civilisation, it was necessary to maintain a high level of education there. From this perspective, Scheidler criticised the tendencies of Europe's societies to weaken their position, decrying pauperism as well as education that excluded many. Instead, a true and good civilisation should agree that humans yearn for 'happiness, perfection, and morality' for all the population. Scheidler believed that education was the chief means to overcome destructive tendencies. Hofwyhl's importance was based on its founder's pedagogy, which inspired the better-known Pestalozzi to turn to all classes of society and combine education in practical economic issues with that in intellectual and spiritual matters of learning.[86]

Policies targeting Russia reinforced the notion that the country was not part of European civilisation. In Germany, it was said that Russia was not of German, Roman or Latin origin, having a non-European kind of Christianity, and lacking freedom and law. It had not adapted to innovations and had not risen to the high standards of European civilisation.[87] The Crimean War of 1853–56 provided more reasons to raise the banner against Russia, when France and the United Kingdom, with some support from Sardinia-Piedmont and Austria, supported the Ottoman Empire in defending its provinces across the Black Sea from Russian occupation. Richard Cobden, always ready to comment on major affairs, called upon the British government to negotiate with Austria and the German Federation, as these countries were 'completely identified' with the cause of Britain and France: '[T]here are grounds for believing, that, for the *future*, Germany may be reckoned upon, by Western Europe, as the bulwark against Russian aggression'. He conceived the threat from Russia as a European question, a matter of

Europe's safety, and concluded that it would be good if a treaty were settled, but even better if the states of Western Europe would enter into a federation to stand against Russia.[88] Another example was that of Emil von Qvanten, from a wealthy Swedish-speaking family in Finland, who pleaded for Sweden to take an active part in the conflict against Russia during the Crimean War. His background played a role in his standpoint, as the Swedish king and aristocracy had ruled Finland for six hundred years, and the pain from that division of the state could still be felt, though more so west of the Baltic Sea. Qvanten's argument was that Finland had its heart in European civilisation and should be welcomed in, while Russia should recognise its duty to turn east, not west, and towards the adolescent and undeveloped countries of the Orient by sharing the European mission to 'advance civilisation'. If Russia did this, it would find support and praise from 'West European civilisation' – but it would have to be forced to take this drastic action, he added from his exile in Stockholm.[89]

In this context of a perceived threat, the mention of civilisation was frequent. 'L'Europe aux Européens' was proposed as a motto by a French historian when he saw the modern European civilisation as inevitably threatened by Tatarian Russia. The two could not coexist: a battle was bound to take place, and one party would lose. The best bet would be to create a European federation to build strength for what was to come.[90] Thus, when policy makers appealed to European civilisation, it was to spur on the unification of Europe for the sake of defending that civilisation.

Discontent with Civilisation

> We find ourselves to-day in the midst of a somewhat peculiar state of society, which we call Civilisation, but that even among the most optimistic among us does not seem altogether desirable.[91]

With these lines, the socialist poet Edward Carpenter began his 1891 critique of civilisation. His words should be read in light of the concept of civilisation, embedded as it was in developments regarding commerce, technical innovation, means of communication, and the production of material wealth. Industrialisation and new modes of production led not only to increasing wealth, but also to harsher working conditions and the marginalisation of older businesses, to the point that these tendencies met with criticism throughout the century. Not only were there revolts against the installation of new machines, and protests against capitalist modes of production, but much was also written about such issues. The social question was a constant, leading to investigations of working-class conditions and criticism of the inhumanity prevalent in the growing centres of industrialisation. This was connected to spreading industrialisation and growing markets, so much so that by the turn of the century all European countries had been affected.

We should not be surprised, then, to learn that not everyone was happy with civilisation. As European civilisation had spread to most European countries it had brought with it poverty, one early critic said. One effect of it was the unequal division of property, to the extent that the bulk of humankind was deprived of basic comforts, which destroyed both body and mind.[92] Carpenter, inspired by this, wrote about the conditions of civilised man. Physically, he said, the dispersal of civilisation had spread illness, and wherever it arrived, inhabitants had begun to suffer from disease. Not only individual people but also the very societies themselves had begun to suffer from disease, which could be blamed on their lack of unity. The effects of this were actual warfare between classes and among individuals, along with mental unrest and an ever-present sense of sin among the population. Carpenter confessed to holding a Communist view and an ideal vision of society, seeing the root of the problem as private property and class government. His solution for the illness of civilisation was more communal unity: 'There is more true social unity, less of disease'. Communities should be established that have mutual respect among their inhabitants, and no division into rich and poor. Although he was not a Marxist, he was rather close to William Morris in developing his cure for civilisation. He outlined the divinity within every human as a general starting point from which to subordinate one's own greed and longing for personal fame, in favour of naturally endowed unity. Beyond civilisation, he saw the new Eden of a simpler life, advocating vegetarianism and more time spent outdoors. A new kind of architecture should try to construct buildings that would preserve the given landscape, with houses 'built for the use of free men and women', not for private lives, but for community life.[93]

Such criticism did not worry the defenders of European civilisation. Though it might have its weaknesses and even be associated with disease, that did not make their civilisation a burden: its positives greatly outweighed its negatives, and it had to be defended. As one defender said, 'the stronger the light is, the more glaring the shadow'.[94]

In Germany, Friedrich Nietzsche merged the concept of civilisation with a call for unity. He was one of the most outspoken critics of the present civilisation in the West, condemning it as decadent, and putting his hope in the future unity of Europe. A new way to consider the concept of civilisation, which would prove to be of importance after the First World War, was instituted. It was then that the unification of Europe was established as a way out of the decay of European civilisation and its inner strife.

When Nietzsche was discussing 'the moral sentiment in Europe', he famously described Europe as a small peninsula that set itself above Asia as representing humankind's progress. Unlike Carpenter, Nietzsche talked distinctly of a *European* civilisation and addressed the issue of European unity. He envisioned European civilisation as marked by moral hypocrisy and nihilism. Nietzsche said that the modern European man was strongly dissatisfied with himself, and largely practised an ugly kind of self-contempt. Progress might appear to help, but it did nothing but add distractions that concealed the true illness. High ideals of civilisation, humanitarianism and democracy were nothing more than seductive costumes disguising the fact that Europe was very sick. In his diagnosis, the free will of Europeans had been cast aside in the pursuit of scientific objectivity and a paralysing scepticism. Modern European man was no longer able to make independent decisions. Some of this fundamental moral capability was still seen in Germany and especially its northern parts, as well as in England, Spain and Corsica, though less so in Italy. Nietzsche remarked that perhaps a growing threat from the Russians would force Europe to wake up and unite to take a stand against its eastern neighbour and share a single common will.[95]

He believed that Europe should be one, and he condemned the severe divisions that had led to violent national struggles, viewing such strife as madness. The estrangement that followed was further enabled by politicians who only managed to see the short term, putting aside the idea that 'Europe wishes to be one'. He saw one Europe – that existed despite its many fatherlands – expressed by great men such as Napoleon, Goethe, Heine, Schopenhauer and, among his own contemporaries, Wagner and Delacroix. These men embodied the European soul. He called for an end to petty politics and renounced the obsession with 'petty stateism'. A new ruling class would need to take over for the sake of Europe's future. When he said that the time of dynasties had passed, it was obvious that dynasties should be replaced by the notion of a united Europe. When he stated that the era of democracies, with its struggles between the wills of the many, belonged to the past, he added fuel to the political philosophy fire, which persists to the present.[96]

Although critics such as Nietzsche existed, the idea that Europe was privileged because of its history, geography and human resources was a strong and inspirational framework. European civilisation ruled the world, bringing order, culture, moral guidance, and progress. The dawn of European civilisation was to be found in Greek and Roman antiquity. European civilisation had brought humankind its greatest achievements. European science was constantly achieving brilliant breakthroughs. Its military forces and military advances had conquered the world, while its celebrated arts had captivated the senses. A certain spirit imbued Europeans with a particular momentum, and during all of this, Europe was considered a single unified entity.

Some progressivists, who believed that Europe was of its time, also depicted Europe as nothing less than an expression of time itself. This was the case with the Swedish author Carl Johan Almqvist, who embodied much of the discontent of the late 1840s. In a novel, he pleaded for more freedom, and claimed that every man and woman should be free to realise their true character. Against inner composure, the truly human, righteousness, and God's voice, he placed external wretchedness and bewilderment. His novel was set in a Swedish mansion but his ambition was to convey something more universal, that the human being was essentially caught in a battle between real human nature and the curses of life as it was. He wrote that everyone had an indisputable right to lead life according to his or her own desires and personality. A departure from societal conventions would therefore kindle the European revolution. Almqvist invoked not only the demands of the people but 'the spirit of the time', 'the words of the time', and the 'European spirit' that could lead all the people on Earth.[97] In truth, it was the future that Europe would introduce us to, would bring into our lives and dwellings, whether we wanted it or not:

> Europe has no issues more important than these . . . no heart in our part of the world is now beating for anything else, no head is thinking about anything else. . . . The European future is standing by us all in the entrance hall and it wants to come in. The one who will not open his door to the knocker will have his door staved in.[98]

One conclusion of this chapter is that the dream of European unity not only had a political dimension, as manifested in the pleas for a treaty, but many other dimensions, including tradition, religion and culture. Aside from the political language of European unity, we also find the cultural language of unity: one language that sets the terms of treaties and federations, and another language of unity that concerns cultural traditions and shared customs. Both can be future oriented, but both can still take inspiration from history. They can be separate and intertwined. Furthermore, in emphasising cultural aspects, the concept of Europe is associated with divisions, between Catholicism, Lutheranism and Orthodoxy, between Russia and Western Europe, between Northern and Southern Europe. Furthermore, the cultural language of Europe privileges one or several nations against the others.

Notes

1. Chakrabarty, *Provincializing Europe*, 7–9.
2. Miettinen, 'The Particular Universal', 66.
3. Fischer, *Oriens – Occidens – Europa*, 78–79.
4. Hay, *Europe: The Emergence*, 25, 51–52.

5. Todorov, *The Morals of History*; Ivanka, *Byzantinische Geschichtsschreiber*, 32–35, 103–5, 85.

6. Montesquieu, *Om lagarnas anda*, 161–64.

7. Herder, *Ideen* I, 40–44.

8. Hegel, *Vorlesungen*.

9. Koschorke, *Hegel und wir*.

10. Said, *Orientalism*.

11. E.g., by Hourani, *Islam in European Thought*, 63–64.

12. Ibid., 10–16, 24–27, 136–39.

13. Schön, *Allgemeine Geschichte*, 58–61; cf. Dainotto, *Europe (in Theory)* for examples from Italy (in the first instance) and France.

14. Venning, *A Geographical Present*, 2, 9, 51–52.

15. Cobden, *Political Writings*, 270–71.

16. Schmidt-Phiseldeck, *Der Europäische Bund*, 69–74.

17. Herder, *Ideen* I, 393–95; II, 291.

18. Todorov, *The Morals of History*.

19. Philippi, *Geschichte der vereinigten Freistaaten*, 1–2; De Gurowski, *America and Europe*, 410.

20. Martineau, *Society in America* I, 199–207; quotation from III, 207.

21. Dumas, *L'Étrangère*.

22. James, *The Europeans*; James, *The American*.

23. E.g., Schön, *Allgemeine Geschichte*, 136.

24. Woodbridge, *Universal Geography*, 166; published in America, it was edited several times in Great Britain. Another popular American textbook that propagated the idea of a white race dominating Europe and its dominions was Pickering, *The Races of Man*.

25. Bluntschli, *Politik als Wissenschaft*, 160–63.

26. The idea of race is discussed in Hannaford, *Race*. Racism is discussed in depth by Malik, *The Meaning of Race*. The term *Rassenhygiene* was invented by Alfred Ploets.

27. E.g., Stein, *Die Vereinigte Staaten von Europa*, 19–22.

28. Bernal, *Black Athena*.

29. Cf. Chakrabarty, *Provincializing Europe*, 7–10.

30. Herder, *Ideen* II, 338, 484.

31. Heater, *European Unity*, 8–11, quotation from 81; Dainotto, *Europe (in Theory)*, 136–37.

32. Burke, *Reflections on the Revolution*; the argument is explored in Thompson, 'Ideas of Europe'.

33. Rietbergen, *Europe*, 259–300.

34. Murray, *History of European Languages*, 3.

35. See, e.g., Arndt, *Über den Ursprung*, 3.

36. Lepsius, *Das allgemeine linguistische Alphabet*, 4–7.

37. This search was conducted at the Hathi Trust Digital Library on 8 May 2017.

38. Hoffmann, *Europa und seine Bewohner*, 377: 'Der Kulturzustand hat in den meisten europäischen Staaten eine Höhe ereicht, wie wir ihn in keinem anderen Weltheile sehen'.

39. Allen, *History of Civilization*; Carlyle, *Lectures on the History*.

40. Verga, 'European Civilization'.

41. Caffentzis, 'Scottish Origin of "Civilization"'.

42. Febvre, 'Civilization'. See also Bowden, *The Empire of Civilization*, 26–34, who claimed that the concept first arose in France in the 1750s, and in Britain only a few years afterwards.

43. We find the following in a geography textbook by an American geographer and education reformer: 'Europe is the smallest of the great divisions of the world, and least

distinguished for the grandeur of its natural features; but in science, arts and improvements it surpasses all the rest. In modern times it has been the central point from which civilisation and knowledge have extended to other nations, and its emigrants have peopled all the civilized countries on the globe'; from Woodbridge, *Universal Geography*, 289.

44. Schön, *Allgemeine Geschichte*, 4: 'ist die civilisation das vorhandene product jener Erziehung'.

45. Hall, *The Effects of Civilisation*, 2.

46. Schmidt-Phiseldeck, *Der Europäische Bund*, 48–55.

47. Mazzini, *De l'Italie*, 353.

48. Woodbridge, *Universal Geography*, 175–76.

49. Verga, 'European Civilization'.

50. Guizot, *History of Civilization in Europe*, 3.

51. Ibid., 3–24.

52. Ibid., 10.

53. See, e.g., the exposition on Guizot by MacLeod, *European Life*, 7–10.

54. E.g., D'Erbigny, *Future Destinies of Europe*, Section V.

55. Buckle, *History of Civilization* I: 210, 225; II: 1, 29, 45, quotation from I: 225. Published in French as *Histoire de la civilization en Angleterre* (Vols I–V), Paris: A. Lacroix, Verboeckhoven, 1865; published in German as *Geschichte der Civilisation in England*, Leipzig: C.F. Winter'schen Verlagshandlung, 1860–1861.

56. See Hazard, *Crisis of the European Mind*, 50–51; Dainotto, *Europe (in Theory)*, 30, 38, 50.

57. A Spanish writer and a Spanish theologian presented this idea with all possible conviction. See Roca y Cornet, 'La civilización', 19: La religion considerada como la base de la civilizacion' [Religion is understood as the basis of the civilisation]. See als Rodrígues Pridall, *Influencia del cristianismo*, 20.

58. E.g., the Reformation plays an important role in the regeneration of European civilisation in Schön, *Allgemeine Geschichte*, 85–95.

59. Guizot, *History of Civilization in Europe*, 3–24, quotations from 17, 24.

60. D'Erbigny, *Future Destinies of Europe*, 56, 84, 106, 130–43.

61. Schön, *Allgemeine Geschichte*, 85–88.

62. Dainotto, *Europe (in Theory)*, 149–50.

63. Balmes, *European Civilization*, 50, quotation from 337; also published in French and German.

64. Balmes, *European Civilization*, 30.

65. Ibid., 37.

66. Ibid., quotation from 375.

67. Ibid., 376.

68. Diezel, *Die Frage der deutschen Zukunft*, 10–51.

69. Bluntschli, 'Die Organisation', 279–80, quotation from 280: 'Die heilige Allianz, dia fast alle europäische Staten beigetragen waren, war . . . ein religiös motivirter Ausdruck derselben Grundgedankens, dass die christlichen Statens Europas dauernd miteinander zu einer wohlgeordneten Rechtsgemeinschaft verbunden seien'.

70. Diezel, *Die Frage der deutschen Zukunft*, 10: 'Civilisation! Sicherlich hat man zu keiner Zeit mehr von Civilisation gesprochen, als in unsern Tagen, gewiss aber auch ist nie ein Wort vergeblicher und heuchlericher in Mund geführt worden als dieses'.

71. Prescott, *Historia de la conquista*; Pumphrey, *Indian Civilization*.

72. Pumphrey, *Indian Civilization*.

73. Schön, *Allgemeine Geschichte*, 58–60; Peyré, *Civilisation*.

74. These binaries are used by Littré, *Études sur les barbares*.

75. Weir, *Modern Europe (1760–1815)*, 28.

76. Cobden, *Speeches on Public Policy*, 21.

77. E.g., Tapa, *Historia de la civilizacion Española*; Ferrer y Suberana, 'La nacionalidad', 68; Martins, *Historia de la civilización Ibérica*; Altamira, *Historia de España*.

78. Scadding, *English Civilization Undemonstrative*.

79. The argument of the leading British commercial firm, the East India Company, when it wanted support to expand further into India was that '[e]very one out of England is now ready to acknowledge that the whole of Asia, from the Indus to the Sea of Ochotsk, is destined to become the patrimony of that race which the Normans thought, six centuries ago, they had finally crushed, but which now stands at the head of European civilization. We are placed, it is said, by the mysterious but unmistakable designs of Providence, in command of Asia; and the people of England must not lay the flattering unction to their souls, that they can escape from the responsibility of this lofty and important position, by simply denouncing the means by which England has attained it'; quoted from Cobden, *Speeches on Public Policy*, 386.

80. Stein, *Oesterreich und der Frieden*, 42: 'Mission, der Träger der Civilisation in dem für Europea neugewonnenen Lande zu werden'.

81. Schön, *Allgemeine Geschichte*, 6.

82. Spaventa, *La filosofia Italiana*, 8–11, 21, 30f, quotation from 31: 'L'Italia apre le porte della civilitá moderna'.

83. Dainotto, *Europe (in Theory)*, 102–8, 128–33, 205–11.

84. Ibid., 46.

85. Quoted from Gowing, *Richard Cobden*, 24.

86. Scheidler, *Die Lebensfrage der europäische Zivilisation*, 1–50, quotation from 25.

87. Gaertner, *Ueber die Provinzial-Rechte*, 79–81. De Gurowski may be quoted from *Russland und die Civilisation*, 2: 'Die europäische oder christliche Civilisation lässt sich von ihren Ausgangspunkte bis zu unseren Tagen durch die Namen von zwei historischen Existenzen Ausdrucken. Die lateinische und die Germanische, welche seit unserer Zeitrechnung die Beherrscherinnen des Occidentes von Europa gewesen sind' [The European or Christian civilisation from its starting point to our present can be expressed through the names of two historic existences: the Latin and the Germanic existence, which have been the rulers of Europe's Occident since our calendar began]. See also Diezel, *Russland, Deutschland*, 18, 29.

88. Cobden, *What Next and Next?*, 48–49.

89. Qvanten, *Fennomani och skandinavism*, 10, 30, 61.

90. Martin, *Russland und Europe*, 119, 289; also published in Swedish in 1870. Another Frenchman concluded for the same reasons that there was a need for a European federation; Talbot, *Europa den Europäern*, 253–56. A similar message outlining a long-term Russian political plan to conquer Europe was published in Switzerland and Germany in 1866: Anonymous, *Europa: wird es republikanisch oder kosakisch?*

91. Carpenter, *Civilisation*.

92. Hall, *The Effects of Civilisation*, 170; published in German as *Die Wirkungen der Zivilisation auf der Massen*, Leipzig: C.L. Hirschfeld, 1905.

93. Carpenter, *Civilisation*, 1–50, quotations from 9 and 41.

94. 'Je stärker das Licht, desto greller die Schatten'.

95. Nietzsche, *Beyond Good or Evil*, 59, 94, 129–30, 147.

96. Ibid., 130, 186–94.

97. Almkvist, 'Det europeiska missnöjets grunder', 29–30, 35, 54–57.

98. Ibid., 26: 'Europa ha inga vigtigare ämnen än dessa;.... men intet hjerta klappar i vår verldsdel nu för annat än detta, intet hufvud tenker på annat.... Europas framtid stå hos oss alla i förstugan, och vill in. Den, som ej låser upp sin dörr för den klappande, får dörren inslagen'.

CHAPTER 4

Performing Communality

Thinking about Europe entails taking an interest in what is occurring in neighbouring states and elsewhere in Europe. Gazes are directed more towards some and less towards others; some countries are more in focus on certain occasions, and others tend to be of interest thanks to their cited advantages or disadvantages. Contacts across borders are a well-known phenomenon, cultivated through travelling and exchanges as well as through institutionalised channels. Countries are compared as news travels from one place to the next. Modern European states are built, and national traditions and values formed, by comparing and imitating. New ideas, arrangements and opportunities, as well as arguments over controversial issues, are often found by looking towards other European states. Transnational research in intellectual history emphasises the impact of cultural transfer.[1] It is possible to see a kind of unity when ideas, concepts, models and theories move across borders, which differs from presenting political, economic or cultural unity.

Europeanisation is often seen as pertaining only to the post-war era, not least in the historical narrative of European integration. Such a presentation can only be justified by considering the development of common European institutions and policies. However, it is inaccurate to assume that the experience of Europeanisation is a solely post-war phenomenon, as is the case in much social science literature. For example, in Ulrich Beck and Edgar Grande's *Das kosmopolitische Europa* – an admirable work in many respects – Europeanisation is treated as an institutionalised process. Gerard Delanty and Chris Rumford point out in *Rethinking Europe* that, in the social sciences,

---

Notes for this section begin on page 128.

Europeanisation is elaborated on using either institutional or comparative approaches to studying the European Union and the resulting integration processes.[2] Looking at where and when Europeanisation is taking place does not entail identifying the pros and cons of the European Union. One should not forget the Europeanisation that was actually taking place long before the Second World War. Medievalist Robert Bartlett has stressed the Europeanisation occurring in the 950–1350 period, which included the dissemination of unifying linguistic elements such as names, the establishment of a religious order across the continent, and a new university system that gave bureaucrats common experience. Compared with earlier periods, communication was distinctly faster and cultural exchange ran more smoothly.[3]

Clearly, there has long been an exchange of community values guiding the countries of Europe in constructing their societies. The German historian Karl Schlögel emphasises that there is a long history in Europe of crossing borders and Europeanisation, which he associates with mutual learning.[4] In Europeanisation, which was a historical phenomenon existing prior to post-war integration, European countries had similar institutional settings, and often largely modelled themselves on one another. This chapter treats Europeanisation as a matter of mutual intellectual inspiration between countries, and of countries adopting similar values and taking similar directions to each other. This kind of Europeanisation is of special interest when exploring the idea of Europe.

When ideas and models move from one part of Europe to another — likely from the centre of Europe to areas on the periphery — it is not a simple transfer. When concepts cross political and cultural borders, they move from one historically specific context to another. It is obvious that cultural transfers are conducted in the hopes of influencing environments and changing them in certain respects, and the Europeanisation concept entails a 'stagist theory of history' (which in this volume applies to divisions and hierarchies within Europe) stating that some countries are the role models for the rest, enabling those countries to have a dominant role in the European mindset. However, we must acknowledge that concepts and models adapt to their new contexts through a process of translation. Sometimes this translation occurs in the open and is easy to observe, but often it requires detailed study, supported by a solid knowledge of the concept (or idea, or model, or theory) and its origins, as well as a good understanding of the new context and how the introduction was staged. This chapter examines the transfer of concepts of community that have taken place throughout Europe, and includes certain cases about which I have special expertise. In earlier case studies on the introduction of the concept of local self-government, I learned that these translations are political and ideological, with implications for the social order.

As a final introductory observation, I note that intellectual Europeanisation is not a result of the idea of European unity, and should not be reduced to a simple device for administrative integration. It occurs in a broader sense and in the context of interaction between centre and margins within Europe, emphasising both Europe's unity as well as its internal borders and divisions. Still, when communal values and standards are implemented and established, they can be taken as necessary prerequisites by countries that are on the verge of entering into multilateral cooperation, in that they produce a common ground for understanding and for shared ideas on how to organise society, as well as for future collaboration. However, that is not the focus of this chapter.

The Quest for Legitimacy: Citizenship and Local Self-Government

An appropriate starting point for examining the Europeanisation of concepts of community is the French Revolution, or rather the period and changes it represents. Starting in the late eighteenth century, some of the most urgent political questions were those related to the state and nation. The responsibilities of the state grew as it expanded and became more centralised. More workers were required and their duties became more complex. To ensure capable officials, forward-thinking regents supported special university programmes, making cadres of workers into professionals. Meanwhile, the people and the nation became important political concepts of the time, with the idea that all forms of government need the approval of the governed. The state was transformed into a nation state whose governance was legitimised when its citizens acquiesced to it. After the French Revolution, it seemed impossible to uphold an autocracy purportedly based on the grace of God. The decisive questions that arose when shaping government concerned how it should be organised and what kind of popular support the exercise of power would garner.

Issues of constitutional and representative government became connected with the political agenda in Europe during the first half of the nineteenth century, as did certain key political concepts that have continued to be of utmost importance since then, namely, democracy, citizenship and legitimacy. The French Declaration of the Rights of Man and the Citizen is indicative of this, and illustrates the merging of citizenship and nationalism; the sovereignty of the French nation was thus vindicated, as was the rule of its people and citizens. Citizenship became closely tied to the state and the elaboration of a national identity, including the attribution of a national community. The events in France were closely followed throughout Europe; associated ideas spread rapidly, and soon the citizenship–state–nation triad became institutionalised in one country after another. The process occurred more quickly in Western than Central Europe, with its multinational states. This triad was the cause of conflicts over which nations were deemed independent, and which were to be subsumed in other nationalities. This was quite often solved by the suppression of minority languages and other cultural expressions. Furthermore, conflicts over citizenship were rampant in Europe, with exclusions being made on the basis of sex and/or an individual's lack of resources.

The extent and scope of citizenship has been discussed throughout Europe, with demands for citizenship to encompass wider swathes of the population in the state. At the same time, a key issue has been the setting of limits regarding who should be included and who excluded. Participation could be broadened among the aspiring elites in trade and industry, but also extended to additional segments of the population. While the elite demanded that only they should possess the resources and wisdom needed to take part in political governance, the extension of participation was often interwoven with the struggle for individual freedom and equality. It was common to include different degrees of citizenship. Kant distinguished between passive citizens, who enjoyed the rights and protection of the state, and active citizens who, in addition to this, were given the opportunity to participate in state activities and design its tasks. Full citizenship was usually based on the ownership of property. When property was understood broadly, as when Kant included in it the capacities of craftsmen, artists and scientists, more people were attributed full citizenship.[5] The issue of participation was particularly controversial at the beginning of the French Revolution. The Declaration of the Rights of Man and the Citizen, proclaimed by the National Assembly in Paris in 1791, states that each and every person is born free and that equal rights are guaranteed for all citizens. It does distinguish between passive and active citizens: only the latter, who pay a certain amount of tax, are given the right to vote for political assemblies. Distinguishing between bad and good citizens was also a common theme: the bad being revolutionaries, and the good having respect for the order and conventions that have long regulated societies.[6]

In her famous tract, Mary Wollstonecraft challenged some of these exclusions, arguing that citizenship ought to be extended to allow women's participation in political life. She was anxious about the economic and social subjugation of women, and argued for equality in public life. Comparing the political rights of women to those of slaves, she said that one way out of this was to provide the same education for both men and women. Only then, she concluded, would it be possible for women to find their place in working life and secure their own income, ending their dependence on men and allowing them to act as enlightened and responsible citizens.[7]

These examples illustrate that participation was central to the concept of citizenship after the French Revolution. It became important to take part in political discussions and decision making, and those who did not share these privileges and duties were excluded. The concept of local government was another answer to the agenda-setting questions of the political discussion in the first half of the nineteenth century, though often neglected in the history books. This concept, which was based on the cities and their bourgeoisie, arose in reaction to the autocracy of the kings and the absolutist state. It was not a plea for the self-rule or independence of the towns, but a modern idea of self-government that assumed the presence of a strong and centrally organised state. The argument for local self-government was its ability to strengthen the state and relieve its bureaucracy by transferring some of its tasks to local property owners. That was the context in which the possibility of local government and its design were drafted, making local government stand out as a promising political idea. In fact, some examples were put forward before the revolution, both in Great Britain and by French physiocrats. The English concept of 'local government' by the gentry was invoked as exemplary in Germany and Scandinavia during the nineteenth century.

In the following decades, local or municipal self-government was manifested in European countries in answer to the questions of the time, in political discussion and in concrete institutions created by the state and established by law. Examples of the latter are numerous. France made the commune the smallest administrative entity in 1790 (and again in 1800). Prussia was also early with its law of municipal self-government in 1808; other German states followed the Prussian example, as did the Netherlands in 1824. A decade of great importance is the 1830s, with its wave of laws establishing local government. The UK, which had a tradition of estate owners settling public concerns, passed the Municipal Corporation Act in 1835. The Belgian constitution of 1830 advocated local government. The Swiss cantons passed laws on local government on various occasions throughout the 1830s. Denmark passed laws in favour of local government in 1837 and 1841; Norway's corresponding laws (*formandskapslovene*) were enacted in 1837, while Sweden's were enacted somewhat later, in 1862.

The new interest in local administrative bodies and their capacity to conduct their own affairs failed to generate a common European terminology, however. In the UK, the terms were 'local government' and 'self-government', whereas the Germans talked of *Selbsverwaltung*, which means only administration on behalf of the state. The French used the expression *libre administration*, stressing the autonomy of administration. Other terms had also come into use. Since the Middle Ages, *Gemeinde* had been used in Germanic languages, while in the Romance languages, a place could be communal like *Terra di commune* (Genoa, 1359) and *Communidades de Villa y Tierra* (Castile, fourteenth century). The French word *commune* connoted a city administered by the burghers. The French Revolution was also decisive for the modern history of the word. The revolutionaries of Paris used *commune* to designate the council of 1789 as well as the most militant revolutionaries of 1792–94. *Commune* was understood as the smallest body of the state, ruled by a mayor and a council, this being legally established by the reform of 1801. At this point, the word '*commune*' had already spread to other countries, such as Denmark and Sweden.

This was a Europeanisation that drew upon a shared concept, which was then recast in various forms. The new laws installed local administrative bodies with varying degrees of autonomy. These local bodies were detached from the administration of the state, and their installation was a way of delegating to the local level in order to promote efficiency and the satisfaction of the local population. More importantly, the delegation provided a new platform for an increasingly active bourgeoisie, which, as opposed to the aristocracy or church, took the lead in introducing local bodies. The old power structure was forced to give way.

From the very beginning, arguments for local government included pleas for active citizen participation. An early and illustrative argument can be found in the works of Karl von Stein, the Prussian prime minister who carried out the municipal self-government reform in 1808. Beginning with proprietors, whom he also called citizens, he specifically referred to artisans and industrialists, arguing that they should help to manage local administration, binding them to the state. Stein believed that the connection between the state and its citizens would need to be created in local administration. This would be where the citizen was connected to the fatherland. By the same token, it would also be where the state could obtain the counsel and active assistance of its citizens, receiving suggestions for improvements and complaints about irregularities.[8]

Stein was horrified that state officials were ruling on local matters while proprietors were being deprived of influence – a right had been taken away from them. It is not clear whether this right should be understood as a natural Lockean right or a traditional one. According to Stein, the problem was that the officials of the provinces were appointed and dispatched by the state, and lacked their own connections to the situations in which they were placed. This echoes a critique of centralised administration and its officials that Stein was neither the first nor the last to articulate. The central thesis of this critique was that the common spirit of society would be seriously harmed by the absence of proprietors in administration. Stein also pointed out that a higher cost was associated with state officials than with local citizens. Of utmost importance, however, was 'the experience of common spirit and citizen spirit', a concept that spread throughout Europe together with the new institutions of self-government.[9]

The concepts of both citizenship and local government feature in discourses on European unity. They hold a prominent position as early as 1821 in the writings of the Danish official Schmidt-Phiseldeck. Among other matters, he presented contemporary examples of representative constitutions and local self-government: the former strengthens the governance and reduces abuses, while the latter relieves the state of commitments and administrative costs through local undertakings by citizens in towns and municipalities.[10] However, he also broke new ground by making a plea for European citizenship, providing citizens of another European state with the privileges and responsibilities of their country of residence. He was likely the first to assign a legal meaning to the idea of European citizenship, and might very well have been the one to coin the expression.[11]

The expression 'Europäisches bürgerrecht' later became established in German. It was mainly used to describe something that belonged to Europe, being used rather oddly by botanists when describing butterflies, insects and birds, and somewhat more naturally by human and social scientists when describing European perspectives. One linguist who referred to the European family of languages said that Hungarians were part of the European family and should thus be accepted as a European nation: they have 'Europäisches bürgerrecht' and should also be included in a future European Federation.[12] Another linguist believed the Turks also had this European citizenship, although their language should definitely not be recognised as European.[13]

The Quest for Modernisation

According to a common nineteenth-century notion, improvements to the social structure were passed down from the more advanced countries in Europe. Those interested in modernisation looked towards other European countries for models to follow, while they considered the knowledge that could be obtained at home to be old-fashioned. One aspect of Europeanisation 'of the mind' was the belief that good examples could not be found at home. When József Eötvös and other Hungarian nationalists attempted to reform the constitutional institutions in Hungary, they noted that, compared with Europe, Hungary was lacking in development. Unsurprisingly, Europe was the standard against which many nationalists in Central Europe measured themselves. When the Czech nationalist František Palacký wrote in 1837 about 'the new European science' and 'the need for new European knowledge', he mainly intended to criticise the limiting and reactionary Habsburg state.[14]

France, Germany and Great Britain often stood out as role models for the rest of Europe, not least due to their higher education institutions and impressive research. They were admired for their technical high schools, social and human sciences, and philosophy. Academic careers took flight after scholars from the rest of Europe attending their universities translated and spread the ideas of French, German and British scholars. There was a belief that French, German and English cultures were advantageous; their art and literature were looked upon as exemplary, so authors and artists made their way to Paris, Berlin and London.

One could view Western Europe either as decadent and outdated, or as a symbol of essential progress via industrialisation and economic development. Both these views were heavily influenced by French and British authors such as Jean-Jacques Rousseau and James Macpherson. They celebrated life in the countryside unspoiled by civilisation, comprehending it as the exact opposite of life in the decadent Western metropolises. Others wished to develop their societies in the direction of the European centres. People spoke of 'the new Europe' that was growing. The Western way was worth following.[15]

Europe was primarily viewed as a role model, but its deficiencies were also often discussed, which could lead to the rejection of Western Europe as a leader worth emulating. One of the most extreme repudiations was that of Polish poet Adam Mickiewicz, who saw Western culture as in crisis due to the epidemic of causal reasoning, the progress of industrialisation, and the beginning of general bureaucratisation. With rationalism, he thought, comes the loss of morals and the Holy Spirit, and the proper governance of the nation would then be impossible. While the West declined, the Slavs, especially the Poles, had a grand mission to fulfil: being unaffected by rationalism and industrialisation, they would have to step up and save the world.[16]

This mirroring also took place farther east. The images of Europe that were cherished on Europe's peripheries or by its neighbours prompted both imitation and repudiation. In the Middle East, Europe's art of war, modern science, and technology were early objects of interest, and some influence could also be seen in architecture and the decorative arts, but otherwise the influence was limited until the late eighteenth century.[17] With its growing success and power, Western Europe increasingly stood out as a role model. Some proposed the Europeanisation of Iran and Turkey, for example, where programmes were implemented to create new manners, new ways of thinking and new ways of life. Europe was considered the progressive centre of the world, and an example for the periphery to follow as far as possible.[18]

The concept of Europeanisation was originally meant to indicate the process by which the leading European powers transformed other regions, be it provinces on the European continent or colonies across the oceans. It turns up in German publications referring to the good effect of German migration into Siebenbürgen in terms of cultivating the Magyar natives. The claim was that the Germans represented European culture, and had long been vital for Europeanising Hungary.[19] The agents of Europeanisation also included other leading nations, and the concept broadened to encompass other continents. Whether or not the natives appreciated it, as one observer put it, they were becoming more European just by being in contact with and becoming colonial subjects of European powers.[20] Istanbul was being Europeanised by new customs from the West, as were the Russians, the Jews, and many 'barbarians'. This was how 'Europeanisation' began to define Europe's place in the world. The earliest examples of this dynamic were found in Germany, and soon thereafter in France; somewhat later we see it in English publications, referring to the civilising value for India of having become part of the British Empire.

The debate continued in the European fringes, where it was disputed whether or not certain countries even belonged to Europe. Finnish nationalists looked westwards, taking for granted that Finns belonged to Europe and did not originate from what they considered the Russian Mongol tradition. They emphasised that Swedish traditions were upheld in Finland and that Sweden had brought civilisation into the country.[21]

In Russia, the discussion concerned whether the country should align itself with Western Europe or claim its own specific culture. When George Brandes gave lectures in St Petersburg and Moscow in 1887, he was seen as a European by the Russian press. The papers did not agree, however, when judging him: the conservative press claimed that Brandes had no feeling for Russian literature, and moreover had not mastered the Russian language. It was said that Russians ought to trust themselves instead of inviting literary critics from the West. Liberal papers stated that Brandes brought European culture to Russia, so it was crucial that he should present his European views.

These opinions were typical of the nineteenth-century Russian discussion of the character of the country. Everyone could agree on one point: there were clear differences between Russia and the Western states. Some aimed to make Russia significantly more European through promoting individualism and rationalism, while others preferred an emphasis on the unique Russian character.

In many respects, the opposition to Western influence in Russia derived its intellectual foundation from German romantic philosophy – in fact, also a kind of Europeanisation – which affected Slavophiles who were hoping for a genuine Russian national culture. Along with Schelling, they claimed that the nation was a kind of organism with its own legislation and ruled by its own logic. They rejected laissez-faire doctrines and the superiority of Western capitalism.[22] One of the first Russian Slavophiles was Ivan Kireyevsky, who listened to Schelling's lectures in Munich in 1830 and eventually became the ideologue of the Russian aristocracy.²³ He stressed that the Western tradition had consisted of rationalism and individualism ever since the Roman Empire, which led Europeans to become independent, isolated, owners of property, and intrinsically bound to their societies. Russians were different, defined by their shared goals and spirit in a society of organic bonds. Their traditions and the significance of the Orthodox Church had been maintained, and their laws were based on customs. There was originally no private property in Russia as the tsar possessed all the land, which meant that it belonged to the entire nation. Russia was substantially a community of faith, land, and nationwide customs.²⁴ Another assessment of Europe was presented by the Westerniser Pyotr Yakovlevich Chaadayev (at least until 1835–36, when he shifted to a more pro-tsarist stance). His position was distinct, however, as he did not uphold an atheistic standpoint like most Westernisers; rather, his idea was to bring religion into European civilisation. Russia was understood as a country lacking in what was typical of the civilised West: traditions of law and order, ideas of duty and justice, knowledge and reason. His vision was of a future united Europe that included Russia, where religious feelings would be engendered in the West, and Russia would be civilised by West European knowledge.²⁵

As we move farther south to Spain, we can see that the loss of its colonies – and other signs that it was no longer an imperial power – prompted debate on the notion of Spain and its future. The modernists desired a turn towards Europe and the shaping of a national identity modelled on those of Britain, Germany, and especially its northern Latin neighbour France. Intellectuals and artists of the so-called generation of 1898 sought an opportunity to create a new image of Spain, and promoted the feasibility and desirability of Europeanisation. The writer Miguel de Unamuno objected to this, insisting that the European spirit and the accommodating modern life were not meant for Spaniards, and he admitted his repugnance at Europeanisation in an essay from 1906. He mentioned that Europeans seek happiness, and believe this to be their ultimate goal. He opposed science and its methods with wisdom: 'Science robs men of wisdom and usually converts them into phantom beings loaded up with facts'. Science, logic and reason are only preparations for more profound wisdom. In conclusion, said Unamuno, Spaniards are incapable of absorbing civilisation.²⁶ The modernists, on the other hand, wanted a revival of Spain, moving away from its inquisitorial and premodern heritage. Ortega y Gasset was deeply concerned with the need for Europeanisation, and repeatedly returned to the issue in pleas to reform education and make scientific progress, opposing the misconduct of Spanish governance and proclaiming that German culture was the most advanced in contemporary Europe.²⁷ He published some of his articles in the magazine he started entitled *Europe*.²⁸ He answered Unamuno, saying that a Spanish revival was impossible without a rebirth and a turn towards Europe: 'Regeneration is our desire; Europeanisation is the means to satisfy it. It is really clear from the outset that Spain is the problem and Europe the solution'.[29]

A similar kind of Europeanisation was illustrated by Swedish modernizers whose gaze was directed towards Britain, France and Germany, as well as towards Belgium and the Netherlands. They wrote about the successful management of harbours and cities abroad, about the evolution of democracy, and the way that local self-government prospered. For example, a conservative member of the Swedish parliament, Magnus Björnstjerna, invoked what had occurred in these countries and the views of their statesmen, philosophers and political writers in order to criticise and offer alternatives to the deficiencies of the Swedish system of governance.[30] In his writings, the liberal Carl Forsell took inspiration from Europe in seeking ways to improve Sweden: in 1820, his focus was on establishing a new transportation route between Sweden's two main cities using steamships to cross large lakes; in 1830, his focus was on associations that promoted sobriety; and a few years later it was on the importance of elementary school. Forsell mainly looked to England, to which he had travelled. There was trade and industry there, and important inventions such as the steam engine and the mechanical loom, as well as the development of economic thought. While Sweden remained a country with inferior transportation, England had hundreds of steamships and even a railway, reported by Forsell as the first of its kind, which ran between Manchester and Liverpool. He had the opportunity to ride it, and, although initially worried that the high speed might cause breathing problems, he reluctantly admitted afterwards how pleasant it was to travel at thirty kilometres per hour, and emphasised the necessity of building railways to improve transportation in Sweden.[31] In his final book, written in 1843, the European perspective was stressed with reference to the common European issues of crime and poverty. He argued for local self-government as a way to deal with such things, and cited continental examples. England was seen as the most advanced example, where the locals dealt with problems instead of leaving them to the officials of the state. Local self-government enhanced community spirit and a common responsibility for pauperism, morality, and economic issues of general interest.[32]

Although Germany and Prussia could be regarded as models for Scandinavia, Europe could also be seen as a model for Germany, especially before unification in 1871 and the economic boom during the final decades of the century. This is the case in the writings of Friedrich List, who around 1820 described national German interests in terms of a shared economy based on free trade and the abolition of domestic customs tariffs. Trade routes should be open from the North and Baltic seas to the Adriatic, from the Vistula River in the east to the Rhine River in the west. His argument was based on what other European states had already claimed and done. Following their example was not only a way to increase wealth, but would also lead to a stronger sense of belonging to one nation when all Germans were politically united. Spiritual culture would blossom and Germany would be reborn.[33] As the years passed he became more pessimistic: Germany continued on a path of fragmentation that had led it away from the might and glory it had possessed five hundred years previously, while England and France had gone from being relatively insignificant to become rich and powerful by constantly striving for national unity.[34] According to List, only large and well-organised countries operating at the highest cultural levels could control their futures and, as such, he recognised only England, France and the United States. Germany was ranked alongside Russia and Spain as states that had some of the prerequisites necessary to attain that higher level. While Russia only possessed strong military power, Spain lagged behind due to weak political organisation. He concluded that one could sense the disappointment of contemporary German liberal modernizers, as their country possessed both resources and culture, but it lacked not only the essential political institutions but also the economic organisation. He seemed to imply that time was running out for the Germans, that it was now or never if they wanted to find future success.[35]

The political backwardness of Germany was also a theme of Heinrich Heine's *Deutschland: Ein Wintermärchen*, in which Europe was compared with Prussia. In Europe there was innocence, freedom and enjoyment, while Prussia could show nothing more than oppression and foolishness. The attempt to unite the country through a customs union and censorship, to shape an economy in order to achieve a spiritual unity, was described with irony by Heine. Despite these powerful aspirations for unity, German souls existed only in the country of dreams.

> The Land belongs to the French and the Russians
> The Seas belong to the British,
> But we own in the airy empire of dreams
> A sovereignty that is uncontested.[36]

The Books

In 1719, an enduring figure was introduced to the public when Daniel Defoe published the novel *Robinson Crusoe*. We all know the story of Crusoe, who survived a shipwreck and then lived his life on a deserted island; how he built, cultivated and created, and how he carefully calculated how to make the best use of his limited resources. Robinson Crusoe is an excellent example of a hero of modern times: he is a man not a woman, he is white, and Man Friday is enslaved. Crusoe toiled to expand his riches. By his hands, the island off the coast of South America was colonised and civilised. We can infer that he longed for safety and feared the unknown, as he built walls to protect himself from any potential enemies. His virtues were marked by bourgeois ethics: he had a strong awareness of duty, and he read the Bible.

Defoe's novel continues to be published widely to this day. He was not the first to use the theme of shipwreck and survival, but his version of it was emulated by many others who followed, making Crusoe a famous literary figure. It is worth noting that the novel was already assigned reading for children and youths during the eighteenth century, which says something about its importance. Crusoe was looked upon as a good example for the young, as the novel clarified the norms of society.

This is only one example of how books have been vital for the spreading of community values in Europe. The elites were happy to read French, German and English, while considerable work went into translation, primarily managed by publishers. In the absence of copyright treaties, they were the ones searching Europe for new, potentially lucrative books for their national publics. Changing community values were often appropriated from books in the late eighteenth century. *Ideen zur Philosophie der Geschichte der Menschheit* (1784–91) by Johann Gottfried Herder not only influenced the architects of nationality in Central Europe, but also attracted nationalists in England, France, Russia and the Scandinavian countries, with its message of a national culture based on language as a natural and dynamic community.[37] There are many examples of such books being central to community discourses in several countries, such as *De l'esprit des lois* (1748) by Charles Louis Montesquieu, and *Du contrat social* (1762) by Jean-Jacque Rousseau.

The Wealth of Nations by Adam Smith, which laid the foundation for political economy around Europe, was published in 1776 and was soon thereafter cited in France. It was a significant influence on moderate reformists at the beginning of the revolution, and later inspired minds such as Say, Constant and Sismondi. Translations were many, and in Germany, for example, one after another was published. Academics and reformist-minded officials in the bureaucracy assimilated its messages that individual self-interest is a blessing and that a free market is needed within a state's borders.

Smith's work became a centrepiece of political economy, a discipline cultivated in several countries where its practitioners read, quoted and criticised one another, all the while interested in a single common problem – wealth. From its inception in the seventeenth century, the discipline had focused on the wealth of the public and of nations, always keeping in mind that the countries studied belonged to Europe.[38] Adam Smith's perspective was very European, and he wrote about Europe's wealth and present state. He even distinguished between those nations belonging to 'Europe' and those belonging to 'modern Europe', the former being mostly concerned with agriculture and the latter favouring manufacturing and foreign trade.[39] The European view of political economy was being stressed by 1800, as evidenced by increased usage of the word 'Europe',[40] and by how the sources of wealth were considered to be the object of the 'solitary and combined efforts of the most distinguished writers among the most celebrated nations of Europe'.[41] The French economist Charles Ganilh cited authors from England, France, Germany, Italy, the Netherlands and Scotland. He discussed what brought wealth to Europe and stated that the keys to growing wealth were the same for all Europe's nations, even claiming that there was a common 'fate of Europe'. Various steps taken by specific nations could be judged by how much they succeeded in bringing wealth and prosperity to 'the system of modern Europe'.[42]

New books and authors came forward after the French Revolution and after the upheavals in Europe settled. Socialists across the continent were reading Charles Fourier, Joseph Proudhon and Karl Marx. Among the works of early English liberals, those by Jeremy Bentham and John Stuart Mill were much discussed on the continent. Stockholm liberals established a centre for Swedish Benthamism, and scheduled plenary debates on Bentham in parliament. Meanwhile in Barcelona, Bentham was extensively published in the journal *La civilización*, which was founded by Europe-oriented writers.[43] The conservative liberal-minded historian and statesman François Guizot presented *Histoire générale de la civilisation en Europe*, which would hold great sway with its many editions, not only in French and English, but also in further translations into German, Italian, Russian and Spanish as well as more minor languages such as Swedish and Danish. One of his British admirers exclaimed that this eminent historian had written 'a book every student of history should read'.[44] A full list of books with pan-European readership would be long. However, regarding concepts such as democracy, citizenship and local self-government, one book stands out in the first half of the nineteenth century. French discussions of how the future mode of government should be realised resulted in the most widely read and quoted book on this issue in Europe in the 1830s and 1840s.[45] By the time Alexis de Tocqueville had published the first part of *De la démocratie en Amérique* in 1835 (the second part appeared in 1840), local government was already an established institution in several European states and the subject of political discussion. The book was still a bombshell, given its proposals for free, self-governed communes with activities shaped and implemented by active citizens. Tocqueville described innovative approaches and presented new perspectives on local government. His book was soon translated into other languages and was constantly cited by anyone with views on local government. The book's examples of local government in North America were frequently cited, and its arguments supported or dismissed. In Austria it was referred to as a critique of the autocracy. In Germany it was promoted by Jacob Burckhardt, and in Great Britain by John Stuart Mill and Nassau William Senior, for whom it was 'one of the most remarkable books of our age'. It was referred to by conservatives and by liberals, by those who were for democracy and by those who were against; it was certainly never ignored.[46]

According to Tocqueville, there was a special future risk in Europe, where local authorities had been disappearing. The state controlled the 'smallest citizens' and their 'smallest matters' in a way that left no room for links between the state and the individual. A national parliament mitigated the drawbacks of strong state power, but could not eliminate them. For Tocqueville, the democratic institutions generated by a powerful central form of government were not enough; rather, the remedy for despotism consisted of the links that were forged in the freedom of the communes.

He also called attention to a problematic aspect of democracy – that it had characteristics of both freedom and obedience. It required citizens who were willing and able to act independently, as well as to be obedient to laws and decrees. Democracy also created an ideal, and a requirement for moderation that made Tocqueville fear a new kind of despotism characterised by equality and moderation, in which the state guaranteed its citizens security, employing power that is 'without limits, detailed, regular, foreseeing and soft'. Democracy could be seen as a form of government in which individuals would not grow up as citizens, in which freedom could become less and less important. The state could turn into the shepherd of a frightened flock, whose wills would become increasingly weak and passive. Tocqueville therefore stressed the need to clarify the limits of state power, and also the rights of individuals in order to safeguard their 'power and peculiarity'.

Tocqueville wanted a communal spirit in Europe like that in New England, which had been kept alive and was still energising local communities. He concluded that a strong and independent commune was a prerequisite for a society of citizens, and that political life originated in the communes. His book and how it was received illustrates the different perspectives evident within the Europeanised concepts of democracy, citizenship and local self-government. Tocqueville himself represents a kind of bottom–up perspective, beginning with the local community and its citizens, understanding the communes and towns as the foundation of political life and legitimate state building. At the same time, he was read and used by those who held a statist perspective, looking at the local community as an efficient tool for implementing projects and gaining legitimacy for the state government.

Tocqueville accorded clear precedence to local bodies: the political life of the nation, in which active citizenship limits autocracy and unhealthy centralisation, rests on the freedom of the communes. This perspective would change somewhat when his ideas were related to specific contexts – for instance, in Sweden, where Tocqueville was much read and both liberal and monarchist papers cited him. The senior historian Erik Gustaf Geijer regarded Tocqueville as an 'excellent thinker' who 'thinks better than everybody we know'; he saw his book as vitally important, 'one of the best books I have read and anybody could read'. Geijer's pupil and friend Pehr Erik Bergfalk, professor of law, read Tocqueville carefully, evidenced when, in the late 1830s, he presented a rather elaborate plea for local government in Sweden. Bergfalk was a liberal, and favourably disposed to local government and the idea of citizenship. He was a member of the law-drafting committee in the 1840s, and president of the constitutional committee in 1859–68. Considering that the Swedish laws on local government were passed in 1862 and followed by a new constitution in 1865, Bergfalk can be considered a key figure in the creation of local Swedish government.[47]

Bergfalk argued that the state defines the local community and gives it status. The commune is a legal institution of its own, just as the state is. Both are legal entities, but the commune is a simpler institution at a subordinate level. The state defines the commune, identifies its properties, gives it certain rights, and makes sure that it does not misuse its freedom. In a logical sequence, the state has first priority, with the local administration deriving its authority from the state by allocation (to use today's technical concept). Bergfalk was inspired by Tocqueville when it came to the amount of activity, development and efficiency generated by self-government. Directly referring to Tocqueville, he asserted that state power was a threat to communal freedom, but he did not share Tocqueville's basic idea of the state's historical and logical precedence. Yet Bergfalk agreed with Tocqueville that local government teaches its inhabitants to look beyond private interests when considering their common matters. His statist perspective, not inspired by Tocqueville, can also be seen when he describes the commune as a tool of the state for producing civic competence.[48] Unsurprisingly, the statist perspective was the one that was realised in practice. Local self-government then became a kind of moderate decentralism administered by, and integral to, the centralised modern state. This perspective emphasised how the local context produces a relationship between citizens and the state. The arguments of Bergfalk and others for local government connect citizens to the state through local administration, while the state safeguards knowledge of local conditions and the deeds of citizens. Civic spirit is thus able to grow. Local self-government is constituted as the foundation of the state. The idea of self-government positions individuals in relation to both the local community and the state. The ideas of Tocqueville can therefore be applied to the Swedish context, with certain adjustments. This case illustrates both the Europeanisation of a concept, whereby intellectuals and reformers were inspired by foreign authors, as well as its adaptations to specific contexts.

European Individualism

Concepts spread in many ways. Individualism is considered a truly European value of old and sometimes even ancient origin, a unique historical feature of Europe.[49] One argument is that the preconditions for fostering capitalism and creating industrial production only arose in Europe.[50] This argument is mentioned when explaining differences between the various parts of Europe – for example, that the lower impact of individualism in Eastern Europe and Russia meant a delay in their development.[51] Furthermore, it has been claimed that the different social structures in Northern and Southern Europe have been generated by different varieties of individualism.[52] This book is not the place to write the history of individualism or discuss its explanatory value. Instead, we will consider how the word 'individualism' entered several discourses, finally being defined as 'European individualism', constituting a further example of conceptual Europeanisation.

Tocqueville declared that individualism was a new word. He was right, even though the idea that the individual was the basic unit of society had already been adopted in some branches of philosophy. The new word 'individualism' was initially used pejoratively to connote something that should be rejected. It was introduced by Restoration thinkers in France around 1820, and viewed as a threat to traditional values such as obedience and duty. As such, individualism represented the consequences of the French Revolution as well as the ideas of natural rights and individual freedom. The idea was later picked up by the disciples of Henri Saint-Simon, who associated individualism with disorder, atheism and egoism, viewing it as incompatible with their idea of a modern industrial society based on religious community. It was soon used by a range of French authors who wrote about the '*l'odieux individualisme*' of society, which was corrupting social life. They associated individualism with the economic doctrine of laissez-faire, and liberal ideas of coherence between individual interests and those of society.[53] Meanwhile in England, Robert Owen was criticising the 'competition of interests' as irrational and to blame for causing the 'individualising' of men, regardless of whether they resided in cottages or palaces.[54] This illustrates that the attractiveness of this kind of argument extended outside of France and, unsurprisingly, the word spread quickly throughout Germany, Great Britain and other European countries, as well as America. At that point, individualism became a main theme on both sides of the Atlantic when comparing

Europe and North America, and it was always said to have gone further in America than in Europe.

As the word spread, it gained more positive connotations, first in America where the freedom of individualism explained its attractiveness to European migrants. In Europe it was only cautiously accepted as a positive description or value. When Robert Owen later talked about individualism, it was understood as a bad practice and an irrational way of organising society, although he did uphold the individuality of man. Still, the 1840s liberals in Britain, France and Germany openly advocated individualism, mostly influenced by German Romantic writers who raved over individuality. Individualism was favoured by some socialists, and even Proudhon declared himself an individualist.[55]

While individualism was apparently a popular notion, it was also occupied by nationalistic discourses. The historian Guizot claimed that it was a German virtue that should have been taken over by the French.[56] Some sources confidently claimed that individualism was a special British virtue: 'the height of self-reliance and self-sufficiency, of initiative and individualism, upon which commerce is based, and which constitute England's . . . mercantile strength' (*The Eclectic Magazine*, 1844);[57] in German, the word individualism was introduced in 1842 by the liberal Karl Brüggemann, who contrasted economic individualism with a specific 'German infinite [*unendlichen*] individualism based on an infinite individual self-confidence to be personally free in morals and truth'. When French liberals used the concept of individualism with more positive connotations, they were condemning the lack of the thriving spirit of individualism that they acknowledged in England and Germany.[58]

National discourses continuously influenced the idea of individualism after the turn of the century. Miguel de Unamuno saw a traditional Spanish individualism that had its origin in the tendency to disrupt community life and separate into different tribes, whereas he hoped that the progress of commercial competition, together with civilised, urban and industrial life, would modify this tendency.[59] The philosopher and sociologist Georg Simmel addressed an 'old individualism' marked by economic ideals and the free individuals of modern times. Against this, he specified a new and qualitative individualism from the German tradition of Goethe, Fichte, and the other Romantics up to Nietzsche, that focuses on the distinctiveness of individuals and their will to develop their own individuality. Thomas Mann underlined the distinction between a Western individualism imprinted with liberalism, and the Enlightenment and a German individualism aligned with community and social thinking.[60]

Individualism apparently had several meanings. Critiques of modernity interpreted individualism as simple egoism that threatened society with anarchy. Many socialists condemned it as an expression of capitalism and the freedom of the market. Yet socialists could also argue, as Oscar Wilde did, that only individualism could offer the fulfilment of human potential. With economic liberalism, on the other hand, individualism was considered a way of defending property rights. Other liberals, such as Leonard Hobhouse, defended individualism as a social freedom and as embodying the ideal equality of human rights, concluding that freedom and equity demanded a social control that was beyond the scope of economic liberalism.[61] There were two basic themes running through the different interpretations of the word: one was that the individual constitutes the fundamental part of society (as opposed to the family, clan, parish, nation, or other community); the other highlighted the ability of human beings to articulate their own truth about what is right or wrong, and how they should act in different situations. These themes have a long history, so even though the word only began to be used after 1820, individualism as a concept has a history that dates back even further. It has been argued that individualism was specifically developed by philosophers, including Thomas Hobbes, John Locke, Adam Smith, Jean-Jacques Rousseau, Immanuel Kant and Johann Gottfried Herder.[62]

Neither the longer history of the themes of individualism nor the frequent use of the word and its apparent popularity throughout Europe initially defined it as a European phenomenon or value. This changed when individualism was made into an object of historical arguments and historical writing. One example – possibly the first – is from America in 1840, and invoked a thousand-year-old history of individualism as strongly influenced by Christianity, and especially by the Reformation. Individualism, it was claimed, was the hallmark of European civilisation, from which it had spread via migration to America and other continents: 'The great feature of this Type [of civilisation] was and is, as I shall call it, individualism; in Government, Religion, Science, Art, Literature, and social life, this long has been and now is, I believe, the great idea'.[63]

The intimate relationship between individualism and European civilisation is recurrently invoked, and it is a main theme of Jacob Burckhardt's *Civilization of the Renaissance in Italy*, which is a broad treatment of life and society, covering state and governance, literature and poetry, culture, religion and customs. In this work, Florence, Venice, and the other city-states of Italy in the fourteenth and fifteenth centuries are envisioned as the birthplaces of modern man – specifically, contemporary Europeans – as these were the sources of individualism. Burckhardt claimed that this was the historical period when the shackles of the Middle Ages were thrown off, initiating the transition from humans seen as members of a community, to being defined as individuals. This transition had to do with the absence of an all-powerful state and the division between worldly and religious power, permitting growing opportunities for private aspirations that could be directed towards amassing riches and individual education (*Bildung*). In these cities, the ideal was that of a comprehensive education that would bring about a versatile individuality.

By 1900, the term 'European individualism' stood on its own as a fully fledged concept with distinctive features. It was frequently used in distinguishing European philosophy, society and religion from their Indian, Japanese and Chinese counterparts, respectively. Russian Slavophiles cited individualism when criticising the West. Moreover, in the emerging social sciences, individualism occupied a key position in determining how society should be treated, especially by economists. The leading economists discussed theories that started from the notion of the rational 'economic man', assuming that the study of society should begin with the economic desires and needs of the abstract individual. Their structuring idea was that man's individual activities shaped the economy. The man they considered was an abstraction who acted out of self-interest. Some of these economists even produced 'Robinsonades' to illustrate their theories. Individualism became a European feature of such self-evidence that its Europeanness no longer had to be made explicit. Robinson Crusoe had become a manifest symbol of this individualism, being used not only in novels but also in sustaining both economic thought and social science.[64]

Approaching Standards and Unification

Throughout the nineteenth century there was a striving to create common standards for the good of commerce and prosperity of society. This was in response to the societal values of efficiency and equal conditions that were associated with the European state model after the French Revolution and the examples laid out by Napoleon. It was certainly important to establish common standards within the state regarding, for instance, weight and measurement systems. However, there was also a drive for uniformity of standards between the countries, underpinning the thesis of Europeanisation and taking place at a far more practical level than the lofty visions and calls for a European federation.

As early as Schmidt-Phiseldeck we see the idea of free trade depicted as a way to knit the world together, bringing mutual dependence and wealth, and to be facilitated by a common monetary standard and credit fund. Throughout the century, calls for free trade across borders had made themselves heard together with pleas for convergence of standards and practices. Industrialisation and improved communications would be facilitated by equalising not only rules of trade but also technological standards. Common standards were driven by industrialisation, which, in turn, brought more trade and further expansion of transport and information exchange. There was a technocratic internationalism fuelled by liberal ideals and discourses of free trade, as well as by the building of new infrastructures.[65] Infrastructure projects were mostly set up to ease trade and communications within states, and with territories abroad in the case of colonial states, strengthening the building of states and empires. The aim was also to expand trade to international markets, leading to international cooperation. Recent research in the history of science has identified a technocratic internationalism among experts, cartels and international organisations that were striving to set technical standards at the continental level. Wolfram Kaiser and Johan Schot have traced the beginning of this technocratic internationalism to the mid-nineteenth century, a period of intensified free-trade agitation and the opening of new arenas for technological transfer, as illustrated by the Crystal Palace Exhibition. At this time the first regional telegraph unions were founded in order to connect national systems, followed in 1865 by an initiative of the French government that led to the creation of the International Telegraph Union. By 1900, a practice was in place for establishing working rules for international cooperation, with the Telegraph Union and Postal Union as the main prototypes cited by experts.[66]

It did not take long for this trend of the convergence of communication standards to be connected to visions of European unification. Bluntschli, the jurist who argued for a federation of sovereign states, said that one of the main tasks of a European 'Staatenbund' would be to manage such special bureaus for post, telegraph and transport between the European countries. He added that further arrangements to facilitate cooperation, such as treaties regarding shipping via international waters, would bring the European states closer to one another.[67] The value of such an arrangement can be illustrated by these words from William Thomas Stead: 'There is a steady approximation to unity throughout the continent'. Stead, hailed as the most important newspaperman of his age when he died in the sinking of the *Titanic* in 1912, campaigned among other things for the peace movement and peace initiatives. Writing in 1898, he greeted the extent to which Europe was moving towards unity, and he had great hopes for the peace conference that was about to take place in The Hague in 1899 for the purpose of preventing war in Europe and giving relief from the burdens of reconstruction.[68]

Through Stead we can observe how the ideas of unity and Europeanisation were given a further dimension, as he was clearly outlining how a versatile unification, or what we would now call integration, was actually taking place at the very moment he was writing. This stands in sharp contrast to the calls for a unified Europe that begin by observing the loss of a former unity. Novalis did this with sadness. Mazzini, on the other hand, heralded an opportunity for democracy when he observed the loss of 'unity of faith' in Europe and of the privileges of the royals and aristocracy, in 'the perpetual inheritance of virtue, intelligence, and honour'.[69]

Stead was neither alone nor the first in claiming that social or even political unification was already taking place. For instance, Schmidt-Phiseldeck noted that travelling brought more unity to lifestyle and culture, also contributing to the growing uniformity of public administration across Europe. Even warfare could have this effect, as armies settled in foreign cities: Danish troops had been in Paris, Germans in Spain, Spaniards in the Netherlands, Italians in Russia, Poles in Italy, and so on. To this, he added, were trade and the scholarly exchange within science. As early as 1821, he claimed that each European capital had been exposed to the entire continent.[70] In an inaugural speech, Victor Hugo addressed the international peace congress of 1869: 'Fellow citizens of the United States of Europe, allow me to give you this name, for the European Federal Republic is established in right and is waiting to be established in fact. You exist, therefore it exists. You confirm it by the union from which unity is taking shape. You are the beginning of a great future'.[71] The ardent peace activist Jacques Novicow was even more eloquent by the turn of the century when he recognised the intensification of travel, economic exchange, and communication following the impact of technical progress. The steam engine and the railway had lowered the cost of trade and facilitated a division of labour that had led to mutual dependence between countries that were no longer self-sufficient. Just as economic interdependence spread, so did intellectual, scientific and cultural exchanges and influences cross borders: 'There has long been a unifying sympathy among Europeans, despite their political divisions'.[72]

In addition, Stead declared that ongoing unification began with the observation that Europeans were becoming more and more conscious of the alleged unity of the continent. Three of the reasons for this consciousness that Stead mentioned should be noted: royalty, diplomacy and communication. The royalty were already forming an international family group on a European scale, offering a kind of forerunner and model for the close unity that the European states were heading towards. For example, the British royalty had connections all over Europe: they attended weddings, mourned the dead, paid attention to one another's affairs, and kept up a careful correspondence with their relatives among Europe's various royal courts – just as relations should have been between the European states. Diplomacy had established a basis for their actions through the system of the Concert of Europe, which Stead looked upon as an embryonic federal European commonwealth. He pointed out that cooperation between the European powers had recently been successful in dealing with the Ottoman Empire, forcing the Turks to leave Greece without having to use heavy military force. His conclusion was that these actions made Europe more accustomed to acting as a unit, and 'will in time bring about the United States of Europe'.

The expansion of means of communication was cited by Stead to exemplify how Europe was able to draw closer to unity. Thanks to the telegraph, news could spread across the continent within hours: social and political gossip could spread rapidly, contributing to a common sentiment in all European nations. The railways made travelling between Europe's countries quick and easy, and large distances could be efficiently traversed via rivers and canals. These links acted like nerves crossing national borders, and there was furthermore a strong tendency to set up international organisations in association with them and other such links: '[E]ach of them may be regarded as an embodied prophecy of the coming of the United States of Europe'.[73] He mentioned such existing 'embodied prophec[ies]' as the Telegraph Union from 1865, the International Postal Union from 1874, the Patents, Copyrights and Trade Marks Bureau and the International Railway Bureau from 1890. Stead's main point in mentioning these institutions was to show that they were recognised as sovereign in their affairs, worked for common interests, and above all, had managed to function in a way that all Europe's states were happy with. We can see that he was demonstrating the Europeanisation of standards – which was necessary when constructing the accessories of modern societies – throughout the European countries. He had great hopes for this idea.

Several discourses advanced the creation of standards – the international organisations that Stead mentioned constituting one example. Stead also stressed the importance of managing international waterways, to protect transportation on the Danube River and between the Mediterranean and the Black Sea through the Dardanelles and the Bosporus. He recognised the commissions overseeing these waterways both as outcomes of the principles of the Concert of Europe as well as examples of how common European interests could be protected.[74] One achievement of the Congress of Vienna was that the victors promised regulation to protect the international interest of movement and trade on waterways that were shared or that ran through several states. For the Danube River and the Black Sea, this promise was realised in the 1856 Treaty of Paris, which lifted restrictions on trade and opened these waterways to international trade. For Lorenz von Stein, a close advisor to liberal-minded ministers in Vienna, who mentioned this matter in 1856, it meant the establishment of the 'European principle of free trade', which would bring the states together into healthy and peaceful competition, establish a truly European way of trading, and contribute to the free development of Europe's commerce. It would benefit all of Europe without causing damage to anyone.[75]

Cross-border arrangements and transnational organisations, such as railway projects, are examples of Europeanisation in practice, which was all about building a Europe that spanned national borders and involved not only cooperation but also regulation. Often such projects were facilitated by a focus on apolitical aims. These projects were not associated with visions of one state taking over another, but simply with prospects of mutual benefit. They were gathered around the warm light of the shared idea of economic progress and the advancement of society. As stressed by Kaiser and Schot, these projects gave experts the task of improving society with the blessing of heads of state and governments.[76]

It has been suggested that, by the nineteenth century, there were certain common experiences that provided a common ground for talking about Europe. In enumerating these experiences, the British historian James Joll referred to the Roman Empire, Christianity, the scientific revolution, the Enlightenment, the industrial revolution, and the increased international trade due to railways and the experience of imperialism since the nineteenth century.[77] To this list should be added the process of unifying community perspectives and values – a cultural exchange – that took place in a very concrete sense throughout the nineteenth century, separate from the more gripping intellectual idea of establishing political unity on a diverse continent. This was a kind of practical integration that occurred without a master plan or organised intentions. It was implemented by reformers and statesmen who took examples for action from neighbouring states or other parts of Europe. It was driven by pressing needs arising from similar challenges and by the simple insight into the advantages of facilitating progress in other European countries. Still, we should not pretend that such Europeanisation implied learning on equal terms, as it was very much a centralising business. It implied that the margins of Europe were the pupils of English, German and French teachers.

In the nineteenth century, Europeanisation was not logically followed by unification, as it took place on a continent crossed by state borders. The aim was usually not to create a real federation, nor to set up a loose alliance, nor to promote the idea of European unity. Rather, the aims were often national: to establish shared community values and strengthen the orderliness of a proper society, to change the direction of development, and often simply to find models for building very concrete public functions. Europeanisation as such did not entail transcending borders but accepting them, and even making them more viable and less likely to disappear. Identifying the Europeanisation of community values can be characterised as a transnational writing of history, a topic that has recently attracted much attention.[78] In the same way that Europeanisation does, transnational research postulates that there are nations, and it studies objects or phenomena that cross borders.

Notes

1. Secord, 'Knowledge in Transit'; Armitage, 'International Turn'.
2. Beck and Grande, *Das kosmopolitische Europa*, 15; Delanty and Rumford, *Rethinking Europe*, 7.
3. Bartlett, *The Making of Europe*, 269–91, quotation from 269: 'The Europeanization of Europe, in so far as it was indeed the spread of a particular culture through conquest and influence, had its core areas in one part of the continent, namely in France, Germany west of the Elbe and north Italy, regions which had a common history as part of Charlemagne's Frankish empire'.
4. Schlögel, 'Europe and the Culture of Borders'.
5. Kant, *Schriften zu Anthropologie*, 151–53.
6. For examples from the history of the idea of citizenship, see Clarke, *Citizenship*; Heater, *Citizenship*.
7. Wollstonecraft, *A Vindication*.
8. Stein, *Briefe und amtliche Schriften*, 389–90.
9. Ibid., 390–94.
10. Schmidt-Phiseldeck, *Europa und Amerika*, 185–90.
11. Schmidt-Phiseldeck, *Der Europäische Bund*: he speaks of 'Europäische Bürger' on 201 and of 'Europäisches Bürgerrecht' and 'Europäisches Staatsbürger' on 269–72.
12. Semmig, *Geschichte der französischen Literatur*, 3.
13. Arndt, *Ueber den Ursprung*, 148.
14. Palacký, 'Předmluwa ke wlastenskému čtenářstwu'. Regarding Hungary, see Bödy, *Joseph Eötvös*, 37–41; Eötvös, *Die Reform in Ungarn*, 13–14, 38, 67–68.
15. See Sziklay, 'Die Anfänge des "nationalen Erwachsen"', 34–38, regarding this phenomenon in Eastern Central Europe. This dichotomy of the European versus the domestic was found not only among Slavic intellectuals, but also in Romania; see Verdery, *National Ideology under Socialism*, 31–35.
16. Walicki, 'Russia, Poland and France', 38–41.
17. Hourani, *Islam in European Thought*, 136–47.
18. Fazlhashemi, *Exemplets makt*, 20–21, 34, 130–35.
19. Schlözer, *Geschichte der Deutschen in Siebenbürgen*, VII, 177, 181, 191.
20. *Göttingisches Taschenbuch 1802*, 83–85; Heeren, *Geschichte des Europäischen Staatensystems*, 400.
21. Svedelius, *Studier i Sveriges statskunskap*, 282; Sohlmann, *Det unga Finland*, 16.
22. Walicki, *The Slavophile Controversy*, 464–70.
23. Ibid., 62–68, 513.
24. Ibid., 134–48.
25. Neumann, *Russia and the Idea of Europe*, 13–39.
26. Unamuno, 'Reflections upon Europeanization', 54–57, quotation from 55.
27. See his articles from 1902–11 that are published in Ortega y Gasset, *Obras Completas I*.
28. Gray, *The Imperative of Modernity*, 85.
29. Ortega y Gasset, 'La pedagogía social', 521: 'Regeneración es el deseo; europeización es el medio de satisfacerlo. Verdaderamente se vio claro desde un principio que España era el problema y Europa la solución'.
30. Björnstjerna, *Grunder för Representationens*.
31. Andrén, *Den europeiska blicken*, 76–79; Forsell, *Plan till Transport-inrättning*; Forsell, *Underrättelse om Temperance-societies*; Forsell, *Anteckningar i anledning av*; Forsell, *Om småbarnskolor*; Forsell, *Utkast till handbok*.
32. Forsell, *Om kommunal-nämnder*.
33. List, *Gesammelte Schriften II*, 16–20, 22–34.

34. Ibid., 367.
35. Ibid., 414–17.
36. Heine, *Deutschland: Ein Wintermärchen*, 9–12, quotation from 24: 'Franzosen und Russen gehört das Land,/ Das Meer gehört den Briten,/ Wir aber besitzen im Luftreich des Traums/ Die Herrschaft unbestritten'.
37. Arnold, Kloocke and Menze, 'Herder's Reception and Influence'; Tronchon, *La Fortune Intellectuelle de Herder*.
38. Petty, 'A Treatise of Taxes', 22–23.
39. Smith, *Wealth of Nations*, e.g., 43, 274, 426–29, 449.
40. Adam Smith (1776) used the word twice as frequently as William Petty (1662), and then James Maitland Lauderdale (*Origin of Public Wealth*, 1804) used it twice as frequently as Smith.
41. Ganilh, *Systems of Political Economy*, 2.
42. Ibid., e.g., 55, 146–52, 173, 309, 377.
43. Swensson, *Den kommmunala självstyrelsen*, 135–38, 360; Roca y Cornet, 'Bentham: Escuela utilitaria', 18–20, 289–305.
44. MacLeod, *European Life*, 6.
45. The rest of this paragraph is a condensation of an in-house report by the author: Andrén, 'Local Government and Local Citizens'.
46. Alexis de Tocqueville, *De la démocratie en Amérique*, 1835–1840; Andrian-Werburg, *Österreich und dessen Zukunft*, 36, 147–48, 190–205. See the two reviews by John Stuart Mill, 'Tocqueville on Democracy in America'. Quotation from Nassau in Simpson, *Correspondence of Tocqueville with Senior*, 3. My presentation of Tocqueville follows that in my earlier book on local self-government in Sweden: Andrén, *Den europeiska blicken*, 28–33.
47. Swensson, *Den kommunala självstyrelsen*, 97–107; Geijer, 'Litteratur-Bladet', 227–28. My presentation of Bergfalk follows Andrén, *Den europeiska blicken*, 45–51.
48. Bergfalk, *Städernas Författning och Förvaltning*, 9, 93–112.
49. Gurevich, *Origins of European Individualism*.
50. See, e.g., Crotty, *When Histories Collide*.
51. Longworth, *The Making of Eastern Europe*.
52. Harskamp and Musschenga, *Faces of Individualism*.
53. Swart, '"Individualism" 1826–1860', 77–90.
54. Cited from Claeys, 'Conceptual Formation, 1800–1850'.
55. For British and French examples, see Swart, '"Individualism" 1826–1860', and Claeys, 'Conceptual Formation, 1800–1850'. For a German example, see Fröbel, *Die deutsche Auswanderung*, 17–18.
56. Guizot, *History of Civilization in Europe*, 77.
57. Anonymous, 'Triumph of Russian Autocracy'.
58. Quotation from Swart, '"Individualism" 1826–1860', 90. See also Claeys, 'Conceptual Formation, 1800–1850'.
59. Unamuno, 'Spanish Individualism'.
60. Simmel, 'Formen des Individualismus'; Mann, *Betrachtungen eines Unpolitischen*, 291–94.
61. Wilde, *The Soul of Man*; Hobhouse, *Liberalism*.
62. See, e.g., Taylor, *Sources of the Self*; Shanahan, *Genealogy of Individualism*.
63. Perkins, *Christian Civilisation*.
64. Andrén, 'Robinson Crusoe och ekonomerna'.
65. Kaiser and Schot, *Writing the Rules for Europe*; Högselius, Kaijser and Vleuten, *Europe's Infrastructure Transition*.
66. Kaiser and Schot, *Writing the Rules for Europe*, 21–36.
67. Bluntschli, 'Die Organisation'.

68. Kaiser and Schot, *Writing Rules for Europe*, drew my attention to William Thomas Stead, *United States of Europe*.

69. Mazzini, 'Europe: Its Condition and Prospects'.

70. Schmidt-Phiseldeck, *Der Europäische Bund*, 49–59, 115–16.

71. Quoted from 'Victor Hugo Central', retrieved 10 April 2022 from http://www.gavroche.org/vhugo/peacecongress.shtml.

72. Novicow, *Die Föderation Europas*, 468–515, quotation from 515: 'So einigen seit langer Zeit zahlreicher Band eder Sympathie die Europäer trotz ihrer politischen Trennung'.

73. Stead, *United States of Europe*, 20.

74. Ibid., 15–38.

75. Stein, *Oesterreich und der Frieden*, 85–115.

76. Kaiser and Schot, *Writing the Rules for Europe*, 25, 53.

77. Joll, 'Europe: An Historian's View'.

78. See, e.g., Werner and Zimmermann, 'Beyond Comparison'; Neunsinger, 'Cross-over!'.

Part II

CRISIS AND DECLINE (1914–1945)

CHAPTER 5

Passage to a New Europe

The First World War

During his New York exile in 1941, the Austrian economist Gustav Stolper reflected on the First World War and how it had changed the world: 'On August 1, 1914, a world that seemed to be built for eternity went to pieces'. This was a world

> where everything was safe, certain, secure . . . where institutions, systems, customs, political frontiers, and economic forces were so much taken for granted that few people troubled to give critical thought to them; how it was to live in a world where progress was a matter of course, moral standards were not seriously questioned, and economic rules were immutable and general.[1]

The war changed Europe. Stolper's own country had collapsed together with Germany and Russia. Historians are able to provide some support for the relative stability of these pre-war empires, and have argued that the war caused their disintegration. In all three countries, the economies had weaknesses but were developing positively. In Austria, issues of nationality were, if not waning, at least abating, and not threatening to disintegrate the empire. In Russia, political separatism was mostly limited to certain circles, with the exception of nationalism among the Poles. Russia had found some stability after the revolution of 1905, and both Austria and Germany were taking steps to integrate the working classes.

Historians have generally seen the First World War as a turning point. For many it is deemed a radical break from the relatively peaceful preceding century.[2] For some it is seen as a discontinuity that people and societies were forced to cope with and muddle through.[3] In terms of the history of the concept of Europe, it is both. There was continuity of certain ideas and ways

---

Notes for this section begin on page 162.

of thinking, which adapted to the new war conditions and re-emerged after the ceasefire. In the interbellum, European unity was one such idea that was reiterated from before the war, incorporating some new arguments. However, regarding the concept of Europe, certain changes were of a more fundamental nature. Instead of a sense of stability, there was one of ongoing crisis. At the heart of these changes was the understanding that Europe would no longer be a continent consisting of a decreasing number of states and dominated by a few empires. The hope for fewer borders was still alive, but it was strongly contested.

In research on the history of the concept of Europe, the First World War has been addressed marginally, with significantly more attention being paid to the interwar period.[4] However, the war saw the development of the concept of Europe really gain momentum, evolving from one of a Europe dominated by several empires and a few additional states, to one of a continent with an increasing number of nation states. This was a time of transition in thinking about Europe, when the war provoked discussions of the role that nationality played in Europe and of how to keep the peace among the many European nationalities. Before we consider the interwar period, we must take a closer look at the concept of Europe during the First World War.

From the first part of this book, we know that the concept of Europe is closely related to unity and borders within Europe, both of which were seriously affected by the First World War. The fact that international cooperation largely broke down when the war began is often cited with reference to trade, workers' movements, and religious groups. However, Jan Vermeiren has emphasised that, during the war, new practices of transnational interaction emerged, as exemplified by cooperation within military alliances, national independence movements in Central Europe, and pacifist groups' activities in the neutral countries.[5] One could argue that cooperation was not new within military alliances, especially between Austria and Germany, nor in the international peace movement. Furthermore, one could say that calls for European unity were raised throughout Europe, as well as within the individual countries at war. Still, these interactions intensified significantly because of the war. The impact of claims of national independence certainly added a new dimension to the discussion. As I am especially interested in how the mindset of the war affected ideas of unity and borders, I will focus on the notion of national independence.

We begin this chapter by taking a look at how intellectuals depicted the war, examining both their increasing nationalism and emphasis of borders, and the ongoing relevance of the idea of European unity. The notion of unity also concerned the unification of distinctive parts of the continent. The most significant of these was the notion of 'Mitteleuropa', widely upheld in Austria and Germany, which was also the title of a bestselling book by Friedrich Naumann. Later in this chapter, we will follow the turn of the tide, away from Central European empires and the idea of 'Mitteleuropa' as the notion of sovereign nation states became established. However, resistance to the establishment of a considerable number of new nation states was great, even among the allies. Two key concepts in this change were those of nationality and a 'new Europe', and the most crucial period was the winter of 1917 and spring of 1918.

The European War

> The European war had broken out. The stream of time, which till that day had borne our destinies along, securely as it seemed, on somewhat troubled and stormy but still not dangerous waters, had now plunged headlong into a vast and wild abyss; and no one knows when and where and through what depths it will emerge, once more to look on the face of the sun, which had smiled upon our face until that fatal day of August 1, 1914.[6]

The conflict was often called 'the war', as it was war on a scale that Europe had not seen for a long time. It went beyond involving just two of the main powers, in contrast to the French–German war of 1870, and was driven by more than Prussia's ambitions to strengthen its position by defeating Denmark in 1866. It played out between highly capable parties, as in the Crimean War in 1855, which accelerated the decline of the Ottoman Empire in the Balkan region, but on a new scale. While most of the bloodshed after the Napoleonic Wars had occurred outside of Europe, in gaining control over colonies, the 1914–18 war involved most of Europe. When they called it 'the European war' or the 'European conflict', contemporary commentators such as Italian writer and historian Guglielmo Ferrero were indicating that it was indeed a major struggle among European powers over their influence. They were implying that this war was something more than just another battle over the balance of power, and referred to it as a 'world war' and a 'great war'. In Britain it became 'The Great War' or 'The Great European War' in which Britain was forced to defend its empire and help its European allies. In Germany it was referred to as 'the war', often with the understanding that it was 'the German war' – an opportunity for the nation to claim its rightful place in Europe and the world. Still, the mental impact of the view that this was a European war was great, and it was believed that this war would decide the future of Europe.[7]

The outbreak of the war was met with much exultation. The optimism of the pre-war era initially prevailed, fuelled by strong nationalistic sentiments. *The Times* reported on 2 September 1914 that there was a 'great rush to enlist', and '4,000 men altogether were enrolled in London yesterday'. One recruiting station was 'crowded all day with enthusiastic contingents of young clerks, eager to exchange the pen for the rifle and hoping they may be so lucky as to share in the risks and adventures'.[8] There was great hope in Britain and France, as indeed there was in Germany, of a victorious and hopefully short campaign.

Many lyricists and novelists welcomed the war. The German poet Hermann Stehr encouraged the German people, who were prepared to drop whatever they were doing to follow the emperor, stand shoulder to shoulder in his armies, and suffer sacrificial death. There was no need to worry, as 'God it is, that speaks through our weapons'; the future belonged to the Germans: 'Now people of Germany, you will be the masters of Europe'.[9] British poet Helen Abercromby found the war to be a 'harvest of glory and triumph, / All honour to those, who for Might and for Right / Laid down their lives, as they plunged into battle / Reaping reward, rich and rare in God's sight!'[10] Poetry and literature embodied ideas about the energising effects of war on both people and society. Novelist Maurice Barrès praised the war for uniting a fractured country and for awakening the soul of the French people. In wartime, citizens operated according to a higher moral standard. Because of the collective French spirit, soldiers bravely faced great risks; they 'leapt forward with enthusiasm to embrace it'. The soldiers, 'when brought forward face to face with the Germans, stood united in strength and effulgent with spiritual beauty'.[11] Neutral countries such as Sweden were no exception to the spreading nationalism, as lyricists and writers celebrated the new war, treating it as a thrilling adventure that brought a new dignity to their nations. The fact that Sweden had not declared war was of no significance to them, as the very threat of being involved had led to reconciliation among the classes and the emergence of a new patriotism. They praised the national troops for their heroism, and noted the unity between officers and soldiers.[12]

The causes of the war were widely discussed. The answers were manifold, with some citing the arming of the military on a new scale, along with the potential for industry to profit from metallurgical and mechanical technologies. Others stressed that competing empires ruled Europe and noted the lack of rational coordination, implying the need for international law or even a European federation. Some blamed the monarchs and elites, suggesting that the war had broken out due to a lack of democracy, a lack of national rights and autonomy, or perhaps a lack of independence for the Western and Southern Slavs.

Guglielmo Ferrero was very clear about what kind of war he considered this to be: a European war. In the piece cited above, which he wrote six months after the outbreak of the conflict, and in another from the final year of the war, he referred to it as 'the European war'. In the former piece, he made a great effort to show that Austria and Germany should be blamed for starting the war, while in the latter, he blamed the German mind. In attempting to explain what had caused the war, he significantly saw it as a crisis of civilisation:

> . . . that unshakable optimism, that blind faith in the progress and strength of man, that unbridled ambition and covetousness which has effaced or at all events dimmed the sense of limitation, of proportion, of the humanly possible and reasonable in the whole western civilization, in the realms of philosophy, religion, art, science, politics, finance, industry and commerce alike. Western civilization was on its way to thinking itself omnipotent.[13]

Ferrero does not give an entirely rosy description of Europe. Modern civilisation had indeed accomplished wonders, giving humans immense power over nearly everything. But while progress had led to the construction of ploughs, ships and railways, and to the invention of the telegraph, telephone and electricity, it had also meant that rifles and explosives were more powerful and deadlier than ever before. The notion of 'progress' now allowed for complete foolishness, Ferrero continued, as unlimited production meant that contemporary progress could occur without consideration for whether innovations were useful or harmful. Progress took no account of what was good or what was evil. Destructive goods such as alcohol and cannons were produced without an understanding or appreciation of limits. Rules and principles were needed to restrict humankind's destructive tendencies, be they aesthetic, philosophical, moral or religious.[14]

The enemies were assumed to constitute the guilty party, and to threaten Europe, its culture and civilisation, with the objective of controlling Europe by infringing on the lawful rights of others. For Paul Rohrbach, an apostle of the German foreign policy of 'Weltpolitik' – the intention to make Germany a world power – England was the foremost enemy of European culture, so its power had to be crushed.[15] The historian Werner Sombart called upon young German soldiers to act as the final defence in preventing the incoming flood of commercialisation from Western Europe and England.[16] In a British paper, one could read that the fighting had become 'less a national cause than the cause of world civilization'.[17] For Gertrud Bäumer, who chaired a German association for women, the war was about which nation would be leading the European collective of countries. She was concerned that enemies would not be able to see that Germany was best equipped for this, having a culture that was open to adopting foreign influences. 'In the streets, which our armies are clearing, will follow all peaceful powers of culture'.[18] Rudyard Kipling warned his compatriots of Germany's aims, being quoted in *The New York Times Current History of the European War* as claiming that Germany had long been preparing for battle, and now their objective was the complete destruction of England's power and wealth. Germany, he warned the United States, was not only a menace to Europe, 'but to the whole civilized world'.[19] Hilaire Belloc, the British-French author, accused the German government of trying to rule the world and 'to overthrow the ancient Christian tradition of Europe', while the British and Latin countries defended the 'sanctity of separate national units . . . and a great deal more which is, in their eyes, civilization'.[20] Henri Bergson claimed that the French were equipped with the moral force of liberty and justice that could transcend the nation, while the Germans had no ideals other than worship of brute force and the will to increase their power.[21]

Ferrero depicted a confrontation between Germanism and Latinism, claiming that the legacy of European civilisation came mainly from the shores of the Mediterranean and from the Latin peoples. North of these countries, the contributions were much fewer and more recent in history. Furthermore, the Germanic and Anglo-Saxon peoples focused too much on the 'indefinite and unlimited increase of human power'. He depicted Germany as a morally meagre country. For over thirty years, Germany had been obsessed with the idea of progress, more so than any other nation. Its success had led to dreams of never-ending triumph. It had a spirit of power and violence that entailed both expansion and the invasion of its neighbouring countries. The hunger for power had become a religion and had led to reduced moral limits. By contrast, the Latin-speaking peoples, guided by the ideal of moral perfection, favoured justice, equity, generosity and loyalty. The spirit of Latinism required that the state and international treaties curb the effects of unlimited commerce and industry; it would entail the enforcement of restrictions and even renunciation.[22] Ferrero was following one of the main strategies of wartime propaganda, emphasising that the enemy was threatening things of great value that were safeguarded by 'our' soldiers.

Werner Sombart believed that the enemy was obsessed with commercial interests. He developed this belief into a major theme, similar to Ferrero's, but here the enemy was England and the Germans were defending the higher cause. To Sombart, it was the spirit of commercialisation that expressed the English philosophy, culture and state. This spirit was both utilitarian and materialistic, permeating the state and setting the agenda for the governing of English possessions on other continents. While the English demanded their rights, the Germans focused on a mission, asking how they could contribute and what they could sacrifice. Instead of business and profit, Germans were concerned with their duty.[23] Sombart took this line of argument to its ultimate conclusion. He supported German militarism as an expression of the highest values of the nation, and emphasised that the German mind was quite exceptional and could encompass everything that human culture had accomplished: 'We understand all foreign people; no one understands us, no one can understand us'.²⁴ What does it matter, he continued, if international exchange in the worlds of culture and learning cease for a decade or two, when we are always the giving ones who do not have much to learn from foreign countries?²⁵

Clearly, the borders and differences between the warring countries were emphasised in all sorts of ways. This phenomenon was prevalent before the war, with the political language of the early twentieth century emphasising the differences between the national cultures, not least between France and Germany. Readers frequently encountered enemy stereotypes in newspapers, essays and novels. In Germany one could read negative stereotypes of the English, and in Britain of the Germans. While France had long been a rival and enemy in the eyes of the British, whereas Germany had been viewed as an ally, after the turn of the century this began to change. In politics, Britain and France started to find peaceful solutions to problems arising from their imperial competition for space and influence, while Germany continued to push to establish an ocean-spanning empire of its own. Germany moreover joined the arms race to challenge the British navy's domination of the sea.²⁶

The decades before the war had seen many efforts to develop and disseminate national traditions. Nationalists introduced practices, rituals and symbols at a large scale, inspiring Eric Hobsbawm to identify nationalism as an invented tradition.²⁷ During the war, nationalism became more obvious than ever, as Europe became a continent of conflicting nations. Depictions of a nation's own strengths and ambitions were coupled with enemy stereotypes to marginalise ideas of a European community. Despite this, ideas of unity managed to stay afloat.

In Spite of It All: Defending Unity

For the Austrian writer and suffragist Rosa Mayreder, it was the concept of nation that had got Europe into its present impasse, with the war almost destroying the larger and more valuable community of European culture. Despite having developed over many years, this cultural community had ceased to exist.²⁸ In an article published in Geneva and Berlin, her compatriot Stefan Zweig lamented that the pre-war European spiritual unity no longer existed and had been almost completely forgotten; the cosmopolitan ideals of the nineteenth century had been thoroughly shaken by the Great War, giving way to growing nationalism.²⁹ Mayreder and Zweig were not the only ones who held on to ideas of European unity at a time when many novelists, artists and scholars were promoting nationalistic sentiments. The notion of European unity survived in spite of the national conflicts and wartime measures in place.

Novelist Gabriele Reuter lamented the propagandistic caricatures of the German people produced in England and France. She declared that many Germans had 'an unbounded love for the universality of European culture', which had driven them to love the artistic and literary works of, for instance, the French, Belgians, Dutch and Scandinavians, and to admire the mystically religious soul of the Russians and the merchant mastery of the English. She deplored the hatred that 'has torn asunder what was believed to be a firmly woven net of a common European culture'.[30]

A sense of shared belonging and purpose was expressed by people who associated themselves with their homeland's rationale for waging war. Shared European culture, encompassing both Shakespeare and Goethe, as well as Homer, Maupassant and Flaubert, was still something many valued, but now it was the enemy who was to blame for dissolving it and causing its destruction.[31] The unity of a common civilisation was still there. One should 'agree in thinking that while our country's cause and the cause of our Allies is just and necessary and must be executed with the utmost vigour, it is not inopportune to reflect on those common and ineradicable elements in the civilization of the West which tend to form a real commonwealth of nations and will survive even the most shattering of conflicts'.[32] The author of this quotation, the British philosopher F.S. Marvin, spoke of Europe's common legacy of law, literature and art, adding science, philosophy, education, and commerce and finance, before ending by emphasising religion as a key factor; he mentioned all these fields as indicators of a civilisational understanding that spanned the whole of Europe.[33] Indeed, the ideas of a shared culture and a common civilisation were still evident.

Some literati continued to advocate European unity. In Barcelona, a group of intellectuals published the 'Manifesto of the Friends of a Moral Unity of Europe' in November 1914, urging their European colleagues to remain faithful to the idea of moral unity, saying that Europe was a commonwealth and all its parts were entitled to the right to well-being.[34] In the Netherlands, the Anti-War Council brought together societies representing political parties, religions, intellectuals and labour. They presented a manifesto that urged the people of the countries at war not to be blinded by strong patriotic feelings, and urged intellectuals to avoid ascribing callous motives or characters to their enemies. Having respect for the foe was implied, because 'faith in the virtues of one's own nation need not be coupled with the idea that all vices are inherent in the opposing nation'. The representatives of the warring nations were to 'remember what unites them and not only what separates them!'[35]

It was not only intellectuals from neutral states who invoked ideas of European unity. In autumn 1914, several prominent French and German scholars, including Albert Einstein, appealed for European unity out of despair at the national enthusiasm for war, highlighting the need to protect shared European culture.[36] Annette Kolb, a German-born writer with a French mother, saw it as her duty to plead for reconciliation, and wrote about the impossible task of annihilating either the French or the German spirit: for the sake of Europe they would have to unite, the Germans assimilating some French characteristics, and vice versa. If they could connect culturally, then they would be able to stand together politically and lead Europe.[37] A similar idea was germinating in the mind of René Schikele from Alsace, though broadened to encompass reconciliation between all European nations. He proclaimed that European unity was emerging in the very experience of the war, with soldiers throughout Europe wanting the same freedom from the war's catastrophic effects, and with the objectives and arguments for the war being the same in all European countries. He concluded that never 'was there a more united Europe, never was the solidarity of people trying to tear themselves apart, so great'.[38] Austrian playwright Hugo von Hofmannsthal turned to a spiritual unity that combined humanity ('*Humanität*') and religion, yielding something holy that went beyond mere utilitarianism and the pre-war era's fiscal concept of civilisation. Such communality could bring about a new focus on the greater deeds of tolerance, forgiveness and patience, but it would not come easily or from current political leaders. Instead, he placed his hopes in the efforts of writers to continue their exchange that transcended national borders, and it was through these activities that a spirit of unity could evolve.[39] Romain Rolland stood out among the French literati as one most concerned with the project of European reconciliation, and therefore received much criticism. In France, he was accused of being a traitor when he repeatedly stated that there were writers, artists and thinkers in Germany who belonged to an idealistic tradition that did not support Germany's oppression of its neighbours nor its menacing behaviour towards Europe's common civilisation.[40] He saw the war as the triumph of nationalism, flooding Europe with destruction. Rolland wished to focus on the idea of unity, and wanted only to safeguard Europe from collapse. In the contemporary 'storms of passion', he recognised that the greatest duty was to shelter 'the spiritual unity of civilized humanity'. He concluded that the countries at war belonged to one common European civilisation with common interests.[41]

In the peace movement, leaders continued to discuss the need to conclude the mutual hostilities of the European nations. To them, Europe represented a special community with the most advanced civilisation in world history. Europe was seen as an entity, albeit one that was in a dreadful state due to the revitalisation of militarism. Its only hope was that its nations would agree to peace for the common good.[42] Women of the peace movement called for solidarity among themselves: while men were at war, it was up to the women of Europe to bring peace, so they would have to stand together and strive for peaceful arbitration and reconciliation.[43] 'We are', read an appeal, 'the women, the mothers of Europe' calling for peace and for making this the last European war.[44]

There was another way to plead for European unity that did not lament what was lost or focus on a unity that existed despite the conflicts. Instead, attention was on the lack of organised cooperation despite all the factors that furthered exchanges between the countries, such as modern technology and means of communication that had made the world more accessible. British author H.G. Wells hoped for a United States of Europe that would consist of a body not driven by nationalism or imperialism, in order to address the commercial frictions and rivalries between states.[45] The British journalist and pacifist Norman Angell blamed the war's occurrence on the fact that 'Europe' as such had not formally existed previously. There was no pan-European organisation to prevent the war from breaking out, no shared law that states had to follow, and no community of mutual protection. War, he wrote in 1917, was the price to be paid for the anarchy of international politics and the lack of common organisations.[46] In general, the peace initiatives noted the lack of formal bodies in place to curb nationalistic excesses, and this interpretation supported initiatives that would eventually lead to the establishment of the League of Nations and to further initiatives for a united Europe.

Pleas for peace regularly included calls for a European federation.[47] Calls for a United States of Europe continued during the First World War. In Berlin, the 'Neues Vaterland' (New Fatherland) was founded, which included leaders of the peace movement and prominent economists, historians and scientists, such as Albert Einstein. In London, the Union for Democratic Control demanded a European federation, as did committees in the Netherlands and Spain.[48] The European Unity League, founded in 1913, with branches in many European countries and especially strong in Great Britain, pleaded for a United States of Europe based on a free market. Its founder, the German-born British citizen Max Waechter, argued that the elimination of trade tariffs would be a means to avoid both war and burdensome military expenses.[49] Such pleas for a European federation treated the war as a menace to civilisation and a harbinger of the collapse of an old order of militarism – for some, also, of capitalism – and said that the only salvation would be to deliver a federation that would shape Europe into the fatherland of all its peoples.[50] According to this line of thought, international disputes led to war because of the old order. A main argument for a federation was that the European states had many shared interests, with their inhabitants meeting in international associations and their politicians at congresses. Instead of fighting, the European states should be complementing each other.

There was no need for them to fear losing power when centralising administration, one of several Swiss federalist-minded intellectuals emphasised.[51]

Promoting the idea of European unity in spite of the war, whether based on a common spirit, culture or civilisation, could well be seen as the project of intellectuals who had little influence on politics. To appeal to unity when countries were fully mobilising for warfare, however, could be interpreted as the only available means of pressing forward. In addition, it was well known that the transnational economy of pre-war Europe was utterly shaken and partly destroyed by blocked trade routes, disrupted financial systems, and the efforts of the nations at war to control enemy assets from the early autumn of 1914. However, for some businesses, this was seen as an opportunity to expand and develop branches promoting mass armament across the borders of allied countries.[52] However, in trade and commerce there were also arguments for continuing business with enemies, despite the war. When Great Britain pleaded for a trade embargo against the Entente, Russia hesitated for fear of ruining its agriculture sector. Russia had substantial trade with Germany, and the Russian Privy Council reportedly opposed an embargo. Italians wanted to uphold trade relations that were still in place with Austria and Germany. In London, there were fierce discussions in both houses of Parliament, with free-trade proponents arguing that the ongoing war should not be turned into a detrimental war of trade. A deputy of the Austrian Reichsrat warned as late as 1917 that certain policies could isolate the economies of Austria and Germany; instead, he backed a strategy that might lead to an economic alliance among the European states.[53]

Nevertheless, calls for custom unions and economic trading blocs were of much greater significance, as they could further entrench the division of the continent between the Triple Entente and the Central Powers. Politicians in both France and Italy initiated meetings and inter-Allied conferences in Paris, where they pleaded for an economic federation that would include England and possibly Russia. A Latin federation was also discussed, which would include Belgium. The French government, led by Aristide Briand, was more eager to form a trading bloc than were their Allied partners.[54] The idea of a bloc encompassing the Allied countries began to take shape. A union between the democracies, including the United States, was one option discussed.[55] The most important and evolved concept under consideration was that of 'Mitteleuropa'.

Nationalism for an Empire: 'Mitteleuropa'

In the early twentieth century, the concept of Europe was associated with calls for expansion, as the dominant cultures were claimed to need space:

Britain already had an overseas empire, French colonies were in place in Africa and South East Asia, and Russia had expanded in the Far East. Would Germany also have an opportunity to expand in similar fashion? It was often said that German culture was significant and, as such, had as legitimate a right to expand as did the other leading European cultures. One of the options proposed as a way to end the war was to ensure that Germany had room for expansion. Even British pacifists expressed such an idea, to the vexation of H.G. Wells: 'I cannot understand those Pacifists that talk about the German right to "expansion", and babble about a return of her justly lost colonies'.[56]

The most noteworthy understanding of a European empire during this period treated the war as a grand and powerful creator of a continent with fewer borders.[57] This idea took inspiration from the historical trend towards expanding political units, with smaller units and less successful national cultures gradually disappearing. It envisaged the successful expansion of German culture through the emergence of a broadly defined 'Mitteleuropa'.[58] As a geographical concept with political implications, the term 'Mitteleuropa' had been in use since the turn of the twentieth century, although the added implications of German expansionism only arrived with the First World War.[59]

Pleas to create a federation of Austria and Germany, together with some of their neighbouring states, experienced a rebirth starting in 1913 thanks to a number of accounts and pamphlets written mainly by Germans, but also by Austrians.[60] Some calling for a federation were conservative while others were aligned with German liberalism. Generally, they agreed with Prussian actions to unite Germany, and argued that the German emperor should take command of the new 'Mitteleuropa'. Its enemies were in the West and the East, and included England, France and Russia. By comparison, Germany had few harbours, no fertile colonies, and no German-speaking populations overseas. These authors considered Germany and Austria-Hungary to be the heart of 'Mitteleuropa', which could include Switzerland, the Netherlands, Bulgaria and Romania, as well as the Scandinavian countries. One of these authors wanted a pact between Berlin and Baghdad that included the Turkish Empire, while another encouraged the Swedes to liberate Finland from the tsarist yoke. After the war broke out, the defence pact of the two German states came under new scrutiny. Apart from that, the same themes from earlier plans for a 'Mitteleuropa' were repeated. These included a trading bloc large enough to compete with the Russian, British and American markets, plans to open up new countries to German farmers, saving the Germans in Austria-Hungary, and rescuing the Dual Monarchy from disintegration.[61]

The notion of a cultural community had taken shape. Franz von Liszt, professor of law at the University of Berlin, saw a specific German culture of language, art, science and technology, which he identified as the foundation of a shared culture of 'Mitteleuropa'. Hans Mühlstein, a Swiss art historian, imagined Germany's mission as one of spreading its culture and attaining world dominance. He based this belief on the spiritual renewal that Germany had undergone in Europe since the sixteenth century, with Luther and the Reformation, the music of Bach, the philosophy of Kant, and the discoveries of Copernicus. It was that spirit that had permeated the nations in the middle of Europe, Mühlstein wrote in the weeks following 1 August 2014, adding, optimistically and excitedly, that the German people represented the heart of humanity, which had only to manifest itself in the form of a shared body.[62]

The federation's organisation was addressed from several perspectives. The economist Eugen von Philippovich was concerned with the prerequisites for a trade and customs union between the two German states. The journalist Albert Ritter wanted a German-led defence union. Liszt elaborated on the legal aspects and was the only one who argued for a people's assembly, which could show the world that Austrians and Germans stood united in the war.[63] Philippovich, Ritter and Liszt were all Austrians, although they had close connections to Germany, and their careers spanned both states. The booklet by Liszt presented the German government's interest in these plans, as he was a member of parliament and a minister. Moreover, in August 1914, Walther Rathenau, an industrialist who advocated strongly for 'Mitteleuropa', was appointed head of the War Raw Materials Department in the War Ministry, and the chancellor initiated discussions in his inner circle of ways to attract allies and neighbours to Germany using economic means.[64] Finally, in a policy statement from 9 September 1914, the chancellor maintained that Germany should aim to establish a large federation called 'Mitteleuropa' in central Europe. He considered France a suitable candidate to join the union, in accordance with hopes for a quick victory against the French.[65] Accordingly, we can agree with the historian David Stevenson that the outbreak of war triggered the idea of 'Mitteleuropa'. Stevenson, who has charted the range of initiatives of the German government, convincingly argues that they lacked support from the industrial sector and were quite unsuccessful in accomplishing economic and political integration. Neither the Austrian nor German governments were prepared to relinquish sovereignty to shared institutions.[66]

Friedrich Naumann's *Mitteleuropa* was a bestseller in its genre during the First World War. Published in 1915, it had sold one hundred thousand copies within a year, and was eventually translated into Italian, French, English and Swedish. It became the most influential of all German writings on the subject.[67] Naumann himself was a liberal of the Wilhelmine era and called for social reforms. He was a theologian who favoured a strong Germany and the notion of its expansion. He had long been acquainted with the idea of

'Mitteleuropa', had argued for such a federation at the turn of the century, and was familiar with the contributions of both Loch and Liszt.[68]

For Naumann it was now or never: blood was being spilled and nations were mobilising, and now was the time to unite the states between Russia and the West. The war offered a unique opportunity for political figures to demonstrate their greatness – afterwards, it would be too late. Writing optimistically early in the war, he encouraged the creation of 'Mitteleuropa'.[69]

Naumann believed that it was important for the two German states to handle the inner borders of 'Mitteleuropa' with care. The differences concerned Protestantism versus Catholicism, industrial versus agrarian economies, business versus leisure-minded mentalities, being at the frontier of technological development versus embodying traditions of the past, centralism versus decentralism, supporting nationalism versus rejecting it, and having a Western and Northern versus a Southern and Eastern mentality. A common worldview outlook would need to be cultivated in order to transcend these borders and forge the two states into a federation with shared ideas, history, culture, work and law. Joint institutions would need to handle electricity and railways, monetary issues and commercial law, customs tariffs and labour legislation. The legal, medical and historical professions would have to be merged.[70]

Naumann's historical determinism makes sense of the development of small states into larger entities. Just as gross production developed within industry, so did the organisation of states develop. The world would no longer contain many states, but rather continents and world states, such as Russia, America and Great Britain, or large federations. He saw a historical shift towards ever larger units, something of which he greatly approved. Thus, it became necessary for him to theorise the formation of the federation of 'Mitteleuropa'. The nationalities of 'Mitteleuropa' with fewer people had no future as independent states, and Naumann concluded: 'It is painful, but that is how world history wants it: political "small businesses" need affiliation'. However, he insisted that there would still be a place for certain smaller nations in 'Mitteleuropa' because Hungary and some of the Slavic nations would be impossible to Germanise as their distinctiveness was too pronounced. He did not recommend assimilating these into the German nationality; the Hungarian and Slavic nations were there to stay, although they would not be able to remain sovereign states. The very foundation of 'Mitteleuropa' would be the German people, with their superior culture, language, and capacity to organise. Yet, harmony would only be achieved if other languages besides German were given room. A 'Middle European' spirit would be necessary, one with consciousness of a shared history and culture, made possible thanks to the historical process of the German awakening during the nineteenth century, which was completed with the unification of the German states.⁷¹ Naumann said that 'a Middle European culture will grow out of German nationality'.⁷²

However, it was seen as impossible to fully civilise the Hungarians and Slavs into 'thinkers, men of reason, technicians, organizers, sober men of reality', like their German counterparts. Therefore, the Germans would need to adapt themselves to other nations, at least to a certain degree. Although German would be the official language, other languages would have to be accepted. In due time, a Middle European type of personality would develop as 'the bearer of a manifold, strong and rich culture that grows from the German nationality'.⁷³ In the end, Naumann believed that only Germans would be able to civilise the region. He saw them as possessing a superior capability to organise, compared with other nationalities in the region, and even with the British and French. Not least did this concern the organisation of economic life, which could weave together a public safety net, encompassing both individual and private interests.⁷⁴

He offered a twofold answer on how to best organise the region. First, a federation would need to be created, with one political leadership and a common economic bloc. Next, a collection of nationalities would need to live together within this federation, with Germany serving as their leader and civiliser.

Advocacy for 'Mitteleuropa' continued following Naumann's book, with many further publications by other authors. His work was mostly praised, and his conception of 'Mitteleuropa' was considered an accomplishment, as the realities of war had forged unity between Germany and the Habsburg Empire. If certain dimensions seemed to be missing, it was only a matter of time until a fully fledged federation would emerge. The arguments mainly focused on the military and economic benefits of having two states, and on the global shift towards larger economic units, but it was also said that a federation would bring increased stability to Europe and strengthen its society.⁷⁵

Still, 'Mitteleuropa' never became one of Germany's main objectives during the war.⁷⁶ Some reactions to Naumann were rather doubtful. His friend and fellow member of the Liberal Party, Paul Rohrbach, had criticisms regarding foreign affairs and colonial questions. He preferred a 'Weltpolitik' directed at other continents, recommending the annexation of European neighbours rather than a joint federation.⁷⁷ Naumann's imperialistic ambitions were milder, while Rohrbach stunned the public with a rigid imperialism. Some social democrats reacted favourably to Naumann's book, which caused Karl Kautsky to mention the idea of 'Mitteleuropa' in several of his writings, unsurprisingly disagreeing with the imperialistic ambitions and undemocratic visions underlying the concept. However, he was optimistic about the idea of a federation, agreed with the need for the states between

Russia and England to cooperate more closely, and especially highlighted the closeness between the two German states.[78] Kautsky and others who promoted the idea of 'Mitteleuropa' were still operating under the assumption that this was a European movement that followed the trend towards larger units. It recognised the complexity involved in the question of nationalities, and found a way to merge nationalism with imperialism.

The Nationality Principle

When H.G. Wells was forecasting the future in 1917, he predicted that the expansion of Europe would eventually end. The expansion of European empires was first halted in America, and it was about to end in Asia, with Africa following suit. The age of empires was drawing to a close: 'The days of suppression are over'.[79] He was correct in this, although it did not happen as soon as he had predicted, and the fall of the empires was a theme that would haunt Europe in coming decades. However, grandiose plans for empires persisted, in addition to the vision of a German 'Mitteleuropa'. Wells himself put considerable effort into predicting how Britain's dominions would continue to be British in the age to come. Britain would need to relinquish some of its control over its territories, and accept that they could have their own interests and a desire to forge new relationships with neighbouring countries. Instead, the feeling of Britishness should be developed, keeping Canada, India and the African and other territories together by encouraging a sense of community, rather than by ruling with a strong hand.[80] Wells reflected on the growing attention that many writers had begun to pay to the conditions of political organisation in Europe and the world, and nationalities were central to this idea.

In 1917 Wells saw a new age dawning, an age of nationalities. He observed that nations were undergoing fundamental growth, and proposed that once a nation had gone beyond its early, barbaric state, it would naturally want to make its own way and would reject foreign oppression. 'Nations will out!', he claimed, meaning that they would want to freely develop their opportunities. The consciousness of being, for example, Egyptian or Polish would endure despite foreign dominion. For Wells the nationality principle was applicable to regions where homogeneous nationalities existed. However, on 'the natural map of mankind', he found other areas that were much more complex. In some regions where religious and/or linguistic borders outnumbered the nationalities, it was better to adopt a Swiss-inspired district system that accepted some differences, but managed to keep the nation together. Moreover, some cities and regions were home to many nationalities and were, in effect, international spaces. He wanted those to be ruled in conjunction with the associated nations, in the form of a union between the peoples who were affected. In Europe, he identified the region between Germany and Russia as troublesome, with nations that were neither mature enough nor large enough to stand on their own. The Poles and the peoples of the Habsburg Empire had unique nationalities that would not allow them to assimilate, and that could continue to cause conflicts if they became independent. A union between the western Slavic nations could have offered a solution for the region, but he believed that it would be impossible to implement because of the interests of Germany and Russia in keeping such a construction under their own rule.[81]

Obviously, Wells saw the end of the era of empires and the dawning of a new one of nationalities. However, although he was half-hearted in rebutting the existence of empires, he could not fully accept the independence of smaller nations as a general pattern for Europe. He illustrated a kind of thinking shared by many others. Arnold Toynbee, the conservative historian, believed that nationality was the optimal organising principle for Europe. Still, he saw no chance of most of the Central and East European nationalities existing as independent states: the Czechs were too dependent on the Austrian and German economies; the Slavic nations of the Balkan Peninsula would do best in a shared customs union; and the nationalities of north-eastern Europe could only express themselves within the Russian Empire. For only a few peoples would nationality lead to independence, and most were 'undoubtedly unripe for it'.[82] The liberal prime minister, H.H. Asquith, declared that Britain would stand up for the nationality principle, and an imperialist-minded London journalist defended the independence of 'many of the smaller nations'. However, when listing them, like Wells and Toynbee, both men only mentioned nation states that were in existence before the war.[83] Similarly, during the 1915 International Congress of Women in The Hague, women from both warring and neutral countries struck the International Committee of Women for Permanent Peace, demanding 'respect for nationality' and a recognition of 'the right of the people to self-government' in a declaration. Occupied Belgium was on the minds of people outside of Germany and Austria, as was the looming referendum of those living in South Tyrol, Alsace and Schleswig regarding which state they wanted to belong to.[84] The Uruguayan-Spanish writer Adolfo Agorio brought up Belgium and Serbia when discussing the ideas of nationality and international justice as the bases for creating fraternity in Europe: these two ideas would deliver a just peace. He said nothing about other nations.[85]

It is possible to make the same observation in other discourses. Many writers and activists blamed imperialism for starting the war.[86] John Hobson, who had popularised the notion among leftists early in the century, saw the war as an outcome of previous European imperialist policies related to militarism and the financial exploitation of foreign countries.[87] Wells singled out Germany as the main imperialist culprit because of its policies, which he found aggressive, cowardly, undemocratic, and lacking in recognition of the rights of different nationalities.[88] In such rhetoric, national independence and the rights of people to determine their own fate were essential for building a lasting peace. However, the focus remained on existing nation states, while the nationality issue in Europe concerned many stateless minorities from the Austrian, German, Russian and Ottoman empires.

Both the Allies and the Central Powers used the nationality issue for their own purposes and took steps to empower nationalist movements, in the hope of diminishing enemy resources. Germany and Austria-Hungary promised nationality rights and institutional bodies to Finland and the Baltic region, to the Flemish in Belgium, to Ukraine and Moravia, and to the Poles in the former Russian possession of Warsaw. Britain offered the exiled Belgian government guarantees of restored independence, made promises to the nationalities of the Habsburg Empire, and raised hopes among the Poles to reunite the divided nation. However, German policies for Poles within the Reich offered them little hope, and those who ruled Vienna refused to increase the national rights of the Slavs, eventually becoming more hostile towards nationality movements when the war broke out. In London, those in power would listen to neither a Welsh campaign for federal autonomy, nor to the demands of the Irish for national rights. Instead, Irish leaders were arrested and, as protests against British rule escalated, people were killed. The new Bolshevik regime of Russia accepted in theory that nations were free to decide whether to form states with other nations or to become independent, and this also applied to its own non-Russian nations. In reality, however, the regime intervened in one way or another in Ukraine, Bessarabia/Moravia, Finland, and the Baltic states after their declarations of independence.[89]

A clear indication that the concept of nationality was growing in popularity was that it had entered the minds of socialists and social democrats, and forced them to consider it worth defending. Conditions had changed since the war began, and they needed to call for more than internationalism. They needed to support the governments of their countries in more ways than just backing the declarations of war in 1914, as during the war they had become more opposed to it. Even Lenin, who ascribed all talk, comments and noise made about nationality to capitalist propaganda, recognised the right of nationalities to be liberated from oppressing states.[90] Some went further, stating that the struggle for national independence was just as important as the class struggle, and noted that there were nationalities that did not have proper states. Leaders of the Social Democrats in Germany and Austria wrote at length on the topic. Karl Kautsky emphasised that freedom was crucial, not only for nations that were large or more culturally developed, but for all nations. He saw their self-determination as one of the main issues facing Europe. However, this did not mean that he welcomed new states, as he drew a clear distinction between self-determination and independence. His notion of a state included economic unity of trade with a free market and external customs, and a military strong enough to defend itself behind borders. He believed that, to form a nation state, it was essential to have community of language, and indicated that some nationalities were simply too small to form states. In that case, a national culture and language were still considered important for democracy and for a minority's right to express itself.[91] In line with these arguments, his party declared in 1917 that occupied Belgium and Serbia ought to retain their freedom, and that Poland, Finland and Ireland should be welcomed as independent states, while other minority nationalities should settle for autonomy within their states.[92]

The nationality question had a special resonance in Cisleithanien, the country located on the River Leitha, officially called the 'Kingdoms and countries represented in the Reichsrat', which consisted of the Austrian part of the Habsburg Empire. Transleithanien, the country beyond the Leitha River, was Hungary.[93] Before the war, the empire had experienced a long period of stability. Conflicts between nationalities did not threaten its reign because the nationalists, with few exceptions, wanted to keep the empire intact. It is true that the pan-German movement of George Schönerer wanted the German parts of Austria to break away and join Germany, but the movement attracted little support and was backed by only a minority within the Austrian Parliament.[94] Slavic nationalists won supporters in their objective to expand national autonomy when they called for the right to use their own languages in civic administration, but most were loyal to the state. More so than in any other groups, it was among the high-ranking officials that Austrian patriotism remained strong, with loyalty and obedience to the emperor trumping nationalist sentiments. The war, deliberately started by the monarchist leaders, changed the Austrian mindset. The army did not meet the standards of modern warfare and could hardly win a battle without the support of German troops. Rumours spread, with people saying that the war would lead to disaster for the Habsburg state, which was soon both militarily and economically in the hands of Germany. A customs union was enforced, and the monarchy was well on its way to becoming an integrated part of a German-dominated 'Mitteleuropa'.[95]

The notion of a German-led 'Mitteleuropa' was criticised as too focused on the economy and blind to anything besides German culture and nationalism. Polish nationalists writing in a journal in Vienna were enthusiastic about the possibility of uniting their divided country within a new 'Mitteleuropa', but they leaned towards the Habsburg Empire, hoping to increase their independence within a multinational state.[96] The historian Josef Pekař was among the nationalists who anticipated that the Czech nationality would occupy a stronger position in a future Austria, because its culture already had ample influence on the region and it would strengthen the Habsburg regime in its partnership with Germany.[97] In revising the notion of 'Mitteleuropa', economist Gustav Stolper emphasised higher aims and religious values when he argued that Austria could add a moral component to the federation.[98] Like Naumann and other Germans, Social Democratic Party leader Karl Renner also emphasised a cultural community in the region, but he did not define it as German or as specific to any other nationality. Instead, he turned to history and shared intellectual, religious and national experiences. Stolper said that Austria had a world mission to spread a specific sensitivity to cultural diversity, and building a new world order on this basis would be the greatest achievement of humanity since Christianity. Christian Social Party leader Ignaz Seipel understood the Dual Monarchy as exemplifying the highest standard of political organisation in existence. Only in a multinational state would it be possible to achieve perpetual peace, while also allowing multiple nationalities to uphold their own agendas – even while organising exchange between national cultures, without which they would not survive. We can see a vision of a federal and multinational Austria that is partly in harmony with the idea of 'Mitteleuropa'. These authors downplayed the idea of German culture as an organisational principle of society, instead seeing Austria as the heart of a region where nationalities were able to live peacefully together and learn from one another.[99] Evidently, they saw no reason for independent nation states.

All these efforts were futile in establishing an Austria of nations with a post-war future, as the Dual Monarchy fell under German control, which eventually undermined its political and economic sovereignty. The dynasty, with its new Kaiser, lost power to its German brother in arms. The ability of Slav nationalists to stay within the Austrian state seemed to promise a future with weak opportunities for self-determination. The military offensive by the Central Powers in 1918 ended in a grand failure, and the state began to break up. It was of no help that the young emperor, Charles, had initiated a plan to reorganise the state according to federal principles. The main nationalities declared themselves independent, and the emperor was forced to abdicate.

A New Europe

After only a few months of warfare, people began to speculate about what Europe would look like when the war was over, as it would undoubtedly not be the same as before. Many insisted that the old Europe was dead, that the aspirations of the Congress of Vienna had finally collapsed, and that neither the Congress System of the Treaty of Vienna nor the coalition system of the pre-war years remained viable, as they were part of the problem. It was time to look to new principles of international relations, for a way to settle border issues without igniting new conflict. Different expectations of the future began to take hold, including hopes for new ethical standards and international law.[100] Some asked for a new way of thinking. The Swiss art historian Hans Mühlstein stated: 'The coming reformation of European politics and culture can only come from a better philosophy than the one that dominates our rulers'.[101] He had defended German expansion in 1914, but after his experiences in the war, he became a pacifist and socialist. However, the focus of the discourse remained the rights of nationalities and rectifying their divisions.

Indeed, there was quite a lot of speculation about post-war Europe. The notion of a new Europe gained traction mainly in the Allied countries with a focus on the concept of nationality as a fundamental asset for the coming political order in Europe. In 1915, the new Europe of Arnold Toynbee consisted of interconnected nations unified by their culture and language. In some cases, a nation represented an economic unit in and of itself, and sometimes nations were assembled into a group. Each nation matured in its own time, which could be seen as a kind of social evolution. Toynbee was adhering to a stagist theory of history when he said that immature nations should follow the more advanced ones in Europe, emphasising that more established nations should refrain from focusing on mere economic interests and from engaging in conflicts over foreign territories. He also added, rather elusively, that nationality should not be the final stage, and hoped that someday there could be an international authority in place by which nations could transcend nationality altogether.[102] Apparently, the early talk of a new Europe was vague, and masked an effort to discredit Prussianism and the current German regime. For Toynbee, Germany was not fit for a new Europe. Its Prussian conduct and dynastic ambitions were not appealing to a democratically inclined public, and did not apply to a political organisation of Europe based on nations. Its concept of nationality represented only brute force and domination; it was 'a menace to our civilization' as it relied on German glory during the Medieval period, and focused on territorial inclusion, while Britain truly represented a modern nation: 'a spiritual experience and self-expression of a human society' that represented democracy and cooperation.[103]

Discussion of a new Europe approached the matter from different perspectives. In *L'Europe Nouvelle*, also written in 1915, the socialist-leaning journalist Paul Louis wrote: 'The expression "New Europe", which is used daily, is very vague, it covers territorial Europe, social Europe, political

Europe', adding that this also concerned a 'moral Europe'.[104] He stated that French, Germans, British and neutrals alike rejected a return to the way things were before August 1914; the Germans aimed for expansion, while the others opposed Germany's push for more territory. For Louis, the war was a historical moment of the same significance as the French Revolution, when an old era was left behind and a new one was dawning. In the new Europe, the will of the people and the nationality principle should rule, such that 'there were no more oppressed, despoiled, mutilated peoples'.[105]

This makes him another example of a socialist who valued nationalities, although he defined a nationality not by language, religion, or historical memory, but by the unity of its people. For instance, one nation can encompass more than one language, and one language may be spoken in several different countries. The new Europe would need to abandon the orders of the Treaty of Vienna and the Prussian, Bismarckian and pan-German doctrines of territorial expansion, whose 'monstrous ambitions' had tortured the French in Alsace-Lorraine, the Danish in Schleswig and Holstein, and, most of all, the western Poles. Louis wrote that referenda could sometimes be useful in letting the people decide where they belonged, but he saw only Poland as capable of forming a new independent state. He believed that Finland should have autonomy within the Russian state and that Austro-Germans, Czechs and Hungarians should form a tripartite state with equal rights for its three nationalities. Other parts of the Habsburg Empire should be included in the expanding territories of Italy, Serbia and Romania. A recurring argument was that nations were supposed to be large and populous enough to form a state. Using this logic, Louis dismissed the pre-war independence of Luxemburg, considering it part of Belgium. He concluded that this would be a Europe without slaves, because each nationality would have its freedom, which would increase the likelihood of peace.[106]

Neither Louis nor his ideological opposite Toynbee viewed Europe as providing an opportunity for new nation states to emerge. However, they reflected changing opinions regarding the significance of smaller nations. In late 1915, a Swedish envoy to Paris wrote in his diary that, after meeting representatives of the government and leading politicians, it was possible to view smaller states with fresh eyes and to appreciate their importance. Not only were these representatives interested in forging closer economic ties with Sweden, but they also spoke of their willingness to support the Finnish claim to self-determination, or even independence.[107] Louis argued that these nations – representing smaller states – without the power or grandeur of the main European countries nonetheless had an important part to play in establishing buffer zones. The free nations of the Netherlands, Belgium, Poland, Switzerland and Denmark would constitute buffer zones between bigger countries, reducing the risk of their direct confrontation. Smaller nations had nothing to gain by starting wars, which they would be bound to lose; rather, they feared war, and their peacefulness offered a kind of balance to Europe. They tended towards democratic and liberal governance, were concerned with the freedoms of their citizens, and offered asylum to expatriates. They were considered progressive in many respects regarding their own countries, civilisation, and international relations. Louis's song of praise concluded that, in a rejuvenated Europe, smaller states would be of greater importance than ever before, although he could not see that any new states should be established.[108] Despite the tributes paid to their literature, art, science, and innovative thought, Louis imagined that the post-war European states would remain almost exactly the same nations as they were before. A reorganised Europe with altered territorial borders? –Yes. A Europe with additional states? – No!

The Czech nationalist Tomáš Masaryk believed in the prospect of new nation states. He proposed an alternative to Austrian, German and Russian dominance of the western Slavic nationalities, and began to talk of a Central Europe composed of free and democratic states. In his earlier books on Czech nationality he did not discuss the concept of Central Europe, nor did he tie the future of the Czech people to that of other Central European nations or espouse an independent Czech state.[109] However, from 1912 onwards, he became increasingly opposed to the governance of Austria, and expressed indignation at the throne, the aristocracy and the Czech elites. He called upon the Czech and the other minor Austrian nations to strive for cultural and political self-determination. Even at that time, he considered the establishment of an independent Czech nation outside the Austrian Empire to be impossible. Only the war, and the possibility of gaining support from the Allies, made him change his mind.[110] It was also the war that made it possible to present Central Europe as an alternative to a German 'Mitteleuropa'. Czech nationalists had known about the latter since at least 1905, when the leader of the Young Czech Party, Karel Kramář, warned citizens of Germany's ambition to expand its power throughout the Habsburg Empire. A customs union would only benefit the Germans, not the Czechs. Kramář confronted a German 'Mitteleuropa' based on his interest in living in a Czech nation at 'the heart of Europe'. Nevertheless, there was still no talk of an alternative idea of Central Europe composed of nation states, as he believed that the Slavic nations of Austria should exist within the frame of a federalist reconstruction of the monarchy.[111]

Forced by the war into exile, Masaryk arrived in England in March 1915, at which point he began to campaign for Czech independence by establishing influential contacts, writing petitions to the minister of foreign affairs, and collaborating with the weekly *The New Europe*. He took every opportunity to petition for the freedom of the peoples of Central Europe, and tried to convince the British public that such an aim was exactly in line with Allied interests and victory. He contended that the Allies would soon defeat a disintegrating Habsburg Monarchy, which would open a path to victory over Germany. This proposed strategy evoked positive reactions from the British government and ministries, but only became part of official British policy in 1918.[112]

In a speech given in London at Kings College's newly established School of Slavonic and East European Studies, as well as in a memorandum to the British government in October–November 1915, Masaryk defined his own position as an alternative to the plans for a German 'Mitteleuropa', and was apparently quite familiar with the German literature and policy on the matter. He wanted a different plan from that of the Allies, a Central Europe free of German domination, where Czech sovereignty was not limited by German power and where the independence of the Slavic nations could provide a bulwark against future German expansion.[113] Cautiously, he wrote that England and France were defending the rights of smaller nations to self-determination, and underlined the assurances of the tsar that the Slavic peoples should be liberated. He was thus able to present his aims as very much aligned with those of the Allies. He did not mention his ambivalence towards tsarist rule in Russia, nor that the Allies' drive for self-determination differed from his for sovereignty. He was more outspoken in his criticism of the Austrian and German empires when he said that they represented a previous era's authoritarian rule, and he insisted that in the modern world a state would need to find common ground if it was to build a nation with a shared language and democratic rule. His European map consisted of a Western Europe with nineteen nations and twelve states. Eastern Europe was dominated by a few large empires and a multitude of smaller nations. Between Eastern and Western Europe he described an 'ethnological zone' with a southern border running from Trieste via Thessaloniki to Constantinople, and a northern border along the Baltic Sea. It included Eastern Prussia, Austria-Hungary, Western Russia, and the Turkish-ruled part of the Balkans. Masaryk called this zone 'Central Europe', and supported his plea for national sovereignty by looking at the national conflicts that had yet to be viably resolved. By releasing them from the empire, they could become more like Western nation states. Masaryk's new Europe began with a new Central Europe composed of independent nation states.[114]

Starting in January 1917, the Bohemian Masaryk began to edit *The New Europe*, in which he promoted democracy and independence for the nations of Austria-Hungary. *The New Europe* was Britain's main outlet for calls for national self-determination, with collaborators from all Allied countries, including occupied Belgium. It supported the right of all peoples to decide whether or not to be independent, and to decide on the degree of autonomy that they should have. The Macedonian people should have the right to hold a referendum regarding their partition among Serbia, Bulgaria and Greece. The 3.5 million Romanians of Transylvania should have the right to an autonomous province within a federalised Hungary.[115] Regarding Luxemburg, an article asked for the assurance of independence.[116] One article spoke of Icelandic attempts to persuade Denmark to agree to expand its self-governance.[117] Another article focused on Åland's petition to become part of Sweden, after Finland had declared its independence.[118] In addition, the journal reported every concession of the Allies to sovereignty. These included the new Russian regime's proclamation of autonomy for all non-Russian peoples, the French recognition of Finnish independence in January 1918, and the Allies' recognition of a Czech legion within their ranks. It also included the recognition by Russian delegates of Ukraine as an independent state four months later in May, and the promises of the British, French and Italian prime ministers to support Poland, Czechoslovakia and Yugoslavia in becoming their own nations in June of the same year. All of this stood in contrast to the Central Powers' insistence 'upon restricting its [i.e. self-determination's] applications to *states*, not nations, and leaving existing frontiers unimpaired'.[119] Guided by the motto 'Pour la Victoire Intégrale', *The New Europe* aspired to offer a new international order for Europe, promoting 'victory for the democratic idea, and for peace without annexations and on the basis of complete self-determination of nations'.[120] Democracy and national sovereignty formed the journal's formula for a new Europe.

In late 1917, national self-determination and sovereignty became options in Eastern Europe. From the beginning of the war, Ukrainian nationalists had declared that their nation had a culture of its own, with the richest musical and poetic traditions in Europe, and that it was capable of forming a unique state of its own. Ukrainian independence from Russia would benefit all of Europe, while it would weaken or even disintegrate Russia, free its subjects from tsarist rule, and relieve Germany and Austria of their eastern threat.[121] These were the claims, and after the October Revolution, Ukraine proclaimed independence from Russia, as did Moravia and Finland. In the Baltic region, under German occupation, national bodies were allowed to develop in order to gain distance from Russia. In early 1918, Estonia, Latvia and Lithuania declared themselves independent. In Austria-Hungary, nationalism became radicalised as the empire was on the brink of collapse due to food shortages, strikes, and a breakdown in transport. The army was running out of men, materials were in short supply, and Slavic troops refused to fight against the Entente. On 6 January 1918, Czech deputies of the Reichsrat and Diets of Bohemia, Moravia and Silesia agreed to a programme for Czechoslovakian independence.[122] Willingness to remain loyal to the empires of Central and Eastern Europe was rapidly declining.

The process leading to the disintegration of the continental empires received further impetus when a manifesto for the future organisation of Europe arrived from the United States. Paul Louis was a witness:

> No document, since 1914, has had more resonance than Mister Wilson's message dated 8 January 1918. The words of the American president have always had the gift of catching the attention of men, because one feels his firm will, clear and at the same time audacious thoughts, a rather rare disinterestedness; but this time, it is not an exaggeration to say that they have provoked a profound shock in both aggressive and neutral countries.[123]

The idea of national self-determination was fundamental to the American president Woodrow Wilson. In his address to congress about the conditions for establishing peace, he set out 'the principle of justice to all peoples and nationalities, and their right to live on equal terms of liberty and safety with one another, whether they be strong or weak'. America represented, in his eyes, a historical development away from empires and towards nation states, while Germany and Austria were the prime examples of outmoded imperialism.[124] Detesting dynastic and authoritarian rule, he frankly declared his belief in democracy and the possibility of improving the world order: '[W]hat we seek is the reign of law based upon the consent of the governed, and sustained by the organized opinion of mankind'.[125]

Although his inspiration came mainly from the independence movements in North and South America, Wilson was aware that the European discourse of the war had inspired aspirations of national self-determination and even independence.[126] The declaration clearly addressed the Polish and Balkan demands for independence but was more conservative when it came to the Habsburg nationalities, to which it offered only self-determination. That limitation was of little importance as Wilson had already made a name for himself as an ardent proponent of moral principles in favour of peace, and his new declaration only further boosted national sentiments. For many, Wilson stood out as 'the recognized prophet of the Allied cause'.[127]

On 10 April 1918, non-German nationalities of the Habsburg Empire gathered in Rome at the Kongress der unterdrückten Völker Österreich-Ungarns, and on 17 May they gathered once again in Prague. The assembled included Slovaks, Croats, leaders of the Yugoslavian movement, Serbian dissidents, Bosnians, Italians, Romanians from Transylvania and Bukovina, Poles from Galicia and Silesia, and representatives from all of the Czech parties. Their declaration referred to hundreds of years of oppression, and envisioned a future of lasting peace that would lead to independence and overall 'a better future of the nations'. Aggressive imperialism would be exchanged for a system of free and equal nations. Wilson's principles left their mark in the resolution: the new future would be 'assured by the world democracy, by a real and sovereign national people's government, and by a universal League of Nations, endowed with the necessary authority'.[128]

The tide was quickly turning in favour of the Slavic nationalists as the Allies viewed the disintegration of the Habsburg Empire as a way to weaken and isolate Germany. By the end of May 1918, the British government and President Wilson praised the Slavic nationalists' ambitions, declaring that their independence and liberty were among the Allies' war aims. However, full sovereignty for every individual Habsburg nationality was not what the Allies had in mind, as sufficient size was thought necessary in order to become a viable nation state. The British spokesman uttered something vague about gathering these nations into a Central European federation. Wilson promised sovereignty to only Czechoslovakia and Yugoslavia, each of which comprised more than one nation.[129] Economic arguments proved useful when attempting to limit claims to national independence. In *The New Europe* it was explained that the southern Slavic provinces needed the mountains, plains, and coastal lands for economic development purposes. Developing trade routes, commerce and industry throughout the inland regions would require connections with the Dalmatian coastal towns, which would then enable trade across the Mediterranean. Trieste and Fiume would have to be oriented towards the Yugoslavian provinces instead of the Austrian centres in the north.[130] Clearly, an independent state should have the most conducive economic conditions.

Hopes for an Allied victory were high in autumn 1918, as the Habsburg Empire had collapsed and it had become clear that it only was a matter of time until Germany admitted defeat. In Copenhagen another journal was established, also entitled *The New Europe*, or in Danish *Det ny Europa*, by leading Scandinavian cultural figures, including the Danish critic Georg Brandes, the Norwegian explorer Fridtjof Nansen, and the Swedish suffragette Ellen Key. They declared that a new Europe was in the making, and they likened the European nations to the sons of a larger common fatherland. By heralding the coming of this new Europe and declaring their love for it, they were giving expression to the strong prevailing currents of hope.[131]

The Wilsonian Moment: An Ending with New Divides

Recently, a researcher aptly called this juncture in 1918 'the Wilsonian moment'.[132] President Wilson was expected to take the lead in organising the new Europe according to his principles. Hopes were high when Germany asked for a ceasefire and accepted Wilson's terms. However, this was also a moment of great anxiety. While some saw Germany as the main threat to a future Europe of national self-determination, others believed that the

German people were not to blame for what its leaders had perpetrated. Ellen Key asked the victors to respect the spirit of the German people: '[T]hose who now want to trample Germany's self-determination, pride, and future opportunities into pieces are beginning a new war in which their grandchildren will bleed and Europe will fall'.[133] That is, the notion of national self-determination should also include Germany.

Wilson's ideals were definitely anti-colonial, and met with resistance from the other Allied leaders, who had no understanding of national self-determination outside of Europe. In fact, Wilson himself believed that few non-Europeans could manage to govern their own countries. Wilson sought an alternative to the imperial system of pre-war Europe that would be more attractive than communist rule. His idea was to establish lasting peace by eliminating reasons for disputes through granting each nationality the right to self-determination, and offering a way to have an international body deal with conflicts.[134]

Intellectuals developed a range of arguments to support such a supranational association. They enthusiastically embraced Wilson's principles, finding that they represented freedom and the peaceful arbitration of international disputes. One argument constituted nothing but historical determinism: in the beginning was love for the family, then grew compassion for the tribe, after that for the nation, and the next step was to embrace a larger, international community. Another argument tried to apply a pedagogical logic: nationalism and a feeling of belonging to one people were necessary to foster internationalism. Only when people understood the complexities of national society would it be possible to extrapolate this understanding to the complexities of interacting nations: 'Only from nationalists could one create internationalists'.[135]

A third argument drew on the experience of wartime cooperation, with the pooling of resources, the unifying of military forces, and to some degree the combining of economic actions through the War Council of Versailles. This council acted as a supranational authority, and had come to signify 'that only a certain voluntary curtailment of the sovereign right of each nation can avail to equip the common cause with the means of victory'. Not only did this approach serve the Allies in the war, it represented the embodiment of a supranational body, illustrating how it would behave when it had the authority to control sovereign nations to address a shared aim. According to this argument, the council put 'the whole task of European reconstruction' on the agenda.[136]

As the expectations of internationalism continued to increase, so did early signs of disputes resulting from the self-determination of nations. When the Moldavian Republic was declared, Romania took steps to extend its territory to the detriment of the new state. Polish troops entered Lithuanian and Ukrainian territory. Bohemian-German parties opposed the creation of a Czechoslovakian state. The dispute over a border town between the new Czech and Polish republics remained unresolved. For the internationalists, and for all who found hope in Wilson's programme, it might have come as a surprise that the wave of nationalism and the establishment of nation states laid the ground for conflicts during the interbellum period.

The end of the war meant the dismantling of the Romanov, Hohenzollern, Habsburg and Ottoman empires, which allowed for the construction of independent nation states. However, this was not easily accomplished, as the nationalities constituting the former empires were not clear-cut entities. Many people were unaware of their national affiliation or were unwilling to belong to a certain nation, but would in any case, with or without their consent, be forced into it by the principle of self-determination. Linguistic and historical demarcation lines were often too complex to offer any obvious borders, as every choice would leave some minorities behind. Rather than solving territorial issues, the principle of self-determination seemed bound to create even more disputes between the European states. Furthermore, the victors were more interested in finding the best possible provisions for themselves than in finding agreements that everyone could live with. It is no wonder that the delegates of the conference in Paris were mostly pessimistic about the results of their deliberations, and were even alarmed at the resulting treaty. A British delegate wrote in a letter that 'the total effect is, I am quite sure, quite indefensible and in fact is, I think, quite unworkable'. John Maynard Keynes felt 'deep and violent shame', and left the conference very worried about the economic chaos that he thought the treaty would instigate.[137]

With the treaties after the war, Russia was removed from Finland, the Baltic States and Poland, Germany lost its foothold in Poland, and the Habsburg Empire was broken into four states. Albania gained its independence from Italy and the sovereignty of Belgium and Luxembourg were confirmed. Apart from that, Denmark signed a treaty that granted Iceland its freedom in all areas except foreign policy and the common monarch. Ukraine and Moravia declared their independence before the new Soviet Union eventually defeated them, and in 1922, the Irish Free State proclaimed its independence from the United Kingdom. This meant that the number of European states radically increased, and also that Europe could be seen as a continent composed of nation states.

Although the Allies were prepared to turn a page and give up their imperial ambitions in Europe, that did not mean they were ready to relinquish their power on other continents. The idea that Europeans had achieved a higher standard of development was still current, and imperial ambitions remained on the agenda. However, the fear of losing that higher position was pervasive and widespread. As a result, a new chapter in the history of the

European idea emerged. While the new prominence of nation states reinforced the conception of a Europe of dividing borders, the fear of a diminishing European role in the world sparked the idea of European unification.

Notes

1. Stolper, *This Age of Fable*, 3.
2. Hobsbawm, *The Age of Extremes*; Karlsson, *Urkatastrofen*.
3. Smith, Mollan and Tennent, *The Impact*.
4. As emphasised by Vermeiren, 'Notions of Solidarity and Integration'.
5. Ibid.
6. Ferrero, *Who Wanted European War?*, 37.
7. Belloc, *Sketch of the European War*, 4: 'This war is the largest and weightiest incident that Europe has known for centuries. It will surely determine the future of Europe. . .'.
8. 'Arms and The Men'.
9. Stehr, 'Der Krieg bricht los', 1185–88: 'und Gott ists, der durch unsere Waffen spricht', 'Nun deutsches Volk, wirst du Europa's Meister'.
10. Abercromby, 'The Harvest (September 1914)', 14–15.
11. Barrès, *The Faith of France*, 1–6.
12. Ahnlund, *Diktare i krig*, 154–57.
13. Ferrero, *Europe's Fateful Hour*, IV.
14. Ibid., 69–72, 222–33.
15. Rohrbach, *Der Krieg*, 99–100.
16. Sombart, *Händler und Helden*, 55, 145.
17. '(The) First Phase'.
18. Quotation from Anonymous, '(Der) Wille zum Frieden', 264: 'Auf den Strassen, die unsere Heeren bahnen, sollen nachher alle friedlichen Kulturmächte einhergehen'.
19. Kipling, 'As They Tested Our Fathers', 106–7.
20. Belloc, *Sketch of the European War*, 47.
21. Bergson, 'The Vital Energies of France', 153.
22. Ferrero, *Europe's Fateful Hour*, 51–68; on Latinism, 51: 'The religion, the political institutions and doctrines, the organization of armies, the law, the art, the literature, the philosophy . . . are . . . the work of those nations which one can, from their position, describe as Mediterranean'.
23. Sombart, *Händler und Helden*, 14–64.
24. Ibid., 135: 'Wir verstehen alle fremder Völker, keines verstehen uns, und keines kann uns verstehen'.
25. Ibid., 136–37.
26. Jaraush, *Out of Ashes*, 53–64.
27. Hobsbawn, 'The Nation as Invented Tradition'.
28. Mayreder, 'Die Frau und Internationalismus', 28.
29. Zweig, *Messages from a Lost World*, 58.
30. Reuter, 'The German Religion of Duty'.
31. Hauptmann, 'A Reply to Rolland'; Hauptmann, 'Are We Barbarians?'
32. Marvin, 'Preface'.
33. Marvin, 'The Growth of Humanity', 304–7.
34. D'Ors, 'Manifesto of Moral Unity'.
35. Dresselhuys, 'Nederlandsche anti-oorlog raad', 133–34.

36. Einstein and Nicolai, 'Manifesto to the Europeans'.
37. Kolb, 'Briefe eines Deutsch-Französin'; Noe, *Die literarische Kritik in 'Die weissen Blätter'*, 149–53.
38. Noe, *Die literarische Kritik in 'Die weissen Blätter'*, 109–10; quotation from 110: '. . .hat ein einigeres Europa bestanden, nie war doe Solidarität der Völker, die sich zu zerfleischen suchen, so gross'.
39. Hofmannsthal, 'Die Idee Europa'.
40. Starr, *Romain Rolland and War*, 3, 50–65.
41. Rolland, *Above the Battle*, 121, 129, 135.
42. Fried, *The Restoration of Europe*.
43. *Report of the International Congress*. See also, e.g., Wägner, 'Hvad säga kvinnorna?'; Qvarnström, *Motståndets berättelser*, 118–21, 162–75.
44. Anonymous, 'In ernster Zeit'.
45. Wells, *What Is Coming?*, 193, 254–62.
46. Angell, 'Introduction', xxv–xxvii.
47. See, e.g., the Swedish social democrat Erik Palmstierna, 'Europas förenta stater' or the Austrian Nobel laureate Alfred Fried, *Europäische Wiederherstellung*.
48. Lipgens, *Die Anfänge der Einigungspolitik*, 36. The secretary of the Dutch committee, Nico van Suchtelen, published *Europe United* (translated from Dutch in 1915; plus other translations, e.g. into Danish in 1916, *Europas forenede stater*).
49. Waechter, 'How to Prevent War'.
50. See, e.g. Blum, 'A European Dialogue'. See also the call to all Europeans in November 1914 by Nicolai, *Die Biologie des Krieges*, 12–15.
51. Wettstein, *Europas Einigungskrieg*, 86–89.
52. Smith, Mollan and Tennent, *Impact of First World War*, 6–12.
53. Battaglia, *Zoll- und Wirtschaftsbündnis*, 706–40.
54. Ibid., 704–7; Stevenson, 'War and European Integration'.
55. Wells, *What Is Coming?*, 46, 210; Angell, *War Aims*; Angell, *Conditions of Allied Success*.
56. Wells, *What Is Coming?*, 238.
57. Vermeieren discusses the political impact of the understanding of Germany's war aims in *The First World War*, 145–82.
58. The following pages on 'Mitteleuropa' are based on Andrén, *Att frambringa*, 149–56.
59. Chiantera-Stutte, 'Space, Großraum and Mitteleuropa'.
60. Meyer, *Mitteleuropa in German Thought*, 145–59, charts the relevant newspaper and magazine articles.
61. Klaein, *Die Kulturgemeinschaft der Völker*; Liszt, *Ein Mitteleuropäischer staatenverband*; Loch, *Der mitteleuropäische Wirtschaftsbloch*; Mehrmann, *Grossdeutschland*; Mühlstein, *Deutschlands Sendung*; Philippovich, *Ein Wirtschafts- und Zollverband*; Ritter, *Berlin-Bagdad*; Ritter, *Nordkap-Bagdad*. From 1913, the only major book treating 'Mitteleuropa' – openly critical of the policy of Bismarck and of the Prussian unification of Germany – was by the agrarian conservative Schuchardt, *Der mitteleuropäische Bund*.
62. Liszt, *Ein Mitteleuropäischer staatenverband*, 16, 42; Mühlstein, *Deutschlands Sendung*, 10–21, 45–48.
63. Philippovich, *Ein Wirtschafts- und Zollverband*; Ritter, *Berlin-Bagdad*; Liszt, *Ein Mitteleuropäischer staatenverband*, 29, 41.
64. Stevenson, 'War and European Integration'.
65. Theiner, *Sozialer Liberalismus*, 150, 239; cf. Fischer, 'Weltpolitik, Weltmachtstreben'. See also Mommsen, 'Die Mitteleuropaidee und die Mitteleuropaplanungen', 14.
66. Stevenson, 'War and European Integration'.
67. Theiner, *Sozialer Liberalismus*, 129–59.

68. Ibid., 50; Meyer, *Mitteleuropa in German Thought*, 195; Naumann, 'Deutschland und Österreich'.
69. Naumann, *Mitteleuropa*, 496–97; quotation from 523: 'Mit disem krieg im Rücken können wir Berge versetzen. Jetzt oder nie wird die dauernde Einheit zwischen Ost und West, wird Mitteleuropa zwischen Russland und den westlichen Mächten'.
70. Ibid., 501–4, 519–22.
71. Ibid., 492–3, 523–33, 543–50, 578–9, 586–7, 595–6, 663–5; quotation from 586: 'Das ist schmerzlich, aber so will es die Weltgeschichte: politische kleinbetriebe bedürfen der Ahnlehnung'.
72. Ibid., 555: '. . .um das Deutschtum herum wächst die Kultur von Mitteleuropa'.
73. Ibid., 579: '. . .Denker, Verstandsmenschen, Techniker, Organisatoren, erfolgreiche Nüchternheitsmenschen ', and 596: ' der träger einer um das Deutschtum herum wachsenden vielgliedrigen starken und inhaltreichen Kultur'.
74. Ibid., 597–612.
75. List, *Deutschland und Mittel-Europa*, 107–9; Dix, 'England und die Mitteleuropäische Verkehrseinheit', 73–75; Stern, *Mitteleuropa*, 726–35.
76. Vermeieren, 'Notions of Solidarity'.
77. Mogk, *Rohrbach und 'Grössere Deutschland'*, 5, 182–83.
78. Kautsky, *Nationalstaat und Staatenbund*, 72–75; Kautsky, *Die vereinigten Staaten Mitteleuropas*, 1–14.
79. Wells, *What Is Coming?*, 239–42; quotation from 242.
80. Ibid., 38–44.
81. Ibid., 192–207, 254.
82. Toynbee, *Nationality and the War*, 476–77; Toynbee, *The New Europe*, 61–62.
83. Cook, *Britain and the Small Nations*. Asquith is quoted by Sydney Brooks, 'The New Europe', 66–78.
84. *Report of the International Congress*.
85. Agorio, *La Sombre de Europa*, 33.
86. Hobson, *Imperialism: A Study*.
87. Hobson, *Democracy after the War*.
88. Wells, *What Is Coming?*, 192–207.
89. Regarding the Russian case, see Seton-Watson, 'The Musings of a Slavophile'.
90. Lenin, *The Imperialist War*, 91, 190.
91. Kautsky, *Die Befreiung der Nationen*, 6, 27–46.
92. 'Memorandum of the Socialists'.
93. Kann, *Das Nationalitätenproblem der Habsburgmonarchie*, 17–39; Zöllner, 'Der Österreichbegriff'.
94. Sked, *Fall of the Habsburg Empire*, 218–39.
95. Ibid., 255–61.
96. Boleski, 'Die Einheit Mitteleuropas'; Gružewski, 'Die koalition Mitteleuropas'.
97. Pekař, 'Kdo založil Rakousko?'
98. Stolper, *Das mitteleuropäische Wirtschaftsproblem*, 100–101; Stolper, *Wir und Deutschland*, 29–30.
99. Renner, *Der Selbstbestimmungsrecht der Nationen*; Seipel, *Nation und Staat*, 31, 68, 92–95, 139; Stolper, *Wir und Deutschland*, 29–32.
100. See, e.g., Agorio, *La Sombre de Europa*, 23: 'Nos hallamos al borde de esta suprema transformación. Ya ha comenzado al gran proceso de todos los valores éticos, la gran revisión de todas las garantías jurídicas' [We stand on the brink of this supreme transformation. The great process of all ethical values has already begun, the great review of all legal guarantees].
101. Mühlstein, *Herrschaft der Weisen*, 3: 'Die kommende Reformation der europäischen Politik und Kultur kann nur von einer besseren Philosophie ausgehen'.

102. Toynbee, *The New Europe*, 61–73.
103. Ibid., 9–18.
104. Louis, *L'Europe Nouvelle*, 6: 'L'Expression "Europe nouvelle", dont un use quotidiennement, est d'ailleurs très vague; elle recouvre l'Europe territoriale, l'Europe social, l'Europe politique'.
105. Ibid., 7: 'n'y avait plus de peuples opprimés, spoliés, mutilés'.
106. Ibid., 12–30.
107. Palmstierna, *Orostid I*, 155–75.
108. Louis, *L'Europe Nouvelle*, 22–131.
109. Andrén, *Att frambringa*, 171–84. The following paragraphs on Masaryk are based on Andrén, *Att frambringa*, 168–71.
110. Garver, 'Masaryk and Czech Politics'. For background on Czech policies of self-determination, see Garver, *The Young Czech Party*.
111. Kramář, *Anmerkungen zur böhmischen Politik*, 4, 90–97.
112. Seton-Watson, *Masaryk in England*, 75, 154.
113. Masaryk, 'At the Eleventh Hour', 186–94; Masaryk, 'Masaryk to Seton-Watson'.
114. Masaryk, 'Independent Bohemia', 117–19; Masaryk, 'The Problem of Small Nations', 135–38; Masaryk, *The Slavs Among the Nations*.
115. Rakovski, 'Transylvania and Macedonia'.
116. Gribble, 'The War Aims of Luxemburg'.
117. Anonymous, 'Iceland and Denmark'.
118. Valentin, 'Sweden and Åland Islands'.
119. Rubicon, 'The Czechs and Austria'.
120. Anonymous, 'Keep to the Left!'
121. Dontsov, *Die ukrainische Staatsidee*, 65–68.
122. Mick, '1918: Endgame', 141, 158; Rubicon, 'The Czechs and Austria'.
123. Louis, *Aspects politiques de la guerre*, 202: 'Aucun document, depuis 1914, n'a eu plus de retentissement que le message de M. Wilson en date du 8 janvier 1918. Les paroles du président américain ont toujours le don de saisir l'attention des hommes, parce qu'on sent une volonté ferme, une pensée Claire en même temps qu'audacieuse, un désintéressement plutôt rare; mais cette fois, il n'est pas exagéré de dire qu'elles ont provoqué une secousse profonde dans les deux combinaisons belligérantes comme chez les neutres'.
124. Wilson, 'The Ideals of Democracy'.
125. Anonymous, 'The Very Stuff of Triumph'.
126. According to Lida Gustava Heymann, the efforts of the women's peace movement and the Hague Conference were of great importance to Wilson's programme for a new Europe; see Heymann, *Erlebtes – Erschautes*, 130–34.
127. Anonymous, 'The Very Stuff of Triumph'.
128. Noser, 'Unrest in Bohemia', 182.
129. Mamatey, 'Masaryk and Wilson', 192–93; Anonymous, 'Lord Robert Cecil'.
130. Djuric, 'The Southern Slavs and Italy'.
131. 'Et nyt Europa'.
132. Manela, *The Wilsonian Moment*.
133. Key, 'Vart Fædreland Europa', 25: 'De, som nu vil trampe Tysklands Selvbestemmelseret, Stolthed of Framtidsmuligheder I Stumpen og Stykker, de forbereder den nye Krig, I hvilken deres Børnebørn vil forbløde og Europa gaa under'.
134. Neiburg, *The Treaty of Versailles*, 11–13.
135. Shaw, 'Nationalitet og Internationalisme', 30.
136. Whyte, 'The Versailles Mustard Seed'.
137. Neiburg, *The Treaty of Versailles*, 74, 76.

CHAPTER 6

Fearing Crisis

The Great War was followed by both optimism and pessimism. Hope and trust were found in the promises of European culture, civilisation and order. There was still faith in civilisation, and expectations of a lasting and fair peace mounted in the mid-1920s. Memorials to fallen soldiers were raised in Belgium, Britain and France.[1] The Great War was often expected to be the last war, so many countries began to disarm themselves. Belgium, France, Germany, Great Britain and Italy resolved further issues between them in the Locarno Pact of 1925, with the explicit aim of guaranteeing peace in Western Europe. This resulted in the leading negotiators – the foreign ministers of Great Britain, France and Germany – winning the Nobel Peace Prize: in 1925 it was awarded to Austen Chamberlain, and the following year it was shared by Aristide Briand and Gustav Stresemann. One observer stated that 'the war is definitely ended, that, whereas we have been living for the last six or seven years in a state of truce, in a state of concealed ill-feeling, of anxiety, dissatisfaction and uncertainty, to-day there is a real cooperation between the Allies and their enemies, and the psychology of war is a thing of the past'.[2] In addition, Briand's attempt at a universal treaty outlawing war was completed in the so-called Peace Pact of 1928, according to which all major powers promised not to invade other countries. As the pact was signed by almost all European countries, happy days seemed once again to be likely.[3]

Still, the discourse of Europe was riddled with pessimism and even despair. In Bremerhaven in February 1923, the Austrian journalist and author Joseph Roth described Europe darkly through the eyes of emigrating East

---

Notes for this section begin on page 186.

European peasants bidding a final farewell to the continent, stressing their experiences of maltreatment and oppression, and their hopes of a better future elsewhere. These were mainly Jews from Poland, Lithuania, Russia and Ukraine. He told of a mother with two young daughters and a twenty-year-old son who 'have been wandering through the sorry, moribund West of Europe'. They had been to Budapest, Vienna and Berlin before a cousin in New York finally sent them tickets to America. These refugees on the emigrant ship *Pittsburgh* now belonged to the lucky ones who could 'get away from Europe, the continent of pogroms'. They were lucky to have their tickets and an address for a brother-in-law, nephew or cousin over there. They were 'fleeing hunger, the plague, and a creeping charity'.[4] To Roth and many others, Europe was a backwater, and Western Europe was dying.

Disputes between European states stoked fears of new wars. The Swedish author and peace activist Elin Wägner wrote, apropos the French seizure of Ruhr in 1923, that Europe was on a road towards disaster, where mistrust and hatred among the nations would end in mutual destruction. The open wounds from the war tainted the European mind: 'If we in thought and action continue in our direction from the war, then we will unerringly tear ourselves apart, and leave our beautiful, wonderful continent destined for foreign races to inherit'.[5]

Crisis and decline remained salient themes in the intellectuals' political and cultural discourse of European unity in the interwar period.[6] In fact, it was impossible to consider Europe without the significant impact of discourses of degeneration that added a new framing of the idea of Europe. Most of all, the crisis was associated with the borders and divisions of Europe. Here, we turn to issues of European decline and crisis, which were ascribed various characteristics and usually accompanied by appeals to take ameliorating action. What kinds of decline and crisis were being represented, and what kinds of rescues? Europe was seen as embroiled in an epic drama with an unknown conclusion. It had risen to a place of might and glory, achieved technological revolutions, freed the mind, and rationally organised society, but its position could no longer be taken for granted.

This chapter begins by outlining the contemporary trepidation regarding the new borders and economic failures of the new European order, illustrating the entanglements of unity and borders. It will then examine contributions to discussions of European crisis, decline and nihilism, illustrating European divisions as well as arguments for moral and cultural unity, while keeping to the conception of European exceptionalism. The findings of this chapter underpin the results of Chapter 5 regarding the fundamental impact of the redefined concept of Europe, emphasising its many national borders. In addition, this and the following chapter give further evidence of the Europeanisation of ideas and concepts as a long-term historical process more pronounced, especially among intellectuals, than in previous periods.[7] We should be aware, however, that the nation was the basis for transnational activities in the 1920s and 1930s,[8] activities that were a way to act within borders, not to create an all-encompassing unity.

Borders: Necessary Barriers or Opportunities for Cooperation

> Europe, whither goest you? – the poignant question of to-day. The pride of Christian culture, the greatest human achievement in history, with, as we thought before 1914, the seal of immortality set upon her, is now perhaps moving towards dissolution and death. Europe has begun a rapid decline, though no one dares to think that she will continue in it downward until she reaches the chaos and misery and barbarity from which she sprang.[9]

British journalist Stephen Graham captured the thoughts of Europe after the war, when history seemed to be taking a new path and progress had turned into its opposite. Through the eyes of this voyager of Europe, conditions had already declined by the beginning of the 1920s. During and after the turbulent ending of the war, Europe had rapidly increased its number of nation states to almost thirty. At each border, it was necessary to have a passport and a valid visa. A visa for travelling could only be obtained for a certain period and needed to be renewed if the visit was prolonged. At each visa office and border one had to queue, the officials might very well insist on asking their questions in their national language, and each monetary exchange entailed a cost, as reported by Graham.[10]

The new borders were not only inconvenient for travellers, but they also illustrated the contemporary anarchy caused by the nationalistic breakdown of the old Europe and a nation state ideology unfit for the needs and awaiting tasks. The shattering of Europe into nation states manifested in the proliferating new borders was increasingly blamed for both the decline and the crisis. Some critics found solutions in ideas of national superiority and a hierarchy among nations. The German conservative nationalist Max Hildebert Boehm warned of a Europe comprising small states that were weak, politically divided, economically shattered, mutually unfriendly, and with disputed borders, adding an urgent need for a European rebirth that included a strengthened Germany.[11] In Vienna, the conservative sociologist Othmar Spann frankly stated that the crisis would end if the Central European states were all made into German provinces. The Balkanisation of Europe, with all its minor states, had brought chaos, and it was the future task of Germany to restore order and peace. Poland, Bohemia, Hungary, the Slavic people in the south, and Greece should belong to Germany. For the pan-Germans, the independence of the minor nations was an illness that could only be cured with an accumulation of German power.¹²

It is true that many nationalists still believed in the blessings of largeness, as Boehm and Spann illustrated. It was the idea of a hierarchy of European peoples that had subjected many nations to the larger states. Elin Wägner satirically represented the dilemma in a vignette:

> An Englishman to an English woman after hearing a lecture: Was that not a gripping appeal?
> The woman: Yes. But of course I think, like my husband, that you really should not help the Russians. It is only good if that race could be reduced, as it is the disruptor of peace in Europe.
> He: But do you really think that the Russians are worse than, for example, the people of the Balkans?
> She: No, I really do not know what we in Europe should do with the people of the Balkans.
> He: In that case, I must say if we are to cleanse Europe, then there is no reason to let the Germans stay here.
> She: The Germans, yes. I had forgotten them. It would of course be a blessing if we could get rid of them as well.
> He: But tell me, then, what is it that makes us English so outstanding and worthy of living compared with others?
> She: We are so human.¹³

For many the decline was caused by the economic circumstances of the war and the incomplete recovery afterwards, which to a significant extent was explained as an outcome of the new borders. The elimination of trade tariffs was often called for. At the Paris Peace Conference in 1919, Louis Loucheur, the main economic advisor to the French prime minister, claimed that economic stability was essential to avoiding a new crisis.¹⁴ In the same year, it was reported that a German economics professor had predicted rapid economic decline unless a United States of Europe was established.¹⁵ Warnings about the peace treaty were widespread, and in everyday speech, the Parisians called it the 'heartfelt rift'.¹⁶ One British representative, the economist John Maynard Keynes, resigned his post and left the conference utterly disappointed at the inability of the victors to formulate a sound treaty. He argued that they would not succeed in bringing economic stability to the decaying organisation of Central and Eastern Europe and its new states, but would instead further misery and disorder.¹⁷ It was observed that the principle of nationality was dysfunctional in economic life, as provinces and states suffered from economic obstacles raised by neighbouring states, and national hostility paralysed Central and South East Europe with no economic gain for any regions. Exports of raw materials were hampered, transit across territories to the sea and other states was blocked, and rail traffic was impeded by heavily discriminatory duties. If this were not enough, from the sovereignty of independent states over their economies followed perhaps twenty other ways to impede the economic freedom of their neighbours, argued the British publicist and labour politician Norman Angell. He warned of a peace treaty that organised the European economy based on the principle of nationality. Instead, he advocated economic movement and the ability to be independent of political sovereignty, with some kind of supreme economic council that could settle disputes.[18]

> The truth is that a settlement on a basis of nationality, involving an absolute sovereignty and 'ownership' of soil, must necessarily conflict with the vital economic cooperation of the world. An international system, under which adequate economic opportunity can only be secured for a people by their complete political sovereignty over the territory [that] contains the raw material necessary to their industry is fatal to the security of nationality itself. The price of secure nationality is a workable economic internationalism.[19]

A range of publications argued that social and economic factors were determining the future, being at the root of the crisis and decline. Only months after the peace treaty, Paul Louis, who had abandoned his vision of a 'New Europe', declared that the capitalist system had put Europe and the world in crisis. Capitalism had led to the war, but to win it, capitalists and imperialists had made promises they had since betrayed. They had promised a new world order with an end to dynastic rule and secret diplomacy, and the dawn of rule by the will of the people. Much of this new order was not realised, as the rulers had not understood that the war had paved the way for worldwide social upheaval and the age of democracy. Now they were ignoring the burdens of rapidly increasing living costs and inflation. In Louis' analysis, the workers who had fought on the front lines now put both capitalism and imperialism in crisis with revolutions in some countries, and strikes and upheavals in others.[20] Louis was right: all the signs of a true economic crisis were in evidence, with sharply reduced production capacity, a lack of raw materials, the abandonment of farming, and overproduction of paper money.

As early as 1920, in an acclaimed and frequently cited analysis, the French geographer Albert Demangeon had already questioned the viability of the sources of Europe's wealth, as the war had exhausted the continent and set it on a path of decline in the world economy. His figures indicated a remarkable decrease in agricultural and industrial output, exports, and birth rates – and, in addition, the states were heavily burdened with war debts. The outcome of the war had been disastrous, as it had 'stopped production, forced Europe to buy overseas, thus turning former debtor nations into creditors; and, as a terrible agent of destruction, it [had] substituted the task of reconstruction for that of creating new wealth for exchange. Above all, in its destruction of life, it [had] dried up the source of energy and vitality'. Demangeon remarked that, in the meantime, the United States and

Japan had increased their capacities and taken over export markets as well as trade routes, de facto putting the major European states under further pressure. Moreover, he predicted that the ability of the European empires to uphold their global hegemony would face pressure from growing national ambitions – a revolution in the relations between Europeans and others would only accelerate the decline.[21]

Economists emphasised the division of Europe between its industrial and wealthy parts in the West, and its agrarian parts in the East and South: the former was dense with roads and railways, while transportation links were scarce in the latter; the former saw the thriving exchange of products, while the latter was underdeveloped. The French economist Francis Delaisi spoke of 'two Europes'.[22] Despite the catchphrase of 'cooperation or downfall', creation of a European market and rational planning at the European level faced opposition from protectionism and dysfunction within European industry. Trade tariffs were repeatedly seen as the main obstacle to progress. In the late 1920s, when the protectionist measures implemented throughout Europe threatened to expand into a tariff war, the reduction of trade tariffs was interpreted as a way to prevent decline and to unite Europe. The message was clear: the continent had been riddled with wars – fought by economic means if not with arms – when it ought to have been governed by order and self-restraint. Europe's eminence was attributed to both economic prerequisites and civilisational accomplishments, and any lack of internal economic cooperation was seen as potentially inviting decline.[23]

The Crisis of Civilisation, and How to Overcome It

The notion of a European crisis was widespread. For many contemporary observers, it was not only that an economic decline was taking place, but also that a far-reaching crisis was developing. Strengthening the European economies was not enough, as the acute economic crisis was only a symptom of a more profound malaise.[24] The military crisis might have been over when the war ended and the peace treaties were signed; it might have been possible to avert the economic crisis, but the European crisis in its totality would not be so simple to resolve, as it had other and even more fundamental aspects, wrote Paul Valéry in 1919. Europe had been seriously shaken and its intellect was disturbed. A generation of young artists and writers was lost, as was belief in a European culture: its moral ambitions were scattered, both realism and idealism scorned, the spirit incapable of saving anything and in doubt of its own capacities, according to Valéry.[25]

Some identified the post-war economic disorder and social crisis as a moral problem. Italian writer, historian and politician of the left and liberal parties, Francesco Nitti, saw Europe as a state of mind that was out of balance. It had been torn apart by war and economic delusions, and only understood the language of violence; it was an unhappy continent that lacked the language of peace: '[O]ne thing is above all others necessary: the resumption, not only of the language, but of the ideas of peace!'[26] For Nitti it still all came down to practical issues: the cynical and greedy peace treaty that robbed Germany of land and resources, by which Europe had been divided into two camps, one heavily armed and threatening the other, which had been 'forced to labour in slavish conditions under the menace of a servitude even more severe'.[27] For a disillusioned Russian socialist and Marxist exile, it all came down to finding a new spirit. He called for Europe to reclaim its moral vision and to focus on what was best for its citizens. When Europe was poor, indebted and without culture, most of its countries plundered, its politicians and parties corrupt, without hope that any social class could take the lead in changing society, then Europe would have to either die or be reborn. Either it would be capable of making a spiritual turn, or it would definitely decline.[28]

Every aspect of the crisis was taken into account when representing the idea of a crisis of civilisation. The British anthropologist, essayist and novelist Robert Briffault, who alluded to Gibbons with his *The Decline and Fall of the British Empire*, wrote in *Breakdown: The Collapse of Traditional Civilization* that 'symptoms of mental decay are noticeable everywhere throughout Western civilization', and that 'all thought exhibits a manifest decadence'. This concerned not only economic and social life, he suggested, but language, literature, and all the arts as well.[29] This way of defining the period was often elaborated on by Austrians and Germans – unsurprisingly considering the effects of the First World War and these countries' declines as leading powers due to their losses of Central and East European provinces, and the German forfeiture of its colonies. The criticism draws on themes, already in place at the end of the nineteenth century, regarding industrialisation, urban migration, and capitalism, as well as individualism, secularisation, and civil rights movements. Max Weber's view of rationalisation and bureaucracy, as forces that constrain human life, also exerted a strong influence. The Frankfurt School of Marxist thinkers criticised modern technology and analysed phenomena of mass culture as its logical outcome. Conservatives cautioned against communism and American culture. Here we find Ferdinand Fried, an advocate of National Socialism who saw a cold and soulless spirit of money and capitalism that had broken the old institutions and traditions, seeking salvation in a spiritual renewal of both the nation and the people.[30]

For some, the crisis of civilisation was rooted in the cornerstones of modern development. Julius Evola, who adhered to Italian fascism, declared the crisis to be an outcome of the breakdown of traditional order.[31] Evola's friend, the writer and esotericist René Guénon, contended sadly that material considerations always come first, giving priority to utilitarianism and economic factors.[32] For the German-French theologian and philosopher Albert Schweitzer, the current crisis of civilisation was due to the restricted compass of ethical standards. It was a mistake to regard civilisation as essentially materialistic, even if that was what it had come to stand for; instead, true civilisation concerned the spiritual life and ideals of human perfection, quite apart from the improvement of social and political conditions. Individuals' spiritual forces would need to take the upper hand in order to overcome the overriding striving for materialistic achievements in the economic, social and political spheres. A true and active civilisation with real freedom would require ethical standards. Issues of meaning and value are essential to establishing a spiritual condition 'in which we again become capable of civilization'.[33]

For others, the crisis was the outcome of a societal divide. The Anglo-French writer and historian Hilaire Belloc saw a decline that began when the Reformation disrupted Christendom, to which he added further factors: 'The conflict between rich and poor, the conflict between opposing national idolatries, the lack of common standards and of the fixed doctrines upon which they used to depend had led up . . . to the brink of chaos'.[34] Many contributors to this discussion shared the sense that they wanted to rescue Europe by instituting common values. Guénon wrote of a 'traditional and supra-human truth', and Belloc of establishing common standards and principles. It is also illustrative that both turned to the Catholic Church: Guénon recognised it as the only organisation capable of uniting the spiritual forces, and Belloc hailed its principles favouring the better distribution of wealth and the effective control of capitalist monopolies.[35]

The societal divide was also an issue for leftists who addressed the decay of capitalist civilisation. Beatrice and Sidney Webb blamed it for poverty, for inequalities in income and personal freedom, and for causing the war.[36] Scott Nearing claimed that the working class would have to build a new culture, responding productively to the decay and forming a new civilisation beyond the present impotent, declining economic system with its class divisions. He looked towards a new social order with world organisations that formed a global society and global association of organised workers.[37]

For feminists who addressed contemporary decay, the divide was between civilisation and culture, with the former representing male oppression. Austrian Rosa Mayreder connected civilisation with technological progress, economic prerogatives, and mechanisation. It overestimated the virtues of technical progress, and ignored the havoc it wreaked. Civilisation suffered from hubris and intemperance, and overemphasised competition and efficiency; in addition, it was built on men's work. The contemporary crisis was the result, Mayreder claimed, of civilisation moving much faster than culture, leaving the latter unable to absorb its innovations. In addition, culture had fallen into decay following the previous century's upheavals of tradition, societal values, and aesthetic norms. Elin Wägner presented a similar view in the early 1940s, identifying war and preparations for war as outcomes of civilisation. For both feminists, men ruled the world through civilisation just as they ruled women. Hope was found in the will to change this, and in the possibility of creating a new culture in which values closer to life and female experiences had the upper hand.[38]

Salvaging civilisation was seen as connected to developing new international orders of cooperation. We are witnessing a process of collapse, wrote H.G. Wells in 1921, likening European civilisation to a sinking ship due to its exaggerated patriotism, which had found its way into schools, national literatures, propaganda, and national selfishness. The only way to save civilisation would be to spread an idea greater than nationalism; otherwise, he feared that an era of prosperity and progress was about to end. Wells preached the gospel of human brotherhood and saw ultimate salvation in a world state ruled by a common law of humankind. He saw world organisations such as the League of Nations as important, as were 'world unifying efforts', expanding patriotism into the motivation to create a world state.[39]

There were also those who saw the solution to the crisis in the idea of a European community. It was only through a common effort, by gathering all European states into a union, that the continent could be rescued, according to Nitti.[40] If the white race wanted to fulfil its mission, wrote Wilhelm Heile, the founder of the Verband für europäischen Verständigung in 1926, Europe would have to organise itself: to stay in the lead, a United States of Europe was urgently needed.[41] The idea of a common crisis triggered pleas for cooperation, not only among the main powers of Europe; the nation states in Central Europe were especially vulnerable to tariffs and worried about international conflicts. Amidst the economic crisis in 1930, Czech foreign minister Edvard Beneš warned dramatically of the final downfall of European culture. The only available choice would be between conflicts and crises leading to new wars and catastrophes, and a new kind of intimate association that would concern economic relations as well as political and moral affairs.[42]

One of the foremost advocates of a united Europe was Richard von Coudenhove-Kalergi, founder of the Pan-European League. He was a strong proponent of the idea of a major crisis of European civilisation, claiming that 'civilisation has turned Europe into a penitentiary and the majority of Europeans into forced labour', such that civilised man had lost his natural freedom. Dependent on machines, states, and unhealthy cities, he was unhappy and unable to enjoy his maximum potential.[43] Coudenhove-Kalergi's pleading for pan-Europeanism was based on the idea of a double crisis concerning the roots of European civilisation, which forged the largest crisis ever faced by humankind. He saw a political crisis emerging from the failure to ensure lasting peace, freedom, and wealth for Europe's citizens, and concluded that Europe could only be saved if it became unified in a federation that could allow the reconstruction of its morals and culture. The basis of the crisis was the downfall of the common worldview, formerly based on Christianity, but that had long been eroding, finally reaching an acute phase with the spread of materialism and the denial of the existence of God after the Enlightenment. This left Europeans with neither higher values nor responsibilities. However, instead of the rebirth of a Christian worldview, he called for responsibilities to be based on the ethics of pantheism, which he found in Goethe's and Nietzsche's heroic ideals.[44]

Richard von Coudenhove-Kalergi saw technology as the heart of the European spirit. The technical revolution was the global mission of Europe; it had truly changed the continent and positioned Europe as the world leader. Not everything was better because of it, as it did bring mechanisation, standardisation, and tasteless mass production, but it also brought the possibility of liberating people from forced labour and improving their lives. Their houses could have gardens, and be warmed and lit by electricity. New means of transportation and communication meant that people could live away from their workplaces in factories, and that large cities could be dismantled. Like many other visionaries, he also managed to find creative and persuasive rationales for his main standpoints. When arguing that the technological revolution was a driving force of a unified Europe, he noted that public transport had lessened distances. Just as trains had imposed the need to overcome local patriotism in Germany and Italy before their unifications, so Coudenhove-Kalergi argued that aviation brought Europeans closer to one another; he urged politicians to seize the opportunity this presented to overcome nationalism in Europe.[45]

Ultimately, von Coudenhove-Kalergi had no doubt about the greatness of Europe and its world mission to free people through technological and ethical means. According to him, the courage to act, as well as the values of dynamic masculinity and romantic heroism, were highly praised traits in Europe. Europeans had a spirit of invention and were able to invest their energy in global projects intended to contribute to its future.[46]

Indeed, there was little doubt that Europe could be rescued. Europe was and would continue to weigh more than the rest of the world combined. Paul Valéry concluded that the European spirit, with its discipline, morals and power, would be undefeatable and would prevail. Wherever this victory occurred, we would 'witness the maximum of needs, the maximum of labor, capital and production, the maximum of ambition and power, the maximum transportation of external Nature, the maximum of relations and exchanges'.[47] Here, there is no shortage of European self-reliance.

Crises of the Mind, and the Quest for Moral Values

One of the best-known and most widely read books on the issues of crisis and decline is *Revolt of the Masses* by José Ortega y Gasset, which was originally published in Spanish in 1930 and quickly translated into English and German, and thereafter into other languages as well. The book made him an important writer outside his native Spain, and his impact as a writer representing European high culture in the discourse on Europe was immediate and to some extent lasting – Albert Camus would write some years later that 'Ortega y Gasset, after Nietzsche, is perhaps the greatest "European" writer'.[48] Other often-read authors such as Thomas Mann and the Dutch historian Johann Huizinga quoted Spengler and other declinist authors, but above all, they cited Ortega y Gasset. In this body of work, we can extract the main themes of the decline as perceived in the 1930s. Several crises were occurring at that point, notably, the Great Depression following the stock market crash in 1929. Ortega y Gasset was writing against the background of a Spain that had lost its colonies and was at war with Morocco. Led by a much-criticised dictatorship, it had entered a philosophical debate about the essence of Spain in relation to modern Europe. In Germany, the political crisis of the early 1930s ended with the Nazis overthrowing democracy. By 1935, not only Germany but also Italy and several other European states had gone from democratic to authoritarian governments. In absolute numbers, more states had taken this turn than not. Fascism was regarded as a viable option in Spain too, where Franco was about to seize power. If it was not so before, now democracy was truly in crisis.

Timely analysis treated issues such as the rise of dictatorships and the attacks on democracy in the remaining democracies as outcomes of the Great War, as well as the longer trend of the decay of representative institutions and shortcomings in establishing authority and efficiency in democratic capitalism. The argument that political fragmentation needed to be counteracted by 'some force that will jump political boundaries and operate in a worldwide manner' recurred.[49] According to the Swiss diplomat and internationalist William E. Rappard, the future of democracy 'depends in the first instance on the maintenance of peace and on the organisation of international relations such as will again allow national governments to strive primarily for the prosperity of their people, and no longer oblige it to subordinate it to the security of their states'.[50]

The decay was not necessarily conceived of as an economic or political fact. Ortega y Gasset said it was something that was much debated and was a feeling that could possess one's mind: 'Europe feels grave doubts as to whether she does rule or not, as to whether she will rule tomorrow'. Indeed, it was even doubtful whether, after three centuries in the lead, Europe could still be seen as ruling the world, and even more doubtful that it would continue to do so, but such simplification of the contemporary was not proof of a factual decadence. For Ortega y Gasset, the concept of decay defined a feeling.[51] Mann envisioned the decline as an abdication of the spirit and reason, which he observed in culture, art, and the spread of irrationalism. This threatened what he stressed as the European ideals of truth, freedom and fairness.[52] Johann Huizinga declared the crises to be cultural, and his examples tended to reflect art and the ideas of intellectuals. He mentioned the Decadent Movement in literature from the late nineteenth century and the pessimism of Spengler.[53]

Still, they agreed that the cultural decay had brought with it serious consequences. For Huizinga this was marked by a turn towards immediate experience marked by advertisements, political slogans, and the way serious matters had been made the subjects of funny games. It included both pupillage and heroism exalting action and the will, but that left no room for reflection or analysis.[54] For Ortega y Gasset the diminishing self-confidence of Europe was followed by the decay of its norms, and a path was set for a new mentality that gave everyone the right to have rights. The old norms had been dismissed without new norms taking their place, and Europeans were left disoriented.[55] Mann saw this as a cultural backlash against the nineteenth century, which had given way to barbarism and threatened people with devastating war and the fall of civilisation.[56]

Modern man was an issue in this context. Ortega y Gasset began from an analysis of the crisis of modernity as caused by the dominance of the masses. His most famous ideas were those concerning 'mass man' and mass movements. He claimed mass man to be the most adequate representation of nineteenth-century civilisation, found in all social classes and considered a specialist: he was confident in his isolated realm, away from other branches of expertise, and incapable of interpreting the consequences of his actions. His specialisation devastated his ability to make integral interpretations. While current civilisation, with its ideal of progress without limits, had produced a radical increase in specialists, it had also caused the decline of cultured men. Civilisation had been allowed to act on its own, which had brought about a 'rebirth of primitivism and barbarism'.[57] Ortega y Gasset sounds like an eighteenth-century liberal by including the state in his critique of modern civilisation, and warning of its development. During the nineteenth century, the state had grown into a cold-blooded monster, a machine as impersonal as the specialist. European civilisation, he emphasised, was in danger due to state intervention absorbing spontaneous social action, 'which in the long run sustains, nourishes, and impels human destinies'.[58]

Ortega y Gasset was most famous for depicting mass movements in which individual efforts were in vain. In fascism and syndicalism, a certain type of man stepped forward, one driven only by will. This man wanted to lead society without necessary competence, accepting no objective moral standards. He did not appreciate future goals or past advances; rather, his prime concern was immediate leisure. The reign of the mass man disrupted society with conflicts and threatened to demoralise Europe. Thus began Ortega y Gasset's pleas on the behalf of minorities and their importance to social progress, and for the importance of establishing a moral code in society, in this recalling both Alexis de Tocqueville and John Stuart Mill.[59] The mass man was a figure that captivated Thomas Mann, who had read Ortega y Gasset closely. Mann depicted the mass man as someone who could talk and write without spirit or thinking, who could turn against reason when he tried to make philosophy, who babbled a lot and then delivered only superficial thoughts.[60]

Ortega y Gasset, Huizinga and Mann all warned of the outcome of the dissolution of moral systems. According to Ortega y Gasset, the essential problem for Europe was the lack of a system of norms that was respected by its peoples. Living together in a society required that people have a sense of 'restrictions, standards, courtesy, indirect methods, justice, reason', which was now threatened.[61] The need for more reason and rational thinking is a recurrent theme in this literature. Huizinga warned against reductive theories of morality, as when historical materialism focused on the economics of society or when Freud turned to drive-based psychology.[62]

Ortega y Gasset moved beyond both Mann and Huizinga in emphasising the limits of nations and nationalism, and in advocating a way forward. He believed that for something new to begin, the decline of Europe was a necessity:

> Is it as certain as people say that Europe is in decadence; that it is resigning its command; abdication? May not this apparent decadence be a beneficial crisis which will enable Europe to be really, literally Europe. The evident decadence of the *nations* of Europe, was not this *a priori* necessary if there was to be one day possible a United States of Europe, the plurality of Europe substituted by its formal unity?[63]

For Ortega y Gasset, the possibility of European unification had become more evident thanks to European decline and crisis. Nationalism had consolidated means of enclosing and excluding, setting out political and cultural boundaries that were now hampering economic and intellectual life. The sense of the decline of nation states was widespread, as was the need for a new ethos of European unity. Ortega y Gasset considered Europe to be a nation, arguing that four-fifths of the cultural heritage of a German, Spaniard, Englishman or Frenchman was common European property. Europe was a common landscape of the nations, and its inhabitants shared a similar way of thinking and a common heritage. He declared the making of a European nation state as the appropriate answer to the contemporary decline.[64]

These works of the first half of the 1930s underline the importance of intellectual, moral and spiritual factors. Still, they were written amidst an acute economic crisis with millions of workers unemployed, fortunes lost, and individuals and families undergoing catastrophes. On top of this, authoritarianism and fascism were gaining strength, exploiting nationalistic chauvinism and racism. Amidst these economic and political pressures, the idea of a shared European spirit was raised as the appropriate answer to the European crisis, which was proclaimed to be both moral and spiritual. Moreover, Europe could only exist as a moral entity, insisted the French author and pacifist Georges Duhamel. The moral dimension was what made it unique compared with America and Asia. Starting there, science and wisdom would be able to flourish once more.[65] The examples of notable European intellectuals who took such a stand are numerous. The sociologist George Simmel focused on spiritual values, and regarded Europe as 'a nexus of spiritual achievements'.[66] Paul Valéry considered Europe to be an intellectual factory, and the European spirit to be the wellspring of many human wonders. The young Czech philosopher Jan Patočka clung to the idea of a European spirit, and considered European civilisation to be universal and the best hope for humankind.[67] Many believed that Europe's spiritual unity was the one remaining way to defend humanist and Enlightenment ideals and rational thinking. Although hatred and misery were triumphing, some saw Europe as a way to fight back: glory in action, clarity of thought, and wealth for its citizens could still be realised, though only through a moral quest.

This was also the point of departure of the French philosopher and novelist Julien Benda, who was perhaps the strongest proponent of European unification as a moral mission. Benda saw man as a primarily spiritual being, and believed that the world should be shaped by morals. Benda argued in part against previous suggestions to bring Europe together through economic change. He did not claim that economic transformation was not needed – quite the opposite. Nevertheless, the moral transformation was essential and would have to transcend the economy, as only then would economic change be possible. The European problem concerned the moral dimension, and it would not be enough to change just the economic or political system. Change would have to be accomplished through practising a new way of thinking and feeling, and by adopting certain common values. These values would differ from those associated with nationalism, which was increasingly spiralling out of control. Common values would negate the practices of dividing the culture and people of Europe, of expansion at the cost of one's neighbours, of claims of absolute sovereignty, of unwillingness to give up the least inch of independence for the sake of other countries, and of the incitement of hatred.[68] Clearly, Benda's focus was on universal values, which he acknowledged as originating in ancient Hellas, saying that it was up to intellectuals to lead away from nationalistic particularism. Interestingly, he denied that European unity would create a new nationalism, even though he suggested using French as a common language. The unification was to be spiritual – the 'realisation of God in the world' – and would shift focus from the waves of political passion to the controlled efforts of reason, initially to save the continent and then the world. Europeans would not feel attached to their land and soil as national belonging could imply, but would instead celebrate reason and universal values.[69]

When we look at these examples together, we can see a concept of Europe defined as going beyond habits and traditions, as a value beyond logic, rational thinking, and the conflicts that were tearing Europe apart. However, this changes when we take into account 'the German-speaking nobles' that Dina Gusejnova has focused on. These writers shared the experience of being elites marginalised by the upheavals at the end, and in the aftermath, of the First World War. They put the desire for feudal cosmopolitanism and transnational nobility into developing ideas of European unity.[70] The Austrian writer Hugo von Hofmannsthal also belongs to this group. He emphasised the spiritual concept of Europe, whose citizens would pursue higher purposes of humanity, religion and the holy, going beyond the utilitarian superficiality of pre-war Europe and beyond simple calls for a civilisational mission. That is to say, his Europe did not yet exist and the task was to construct it. We can see a similar approach in Julius Evola, who emphasised the missing spiritual unity of Europe, though here we see a distinctly more authoritarian mind at work. Hofmannsthal asked for tolerance, forgiveness and forbearance. Evola wanted to see hierarchies, values and fidelity. A leadership was needed that could take on both the political and spiritual powers.[71] Evola's trajectory was clear – towards leaders such as Mussolini and Hitler.

By contrast, many intellectuals of the interwar period belonged to a loose network, as noted by Paola Cattani. They included Benda, Duhamel, Huizinga, Mann and Valéry, and were characterised as having an 'inclination towards a sort of collectivity [that] is both transnational and tolerant of liberal values'. They disentangled concepts of homeland and patriotism from the nationalism of the First World War, and associated them instead with pacifism and internationalism. Perhaps surprisingly, they clung to the concept of the nation, albeit advocating, as foundational to European unity, a European nation that acknowledged others and did away with egotism. Cattani stresses the affinity of some of them for a definition of nation based on the idea of individuals giving up some of their freedoms for the sake of finding common ground, underlining the liberal content of their Europeanism. However, her analysis also demonstrates standpoints that are not obviously liberal – notably, that these intellectuals furthered a common heritage with shared values and experiences, and assessed European unity to be a moral commitment.[72]

Anne-Isabelle Richard has clarified another dividing line marking a certain tension among intellectuals who discussed the European spirit in the 1930s, between those who advocated and actively strove for unification, and those who held neutral positions. At stake was an understanding of the European spirit as based solely on mutual understanding or as needing defence from nationalism and the use of force. The two standpoints were clearly expressed at a two-day seminar in October 1933 organised by the French Federal Committee for European Cooperation. Intellectuals from several countries were invited, including Benda, Huizinga and Valéry, to discuss the future of the European spirit. Political issues were avoided, and those who raised them were rebuked by the chair with the argument that 'intellectual cooperation must be universal and must, as much as possible, be independent of politics'. Richard concludes that this view was the main one of the decade.[73] However, Ortega y Gasset, who joined the Pan-European League, belonged with the activists. Huizinga did not hesitate to question the understanding of the nation advanced by intellectuals loyal to the German regime. Benda rejected the existing concept of the nation, and Thomas Mann began to criticise fascism in the late 1930s.

Rationalism Contested: European Reason and European Nihilism

So far, the theme of European crisis and decline had been aligned with the idea of a special European spirit, and of writers holding reason in high esteem. Some writers went one step further when they asked whether it was the European concepts of rationalism and reason that were the root of the problem. According to one argument, the crisis was an outcome of the kind of knowledge and thinking that dominated the modern world. For some this was because of its far-reaching materialism: 'It seems that nothing exists for modern men beyond what can be seen and touched', said René Guénon, seeing the modern mind as preferring what is measurable, weighable and countable.[74] Johann Ludwig Fischer, a professor from Olmütz (Olomouc), criticised European culture for being too mechanistic and rationalistic, favouring technological advancement over human considerations.

To him, modern writing's naturalism and surrealism, as well as contemporary architecture and film, were nothing but reflections of the materialistic and capitalistic spirit. To find hope of something else, one would need to turn to the reactions against such mechanistic approaches in the new physics, to pragmatism in philosophy, and to vitalism and new trends in psychology. In the future Europe, Fischer hoped that consideration would be given to what would be best for individuals as humans rather than as passive devices acting for capital. This sounds like socialism and Marxism, but he dismissed them as materialistic ideologies to be left behind, together with the cultural prototype of the mechanical mind. Fischer's final call was to humanise all kinds of modern inquiry.[75]

The notion of a unified spirit that could transcend national differences was widespread among philosophers who criticised mechanistic thinking and scientific reason. Martin Heidegger, who recognised Asia as threatening Europe from outside, contended that Europeans suffered from fragmentation and rootlessness, and could only be saved by seeking unity at the very beginning of European thinking, in early Greek philosophy. If this did not happen, then Europeans would succumb to Asian peoples.[76] Edmund Husserl, who also turned to ancient Greece to find the origin of the European spirit, proclaimed a crisis of European science following the reign of positivism and the sole focus on objectivity when classical physics and mathematics were held up as ideals. This crisis had also invaded the humanities, which seemed to be losing their sense of meaning. Based on this, Husserl concluded that it was not enough to study facts, but that the humanities – and especially philosophy – would have to look for the meaning of things from the perspective of historical circumstances, which included norms, values and objectives.[77] For Jan Patočka, the European spirit was based on rational thinking. However, he saw two kinds of reason: one tries to master reality, is theoretical, and operates in science, while the other is mythical and practised in Christianity. The problem is that the first kind wishes to subsume the second. Patočka clearly agreed with the others in his criticism of rationalism.

The crisis of reason was also accompanied by a crisis of European self-understanding. Europeans had thought of themselves as godlike beings who had created the world by themselves, to cite the Spanish philosopher Maria Zambrano. She presented one of the most intriguing views of the matter in several publications, including 'La agonia de Europa' from 1940. To this pupil of Ortega y Gasset, the European crisis concerned the notion of reason; it demanded new ways of thinking and new references, which were principally offered by art, from which the traditional idea of reason, hailed by philosophy, radiated.

Zambrano identified violence as an important part of the European heritage, a part that actually signified the old Europe. Now this violence was threatening to destroy the European nations, signalling the death of Europe. Any possible new Europe would require a new man who did not create the world outside of himself; this Europe would require more humility and peaceful coexistence in community with others. Zambrano sought to overcome fragmentation and the limited reason of modern culture that subjugates life, as philosophy and scientific knowledge had replaced religious forms of experience, leaving us with far too strong an adherence to conscious thinking. Her alternative was to find a new unity that inhered in both community life and the expressiveness of subjectivity.[78] By featuring a poetic understanding of individual life and communal being, she hoped to expand the range of European reason. The crisis was then conceived as the outcome of an old European tradition that had been allowed to subsume another tradition, which was just as old and as European – one being rational and the other expressive.[79]

Notions of European nihilism evolved alongside the concepts of crisis and decline. Nihilism echoed the recurring 1930s theme of the depletion of culture through atomisation, mechanisation, and the dissolution of values, but it was rooted in German philosophy of the early nineteenth century, and had spread throughout Europe. The concept was used to describe Russian revolutionaries as well as the dissolution of religion and Christian dogmas, symbols and morality.[80] Oscar Wilde satirically reduced nihilism to the pure will to destroy: to stab and to poison, to strangle one's own inclination towards love, 'to set father against son, and husband against wife', to leave fear, hope and future behind, in order 'to suffer, to annihilate, to revenge'.[81] One writer, the wife of a Ukrainian aristocrat, wrote after fleeing the civil war that a nihilist would destroy anything without considering what would come after.[82] Nietzsche, who was central to this discussion, referred to cultural degeneration and coined the term 'European nihilism'.[83]

The concept of nihilism was readily available to discourses of culture and society. During the First World War, several German intellectuals wrote extensively within this critical tradition. The best known was Thomas Mann, who distinguished between German culture, which was anchored in values, and French civilisation, which had no future. For him, a criticism of civilisation was also a criticism of nihilism.[84] Rudolf Pannowitz agreed with Nietzsche that the dilution of Christian and noble values had led to a crisis of all values, which in turn led to the revolution of nihilism in Europe.[85]

The interwar years saw the distinct usage of the concept of nihilism, regarded as the force behind unrestrained technology, degeneration, and other depleting dimensions of modern culture. This critique of civilisation did not regard technology as the fundamental problem, nor was it the fault of machines or the idea of progress. The modern master was nihilism, which caused degeneration and enslavement. Nihilism underpinned positivism, the denial of moral and inner values, technology without boundaries, and the separation of God from humanity. It was regarded as a European phenomenon that had spread around the globe, according to philosopher Martin Heidegger.[86] His colleague, the Heidelberg professor Karl Jaspers, related the growth of nihilism to the fact that people had been uprooted and had lost faith in an afterlife. They felt imprisoned and powerless; they were beset by the awareness that everything would perish, by constant questioning, and by an endless whirlwind of self-deception. In the spirit of Weber, Jaspers coined the term de-deification (*Entgötterung*) to describe the legacy of Protestantism and scientific thought. The result was the rationalisation and mechanisation of production and organisation, as well as the triumph of methodical thinking. Technology had squeezed its way into everyday life, making human interaction impersonal. He characterised the modern world as the era of the machine, reducing individuals to cogs. Nations and cities, factories and shops had become bureaucratic mechanisms from which one could not see beyond the present. As a result, people had lost their sense of the past and of the future. The only thing that mattered was their ability to operate the machine in the here and now.[87]

The concept of nihilism easily meshed with fascist ideology and was used by its intellectuals in describing the despised modern world with its decline and breakdown of traditional order. Julius Evola became even more committed by the end of the 1930s as he entered the inner circles of both Mussolini and leading German Nazis. He pitted the spiritual energy of 'authority, hierarchy, order, discipline and obedience' against nihilism.[88] However, during the Second World War, the idea of nihilism was often associated with the Nazi regime by its antagonists. A book with the significant title *The Revolution of Nihilism* was published in 1938 by the German émigré Hermann Rauschning, a conservative nationalist who was briefly a member of the Nazi party from 1931, but then left the party in 1934 and resigned from his post as senate president of the free state of Danzig. He fled Germany in reaction against Nazi violence, and over the following years wrote several books criticising the regime. Rauschning considered the revolution of nihilism to be the fundamental feature of National Socialism, unleashing destructive forces and disregarding moral obligations. The acts of the Nazis had revealed their lack of ethical standards and of political doctrines, and a worldview that was nothing but scenery. The only thing that mattered to them was holding onto and extending their power, and they were therefore not to be trusted. They had revolutionised German society by destroying, but without being able to build anything new; their policy was one of devastation in order to hold onto power. Rauschning concluded that Nazism offered no ethical basis for the population beyond the use of violence.[89]

From this reading of the political events in Germany and of the mind of Hitler, it is not such a leap to interpret Nazism as the outcome of nihilistic thinking: '[T]he political nihilism of the Nationalist Socialist elite is nothing more than the populist degeneration of [the thinking of] the intellectual elite thirty or forty years ago'.[90] Another exile, Karl Löwith, who was a pupil of Heidegger and terrified by his teacher's flirtation with Nazism, was even harsher: 'As the negation of existing civilization, nihilism was . . . the only real belief among truly cultured individuals at the beginning of the twentieth century. It is not simply a result of the war, but [is] on the contrary its presupposition'.[91] Löwith cited modern authors such as Mann, Proust, Joyce and Céline to exemplify writers who were only interested in depicting the nothingness of modern man, rather than envisioning how to overcome it. Rauschning and Löwith frequently referred to the nihilism of philosophy by citing figures such as Hegel, Marx and Kierkegaard, but it was Nietzsche, especially, who became the focus, as they found his nihilism to be responsible for opening the floodgates, when he declared that God was dead.[92]

Although nihilism was strongly connected to German Nazism, it was still evoked as a European phenomenon. The difference was that it had got out of hand in Germany. In this critique, nihilism grew in strength throughout Europe, eschewing all values and authorities, forcing loyalties to be reconsidered, and demanding a new beginning. 'In the beginning was the act', said Faust, and Thomas Mann later repeated this in *Dr. Faustus* (1947), his 'showdown' with National Socialism. It is obvious that Rauschning and Löwith also situated National Socialism in the nihilist context. The outcome of this could be seen as more or less pronounced pessimism, and for Löwith 'our final word is a nihilism that has become active'.[93]

The discussions of the 1920s were, as Jan Ifversen has stated, 'a major re-evaluation of all the principal themes and concepts related to "Europe" and "civilization"'.[94] However, these discussions also covered the breakthrough of the ideal of sovereign nation states – both their advantages and disadvantages, and they intensified anti-modernism. The concept of Europe promised progress and prosperity, together with claims that peaceful cooperation could prevent new wars on the continent. This was quite often the view expressed in historical presentations. It is striking, however, how close the concept of Europe was to perceptions of crisis and decline. Intellectual historian Jonathan Israel has emphasised that the idea of progress, with its forecasts of both technical and moral advance, was already much contested from the beginning of the eighteenth-century Enlightenment.[95] It does not seem far-fetched to suggest an even closer connection that has to do with the notion of conditions changing for the better. It is difficult to imagine that the improvement of the human condition would not coincide with worries that progress could stop and yield to decline.

The interwar period offered a multitude of stances towards the European crisis and decline, most of which defended claims that Europe should lead the world. Unification was proposed to shelter what Europe and its civilisation had accomplished: power, trade, prosperity and progress, culture and civilisation. In this way, unification became equated with the conservation of past achievements, much as the Congress System had been when it was introduced in 1815. Claiming to salvage Europe, ideas for unification were abundant; they were forward looking and intended to change Europe. In comparison with the Congress System, these plans advanced the idea of unification, but with a significantly broader backing from the public sphere.

Notes

1. Winter, *Sites of Memory*, 78–90.
2. Zimmern, *The New International Outlook*, 4.
3. Hathaway and Shapiro, *The Internationalists*, 288–89: 'Ten years after the war Germany was full of peace. It dripped with peace, we swam in peace, no one knew what to do with all the German peace. . . . they talked of French art. . . . They liked the English very much, and they were sorry about the war'.
4. Roth, *The Hotel Years*, 14–15.
5. Wägner, *Från Seine, Rhen och Ruhr*, 31–35, quotation from 34: 'Fullfölja vi i tanke och handling den inriktning, som vi fingo under kriget, då komma vi ofelbart att sönderslita oss själva och lägga vår vackra, underbara världsdel öde för främmande raser att ärva'. Typically enough, and like several others in the interbellum, she did not hesitate to relate European prerogatives to the concept of race.
6. A most valuable contribution to this research field is Ifversen, 'Crisis of European Civilization', who stated that in 'Europe the intellectual response to the First World War was a heightened sense of crisis' (14).
7. Reijnen and Rensen, 'Introduction: European Encounters'.
8. Clavin, 'Introduction: Conceptualising Internationalism'.
9. Graham, *Europe – Whither Bound?*, 11.
10. Ibid., 31, 56.
11. Boehm, *Europea irredenta*, 4–5, 312–15, see also 235: 'Soll Europa sich in diesem sinnlosen Grenzkampf aller gegen alle nicht völlig verzehren, so werden in letzter Stunde Formen kontinentaler, raumpolitisch gesunder Neugliederung gefunden werden müssen, in denen sich der kleine unbeschadet seiner völkischen Eigenart und Selbstverwaltung in die gefolgschaft des grösseren Nachbarn begeben und gemeinsam mit ihm nötigenfalls die vereinte Kraft gegen den wirklichen Feind richten kann' [If Europe is not to be completely consumed in this senseless border struggle of all against all, forms of continental, spatially healthy reorganization will have to be found in the last hour, in which the small neighbour, without prejudice to its folkish individuality and self-government, will follow the larger neighbour and, together if need be, he can turn this combined strength against the real enemy].
12. Spann, *Der wahre Staat*, 101–2.
13. Wägner, *Från Seine, Rhen och Ruhr*, 116–17: 'En engelsk herre till en engelsk dam efter åhörandet av ett föredrag: Var det inte en gripande vädjan? / Damen: Jo. Men jag tycker förstås som min man att man egentligen inte skulle hjälpa ryssarna. Det är bara bra att den rasen förminskas, den är fridsstöraren i Europa. / Han: Men tycker ni egentligen, att ryssarna är

värre än till exempel balkanfolken? / Hon: Nej, jag vet egentligen inte, vad skall vi med balkanfolken att göra i Europa. / Han: I så fall måste jag säga att det är ingen mening, om vi skall göra rent i Europa, i att låta tyskarna vara kvar. / Hon: Tyskarna, ja. Dem hade jag glömt. Det vore naturligtvis en välsignelse om vi kunde utrota även dem. / Han: Men säg mig då, vad är det för egenskap hos engelsmännen, som gör vårt folk så framstående och värt att leva framför andra? / Hon: Vi är så mänskliga'.

14. Carls, *Stephen D. Carls*, 99, 150–53.
15. Krüger, 'European Ideology and European Reality'.
16. Reported by Wägner, *Från Seine, Rhen och Ruhr*, 31–32.
17. Keynes, *Economic Consequences of the Peace*, 3–8, 226.
18. Angell, *The Peace Treaty*, 99.
19. Ibid., 93.
20. Louis, *Le bouleversement mondial*, 1–30, 149–52.
21. The Demangeon quotation is from Clout, 'Albert Demangeon, 1872–1940', 9. See also Demangeon's *Le déclin de L'Europe*, in the English translation *America and the Race for World Domination*.
22. Delaisi, *Les Deux Europes*, 9.
23. Herriot, *Europe*, 9–17.
24. Kellersohn, *Contre un cataclysme économique*; Benda, *Discourse à la nation européenne*, 203–4.
25. Valéry, 'Crisis of the Mind'.
26. Nitti, *The Wreck of Europe*.
27. Nitti, *Peaceless Europe*, quotations from page xiii.
28. Blum, *Trümmerfeld Europa*, 138–41.
29. Briffault, *Breakdown*, 88; Briffault, *Decline of the British Empire*.
30. Fried, *Das Ende der Kapitalismus*; Fried, *Das soziale Revolution*, 33–37.
31. Wolff, 'Apolitía in Julius Evola'.
32. Guénon, *Crisis of the Modern World*, 82–88.
33. Schweitzer, *Civilization and Ethics*, 1–10, quotation from 10.
34. Belloc, *Crisis of Our Civilization*, 4.
35. Guénon, *Crisis of the Modern World*; Belloc, *Crisis of Our Civilization*, 194, 217.
36. Webb and Webb, *Decay of Capitalist Civilisation*.
37. Nearing, *Where Is Civilization Going?*, 77–94.
38. Mayreder, *Geschlecht und Cultur*, 5–25; Wägner, *Väckarklocka*. Both notions of civilisation are skilfully presented by Katarina Leppänen in *Elin Wägner's Alarm Clock*.
39. Wells, *The Salvaging of Civilization*, 2, 20–26, 44, 68–73.
40. Nitti, *Peaceless Europe*.
41. Heile, *Nationalstaat und Völkerbund*, 24–25.
42. Herriot, *Europe*, 51–55.
43. Coudenhove-Kalergi, *Revolution durch Technik*, 11–12.
44. Coudenhove-Kalergi, *Krise der Weltanschauung*, 8, 18–36.
45. Coudenhove-Kalergi, *Revolution durch Technik*, 40–80. The idea of technology as a unifying force is also mentioned by Stefan Zweig in a lecture from 1932; see Zweig, *Messages from a Lost World*, 107–10.
46. Coudenhove-Kalergi, *Revolution durch Technik*, 25–30.
47. Valéry, 'Crisis of the Mind'.
48. Quoted from Gray, *The Imperative of Modernity*, v, 6.
49. Bonn, *Die Krisis der europäischen Demokratie*; Laski, *Democracy in Crisis*; Madariaga, *Anarchy and Hierarchy*; Wells, *After Democracy*, quotation from 242.
50. Rappard, *The Crisis of Democracy*, 266.
51. Ortega y Gasset, *The Revolt of the Masses*, 132.

52. Mann, 'Appell an die Vernunft'.
53. Huizinga, *I morgondagens skugga*, 9–10.
54. Ibid., 7–10, 102–4, 131–45.
55. Ortega y Gasset, *The Revolt of the Masses*, 134–35.
56. Mann, 'Appell an die Vernunft', 92.
57. Ortega y Gasset, *The Revolt of the Masses*, 107–14.
58. Ibid., 115–24, quotation from 120.
59. Ibid., 134–35.
60. Mann, 'Appell an die Vernunft', 87.
61. Ortega y Gasset, *The Revolt of the Masses*, 75, 134.
62. Mann, 'Appell an die Vernunft', 103–6.
63. Ortega y Gasset, *The Revolt of the Masses*, 139.
64. Ibid., 145–50, 179–86.
65. Duhamel, *Mon Europe*, 9–19.
66. Simmel, 'Der Krieg und geistigen Entscheidungen', 168f.
67. Valéry, 'European Man'; Patočka, 'European Culture'.
68. Benda, *Discours à la nation Européenne*, 5–10, 41, 60.
69. Ibid., 25, 67–68, 106, 113–14.
70. Gusejnova, 'Noble Continent?'
71. Hofmannsthal, *Gesammelte Werke*, 43–54, 454–56; Evola, 'Über die geistigen voraussetzungen'.
72. Cattani, 'Europe as a Nation?'
73. Richard, 'Huizinga, Intellectual Cooperation'; quotation of Gilbert Murray cited by Richard on 246.
74. Guénon, *Crisis of Modern World*, 82–88, quotation from 83.
75. Fischer, *Über die Zukunft*.
76. Heidegger, 'Europa und die deutsche Philosophie'.
77. Husserl, *Krisis der europäischen Wissenschaften*, 1–4.
78. See the groundbreaking dissertation by Källgren, 'Subjectivity from Exile'; also published as a book: Källgren, *Zambrano's Ontology of Exile*.
79. Gingerich, 'European Frenzy', 206–7.
80. See, e.g., Guyau, *L'irréligion del'avenir*, 82–99.
81. Wilde, *Vera or the Nihilists*, 19.
82. Jarosynska, *Ett minnesrikt år*.
83. Burch, 'On Nietzsche's "European Nihilism"'.
84. Mann, *Betrachtungen eines Unpolitischen*, 102–3.
85. Pannwitz, *Krisis der europaeischen Kultur*, 64–70, 191, 217, 247. Austrian intellectuals such as Stefan Zweig and Hugo von Hofmannsthal applauded Pannwitz; see Vermeiren, 'Pannwitz and the Idea of Europe', 136–37.
86. Heidegger, *Nietzsche: Europäischer Nihilismus*, 2–16.
87. Jaspers, *Die geistige Situation der Zeit*, 5–31.
88. Wolff, 'Apolitía in Julius Evola', 258–73.
89. Rauschning, *Die Revolution des Nihilismus*.
90. Ibid., 111–12.
91. Löwith, 'European Nihilism', 197.
92. Rauschning, *Die Revolution des Nihilismus*, 111–12; Löwith, 'European Nihilism', 197–208.
93. Löwith, 'European Nihilism', 193.
94. Ifversen, 'Crisis of European Civilization'.
95. Israel, *A Revolution of the Mind*.

CHAPTER 7

Organising for Europe

During the late interwar period, quite a few novels were published representing ideas of European unification.[1] In the 1935 novel *Europa*, the British anthropologist and author Robert Briffault offered three suggestions for establishing European unity. The first was to look to the past and the Roman Catholic Church to find values around which people could unite. This option went further, actually organising Europe into one society. In the eyes of Briffault's Catholic cardinal, Christendom was the essence of Europe:

> The unescapable tradition of the European world, that world which has been carved out of the Roman Empire, is the tradition of Christendom. Do what it will, the spirit of Europe cannot escape from its source. The waters are carried through changing landscapes, but they remain the same. They are unchanging, unless European civilisation should be wiped out. . . . Of that tradition out of which the European mind has grown, the Roman Church, catholic and apostolic, is the guardian.[2]

One character in the novel, a German professor, repudiated both Christian traditions and nationalism, calling for new values:

> The disaster, which reduced Europe to a stupefied continent, similar to the stupefied countries of Catholic peasants of today . . . was renewed by the fatal monk, Luther, who not only restored the Roman Church, but what was a thousand times worse, restored Christianity at the very moment it was lying prostrate. Europe has thus been robbed of all intelligence and meaning. . . . Crazed by the neurosis called Nationalism and the paltry politics that go with it, European man has before him the gigantic task of transvaluating the values handed over to him by degenerate Christianised Rome. Not until that task shall have been accomplished will he be able to begin to be civilised, to surpass himself.[3]

Notes for this section begin on page 220.

A third view was represented by Briffault's main character, who expressed a longing for European countries to form one community, where it would be difficult to tell whether people were natives or foreigners, where there were no passports as European life had become international, where the idea of killing one another was absurd, and 'the age of wars among civilised people was past'.[4]

In Chapter 6, we read about the desire to return to tradition and to reformulate shared values. In some instances, this desire led to pleas for a shared economic and political organisation of Europe. In this chapter, we will focus on attempts to form a European society beyond economic and political borders, and how such efforts also apply divisions.

Based on the earlier chapters, we understand that the European idea took up themes such as peace, weakness, and threats from outside Europe. We can also state that the European idea could be related to conservative, liberal and socialist political ideologies alike. From the previous chapter we learned that the interwar concept of Europe was charged with notions of far-reaching crisis, decline and nihilism, as well as with the perception of a radical and destructive division of the continent into independent nation states, and that European unification was often declared the solution. The interbellum idea of European unity in some ways revisited and reinforced themes from the previous century such as peace, free trade, Europe's place in the world, and both political and cultural unity. In this chapter, we will explore how the idea of European unity stood in relation to political ideologies of the interwar period, and what happened to it during the Second World War. We will focus on Europe as practice, bringing forward calls, plans and initiatives to create a European federation from the 1920s up to 1945. Several of these plans proved influential for postwar integration, partly by inspiring key politicians and partly by offering some of the cornerstones of European thought for public consideration. These initiatives included the creation of various organisations to launch the European idea. Here we come to a significant aspect of the history of the European idea in the 1920s: Europeanists organising themselves in the interest of creating a federation. Various organisations and networks were instituted and maintained to present Europe as both a unifying and a dividing concept.

First, we will look at pamphlets and books. Second, we will turn to organisations that had unification as their main mission, especially to the Pan-European League, whose ideas can be found in their journal, *Pan-Europa*. Third, we will demonstrate how wartime visions of European unification were tied to national interests of domination as well as freedom.

A Pan-European Discussion

After the collapse of the Habsburg, Russian and Ottoman empires, Europe had more borders than ever before. Sovereignty was claimed by more nations, and multiplying. This paradoxically hollowed out the content of sovereignty, because, more than larger ones, smaller states needed trade, communication, and many other kinds of exchange with other countries. All European states were weakened after the Great War. Three mighty empires had collapsed, and even though France and Great Britain stood strong with large possessions, it was only because of the American intervention that the war had been won. In the eyes of contemporaries, it was obvious that the age of European world power had ended.[5] It was not much of a surprise, then, that considerable attention was paid to the European idea. After the Great War, dreams of a united Europe were very much alive – Perry Anderson, for example, claims to have found over six hundred contemporary publications that mentioned a united Europe.[6] Relevant books, articles and speeches were widely circulated, cited and translated into other languages, ultimately contributing to a vigorous pan-European discussion.

Among other proponents of European unification were a Russian socialist who fled the Bolshevik Revolution and became a German social democrat,[7] a French socialist and pacifist who may have coined the expression 'Europe must unite or die',[8] an Italian industrialist who was the founder of Fiat,[9] an Italian writer and monarchy-minded marquise who, in an acclaimed novel, combined free trade with free love,[10] an Italian writer and fascist who feared that both American and Russian values threatened the European mind,[11] and the leader of the exiled Italian anti-fascists Carlo Sforza, who thought that the nineteenth-century nationalities 'were only a step toward a wider European ideal', while twentieth-century nationalism had 'the traits of a religious movement'.[12] Then there was the French economist who flirted with fascism and was impressed by Hitler,[13] and a Spanish philosopher who looked for a grander project than the nationalisms that had reached and passed their zenith. Now it was only the notion of European unity that could bring about a new mission for Europeans and uphold their spirit of expansion.[14] There was also the British statesman and lord who had learned from his efforts to reorganise the British Empire,[15] and a British scholar and conservative-minded baron who pleaded without enthusiasm for the formation of a possible league of European nations. He said, 'in France, in Germany, in Spain, in Czechoslovakia, the evidence as regards not only public opinion, but also official opinion, is overwhelming for something called "The United States of Europe". Strong, however, as is the feeling behind such a conception, it is difficult to obtain any clear and precise definition of it'.[16] Indeed, the difficulties in defining such a union were plain to see. For some, Great Britain, including all its colonies, was considered part of Europe, while others considered it a union unto itself. Russia was sometimes seen as a possible future member state, but that was difficult for most observers to imagine. Some wanted states founded by Europeans and occupied by European nations to join in a common federation, including, for example, the United States as well as the countries of South America.

Triggered by a determination to avoid new wars and by the Wilsonian declaration of a new international order, new initiatives took hold among intellectuals to establish transnational exchange. There was 'no doubt', intellectual historians Carlos Reijnen and Marleen Rensen have claimed, 'of the great extent to which the intellectual scene of interwar Europe crossed national boundaries', with many new initiatives emerging to defend and increase international cooperation in an era of proliferating borders.[17] The intellectual scene encompassed artistic movements, literary conferences, and cultural events. Many intellectuals took action to organise transnationally. Romain Rolland led the organisation Pour L'Internationale de l'Esprit from France, the PEN Club was founded, and Henri Barbusse initiated Clarté with its periodical and subgroups in many countries. T.S. Eliot published *The Criterion* and Albert Crémieux *Europe*, literary journals that were important for translating and introducing foreign authors to English and French publics, with the aim of transcending national borders. Research has described a cultural internationalism intended to foster understanding across national borders, including both bodies such as the League of Nations' Organisation of Intellectual Cooperation and amorphous activities such as the International Studies Conferences and the Council of Intellectual Workers. Two renowned conferences were 'L'avenir de la culture' in Madrid, 3–7 May 1933, and 'L'avenir de l'esprit européen' in Paris, 16–18 October 1933.[18] Carlos Reijnen and Marleen Rensen have argued plausibly for a strong connection between transnational intellectual exchange, the understanding of Europe, and the European idea.[19]

In addition, peace activists linked pacifism with the European idea. As we saw in Chapter 1, pacifists had already pursued the idea of a European federation before the war, and after the war the quest for peace had become more important than ever, in order to strengthen the European idea.[20] The early 1920s saw an increase in peace activism marked by large demonstrations against new wars and by the establishment of many new groups. The range of peace organisations was broad and included communists, right-wing groups, feminists, republicans, and religious groups. Many intellectuals joined committees, and contributed to journals such as the one published by the Carnegie Endowment for International Peace. These groups were local and national, but many were also part of a transnational network organising exchange visits and participation in international peace meetings and congresses. An international structure emerged, starting with the International Peace Bureau in 1891, which continued its activities alongside the Women's International League for Peace and Freedom, founded in 1915. There were newcomers such as War Resisters' International founded in 1921, the Joint Peace Council founded in 1930, several Christian organisations, and the institutional body of the Peace Pledge Campaign, which succeeded in persuading hundreds of thousands of signatories to promise not to take part in any new war. Not least were the French and German groups that undertook exchanges in an effort to decrease the risk of new wars, reluctantly at the beginning and then more frequently, with visits, speaker tours and youth exchanges.[21]

The cultural unity of Europe was often highlighted in these ventures, for example, in the short-lived journal *Det nye Europa* (A New Europe) where well-known figures from Scandinavia and Germany asserted the need for a European culture and for cooperation across borders, urging all sensible Europeans to unite. The notion of a coherent European culture continued to be seen as an attractive alternative to international conflict.[22]

Leading philosophers and authors from European countries turned to the subject of cultural unity. The historian Christopher Dawson identified a cultural unity nearly a thousand years old that he prioritised over the nationalities: 'The ultimate foundation of our culture is not the national state, but the European unity'; it was important to 'develop a common European consciousness and a sense of its historic and organic unity'.[23] The Baltic German philosopher Hermann Graf von Keyserling criticised the self-presumption of contemporary nationalism that concealed that the European nations were only variations of a larger community with a single spirit at its heart. He predicted that Europeans would increasingly identify as belonging to one culture as they became more aware of their differences from both Americans and Russians. In European culture he found a spirit of individuality that emphasised individual initiatives and responsibility, resisted Russian and Soviet collectivism that left no room for the individual, and resisted America, where the individual was replaced with sameness and the 'tyranny of the majority'. For Keyserling, Europe represented the light in a dark age to come, and the hope for humankind. Thanks to their Christian heritage, Europeans possessed the ability to think logically and behave ethically, beyond all others, as proven by Europe's impressive history of scientific breakthroughs.[24] Although Europe had lost its economic power and would therefore lose its material head start, it was ahead of the rest of the world in terms of culture, spirit and psychology.

Stefan Zweig bowed down to Nietzsche, worshipping him as a prophet who had warned of nationalism and seen its dangers of egocentrism, brutality and particularism. In place of nationalists, supranational Europeans were urged to step forward.[25] In a speech given in Florence in 1932, Zweig gave a full account of the key role played by European culture, recognising its unifying heritage passed down via the ancient Romans and the Roman Catholic Church, and by the European spirit developed by the Renaissance humanists, a spirit longing for unity. He identified a shared European way of thinking, a shared European feeling, as well as shared experiences starting in the early nineteenth century. He believed that 'Europe uniformly lives, think, feels and experiences specific conditions', which could be best expressed by philosophers, poets and novelists. He concluded his speech by telling of the paradox of contemporary Europe, where nationalism and protectionism were stronger than ever, while the consciousness of a shared economic and political destiny also remained salient. His message was that the European nations should stand united if they wished to lead the world in the future, as they had in the past, especially during the eighteenth and nineteenth centuries. Another part of his message was not to turn to economics or politics for examples of, or the legitimisation for, European unification, but rather to look to the intellectuals and the world of learning and culture.[26]

Zweig focused on nationalism as opposed to European cultural unity. For others, the plea for European unification also related to cultural divides, emphasising the national soil of culture, in a Herderian way, and that all great artistic achievements had national roots. A gap between culture and the economy was thereby hinted at. On the one hand, the call for cultural diversity prioritised qualities that made nations somehow unique, while on the other, the call for economic unity nurtured a degree of standardisation across national borders. One needed national cultural achievements, but to do away with borders one needed economic unity. For pan-Europeanists this was not necessarily a problem. Rather, Bronislaw Huberman saw this as an opportunity, as he claimed that what made nations unique would be able to flourish even more without economic borders.[27] For Keyserling, intellectual exchange was essential to cultural achievement: the high culture of one country was always the result of influences from abroad, as exemplified by the influx of Russian intellectuals to France, the number of well-known Englishmen with some Irish or Scottish blood in their veins, and the many intellectuals around Europe who had some Jewish ancestry.[28]

Even with the issue defined in this way, one should bear in mind that transnational connections and encounters did not always transcend cultural borders. The opposite was also seen, as the transnationalism of the interbellum period had the nation as its point of departure. In many cases, the international conferences and gatherings held in the name of European unity turned out to be sites of national contestation. Many intellectuals defended their own nations and the idea, Patricia Clavin has recently argued, was not to go beyond national borders, but to exchange among and learn about national cultures. In a recent article, Geert Somson has pointed out some truly internationalist proclamations made by scientists, but he sees them as exceptions and shows that the scientific community was not as keen on international cooperation during the interwar period. The Treaty of Versailles excluded German scientists from international fora, and the practices and requirements of the scientific work of, for example, chemists were marked by 'cognitive fragmentation'. This created a fundamental ambiguity. On the one hand, the national ideal was held up as superior to the universal, while on the other, intellectuals such as Huizinga, Valéry, Keyserling and Zweig, who all took part in intellectual exchange across national borders, advocated forming a community of the mind and of intellectuals, that would transcend political and national belligerence and set the path for the future of Europe.

Economic and Political Arguments for European Unity

The role played by America in the formation of European unity has been largely forgotten. Even before and during the Great War, the Pan-American Union had attracted considerable attention as an example to follow in gradually removing the incentives for warfare by entering into close cooperation in key areas. In the late 1920s, this model was once again recognised. All of the American republics were represented in the Washington-headquartered union, which dealt with their relations and facilitated and promoted economic, cultural and scientific exchange. The union organised congresses where controversial issues were on the agenda, and established arbitration procedures. Both Alfred Fried and the former French prime minister Édouard Herriot said that, although the focus was on economic and social but not political cooperation, the Union had, since its beginning in 1889, fostered trust and a spirit of peaceful conflict resolution. Herriot concluded that the pan-American model should be followed in the European attempt to set up a union, with regularly held conferences – a permanent organisation that could prepare meetings, as well as special bureaus that could implement decisions.[29]

When the post-Great War depression set in, Europe's economic borders became further stressed. It was at this time, if not before, that the calls for unity and forming a federation became calls for a free market and free trade. The tariff systems were considered a disadvantage for the competitiveness of European industry and, outside the government, some economists and businessmen formed groups to promote further customs unions. A cartel was formed in 1926 by steel producers from Germany, France, Belgium and Luxembourg to regulate excess production capacity. Émile

Mayrisch, director of the Luxembourg steel group ARBED, promoted understanding between France and Germany, and succeeded in involving the governments in the cartel negotiations. This cartel encouraged the idea of unity and was seen as a step towards further cooperation. If production and markets could be rationally managed, this could lead to the realisation of European unity.[30]

Calls for European cooperation were made by ministries of the main European powers. These calls included the German foreign policy of Walther Rathenau and Gustav Stresemann, who strongly favoured cooperation with Germany's neighbours, and were affirmed by the French governments of Édouard Herriot and Aristide Briand.[31] In the British governments, the calls echoed, although they were not embraced, as the unification of the British Empire was preferred.[32] The Italian prime minister Francesco Nitti was zealous for a European version of the United States that could dismantle European borders. He saw this as the only way to bring peace and renewed welfare to war-torn Europe.[33]

The idea of political unification had an interwar peak in the second half of the 1920s. It was possible to detect growing interest among socialists who took a stand against rising nationalism – 'Splitternationalismus' should be met with 'Kontinentalpolitik', according to a German socialist magazine. The socialists pleaded for closer cooperation between France and Germany, to build unity through wide-ranging cultural and economic entanglements between European nations and realise the possibility that a European federation could create an orderly and prosperous economy.[34] Political leaders publicly supported the European idea. French prime minister Édouard Herriot gave a speech in 1925 calling for a United States of Europe; British colonial secretary Leo Amery professed to a Berlin daily his belief that the borders of Europe could be dismantled and that a European federation could be created; and German foreign minister Gustav Stresemann said in a speech that he hoped for a United States of Europe.[35] In the transition from the 1920s to the 1930s, prospects for unification were taking shape, and rapid and successful negotiations were being anticipated. In September 1929, an intergovernmental conference on the unification of Europe was held with France and Germany as main participants. The French prime minister Aristide Briand, leading the Republican-Socialist Party, and Gustav Stresemann, from the liberal–conservative German People's Party, both pleaded for the cause in inaugural speeches.[36] A conference with the express purpose of beginning the process of forming a union by reducing trade tariffs was held in February and March 1930, with twenty-six European governments represented. The results were meagre, although the convention declared itself one of the first steps towards economic cooperation in Europe.[37] In May 1930, Briand and the French government circulated an appeal to the

European governments to organise a European federation/union. In this case, the focus was instead on political unification. The suggestion was to begin by cooperating more closely politically; only when the political federation was established would the nations then move on to economic unification. In this way, weak nations could continue to have the means to protect themselves, and it would be possible to build trust. In a second step, the federation would eventually move forward with measures to eliminate tariffs and other trade barriers.

Interestingly, it is possible to read Briand's memorandum from the conference as an answer to the discussions of crisis and decline, lack of shared morality, and the quest for viable values. The beginning of the first paragraph states the necessity of a treaty that would facilitate the *moral* union of Europe, confirming solidarity among its members. It ends by calling for governments to be responsible and take action 'for the good of the European community and humankind'.[38] Briand's draft stressed the need for solidarity and stability in times of danger. He hinted at the shared culture and the racial affinity of the European nations. The inclusion of morality, culture and race in this political document illustrates the entanglement of the European idea with many other aspects of the concept of Europe.

The proposal endeavoured to adapt to the international order established after the war. Under no circumstances should the union threaten the states' independence. It was to operate within the League of Nations – that is, to include only European countries that were members of the league (thus excluding Russia), following its framework for resolving international disputes and holding meetings during the league's sessions in Geneva. Although the proposal was indeed bold, it had weaknesses in mostly appealing to the goodwill of governments and limiting itself to being an extension of the nineteenth-century Congress System applied to the framework of the League of Nations.

Overall, the proposal received only half-hearted support. Neither the reviews in newspapers and periodicals nor the responses from Europe's governments were overwhelmingly positive. However, the initiative was widely discussed and met with some support, including promotion by French and German committees and adoption in Austrian and Scandinavian initiatives. A further government conference in Geneva was held in September. The leader of a large German company argued for extensive economic unification at a meeting of the German Industry Federation.[39] In Britain, the proposal was supported by Norman Angell in *Foreign Affairs* and John Maynard Keynes in *The Nation*, among others. However, the draft was eventually rejected, and when the United Kingdom voiced its objections it was politically dead. Briand himself announced his resignation as prime minister only a few months afterwards.[40]

For a short period in the late 1920s and early 1930s, the idea of economic cooperation as the salvation of Europe was discussed, often in combination with pleas for a United States of Europe, and frequently expanded outside Europe to include European colonies. Plans that incorporated the joint exploitation of Africa were frequently discussed, for instance, by advocates of the Pan-European League, and were launched by politicians from the colonial powers, including Germany and Italy, which had lost their own colonies as a result of the Great War. For a period, these plans were an issue on the political agenda and the subject of diplomacy. Related political initiatives were undertaken and networks were established, especially between France and Germany. It was argued that such a joint Eurafrican project could not only solve the economic crisis, but also unite Europe. This colonising project engendered a feeling of optimism amidst the ongoing economic crisis. At the Great Colonial Exposition that took place in Paris in 1931, general commissioner Hubert Lyautey advocated a new Holy Alliance of the colonial powers 'for the greater moral and material benefit of all'. The project was even on the agenda of French–German deliberations in 1936–37.[41]

Still, the pleas for economic measures remained largely focused on Europe and the potential of a continent-wide home market. In a 1930 speech delivered in Cologne and Barcelona, American engineer Dannie Heineman suggested that Europe would need to face the crisis using the common pillars of economic life, which included not only free competition and a common financial and banking system, but also permanent collaboration in transport and communication. Referring to how trade had fostered unity and wealth in the United States, he concluded that 'it is internal trade that cements political unity', and recommended building more roads in rural Central Europe, in particular. Heineman, as an engineer, claimed science and technology to be among the main factors that could bridge the industrial and agrarian divides of Europe. By establishing networks of communication, internal trade would increase, and electricity, the new form of energy, would benefit peasants in Eastern and Southern Europe. Overall, this would provide a solid basis for the federation that he saw as essential to Europe.[42]

Heineman was not the only one to invest hope in hands-on measures of technology and engineering. In the early 1930s, large-scale projects were proposed to address the economic crisis, inspired by Briand's initiative for a European federation. The committee of inquiry that was set up invited proposals for furthering the idea, and the International Labour Office (ILO) suggested a radical extension of infrastructure that could help to overcome divisions and mistrust. Large-scale public works would not only create jobs, but also foster a pan-European spirit. The ILO director, Albert Thomas, suggested developing waterways, electricity transmission lines, railways and especially motorways that could connect the capitals, particularly of the Central and

West European countries. Networks were set up and congresses were held with the sole purpose of gathering road planners to discuss inter-European motorways.[43] Inspired by Thomas, a retired Italian diplomat, Carlo Enrico Barduzzi, projected a huge railway venture that could connect the different parts of the continent. Europe would immediately prosper from building these railways, as it would employ millions of workers and, in the longer term, the improved transportation and communication links between the agricultural and industrial parts of Europe would create a new unity. Barduzzi argued that railways from the north to the south and from the east to the west would make Europe more prosperous and peaceful, nurture solidarity among Europeans, further economic cooperation, and support political unity. They could also bring the colonies closer to Europe, as the plan included one route extending from Paris to Istanbul, via tunnels below the Adriatic Sea and the Bosporus, and then on to New Delhi, and all the way to Saigon in French Indochina; another route would start in Lisbon and end in Odessa; and a third would extend from Antwerp to Africa, via a tunnel from Gibraltar. This grandiose draft proposal failed to gain approval from either Italian officials or international leaders, and very few major railways were built in Europe during these years. However, in addition to Baruzzi's draft, there were many other plans and proposals for railways intended to bring Central European or Latin countries closer together.[44] In Germany, the architect Herman Sörgel drafted ambitious plans to lower the Mediterranean by building dams across the Strait of Gibraltar and the Dardanelles in order to create more land and better opportunities to make inroads into the African continent. This macro-technological project was fascinating to the public, and papers reported on it across the globe. It set the stage for films and for several novels, sometimes supported by Sörgel himself.[45] Both the economic argument and the macro-technological projects became closely intertwined with the European idea and, in the case of Sörgel, with the idea of Eurafrica. These projects drew on the perception of a Europe in decline, contested from both the West and the East. Sörgel saw the threat arising from 'the probable combination of the three Americas, on the one hand, and the yellow peril that arises from the racial antipathy of India, China and Japan, on the other'.[46] As Michael Odijie has pointed out, the rumours of a 'yellow peril' eventually found their way into the European unification discourse of the interbellum.[47]

European Movements: Organising for the Sake of Unification

Contemporary observers understood that the League of Nations would not acquire the authority necessary to evoke mutual trust among the European states, and that it exhibited 'a preference for regional agreements'.[48] Mistrust of its aim to marry the cosmopolitanism of the pre-war era to the notion of national sovereignty grew when aggressive nationalism began its advance. Even though the league presented a theoretical universalism and initiated sub-bodies with the aim of enhancing cultural exchange and cross-border understanding, it remained preferential towards national cultures, celebrating national art and folkloristic traditions. Indeed, it 'never took a precise stand against the disgraces of dictatorships', Annamaria Ducci has written.[49] Moreover, the internationalism of the League of Nations was hampered in another way. It had been created by European states and used the means of European diplomacy. The languages of the organisation were English and French. The staff was dominated by West Europeans and, more precisely, by white West European men. In a study of the league's employees, Klaas Dykmann has stressed their internationalism as expressing a 'vision of international co-operation guided by a national compass', and a European understanding of international order.[50] Ducci has remarked that the league always focused on the problems of Europe, as the guidelines for its cultural initiatives were all European. This was true of many of its initiatives regarding transnational exchange, which, in reality, were largely oriented towards Europe in service of European interests.[51] This constrained internationalism is well illustrated by one of the league's more successful organisations, called the Fédération Internationale des Unions Intellectualles in French, while its German name, Europäischer Kulturbund, indicated that its focus was on European cooperation.[52]

It was not at all clear how Europeanists should be able to recognise internationalism. For some, the unification of Europe was a sub-target on the journey towards the final objective of unifying all humankind. They found it necessary to begin with a European federation, as the national and economic conflicts on this continent were a threat to world peace.[53] Others saw the European idea as opposed to internationalism, in accordance with criticism of the emerging international order of the League of Nations. In such cases, intellectual ties to nationalism from radical right-wing groups were frequent, as we will see in the following section. Here it was clear that Europeanists represented a dividing line within the European idea, between full-blooded Eurocentrism and an internationalism that extended beyond Europe's national borders.

In the 1920s, Europeanists began to set up organisations with the aim of expanding the sense of European unity. Some aimed for economic cooperation and others for cultural exchange, some avoided politics while others reached out to politicians. French–German antipathies were high on the agenda, and improving relations between citizens and their leaders was another key issue. The heyday of these networks was the late 1920s, following the success of the Locarno Treaty of 1925, but set against the uncertainties and struggles of the economic crisis and the rising nationalism of the early 1930s.[54] Without going into detail about the organisations that promoted such ideas, we note that there were many of them: there were nationally confined groups – like Vereeniging ter Bevordering van de oprichting der Vereenigde Staaten van Europa and Bloc d'Action Européenne – that promoted European cooperation in the Netherlands and Belgium;[55] there was also the Union Young Europe, the Institute of European Economy, and a body for European Cooperation called the Comité Fédéral de Coopération Européenne.

Some of these groups were mainly smokescreens for nationalist interests. Among the more influential was the Verband für europäischen Verständigung/Fédération pour l'Entente Europeenne, run primarily by Wilhelm Heile. He had worked closely with Friedrich Naumann, and held views of German superiority; his call for a European federation was a way to further national interests and keep the ambitions of a German-led 'Mitteleuropa' alive.[56] Some were mainly interested in free trade and common markets in Europe. Initially, we found such ambitions in the Mitteleuropäische Wirtschaftstagung, a free-trade movement that was wary of German domination. The initiative attracted mainly businessmen and politicians from the post-Habsburg states, but also included representatives from France and Great Britain. They opted for improved economic cooperation and discussed the need for a Danube federation that might include France.[57] In a similar appeal, the Comité international d'Union Douanière Europeenne/ Europäische Zollverein urged all Europeans to support a shared customs union without impairing national cultures or sovereignty. This organisation was set up by a transnational group of economists and politicians from Great Britain, France, Germany, and other countries, and managed to establish groups in more than seven additional countries.[58]

Focusing on cultural exchange and unity, the Austrian-Bohemian aristocrat Karl Anton Rohan initiated the Féderation Internationale des Unions Intellectuels/Europäische Kulturbund and its journal *Europäische Revue* in 1922. It attracted conservative thinkers such as Hugo von Hofmannsthal, Carl Schmitt and Paul Valéry. Individuals joined from the Baltic states to Portugal, and established main offices in Austria, France, Germany and Italy – more than fifty local branches in all. Rohan himself was the editor of the journal *Europäische Revue*, which had a circulation of 2,500. Yearly congresses gathered three hundred members who discussed economic and cultural exchanges, while political issues were banned. Rohan's aim was to gather the spiritual aristocracy of Europe in a venture to overcome divisions of the European mind. Inspired by Nietzsche, Rohan found himself in a new era that was replacing the nineteenth century with its scientific rationalism and materialism. He declared nationalism to be a necessity that did much good, but also said that it demanded a synthesis called Europe. Communication, trade, industrial cooperation, and rationalisation were forces that made territorial state borders obsolete. Because of this, he demanded organic thinking and organised a new aristocratic elite in order to advance a future-oriented spirit of shared European culture that was essential to unification.

From the outset, Rohan and the organisation espoused conservative standpoints and had ties to conservative and Catholic reformist movements.[59] Through the 1920s, the organisation radicalised towards the right, rejected liberalism, parliamentary democracy, internationalism, pacifism, and Briand's memorandum, and declared itself antagonistic towards that most important of Europeanist organisations, the Pan-European League. Rohan saw the future of Europe in the ideas of Italian fascism and in its successful rejection of the results of the French Revolution. Clearly, there were significant differences between Rohan's conservatism and German National Socialism. Still, the organisation collapsed after a series of internal conflicts and the Nazi takeover in Germany. He published the journal for another decade with support from the German regime, soon becoming a member of the Nazi party and declaring that his movement was closely tied to Nazism.[60] Well in line with Nazi ideology, he stated that Europe, European culture, and the white race, which were all destined to rule the world, had been subsumed under the banner of American and communist colonialising.[61]

Pierre Viénot founded the Comité franco-allemand d'information et de documentation/Deutsch-Französische Studienkomitee in 1925, with support from Émile Mayrisch, the owner and head of a large Luxembourgian steel concern. The group's programme was to organise talks and personal meetings between both French and German elites, including industrialists, bankers, university professors, and higher officials. Through its bureau in Berlin, it spread news and information about France, while its Paris bureau did the same regarding Germany. The main goal was to deconstruct what Viénot considered false images and the main reasons for the antipathy of the elites and the public towards each other. There were personal ties between Viénot's and Rohan's organisations, with overlapping memberships, and Viénot taking part in Kulturbund activities. From the beginning, Viénot partly shared Rohan's conservatism, although he never approved of Italian fascism. Although Viénot's committee clearly attracted more elites with nationalist and conservative leanings, it also appealed to liberal minds. These elites had a common understanding of European cooperation as something that could yield national advantages. When the 1920s gave way to the 1930s, the committee followed the lead of Rohan's Kulturbund and took more conservative and radical-right stands, while Viénot himself drifted into socialist views and finally left.[62]

The organisation 'A New Europe' introduced a companion journal *The New Europe* in 1924; the introduction to the first issue, written by the Dane C.F. Heerfordt, addressed the management of a future European federation. He managed to encourage intellectuals, politicians and industrialists to form national committees for the cause, and one hundred prominent Scandinavians declared their support for him. A letter that had been circulated among the representatives of various governments was used by Heerfordt to further international interest in a 'Federation of European Nations', which could guarantee a member state's security both internally and vis-à-vis foreign enemies, and facilitate economic cooperation. Heerfordt's more concrete suggestions concerned disarmament, the establishment of a federal court to resolve conflicts between the member states, a shared parliament with the member states represented in order of importance in the union, and a shared government to handle defence, foreign affairs, and financial and customs administration. Financial and customs administration would be especially appropriate to start with. Heerfordt later concentrated on obtaining French support. In appeals from 1928, Heerfordt tried to convince the French minister of foreign affairs, Aristide Briand, that it was high time for France to take political responsibility. Soon he would be heeded.[63]

It is true that many of those involved were active in more than one organisation. It is also true that there was rivalry both within these organisations and between them, as they bickered among themselves. Wilhelm Heile wanted his Verband für europäischen Verständigung to be a mass movement, just as did the leader of the Pan-European Union, Coudenhove-Kalergi. They each wanted their organisation to be the true representative of the European movement, so they sought to discredit each other.[64] Historian Guido Müller, who has specialised in the networks of the interwar period, concludes rightly that aristocrats with a conservative ideology exerted a remarkable influence on these organisations. These aristocrats were, together with intellectuals and artists, looking for ways to avoid new wars in a Europe they regarded as contested by America and Russia. Their organisations were elite groups that distrusted mass movements, and they viewed democracy with a great deal of scepticism. Müller concluded that the conservative Europeanists of the 1920s sympathised with the anti-liberal, authoritarian and fascist notions in the making in Europe. They supported tolerance and cultural understanding, but they put their trust in elite accomplishments rather than in a democratic notion of Europe.[65] Rohan and his organisation's turn towards the radical right illustrates the dividing line between those nationalists who took internationalism to be their enemy and those affiliated with international cooperation and integration. In the interwar period, the former might have called for a unity of Europe that was cultural and also included ideas of closer economic and political cooperation, but that opposed the multilateralism of the League of Nations. Moreover, the detailed research of Müller shows how, in their early years, these organisations attracted minds with different ideologies: Rohan's Kulturbund and Viénot's Studienkomitee initially comprised socialists and liberals, whereas by 1930, both had been 'cleansed' and become exclusively radical-right organisations.

Pan-Europe

The group with the most outreach activities and most influence was the lobbying organisation for a European federation founded by the Czech count Richard von Coudenhove-Kalergi, who first presented his plans in 1923. His argument was clear-cut: the new Europe that emerged after the war was anarchic in its logic, with many independent nations whose conflicts constituted a latent state of war. The alternative was to bring most of Europe together. While the European states were all busy building separate economies and investing in armies of their own, states in other parts of the world were cooperating with their neighbours. The key was thus cooperation. He became inspired by the Pan-American Union, and he named his movement Pan-Europe: 'There is still time to save Europe from this destiny. The salvation is Pan-Europe: the political and economic merger of all states from Poland to Portugal into one federation'.[66]

Once again, and significant to this period in particular, we see the claim that political unification was founded on belief in a shared cultural heritage, mainly drawing upon Christianity but mixed with a dose of individualism and rational thinking from Greek antiquity. The claim utilises the notions of reason and will: it is rational to unite, but the Europeans would have to want to do so. Coudenhove-Kalergi espoused Europe's vigour; while other cultures had declined, the Europeans had been victorious around the globe, to such a degree that Japan, Persia, Turkey, Egypt, and others were now following its example.[67]

It was typical that this call for European unity included warnings of new threats after the catastrophe of the Great War, of divisions between the European states, of the Soviet Union on Europe's eastern border, and of the rise of Bolshevism and anti-individualism in Central and Western Europe. Both Eurocentrism and colonialism were seen as playing significant roles when he declared European culture to be superior, as it had risen to world domination. It had surpassed all other cultures and was the culture of the white race. The colonies were presented as integral to the pan-European project, as objects of mutual perpetuation because they supplied Europe with raw materials.[68]

His unconcealed racism is also significant. Although the interwar period had seen many attempts to distinguish between different European races,[69] some continued to cling to the idea of a common white race, as Coudenhove-Kalergi did. For someone who considered it rational to look upon Europe as one nation, and the existing nation states as only a historical step on the road to the European nation, it was also necessary to defend the idea that all these Europeans belonged to one single race, giving rise to a common culture. Still, cultural divergences were used in the pan-European movement to support calls for unity. The United States of America was contrasted with the shattered states of Europe. America was an offspring of European culture. Due to its successful unification, the United States was now the strongest power in the world, dominating its own continent and challenging European dominance elsewhere. Asia had a culture of its own, from which Europeans could learn about ethics. Asia showed how to attain harmony and individual self-control, even though Asia lacked the energy and dynamic force of Europe. Coudenhove-Kalergi also compared Europe with Africa, from which he believed nothing could be learned. It was solely a continent of resources, an open field for plundering, which Europe urgently needed to exploit. Europe was urged to continue to embrace its global mission, using its energy to spread its technical proficiency, bring richness, and make the world a better place in which to live.[70]

He nevertheless concentrated on the development of European unification, and claimed that the peoples and states should be joined together in Pan-Europe, in defiance of chauvinism, communism, militarism, and protective tariffs. A broad and mutual patriotism among Europeans was seen as replacing nationalism. Coudenhove-Kalergi's programme declared that the time of small states and national states was over, that partnerships between states and people were to be forged. The British, Russian and Chinese kingdoms were cited as examples, alongside the Pan-American counterpart he considered under construction. If there was to be a future Europe, then it would have to be Pan-Europe, including neither Britain nor Russia, according to Coudenhove-Kalergi. Britain was large enough on its own, and his criterion for excluding Russia was its strong Asian Mongol heritage, while European culture included Christianity and the historical tradition extending back to Classical antiquity. Europe's was a rational and scientific culture; it had Christian ideas of community blended with individualism, which was not part of Russian culture.[71] He perpetuated the long-standing Western discourse that excluded Russia from Europe as Asian, or as not quite European enough.

His movement was not without success. It never did become the mass movement that its founder had hoped for, but it gained respect from intellectuals, statesmen and politicians all over Europe. He collaborated with

Heinrich Mann, who argued in 1927 that 'Pan-Europe was in the beginning the dream of a few intellectuals, but is now not far from being the practical goal of businessmen and politicians'.[72] Among the intellectual supporters were Mann's brother Thomas and nephew Klaus, Albert Einstein, Stefan Zweig, José Ortega y Gasset, Salvador de Madariaga, Fritjof Nansen, Selma Lagerlöf, Bernard Shaw and Paul Valéry. The government in Austria, led by Ignaz Seipel, made premises available for the movement in the Hofburg, the former Austrian imperial palace. Both the German foreign minister Gustav Stresemann, and the young mayor of Cologne, Konrad Adenauer, who as federal chancellor of West Germany after the Second World War took part in establishing the European Steel and Coal Community, were to attend the Pan-European League congresses. The president of Czechoslovakia Edvard Beneš, Winston Churchill, and the British colonial secretary Leo Amery were also in attendance. Among the French who had pledged their support was the young Maurice Schumann as well as the two former prime ministers, Édouard Herriot and Aristide Briand.[73] Coudenhove-Kalergi's efforts to gain provisions included engaging leading bankers and industrialists who offered financial support, underlining the elitist image of the movement.[74]

Coudenhove-Kalergi began ambitiously publishing the book *Paneuropa* in 1923, writing that it was destined to set the stage for a movement supporting a new Europe. Through the awakening of the European peoples, the political pressure for unification would become irresistible.[75] Unification was considered a necessity, he wrote in the first edition of the journal *Zeitschrift Pan-Europa*, which he initiated in 1924: 'The European issue is this: Is it possible for 25 states on the small European peninsula to live together in international anarchy, without this ending in a horrible political, economic, and cultural catastrophe?'[76] Instead of anarchy, he stressed rationality, which was a key notion for Coudenhove-Kalergi: the international and economic orders should favour planned action and cooperation – for example, building continent-wide communication systems. At times, he argued that Europe should be or become one nation, but the model he and others in the Union preferred featured a division between economics, on the one hand, and politics, on the other. The idea of unification was often spoken of in connection with economic matters, particularly the expansion of international trade, as well as with political autonomy.[77]

The model for European cooperation would initially need to be that of the American states and the Pan-American conferences. Then it would be time for a European arbitration court, even more far-reaching treaties, and a common defence to reinforce Europe's eastern borders against the Russian threat. Only after that could economic borders be relaxed in favour of a free market and a common currency. The creation of a federation based on a constitution would finally happen. Not much was actually said about the governmental and administrative bodies or the constitution, beyond equal rights for all European languages within the union.[78]

To begin with, only Coudenhove-Kalergi wrote articles for the journal, but after a year, he began to write with a collaborator and included articles by other authors. Still, the journal was always very much the product of its editor. He stated his views on contemporary political issues, and connected them to the pressing need for European unification. He wrote an open letter to the National Assembly in Paris urging the French to see that they shared their destiny with the Germans and should strive for closer cooperation – republicans, socialists and pacifists should all form an alliance with their German counterparts. If France wanted to remain a world leader, then it would have to allow Germany to be great as well.[79] He hailed the peace movement and delivered a speech at the World Peace Congress in Berlin in 1924.[80] He criticised German nationalism for not seeing things from a European perspective, arguing that this could lead to new disasters, for both Germany and the rest of Europe.[81] He wrote an open letter to the General Secretariat of the League of Nations to argue for its decentralisation into continental blocs that could drive the creation of a European federation. Decentralisation would also make it more attractive for both the Americans and Soviets to join, the former as the leading nation of Pan-America, and the latter as it would be recognised as a separate part of the league. Both China and Japan would be recognised as separate blocs as Britain was, while Africa, Australia and parts of Asia would be included within Britain or Pan-Europe.[82]

He made suggestions for moving forward. A new convention would create a European commission for passports, removing the constraints of visas and establishing a body to which citizens could apply for a passport valid in all member states. A common anthem would be a further visible manifestation of European unity.[83] Coudenhove-Kalergi's comments and analysis always returned to the idea of a pan-European federation as a solution, often presented with enthusiastic praise for the new Europe. The same could be said of other articles from the journal. Julius Wolf, one of the main Austrian propagators of 'Mitteleuropa', declared Pan-Europe to be a good idea that ought to attract increased support. Vilma Kopp wrote that the movement was opening women's eyes to the importance of the European spirit, and she encouraged women to give it their support. Only Pan-Europe could offer the things that women were longing for – namely, peace, hope for the economy, and a spiritual basis for the struggle against social misery; therefore, Pan-Europe was their destiny.[84] Salvador de Madariaga, the Spanish diplomat and scholar, praised the richness of the European spirit and its potency in creating value in art, science and politics – the unifying of Europe was the method to perpetuate this spirit.[85]

Coudenhove-Kalergi apparently had both energy and charisma. Every now and then he was lauded for his vision and achievements in moving the organisation forward, and a young poet even paid him homage with a poem.[86] National committees were established in Belgium, Bulgaria, Denmark, Estonia, Finland, France, Hungary, Latvia, Lithuania, the Netherlands, Norway, Poland, Rumania and Switzerland,[87] each with some members of prominence. In a small country such as Estonia, the committee included more than two hundred members from academia, industry and politics. Estonian dailies published over a dozen of Coudenhove-Kalergi's articles. Leaflets were translated, and one of them, *Paneuropa ABC*, was disseminated free of charge. Estonian newspapers paid significant attention to the pan-European programme in a number of articles over the years.[88] Pan-European student groups formed in Austria, Czechoslovakia, Germany, Hungary and Switzerland.[89] By the end of 1926, the journal prided itself on having offices in fourteen countries and being published in English, French, German, Czech and Greek. It advertised its activities in various countries, reviewed new books on Europe and European affairs, and featured articles by a range of authors.[90] Coudenhove-Kalergi could indeed claim success.

Over the years, Coudenhove-Kalergi made fervent efforts to mobilise politicians. He wrote letters to hundreds of publicists, premiers and ministers, professors and authors in Germany, France and Central Europe to ask whether they believed that a United States of Europe was necessary or even possible. Answers of various lengths were submitted, overwhelmingly positive, and all were published in his journal. He listed the political leaders who had declared themselves in support of the pan-European movement.[91]

In this respect, the first congress of the Pan-European Union was a huge triumph. Held in Vienna in October 1926 with two thousand participants, it included official representations from the League of Nations, Austria, Belgium, Finland, France and Greece, as well as official greetings from the Czech president Tomáš Masaryk, the German and Danish prime ministers, the French minister of war, and the British colonial secretary. The Hungarian philosopher and communist party member, Georg Lukács, gave an inaugural speech. Altogether, there were speakers from twenty-seven European states. This range of participation bore witness to the movement's strong appeal to statesmen from the main continental powers, as well as from the minor ones. The former Estonian prime minister C.R. Pusta, who saw European unity as safeguarding the future well-being, existence, and cultural development of small states, said that 'small states find an echo of solidarity in the idea of Pan-Europe'.[92]

What an event it was, renewing hopes of overcoming divides and of establishing a path to peace. Contentious issues were the threats of a new war, minority rights, and which countries to include in an upcoming federation and European parliament. The session on the economy opened with a critique of the nation state organisation of the industrial sector, which had led to more expensive production, trade hindrances, higher living expenses, and colonial conflicts. The basic idea was clear: the European nations would need to respect one another's political independence at the same time as they transcended economic borders, preferably by creating a common trade area with a single currency.[93] In the session on culture, speakers espoused a common European spirit, either to be fostered by better educating Europe's younger generation or to be found in science or among the great Europeans of the past.[94]

On the wall outside the main venue hung large portraits: Immanuel Kant, the author of the tract on eternal peace; Napoleon, because of his strong pleas for unification; Nietzsche, who rejected small states; Jan Amos Komensky, who espoused universal education; and Abbé St. Pierre, Giuseppe Mazzini and Victor Hugo, who all supported the formation of a European federation.[95] Coudenhove-Kalergi himself assigned considerable importance to a shared cultural history. The portraits also showed that the European heritage was French and German in origin, although complemented with a Czech (who could be considered German as well) and an Italian. Moreover, the portraits illustrated the male character of the movement and the journal. The conference did discuss the importance of women to Pan-Europe, and Anita Augsburg emphasised that it was easy for women to think about and act in accordance with European unity: 'Pan-Europe is nothing alien, new . . . [women are] used to thinking and feeling internationally, to seeing the world as a whole and humankind as a unity'.[96] Still, only three women spoke at the conference. When Vilma Kopp wrote that peace was a task for women, she was one of very few women who had been published in the journal.[97]

Coudenhove-Kalergi wanted to appeal to as many groups as possible, and argued that the idea of Pan-Europe stood above political parties. This entailed not taking a stand against fascism when democracy was in peril in the early 1930s. In an article from May 1933, Coudenhove-Kalergi wrote that 'Pan-Europe is neutral in the struggle between democracy and fascism' and that 'the Pan-European movement is neither fascistic nor anti-fascistic, neither democratic nor anti-democratic'. Moreover, he added that his philosophy of governance 'never was democratic but aristocratic'. He did not support parliamentarianism, and maintained that personalities made a difference in history: strong leaders were expected to unify Europe, winning the people's support for that goal.[98] He attempted to involve Mussolini in his movement in 1923, published an article by him in 1934, and met him as late as 1936.[99] These were not just signs of poor political judgement, but were the outcome of his fundamental political beliefs.

By 1933 the pan-European movement was waning, and so was political and public interest in both European unification and international cooperation within the League of Nations. *Pan-Europe* was publishing many fewer notifications of meetings and events in the sections on various countries. Declarations of official support and recognition were still mentioned at the conferences, but the momentum had faltered. Some of the journal's writers opposed democracy, such as Kurt Hiller, who leaned to the extreme left, and Julius Evola, who supported fascism, at the same time as other writers had ceased appearing. Once again, the content was mostly Coudenhove-Kalergi presenting his own views. His response to the political events of the day was to unify Europe, the same as always.[100]

Coudenhove-Kalergi's programme was greatly debated. Even though leading politicians supported it, the programme was never adopted by the states, with the exception of Briand's government. Some saw it as competing with the League of Nations, although Coudenhove-Kalergi denied this. In large states, the programme was seen as threatening those with grander ambitions; in small states, it was seen as offering security and peaceful cooperation, while threatening economic independence and cultural development.[101] The Pan-European League was accused of being snobbish, and indeed it was an elitist movement driven by the energy of a single person. Its leadership was autocratic and did not allow autonomous initiatives from the sections, leading to internal tension.[102] Given Coudenhove-Kalergi's heroic style of writing, it comes as no surprise that he was compared to Oswald Spengler and other representatives of the so-called conservative revolution of the era. He belonged to a group of nobles who clung to the European idea espoused by Dina Gusejnova, who also highlighted his role as an 'aristocratic radical'.[103] Clearly, Coudenhove-Kalergi did not represent a democratic worldview. In texts written before he began to promote the pan-European ideal, he dismissed the idea of universal suffrage and the parliamentary system; moreover, he espoused a neo-aristocratic principle, in which only the cultivated and wise were destined to rule.[104]

The pan-European concept and Coudenhove-Kalergi continue to fascinate scholars. In the literature, we find overly positive representations of the movement, its leader, and its core ideas. The more critical research downplays the significance and meaning of the pan-European programme for present-day European integration, solely because of Coudenhove-Kalergi's undemocratic ideas. Ulrich Wyrwa has emphasised his disregard for the harm Europe has caused throughout history, concluding that Pan-Europe is 'only possible to understand in the context of the interwar period, and that it is hardly possible to make connections to the contemporary intellectual and political debate on Europe's present and future'.¹⁰⁵ In Coudenhove-Kalergi we meet a representative of a conservatism that has difficulty accepting democracy. Still, we know that socialists such as Kurt Hiller, Georg Lukács and Heinrich Mann supported him, as did the French socialist Aristide Briand, the Austrian social democrat Karl Renner, and the German social democrat Vladimir Woytinsky. In 1930, Woytinsky's book was published by Pan-Europa Verlag, in which he gave much credit to Coudenhove-Kalergi.¹⁰⁶ We also know that Coudenhove-Kalergi gained support from liberals such as Édouard Herriot, Salvador de Madariaga and José Ortega y Gassett, as well as from the national liberals Edvard Beneš and Tomáš Masaryk. Clearly, different political ideologies were represented among his supporters; not all of them supported democracy, but most remained democrats throughout the interbellum. Konrad Adenauer and Bruno Kreisky, two young supporters of Coudenhove-Kalergi's movement, became trustworthy post-war democratic leaders of the West German and Austrian republics while upholding the ideals of European unification. It should also be noted that his movement was condemned by German and Italian nationalists.

However, Coudenhove-Kalergi has long been criticised for his reactionary viewpoints and for building an undemocratic organisation that was both fascist and imperialistic.¹⁰⁷ Indeed, democracy was questioned within the Pan-European League during the congress proceedings of 1926. We can read that the issue of democracy was raised and then criticised by Kurt Hiller as something that could only work among an aristocratic elite, but that in a parliamentary system it only led to squabbling among political parties. The president of the session immediately countered that Pan-Europe would only become a reality through democratic means by the governance of the people.¹⁰⁸ The pan-European movement apparently involved itself in arguments about democracy, and there are good reasons to agree with Wyrwa that Coudenhove-Kalergi and his organisation were closely connected to specific political and ideological contexts. Although one should definitely be critical of Coudenhove-Kalergi's failure to dissociate himself from fascism, his importance should not be underestimated. Wyrwa cites research showing a sharp juncture in European history with the European cooperation that began at the end of the Second World War. However, this view fosters blindness to historical tradition and to the developments and even innovations that occurred regarding European integration during the interwar period. Anita Prettenthaler-Ziegerhofer has rightly stressed Coudenhove-Kalergi's significant contribution in taking the idea of unification to the governmental level.¹⁰⁹

A War for the Sake of European Unity

Let us consider the European idea during the war. One might imagine that the outbreak of the Second World War would have effectively erased any inclination to unify Europe, by simply making it impossible or at least very unlikely ever to happen. But this was not the case, although changing conditions had to be accommodated. Few advocated a united Europe during the First World War, and those who did were outsiders, mainly scholars and intellectuals who denounced war. This was not so during the Second World War, however, when calls for European unity were widespread, even among statesmen. The design of a 'New Europe' was on the agenda, one that would be the result of the war. Would it be dominated by one state or organised as a union of equal partners? Should it consist of independent nation states, of partial federations (the Balkans, Central Europe, the Mediterranean, Scandinavia, Western Europe), or constitute only one unitary federation? There was talk of Europe's rebirth, reconstruction, and new beginning. Scholars of law proposed the transfer of certain rights from national sovereignty to common institutions and a higher authority. The discourse comprised political manifestos and constitutional drafts, continuing to rely on economic arguments, the conviction of a common culture, and the seriousness of the task. Many of the relevant texts were written in a strictly factual manner.[110] However, Thomas Mann's widely disseminated radio address of 29 January 1943 stands out in contrast for its remarkable rhetorical strength, and its introduction is well worth quoting. Mann endorsed the idea of unification, illustrating its broad ideological appeal as the alternative to the brutality of nationalism.

> European listeners! I speak to you as one of you; as a German who has always considered himself a European, who knew your countries and cultures, and who was deeply convinced that the political and economic conditions of Europe were outdated; this division into arbitrary border States and sovereignties that has brought about the misfortunes of the Continent. To me, and to those like me, the idea of European unity was dear and precious; it was something natural to our thought and will. It was the opposite of provincial narrowness, petty egotism, nationalist brutality and boorishness; it meant freedom, spaciousness, spirit and kindness.

In Britain, the long tradition of hesitance to join a European community is well documented.[111] In 1940, H.G. Wells declared that he belonged to 'the great English-speaking community' stretching from Asia to America, where he would take offence if called a foreigner. He found the thought of following 'the flag of my Austrian-Japanese friend [i.e. Coudenhove-Kalergi] into a federally bunched-up Europe' extremely unattractive.[112] Despite such sentiments, a sense of Europeanness blossomed when war broke out – some say more than ever before or since. Soon after war was declared, Arnold Toynbee suggested a union between France and Great Britain, and Labour leader Clement Atlee exclaimed that a new international order was bound to endow an 'international authority superior to the individual states' and that 'Europe must federate or perish', triggering more radical socialists both inside and outside the party to take a stand for the socialist unification of Europe.[113] Beginning in February 1940, British and French civil servants started to devise plans for a union between the countries – notably involving both Jean Monnet and Arthur Salter, who would play significant roles in the post-war making of the European Community. As France was about to collapse in the summer of 1940, Winston Churchill conveyed the eagerness to keep France involved in the war by promising British citizenship to all Frenchmen, and declaring France and Britain to be one union with shared institutions.[114] The main forum for the Europeanists was the Federal Union, which had branches all over Britain where politicians and civil servants met journalists and academics. Initially, there was remarkable activity at the union, including meetings, conferences and publications.[115] When war aims were discussed, European unification was often emphasised as an alternative to the failures of the League of Nations. Rather than trying to embrace the whole world, it was deemed better to build a European federation with a democratic foundation strong enough to withstand the United States and the Soviet Union.[116] In addition, there was great interest in proposals for an Atlantic Union with the United States and a union of democratic states proposed by the American journalist Clarence K. Streit just before the war began. There was also emerging interest in a universal confederation of all the world's nations, which some regarded as inspiring the framework for the European federation.[117]

As before, intellectuals presented various political visions of European unification. Hilde Meisel's idea for the post-war world was a socialist European unity:

> European Unity – this demand is vital for political and economic, and, one might say, for moral reasons. Politically it appears to be the only practicable method of achieving security for the peoples of Europe. Economically, it opens the avenues for a beneficial co-operation that could not possibly be so close and so safe if it were subject to the changing policies of a multitude of sovereign governments. And the moral reason is that the price paid by millions in two world wars imposes the obligation on those who survive, to insist on achieving a peace which is more than a temporary makeshift for the period between the end of this and the beginning of the next world war.[118]

Hilde Meisel, who wrote under the pseudonym Hilda Monte, is not included in the narratives of the European idea, but should be remembered as an important Europeanist at a crucial historical moment. One can easily cite three reasons for her exclusion: she died before the post-war endeavours of the European movement began and political initiatives took off; she was a woman, while history has almost always recognised only men; and her ideology was not only socialist and social democratic but also Marxist, so it did not fit well with the anti-communist notions that prevailed after the war. Yet, she represented the European idea, and her place in its history should be acknowledged.

Born into a Jewish family in Vienna in 1914, Meisel grew up in Berlin and lived in exile from 1933. She undertook several secret missions to Germany and later Nazi-occupied Europe on behalf of exiled resistance groups and the British intelligence service. She attended the London School of Economics and wrote many articles on economics, working as a journalist for the socialist and labour press. On 7 April 1945, she was shot dead at the Liechtenstein border while escaping from a secret mission in Austria. Hilde Meisel was not unique in taking a socialist approach to Europe's unification. In April 1942, groups from six countries met in London and drafted a resolution in favour of a post-war European unity that abstained from national sovereignty and the international order of power blocs, in favour of a political federation and economic unity based on a socialist organisation of the economy and social life, avoiding subjugation to the United States or the Soviet Union.[119] Of the socialist approaches to unity during the war, the plan presented in Meisel's 1943 book, *The Unity of Europe*, was the most extensive and overall one of the most developed of this period.

Like so many other proposals for European unity in the twentieth century, Meisel's used the common argument against smallness: 'all nations of Europe are too narrow to achieve economic prosperity, [or] a rational system of communications'. To this she added the argument that shared economic and foreign affairs policies would not 'reduce the variety of . . . cultural life', but rather the opposite: they might intensify it 'by establishing closer relations between different national cultures'.[120] However, smallness was not the only problem. Regarding the assessment made by Francis Delaisie in the late 1920s, she stressed the economic gap between industrialised and agrarian parts of Europe, and the need for their close collaboration: the eastern regions were in need of economic progress, which could open up new markets for Western industry. Like other economists, she emphasised the importance of bringing Europe together, invoking a notion that would shape post-war political language when she demanded the 'economic integration of Europe'. Together with smallness came 'the changing policies of a multitude of sovereign governments' that threatened the security of the peoples of Europe.[121] She reiterated the moral obligation to insist on a lasting peace after the price millions of people had paid during two world wars. We will see these arguments repeated in various ways during the late 1940s.

Obviously, Meisel's socialist pleas for a common European plan that removed class privileges, the shackles of poverty, and social insecurity bore a Marxist stamp, featuring notions such as monopoly capitalism and the exploitation of the masses. However, her socialism came with a cautious rejection of the Soviet Union, which she regarded as a totalitarian state to be excluded from any future unified Europe. She wanted economic planning, but not coercion, socialist rule with individual and political liberties that offered greater opportunities to the individual for 'shaping his life, developing his capacities, choosing his profession and assisting in the progress of the community'.[122] Hers was a socialism that adhered to a set of common ideals vital to the post-war concept of European unification. This is especially apparent when we consider how she imagined the organisation of a European federation, emphasising that the advantage of self-governance was that 'people determine their own affairs' through their local authorities, and that a central authority would manage joint economic enterprises in transport, airlines, postal services, and the like. One might say that she was more forward thinking when she imagined a central police force and a European investment board. She definitely kept to her socialist convictions when it came to the need for a central authority to regulate labour and social services, and the need to strive for a more equitable distribution of income and consumption. However, it is worth noting that these demands were at odds with the conclusion of general progressivism, that it would take 'a considerable span of time before wage standards and social policy [are] approximately the same all over Europe'.[123]

Inter-war fascism in Austria, Germany and Italy was strongly predisposed to nationalism, in terms of both the rhetoric of special national cultures/races and political measures. Nevertheless, nation-state borders were transgressed by transnational networks and visions of a new Europe.[124] Mussolini associated European unity with a new fascist society, both of which were needed to resist the moral and cultural threat of American capitalism and Russian bolshevism. Among Italian fascists, there was no consistency as to the aims of this new society: some were traditionalists, while others looked forward to a new technological society from which a fascist Europe could emerge.[125] However, there was no doubt about the means to achieve European unity: central to the fascists' idea of creating European unity was the notion of their military might. The writer and Fascist Party member Marquis Giorgio Quartara enthusiastically declared in 1941 that the Axis powers were de facto implementing Briand's plan; whereas earlier efforts had failed, it was now thanks to the Axis that the miracle had occurred and a New Europe had been established.[126]

Consequently, this was also the central notion of the German Nazis' concept of Europe, initially quite insignificant in the official rhetoric, even though the regime embraced some Europeanists such as the Austrian Karl Anton Rohan. Hitler himself condemned the unification of European nation states, and had nothing but disdain for Coudenhove-Kalergi, as a half-breed who embraced racial diversity.[127] Yet, as Germany's forces conquered neighbouring countries, the idea of European unification played a role in German propaganda, and the linguistically useful word 'Neuropa' was willingly adopted.[128] 'The new Europe of the future will certainly bring more advantages than disadvantages to those who belong to it and benefit from it', wrote Joseph Goebbels.[129] Dutch Nazi leader Anton Mussert and the Norwegian Vidkun Quisling dreamed of a Germanic confederation in which their nations and Germany would dominate Europe: 'Europe can only unite under the protection of a leading power, and this can only be the Great German Reich, which lies at the centre of Europe', Quisling wrote, insisting that Germany needed support to achieve this goal: 'If Germany is to guarantee the unity and peace of Europe in the long term, it must rely on the superior strength of a Germanic confederation', including the Dutch and Scandinavian peoples.[130] More developed Nazi plans and arguments for European unification saw the necessity of organising Europe as a *Grossraumwirtschaft* ('large-space economy'), to include industry, agriculture and raw-material production. It would need to be designed and led by the people with the best abilities. While some of the arguments were inspired by economics and some simply repeated Nazi eugenics,[131] others invoked the unity of European artistic culture,[132] and still others identified how a sense of unity had emerged from Europe's defending itself from Asian and Islamic threats.[133] Historian Paul Herre paid homage to Adolf Hitler and gave voice to the Nazi idea of Germany's mission to shape a European order out of the variety of its peoples. Logically, there was a need to co-ordinate the manifold nations located within a limited area of the globe. In 'the new Europe', unification would be based on the consciousness of belonging to the same culture, and would aim to make continental Europe a world power equal to Britain. Repeating many of the nineteenth-century historical narratives of European civilisation, Herre continued by saying that some people had reached a higher cultural level than others, adding that the Germans were the core people of Europe.[134] Certainly, the Nazi concept of Europe was a simplified upscaling of the previous notion of a German-led 'Mitteleuropa', but additionally reiterating much of the conservative and nationalistic interwar rhetoric on Europe, propagated by Rohan, for instance.

Still, according to the fascists, their ideas and movement went beyond nation-state borders, and references to the concept of Europe served as a mobilising device for their cause.¹³⁵ For some advocates of a unified Europe, fascist rule provided the means to create a unified Europe. In occupied France, under the collaborative governance of Vichy, several politicians and intellectuals supported the idea of Neuropa. Some of them had long supported economic cooperation or even a European federation, and they saw the possibility of realising their visions in the realities of victory and defeat. The professor of law Joseph Barthélemy acceded to Briand's plan in 1930, and later joined the Vichy government. The journalist Francis Delaisie, who through his writings earned himself a reputation as an economist, was a long-standing member of the Pan-European League. He took an active part in several other organisations working towards European cooperation. In 1942, he speculated that, for the European economy to recover, it would need to side with the Nazis: on the one hand, he condemned the liberal economic system for causing crises and wars; on the other, he praised the economy of the National Socialists and all it had achieved in Germany in only a few short years.¹³⁶ This was in line with the former socialist minister Marcel Déat, who created the Nazi-influenced party Rassemblement Nationale Populaire (the National Popular Rally) in 1941. The party's policy was to create a united Europe led by Germany and France.¹³⁷

Within the resistance movement, the idea was widespread that groundwork was being laid for a new Europe. To some, the resistance movement was a forerunner of what would become a federation of nation states. In the Ventotene Manifesto from 1941, the document that launched the Movimiento Federalista Europeo, Italian adherents of the resistance had already made a future federal Europe their goal. In 1942, the French resistance movement Combat advocated a 'United States of Europe . . . on the basis of liberty, equality, fraternity, and the rule of law'. Albert Camus, who had joined the group, called for Europe to be 'the country of the spirit . . . a privileged arena where the Occident's battle with the world, with the gods and with itself has reached its peak'.¹³⁸ Taking on socialist demands for social reforms, British works on federalism, and ideas disseminated by the Federal Union, Ernesto Rossi and Altiero Spinelli considered the system of sovereign nation states to be antiquated and reactionary. Now the wish was for a United States of Europe. In 1944, a branch of the Federalist Movement was established in France. It was possible to see continuity from interwar themes of crisis and the decline of moral values, to the present strong commitment to enriching moral values and individual liberty. Members of the Federalist Movement kept to this agenda during the years immediately following the war in their articles, novels, memoirs and essays, and, according to historian James D. Wilkinson, they influenced the decolonisation, peace movement, and European integration of the 1950s. Although the influence on the 1950s integration process was weaker than Wilkinson claimed, the federal movement certainly contributed to the history of the European idea.[139] There is no doubt that the war, and the accompanying resistance movements, pushed the European idea forward.

The war should not be considered a crisis for the idea of European unification among the major states of continental Europe. Rather, it strengthened the idea, which was now deemed a necessity, and made it clear that European unity could be organised in different ways and be built on radically different foundations. From a small-state perspective, the future European order was approached slightly differently, often taking into account the possibility of cooperation among smaller nations. Several main alternatives for this future order were on the table in Europe: a United States of the World comprising all nations on all continents; a Union of Democratic States as proposed by American journalist Lionel Curtis, with the democratic states controlling the world and letting other states join the union when they became solid democracies; regional federations, especially a United Europe based on the interwar work of the League of Nations, or a Pan-Europe in line with Coudenhove-Kalergi's suggestion; and proposals for a Europe comprising several regional federations. It was this final alternative that caught on in the neutral Swedish context, evoking great interest in the idea of Nordic heritage shared by the Scandinavian countries and Finland, and in creating a Nordic defence community and even 'The United Nordic States'.[140] Swedish social scientist Alva Myrdal expressed her country's interest in establishing a stable international order, but was more resistant to joining a unified Europe. It was in the best interests of Sweden and Scandinavia to have strong ties to the United States, Canada and Britain, while Portugal and Central Europe were less important: 'a Nordic Union is a better alternative'. She denounced any kind of isolationism, whether Swedish or Scandinavian, and advocated the 'limitation of national sovereignty in favour of supranational institutions'.[141]

Apart from the Nordic Union, there were proposals for 'Dutch–Belgian Cooperation', a 'United States of the Danube', a 'Mid-European Confederation', a 'Central European Federation', and a 'Central Eastern European Federation', all of which would promote the security and welfare of small states.[142] The notion of regional federations was affirmed by exiled governments in London through Czech–Polish, Greek–Yugoslav and Belgian–Dutch agreements. Joseph Retinger, the Polish scholar, critic and socialist, was impatiently arranging meetings between state leaders exiled in London.[143] For him, the regional blocs were only the first, albeit necessary, step towards the goal of uniting Europe. Regarding other representatives of occupied Central Europe, the Czech Beneš brothers– Edvard the president, and Vojta the historian – reissued Masaryk's proposal for a Central European

Confederation. The idea was that if several small states joined, then others would follow, and in due time the different European confederations could fuse into one. They distinguished between nationhood, to be defended, and sovereignty, which should be neither upheld rigidly nor sidestepped in a hierarchy of states, because 'the Europe of tomorrow cannot tolerate any Herrenvolk rule over non-German peoples'. In addition, the Beneš brothers offered cultural and moral arguments for the mission of the smaller nations, emphasising that they 'also had an important contribution to make to the world's culture' and had a certain moral capability that histories of oppression by mightier neighbours had taught them. The Central European states would 'resume their historic mission' to defend culture and spiritual values, and to preserve peace and friendship. It was those states that could represent the interests of all mankind, that would defend the 'highest values' of civilisation.[144] In conclusion, the combination of small-state interests and federations was supported throughout the continent, often as an alternative to an all-encompassing European Union.

As every war does, the Second World War eventually ended. This time it was obvious to everyone that the former major powers of Europe could no longer claim to be world leaders, even though France and Britain insisted that they should remain great powers. France fervently sought friendship with America, which was manifested in the summer of 1945 when de Gaulle flew to Washington and gave a speech declaring that the United States was the leading world power. In May of that same year, Churchill spoke of an iron curtain descending across Europe, hiding the true state of Communist affairs from Western Europe, and consigning the countries to the east to Soviet rule. Germany was in ruins and was keenly aware of what the Nazi government's bid for world power had wrought. Its new leaders fully accepted that Germany was no longer a main European power, let alone a world power.

This was a critical juncture in thinking about Europe. Europe accepted that its global position had declined, and that the United States and the Soviet Union were now the only real world powers. 'On the morrow of the Second World War, the dwarfing of Europe is an unmistakably accomplished fact', Arnold Toynbee wrote in 1948.[145] This diminishment was underscored by the partition between Western and Eastern Europe. The threat of Bolshevism and the potential expansion of the Soviet Union to the Atlantic coast were tangible, reinforced by the Communist takeover in Czechoslovakia. This bore out Coudenhove-Kalergi's contention that the Soviet threat was the main rationale for forging the West European states into a union.[146]

Notes

1. Spiering, 'Engineering Europe'.
2. Briffault, *Europa*, 54.
3. Ibid., 13.
4. Ibid., 100.
5. Tooze, *The Deluge*, 5–6.
6. Anderson, *The New Old World*, 495.
7. Woytinsky, *Vereinigten Staaten von Europa*.
8. Riou, *L'Europe: Ma patrie*.
9. Agnelli and Caiati, *Federazione Europea*.
10. Quartara, *Gli Stati Uniti d'europé*; Passerini, *Women and Men in Love*, 27–30.
11. Evola, 'Über voraussetzungen europäischen Einheit'.
12. Sforza, *Europe and Europeans*, 302–3.
13. Jouvenel, *Vers les Etats Unis d'Europe*.
14. Ortega y Gasset, *La rebelión de las masas*, 212–47.
15. Kerr, *Pacifism is Not Enough*.
16. Salter, *The United States of Europe*, 89–90.
17. Reijnen and Rensen, 'Introduction: European Encounters'.
18. Laqua, 'Transnational Intellectual Cooperation'; Cattani, 'Europe as a Nation?'
19. Reijnen and Rensen, 'Introduction: European Encounters'.
20. See, e.g., Montfrans, 'Pacifism and the European Idea, 161.
21. Laqua, 'Reconciliation and the Post-War Order', 212–18; Ingram, *The Politics of Dissent*.
22. 'Introduktion til den danske læseverden!'
23. Dawson, *The Making of Europe*, 20–21.
24. Keyserling, *Das Spektrum Europas*, 440–44, 472–91.
25. Zweig, *The Struggle with the Daemon*, 297, 329–31.
26. Zweig, 'Der europäische Gedanken', 316.
27. Huberman, 'Mein Weg Zu Paneuropa'.
28. Keyserling, *Das Spektrum Europas*, 469–70.
29. Fried, *Europäische Wiederherstellung*, 122–23; Fried, *Pan-Amerika*; Herriot, *Europe*, 16–19, 246–58. An indication of the further spread of the American example is provided by the Swedish social democrat Palmstierna, 'Europas förenta stater'.
30. Stirk, 'Introduction: Crisis and Continuity', 13–15. See also Müller, 'France and Germany'.
31. Krüger, 'European Ideology and European Reality'.
32. Boyce, 'British Capitalism and European Unity'.
33. Nitti, *Peaceless Europe*.
34. See the following articles in *Sozialistische Monatshefte*, 1929–1930, a leading journal for reformist German socialists: Kleineibst, 'Entscheidung über Europa'; Herrmann, 'Zum Europaproblem'; Kühnert, 'Europaproblem'; Schmidt, 'Das Herz Europas'; Stössinger, 'Kontinentalpolitik Beginn der Neuzeit'; Cohen, 'Für deutsche Europapolitik' and 'Wege nach Kontinentaleuropa'; Peus, 'Politik aus weite Sicht'; Maas, 'Briands Europainitiative'; and Kranold, 'Nun erst Kontinentalpolitik!' See also Buschak, *Vereinigten Staaten von Europa*, 83–87, 153–55.
35. Amery, Herriot and Stresemann were quoted in *Zeitschrift Pan-Europa* 3(1) (1927), 35–37.
36. Reported in *Zeitschrift Pan-Europa* 5(8) (1929), 1–2.
37. Roobol, 'Aristide Briand's Plan', 32–46.
38. Briand, 'Organisation eines europäischen Bundessystems', 201: 'zum Wohl der europäischen Gemeinschaft und der Menschheit'.
39. Heilner, 'Europäische Zollunion', 11–21.

40. Coudenhove-Kalergi, *Paneuropa*, 18–25, 149–52; Briand, 'Organisation eines europäischen Bundessystems'. On Briand's memorandum, see Heater, *The Idea of European Unity*, 130–46; and Herriot, *Europe*, 83–89. Pegg, *Evolution of the European Idea*, emphasises Briand and his impact.

41. Hansen and Jonsson, *Eurafrica*, 26–31, 44–57, quotation from 55. See also Adamthwaite, *Grandeur and Misery*, 148.

42. Heineman, *Outline of a New Europe*, 35.

43. Schipper, *Driving Europe*, 83–116.

44. Anastasiadou, *Constructing Iron Europe*, 80–95.

45. Spiering, 'Engineering Europe'.

46. Sörgel, *Mittelmeer-Senkung*, 38.

47. Odijie, 'The Fear of "Yellow Peril"'.

48. Zimmern, *Europe in Convalescence*, 136.

49. Ducci, 'Europe and Artistic Patrimony'.

50. Dykmann, 'How International was the Secretariat?'

51. Ducci, 'Europe and Artistic Patrimony'.

52. Cf. Laqua, 'Reconciliation and the Post-War Order'.

53. Illustrated in Woytinsky, *Tatsachen und Zahlen Europas*, 10.

54. Müller, 'France and Germany'.

55. See Richard, 'In Search of a Suitable Europe'.

56. Conze, *Das Europa der Deutschen*, 212–13.

57. Frommelt, *Paneuropa oder Mitteleuropa*, 23–25.

58. Ibid., 18–20. The members came from Great Britain, France, Germany, Hungary, and a few other countries.

59. Müller, *Europäische Gesellschaftsbeziehungen*, 315–23.

60. Ibid., 437–56.

61. Rohan, *Schicksalsstunde Europas*, 11.

62. Müller, *Europäische Gesellschaftsbeziehungen*.

63. Heerfordt, 'Introduction'. Heerfordt published *Et nyt Europa* in 1924, which soon was available in English, French and German, and followed up with several other writings, see e.g. the telling titles *Program für die skandinavische Initiative* (1926); *Eine Hinwendung an die hiesigen Ausserordentlichen Gesandten und bevollmächtigten Minister für Belgien, Deutschland, Finland, Frankreich, Grossbritannien, Italien, die Niederlande, Polen, die Schweiz, Spanien und die Tschechoslovakei* (1926); *Adresse de l'Initiative Scandinave à monsieur Aristide Briand Ministre des Affaires étrangères de la France* (1928); *Quelques Explications et Edaircissements spécialement adressés a monsieur Aristide Briand Ministre des Affaires étrangères de la France* (1928); and *Esquisse d'un Projet Franco-Scandinave* (1929).

64. Conze, *Das Europa der Deutschen*, 214.

65. Müller, 'France and Germany', 104–8.

66. Coudenhove-Kalergi, *Paneuropa-Union*, 25: 'Noch ist es Zeit, Europa vor diesem Schicksal zu retten. Die Rettung heisst *Paneuropa*: der politische und wirtschaftliche Zusammanschluss aller Staaten von Polen bis Portugal zu einem Staatenbunde'.

67. Ibid., 32.

68. Ibid., 32, 194–95, 284–95.

69. See, e.g., Lenz, 'Die Erblichkeit der geistigen Begabung'; Günther, *Kleine Rassenkunde Europas*.

70. Coudenhove-Kalergi, *Revolution durch Technik*, 25–31; Coudenhove-Kalergi, *Paneuropa*, 61–63.

71. Coudenhove-Kalergi, *Paneuropa*, 32–33.

72. Schonfield, 'Heinrich Mann's Political Essays'; Heinrich Mann, *Sieben Jahre*, 381: 'Paneuropa war zuerst der Traum einiger Geister, ist aber jetzt nicht mehr weit davon, das praktische Ziel von Geschäftsleuten und Machtpolitikern zu werden'.

73. Gossman, 'The Idea of Europe', 260–61.
74. Prettenthaler-Ziegerhofer, 'Richard Nikolaus Coudenhove-Kalergi', 98.
75. Coudenhove-Kalergi, *Paneuropa*, 5–6; Wyrwa, 'Richard Nikolaus Graf Coudenhove-Kalergi'.
76. Coudenhove-Kalergi, 'Das Pan-Europa Program', 11: 'die europäische Frage lautet: "Ist es möglich dass auf der kleinen europäischen Halbinsel 25 Staaten in internationale Anarchie nebeneinander leben, ohne dass dieser Zustand mit einer Furchtbaren politischen, wirtschaftlichen und Kulturellen Katastrophe endet?"'
77. Delaisi, 'Europa als Wirtschaftseinheit', 6–10.
78. Coudenhove-Kalergi, 'Das Pan-Europa Program', 3–9, 17.
79. Coudenhove-Kalergi, 'Offener Brief an die französische Kammer'.
80. Coudenhove-Kalergi, 'Pazifismus'; Coudenhove-Kalergi, 'Paneuropa und der Völkerbund'.
81. Coudenhove-Kalergi in *Zeitschrift Pan-Europa* 1(7–8) (1924).
82. Coudenhove-Kalergi in *Zeitschrift Pan-Europa* 2(4) (1925), 14–16.
83. Coudenhove-Kalergi, 'Europäischer Pass'; Coudenhove-Kalergi, 'Paneuropa: Hymne'.
84. Wolf, 'Europäische Sanierung'; Kopp, 'Die Frauen und Paneuropa'.
85. Madariaga, 'Europäischer Geist'.
86. Vegesack, 'Stimmen brausen': 'Stimmen brausen. Immer näher, näher./ Unaufhaltsam dröhnt der Zukunft Schritt./ Brüder, reist die Brüder mit:/ Unter diesen Sternehimmel tritt/ Frei und Aufrecht hin: der Europäer' [Voices roar. Ever nearer, nearer./ The future roars unstoppably./ Brothers, travel with the brothers:/ Step under this starry sky/ Free and upright: the European].
87. See reports in *Zeitschrift Pan-Europa* 2(10) (1925), 22–23, and in 2(11–2) (1925), 33–34.
88. Heikkilä, 'The Prons and Cons of Paneurope'.
89. See reports in *Zeitschrift Pan-Europa* 3(5) (1926), 28–30, and 3(9–10) (1926), 29.
90. See reports in *Zeitschrift Pan-Europa* 3(3) (1926), 28, and 3(9–10) (1926), 29.
91. In 1925 his list included Herriot, Briand, Painlevé, Jouvenel, Loucheur, Thomas, Caillaux, Nitti, Marx, Loebe, Koch, Simons, Seipel, Renner, Dinghofer, Sforza, Scjaloja, Skrzynski, Masaryk, Beneš and Vandervelde. See Coudenhove-Kalergi, 'Drei Jahre Paneuropa', 21. See also *Zeitschrift Pan-Europa* 2(1–3) (1925), 2(4) (1925), and the cover to 4(9) (1927).
92. 'I. Paneuropakongress', 16.
93. Ibid., 33–35.
94. Ibid., 45–51.
95. Ibid., 7–8. For Coudenhove-Kalergi's arguments for giving prominence to Kant, Napolean and Nietzsche, see *Europa Erwacht!*, 100–101, 280.
96. 'I. Paneuropakongress', *Zeitschrift Pan-Europa* 3(13–14) (1926), 53–54: 'Paneuropa ist ihr nicht Fremdes, Neuartiges; international denken, fühlen, die Welt als sein Ganzes, die Menschheit als Einheit zu sehen, ist ihr vertraut'.
97. Kopp, 'Die Frauen und Paneuropa'.
98. Coudenhove-Kalergi, 'Paneuropa und Faszismus', 129–33.
99. As Prettenthaler-Ziegerhofer argues in the very informative and otherwise dependable article, 'Richard Nikolaus Coudenhove-Kalergi'. See also, Benito Mussolini, 'Europäischer Völkerbund'; Wyrwa, 'Richard Nikolaus Graf Coudenhove-Kalergi', 117–19; Conze, *Das Europa der Deutschen*, 220–21.
100. *Zeitschrift Pan-Europa* (1930–1934).
101. Heikkilä, 'The Prons and Cons of Paneurope'.
102. Richard, 'Huizinga, Intellectual Cooperation'.

103. Gusejnova, 'Noble Continent?'
104. Wyrwa, 'Richard Nikolaus Graf Coudenhove-Kalergi', 117–19; Conze, *Das Europa der Deutschen*, 220–21.
105. Wyrwa, 'Richard Nikolaus Graf Coudenhove-Kalergi', 121.
106. Woytinski, *Tatsachen und Zahlen Europas*. Woytinski differed from Coudenhove-Kalergi by including Britain and Russia in the European federation.
107. Frommelt, *Paneuropa oder Mitteleuropa*, 18–20.
108. 'I. Paneuropakongress', *Zeitschrift Pan-Europa*, 49.
109. Prettenthaler-Ziegerhofer, 'Richard Nikolaus Coudenhove-Kalergi', 89.
110. Lipgens, *Documents on European Integration*.
111. O'Toole, *Heroic Failure*; Spiering, *A Cultural History of Euroscepticism*.
112. Wells, *New World Order*, 103–4.
113. Beloff, *The Intellectual in Politics*, 173–99; Attlee, 'The Peace We Are Striving For', 106; Ridley, *Unite or Perish*; Ridley and Edwards, *The United Socialist States of Europe*.
114. Beloff, *The Intellectual in Politics*, 173–99.
115. Pinder, 'Federal Union 1939–41', 26–34; Heffernan, *The Meanings of Europe*, 176–8; Amyne and Pinder, *Federal Union*. See also Jens Norrby's dissertation *Visions Beyond Empire: British Federalism and Post-Imperial Britain, 1884–1949*, to be presented at Gothenburg University in 2023.
116. Cole, *War Aims*.
117. Streit, *Union Now*; Wells, *New World Order*.
118. Monte, *Unity of Europe*.
119. Lipgens, *Documents on European Integration*, vols 1–2, 671–72.
120. Monte, *Unity of Europe*, 35.
121. Ibid., 27–29, 36.
122. Ibid., 38.
123. Ibid., 139–45. Quotation 139.
124. Dafinger and Pohl, *A New Nationalist Europe*.
125. Heffernan, *Meanings of Europe*, 138–41.
126. Passerini, *Women and Men in Love*, 68.
127. Rohan, *Schicksalsstunde Europas*; Mazower, *Hitler's Empire*, 557.
128. *Europa als Lebenskampfgemeinschaft*.
129. Salewski, 'Ideas of the National Socialist'; Goebbels, 'The New Europe', 108.
130. See the documents of Anton Mussert, 'The Dutch State'; and Vidkun Quisling, 'Norway and the Germanic Task', both from 1942.
131. Daitz, 'Das europäische Sittengesetz'.
132. Hotz, 'Die Einheit Europas'.
133. Maschke, 'Die Verteidigung Europas'.
134. Herre, *Deutschland und die europäische Ordnung*, 8–12, 177–85.
135. Alcalde, 'The Transnational Consensus'.
136. Delaisi, *Die Revolution der Europäischen Wirtschaft*, 12.
137. Brender, *Collaboration in Frankreich*.
138. Montfrans, 'Europe is the Country of the Spirit', 126–28.
139. Wilkinson, *Intellectual Resistance in Europe*, 173–76, 252, 276–78; Loughlin, 'French Personalist and Federalist Movements', 197; Pinder, 'Federalism in Britain and Italy', 215–16; Spinelli and Rossi, *Ventotene Manifesto*, 75–96; Pasture, *Imagining European Unity*, 158–59, stresses the Ventotene document as a socialist manifesto.
140. Degerman, *Vägar till fred*; Waern-Bugge, *Grundvalen för världens framtid*.
141. Myrdal, 'När fredens värld planeras'.
142. See Lipgens, *Documents on European Integration*, vol. 2, 373–404, 470–75, 638–40, 644–48.

143. Pieczewski, 'Retinger's Conception of European Integration'.
144. Edvard Beneš, 'Future of the Small Nations'; Vojta Beneš, 'The Mission of Small States'.
145. Toynbee, *Civilization on Trial*, 125.
146. Coudenhove-Kalergi, *Die europäische Nation*, 15, 34.

Part III

INTEGRATION AND IDENTITY (1945–)

CHAPTER 8

Claiming European Unity and a Europe of Nations

Unsurprisingly, contemporaries considered the Second World War and its end to be crucial events. In its final year, the war was more devastating than ever, with ruthless fighting on all fronts, heavy bombing, and ongoing extermination in the concentration camps. In the spring of 1945, reports and pictures of their liberation sent shockwaves throughout not only Europe but the rest of the world. After the ceasefire, much of the continent was in ruins, millions fled in search of security, ruthless transfers of minority populations occurred across borders, and former prisoners were trying to return home. Contemporary observers had good reason to wonder whether decline and nihilism had gone so far as to cause the ultimate downfall of Europe and its culture. Added to this was the fear of a new war and the awareness of the atomic bomb, which threatened the survival of Western civilisation.[1]

European Union historiography emphasises the aftermath of the Second World War, especially the 1950s, and the conclusion of certain key politicians and bureaucrats – called the founding fathers of Europe (there were apparently no mothers of Europe in this historiography)[2] – that unification was the road to future peace and prosperity. Among them we find Winston Churchill, along with others from the six founding member states: Konrad Adenauer, Alcide de Gaspari, Jean Monnet, Robert Schuman, Paul-Henri Spaak and Altiero Spinelli. Their idea was appealing: European nation states would need to give up some degree of sovereignty in exchange for lasting peace, economic development, and prosperity benefiting everyone. Considering this narrative is valuable for understanding the political drive towards economic and political unification as a movement for unity, despite some

Notes for this section begin on page 264.

hesitance, confusion, and vested interests. However, when we consider the concept of Europe, the situation appears somewhat different. It was instead the First World War that laid the groundwork for the thinking that ultimately led to the negotiations for and finally the signing of the Treaty of Rome in 1957. The disintegration of the continental empires was crucial, as was the breakthrough of the ideal of national independence, which set aside the previous dominant idea of the evolution of social communities into ever larger units. It challenged the assumption that viable states, cultures and languages were increasing in size at the cost of smaller nations. Europe was not moving towards fewer and fewer states and nations – quite the opposite. The First World War changed the conception of Europe from being a continent of few empires to one of many nation states, leaving open the question of how best to deal with divisions and disputes.

Attempts to manage this new situation began in the 1920s, when the idea of unifying Europe became energised, as we saw in the previous chapter. After 1945, the arguments for unification were rooted in the same conceptual framework, but with some significant amendments and modifications. First, the idea of cultural unity was launched in the context of the material devastation and human suffering of six years of war. Second, these arguments entailed the development of a conception of the nation that excluded nationalism. This was not a new idea, but one that grew following the fresh insights from the war. It was important to develop the idea of a common European culture that comprised diverse national cultures. This cultural conception charged the notion of European unity with new relevance when several European countries and their citizens celebrated national freedom after years of occupation, while Austria, Italy and Germany had to find their own ways forward as post-fascist states. Third, European unity became married to the notion of integration. This concept slipped into the political language of Europeanists, and developed into a key asset for the economic and political unification process that took place in the 1950s, indicating the direction of the institutional Europeanisation of coming decades, and signifying a tension characterised thus by historian Bo Stråth: 'Long-term dreams about a federal Europe co-existed with short-term operational questions'.[3]

Our history of the beginning of post-war European unification is distinct from the massive, classical work by Walter Lipgens from 1977 to 1985. Lipgens wrote four volumes totalling more than three thousand pages that, apart from introductions and assessments, comprise a huge range of documents – daily newspaper articles, journals, books and archives on plans for a European union – covering the breadth of political ideologies in the years 1939–1950.[4] However, while he focused on the emergence of political groups and parties organised to promote European cooperation, we can also see the issue of European unity from the perspective of the transnationalism of intellectuals. While Lipgens followed the efforts to implement federalism and overcome the nation-state agenda, I am inspired by Alan Milward who, in 1992, turned much previous historical research on integration upside down by insisting that integration was actually a tool used to strengthen nation states. Milward contended that this approach was a fundamental reaction to fascism and to the suffering of most countries in Europe during the Second World War.[5] Partly in accordance with his view, this chapter considers how the concept of Europe was configured within the context of the early post-war years. The importance of this period in the formation of the cultural and political language of European integration was recently emphasised by Rosario Forlenza, who views the Christian Democrat concept of Europe as a 'process of meaning-formation' occurring in its transnational networks.[6]

Here, we assess the concept of Europe of the late 1940s and early 1950s with a focus on the idea of a shared culture, and the distinction between nation and nationalism with reference to transnational considerations. That is, we identify the entanglement of the idea of unification with the notion of borders within Europe at a time in history when both were being stressed. This chapter also outlines the basic features of the frame of mind supporting European unification, by assessing certain key junctures, and finally explores the concept of European integration itself.

'The Spirit of Europe'

In his opening address to the congress 'The Spirit of Europe', held in Geneva in September 1946, Julien Benda declared his disenchantment: Europe was itself responsible for the war; a spirit of common interests, passions and consciousness had never really been in place; and it had to be acknowledged that divisions had instead increasingly been stressed by fostering the development of nations and making them as independent as possible.[7] The Hungarian Marxist philosopher György Lukács pointed out a crisis that had begun with the French Revolution and grown in strength after the First World War – a crisis concerning democracy, the idea of progress, and the belief in reason and humanity, all of which had been disrupted by fascism. According to the British essayist and poet Stephen Spender, Europe had now realised its smallness, weakness and decline, and he argued that it was impossible to return to the pre-Second World War civilisation of richness and strength.[8] Nihilism was repeatedly mentioned during debate at the congress. Nihilistic literature might have been the cause of pre-war decay, said Benda. Nihilism had married with totalitarianism, declared the Swiss intellectual historian Jean Starobinski. The discovery of nuclear fission embodied the idea that morals had fallen into a sort of nihilistic crisis, according to the French writer Georges Bernanos. Europe had lost its self-awareness and religious faith, and did not know what to do with its nihilism, according to Karl Jaspers.[9] Apparently, the interwar themes of decline, crisis and nihilism were not only still relevant when interpreting Europe's condition, but the Second World War had even amplified them.

Still, bids for a common European spirit were also being made. 'Gentlemen, we refuse to liquidate Europe', proclaimed Bernanos at the same congress, stressing that the crisis was one faced by all of humanity, not only Europeans. The crisis could be blamed on a lack of tradition and spirit, on reducing civilisation to mere enjoyment and profit, a state that could be found all around the world.[10] Benda returned to the need to inculcate a European spirit through a common language, education on the unifying rather than dividing historical values, and European nations giving up some of their unique qualities and individuality for the sake of a common spirit.[11] The Italian writer Francesco Flora recognised European unification as a moral duty and a way for the civilisation of humanism to continue.[12]

Indeed, claims of a common European culture were evident from the end of the war. They can be interpreted either as attempts to hide differences and conflicts, or as assuming the task of overcoming the war's legacy. However, the fact is that these claims were continuously being made. Some underscored the unity of European culture based on Christianity and its influence on moral issues, art and law, just as T.S. Eliot did when he warned of its complete collapse.[13] Ortega y Gasset also defended the idea of a common culture of Europe, marked by shared customs, practices, opinions, and other common social phenomena. Still convinced of the strength and prominence of European culture, he warned that chaos could ensue if Europe was unable to recuperate from its crisis and once again set itself on top by reclaiming its historical unity and constructing a European nation on the basis of the historical proximities of its national cultures.[14] Attempts to explore possible foundations of a European culture persisted, made up of both nostalgia and utopianism, in addition to much confusion.[15]

Others issued warnings regarding specific aspects of European culture, such as Spender, who was suspicious of its nihilism. European nihilism furthered discussion of a European culture, particularly among German intellectuals. Hermann Rauschning wrote from exile in America that the end of the war meant neither that the crisis was over nor that nihilism would end. Rather, a common goal was necessary to retain the credo of society: a culture of Western ideas and principles, the legacy of antiquity and Christianity, of rationality and humanity.[16] In his contribution to the Geneva conference in 1946, Karl Jaspers responded differently, one might say more philosophically, addressing the potential for human beings to dwell within themselves and cultivate their own abilities. The alternative to nihilism was not about finding new heroes, prophets or demagogues, but rather would be found in the seemingly trivial events of everyday life, where real changes might occur. In accordance with his 'Existenzphilosophie', he included the meaning of life in his call for freedom and the ability to go beyond oneself to become something more.[17] In this period, he also presented his concept of Europe in a radio speech that was driven by a single thought: nihilism could not be allowed to take over; people should not adopt a nihilistic attitude.[18] He drew upon Christianity, Hegel and history to define Europe as a cultural entity comprising a common spirit expressed by great artists and writers, reflected by towns, monuments, and the culture they carried. Referring to Kant, he said that future European culture should be defined by a few principles, of which freedom of thought was the highest, setting the stage for the spirit of Europe. Jaspers was also careful to note that the terms and conditions of freedom were tied to the eternal flux of history and the contradictory nature of European history, situated between church and state, Catholicism and Protestantism, science and faith, and 'real world' materialism and transcendent idealism. Political freedom entailed restrictions: as the truth was diverse and shifting while science was finite, both liberty and the European enterprise would always fall short of perfection.[19]

While Jaspers was pleading for the dismantling of the colonial empires and granting independence to the nations of Africa and Asia, others lamented such measures. Parisian journalist Louise Weiss regarded this decolonisation as a stunting of Europe caused by 'Third World' nationalism and the weakness of liberal values, leaving Europe behind the United States, the Soviet Union and China. Weiss, who before the war had been an ardent internationalist who believed that decolonisation would cure the dangerous self-interest of nations, and who was critical of German suppression of national independence in Europe during the occupation, now saw the situation differently. The Europeans had brought knowledge and tried to shift the colonies away from their ignorance, despotism and feudalism. For some of them, thousands of years 'of mental evolution separate us – you and me, gentlemen and Europe in general', and they were certainly not ready to have 'our European right to vote, conquered after so many struggles and so many hard-won shifts in public and private consciousness'. The only responsible way to treat them was with paternalism: 'Practiced in many different forms, while these peoples advance step by step from one mental age to another, paternalism has given excellent results from the human point of view'.[20] By 1949, Weiss had moved politically to embrace conservatism, and she sympathised with Gaullism. Nevertheless, her idea of the West's civilising mission reflected widely held opinions from the left to the right, in France and in other parts of Europe.[21]

Connected with this paternalism was the notion of European exceptionalism, often related to claims of European universalism, but varying with different philosophical and political views. Gonzague de Reynold, a Swiss author and radical conservative activist whose political ideal was an authoritarian Christian state, defined Europe as unique, both geopolitically and culturally. Geographically, it stood out from other parts of the world because of its exceptional climate and the development of a shared civilisation with a distinct culture. Now, in disrepair and having lost its high global status, Europe needed to restore its spiritual core of Christian values. Instead of continuing the decline arising from divisive nationalism, de Reynold believed that Europe would need to understand the universal character of its Christian culture. Only Europe had accomplished universality: if Europe could not achieve peace, then the world would be lost.[22] In contrast to de Reynold, enlightenment values were represented by liberal writers on the left. Francesco Flora wanted European culture to focus on a universalistic humanism.[23] Stephen Spender pleaded for the rebirth of Europe as a universal civilisation characterised by an 'unselfish search for truth, love for the beauty, human brotherhood', against the backdrop of the impossibility of conducting war with the new atomic weapons that threatened to extinguish humanity. Europe, he proclaimed, had a unique opportunity because it had been through the most devastating war the world had ever seen; now it understood better than did any other parts of the world the urgent need to establish universal values.[24] A Catholic-inspired approach could also espouse European exceptionalism by referring to the old traditions of Western civilisation. The British economist Barbara Ward began her 1948 book on European unity with the following grandiose assertion: '[No] corner of the world – except perhaps ancient Greece – has contributed as much as Western Europe to the development and enrichment of mankind'. From Europe came the spirit of freedom with the belief in 'a moral order of right and wrong, and good and evil, which transcends every particular interest ... and is the yardstick by which they are judged'. Ward found this in Greek philosophy, Christian teachings, and medieval ideas of natural law, relating it to individual freedom of choice and responsibility, and to the notion of governments existing for their citizens, rather than the reverse.[25] For Ward, this was not a case for European universalism, but for the supremacy of its civilisation.

After a few years, optimism regarding European culture re-emerged. The concepts of European decline and crisis were interwoven with new possibilities arising from the power and beauty of Europe's culture: something new could grow or was already growing. Ortega y Gasset declared in 1949 that, despite all the lamentable death and agony, Europe had demonstrated that 'a new form of civilization is germinating in us; that therefore under the apparent catastrophes ... a new form of human existence is being born'.[26]

Salvador de Madariaga emphasised the common European spirit, as well as the privileges of some nations over others, and concluded his *Portrait of Europe* in 1952 by saying:

> From the Mediterranean, the spirit of Europe gathers to itself the divine light of Greece and Italy; from the Baltic and the North Sea, the colder and quieter light of the North; from Flanders and The Netherlands, the light of homes and families, shining with human warmth in dining rooms and kitchens – and so, rich and flavoured with its many lights of forest and cornfield, vineyard and pasture, the spirit of Europe ever more and more precise, reaches the West and branching into its three best defined peoples – of action, England, of thought, France, of passion, Spain – flows now earthless and magnetic, as through three electric points – to quicken America beyond the seas.[27]

The change was indeed remarkable. Optimism had returned, and occasionally without reservations, such as when the Swiss author Denis de Rougemont discussed the fascist and communist threats to freedom, writing that 'Europe is the great hope'.[28] Those who had previously preached of European unification found new hope. The president of the Pan-European League, Coudenhove-Kalergi, alleged that the rebirth of Europe as a nation was on the agenda, along with a new awareness that it was a community of culture and destiny. However, his nationhood was not one of blood, geography, or even of language and history, but one of a patriotism that defended values of freedom, brotherhood and chivalry. Remarkably, he averred that such nationhood was already in place.[29]

After the Second World War, the proposition of cultural unity in Europe was once again used as an argument for political unity: with cultural unity already in place, Europe should use it as the foundation on which to build a political union. This was the view of traditionalists who turned to history to support their position. From de Rougemont's perspective, Europe had existed before the nations, whose development was nothing but a backdrop to history and had to be amended by creating a super nationality within the frame of political unity; only by doing this could Europe's common culture survive.[30] He shared this view with T.S. Eliot, who saw a common European heritage in Christianity and the ancient cultures of Greece, Rome and Israel, with many shared components that constituted 'the true bond between us'. From this common ground, Eliot reasoned, diverse specific national and cultural elements had developed over the centuries, resulting in different national loyalties, but not erasing the common European tradition.[31] Parisian sociologist Raymond Aron contended that the European nations had common traditions and shared values to an extent that merited 'recognition as one and the same historical civilization'; now Europe would need to unify economically and politically, effectively melting the nation states into a larger, superior political form.[32]

The views of Guizot, Ortega y Gasset, and other nineteenth-century and interbellum intellectuals on the diversity of this shared culture were essential for post-war writers who sought to clarify Europe's new situation. They found encouragement in Ortega y Gasset's post-war declarations that Europeans had always lived simultaneously in two societies – one extensive and one narrow, one Europe and the other the nation, province, or local society.[33]

In discussing Europe, the pairing of cultural unity and diversity had different meanings, implications and motives. Ernst Jünger charged the issue of unity and diversity by following an anti-statist branch of nineteenth-century German conservatism. He called for a unity of organisation with a diversity of national cultures; he believed that Europe should also have a global empire, alongside the other major players in the world, but that it should retain its diversity. He used the expression 'unity and diversity', whereas de Rougemont spoke of 'unity in diversity'. They both contended that, despite its national cultures, Europe did possess cultural unity. Jünger pleaded for 'territorial and political unity while preserving historical diversity', distinguishing between technical achievements that applied to 'industry, commerce, communications, trade weights and measures, and defence', and the organic world of men with 'their history, their speech and race . . . their customs and habits, their art and religion', where there 'cannot be too many colours on the palette'. Jünger distinguished between the suppressing technocracy of the modern state and the freedom and diversity of national cultures. However, while the distinction had previously been drawn in criticising Bismarck's unifying of the German states and the Prussian conformity of modern life, for Jünger it made sense to have a European constitution and state that took responsibility for the technical achievements of society, while culture should be left to the diversity of the nations.[34]

As a critic from the socialist left, Jean-Paul Sartre denied that there was a cultural unity at all, adding that the national cultures were under the threat of extinction. If the continent were to unify itself, then perhaps these cultures could be saved, and he conceived of cultural unity as 'the only one capable of saving what is valid in each country's culture'. For the national cultures to survive, 'they must be integrated within the framework of one great European culture'. However, cultural unity could not survive on its own, but needed economic and political unity as well. Sartre thus believed that it was disunity that threatened Europe and its nations, including his own France, while the unifying of culture and of politics had to go hand in hand.[35]

Europeanists repeatedly described the unity and diversity of Europe, as when Salvador Madariaga addressed 'the play between unity and diversity which is typical of Europe'. Europeanists referred to the French–German cultural border, in particular. For Madariaga it signified two different spirits and ways of understanding life. In essence, this border divided a Latin way, also including Italy and Spain, from a Germanic one, also including Austria and Scandinavia. The French spirit was like a crystal, and the German like a stream. The French referred to a text as an authority conveying holy dictums that invoked differences of space, whereas for the Germans, the very same text signified the passing of time through specific historical moments. On one side of the Rhine the focus was on space, and on the other it was on time. Britain and the small nations on the banks of the Rhine shared the gifts of both, and the small nations had additional features of their own. Altogether, Madariaga concluded that the Rhine was 'the chief feature of Europe, her very backbone'.[36] His exposition was significant to the concept of Europe, and when Europeanists drew on the French–German borderlands as representing the European spirit, they were focusing on the West; behind the Iron Curtain, Central and Eastern Europe were downgraded as less important when the Rhine was identified as the central cultural border.

The Romanian professor of religion at the Sorbonne, Mircea Eliade, saw things differently and considered the Danube to be the quintessential European river. Opposing the tendency to identify European culture with the areas west of the Iron Curtain, he demonstrated that there was also significant diversity in both Central and Eastern Europe, with a variety of churches, languages, philosophies, poetries and historical influences. These cultures also belonged to the larger European culture. Eastern Europe was Europe as well, and Europe was unified by its cultural exchanges with the Middle East and the unifying role played by Christianity, and supported by its defence against Islam.[37] Thus, the focus on Western Europe was contested. However, both definitions of Europe rested on the notion of a common enemy, either communism or Islam.

It is no coincidence that the formula 'unity in diversity' is a cornerstone of the political language of European integration. Although the motto 'unity in diversity' has only been used in official EU rhetoric since the 1980s,[38] it has been on the agenda ever since those heated discussions after the Second World War. Intellectuals of different nationalities and ideologies defended the richness of the national cultures, and stressed the advantages of their variety. This call to blend unity with the actual diversity of national cultures was common, and was something that pleas for peaceful cooperation or unification would have to address, sooner or later. This illustrated the tension that came along with the dreams and plans of unity in a diversified context.

Europe with Nations, Europe without Nationalism

The Britain-based Spanish writer Salvador Madariaga described the two world wars as the 'birth pangs of Europe' – the continent was now creating itself.[39] He and many others were fully aware of the collapse of the idea of a European federation in the early 1930s, and took that time's lack of cooperation and abundance of explosive nationalism to be the main causes of the war and the disaster it had inflicted on Europe. For many intellectuals, the main question of the day was what to do about nations and nationalism. On one hand, the pre-war notion of a shared European culture had been reclaimed; on the other hand, it was obviously important to both disarm and demarcate nationalism. The issue now became how to align European culture with the individual nations and their national cultures.

This section and the one that follows examine a group of liberal-minded intellectuals and their search for a concept of Europe that included nations but excluded nationalism, beginning in 1945 and continuing into the early 1950s. The focus is on the idea that a Europe of nations must be a Europe without nationalism. This group of intellectuals represents the direction that mainstream Europeanist thinking took in the post-war era – that is, that unification must build on the nations and nation states rather than erase them, that the nations should not cease to exist within a shared community, that nationhood and national culture could and should be separated from nationalism. This is the thinking that underpinned the European Commission's slogan 'unity in diversity', which was launched in the 1980s.[40] However, the group we will examine represents this mindset without using the concept European integration, as this concept had not yet been established in the political language, which is something we will return to in the last section of this chapter.

To investigate a mindset that defends national culture while rejecting nationalism, I have chosen four writers to illustrate the transnational context. Born in the late nineteenth century or first decades of the 1900s, they became established writers in the interbellum and experienced the rise of Nazi Germany. Karl Jaspers (1883–1969) was an academic philosopher in Germany who was forced to leave his professorship at Heidelberg when he refused to pledge allegiance to Hitler. He refused to divorce his wife, who had Jewish ancestry, and the couple only managed to avoid deportation to Ravensbrück concentration camp because the American forces entered Heidelberg in March 1944.[41] Salvador Madariaga (1886–1978) was a novelist, critic and historian with a long history of activism for international cooperation in various bodies of the League of Nations. He was a diplomat who was appointed minister of the Spanish republican government, and later its ambassador in Washington and Paris. From the late 1930s, he lived and taught in Oxford. Denis de Rougemont (1906–1985) was a Swiss historian and cultural critic who began his efforts to organise a movement for the federation of Europe in 1930.[42] Stephen Spender (1909–1995) was a British poet, novelist and essayist. In the 1930s he was known to sympathise with the socialists, and for a very short while he was even a member of the Communist Party, which he left after criticising the Soviets and Stalin. These four, as we will soon see, were loosely associated with one another in a transnational community of intellectuals. Using one of Karl Mannheim's classical devices for the sociology of knowledge, we can say that this group existed based on their conscious and rational will. They represent two generations, Jaspers and Madariaga being in their sixties in 1945, while de Rougemont and Spender were in their late thirties. Madariaga and de Rougemont had been Europeanists before the war. The group thus illustrates both transmission and fusion between the generations, making it impossible to define their viewpoints regarding Europe as phenomena connected with a single generation. The formative experiences of both generations were the two world wars triggered by conflicts between European states.[43]

In examining their views, I will first turn to the transnational context that brought together Jaspers, Madariaga, de Rougemont and Spender. Then we will look at how they situated Europe in the post-war era and in history, their quest for a European spirit, and how they believed the European nations could cooperate within a political federation, while leaving nationalism behind.

The entanglement of Europe with nations in the writings of Jaspers, Madariaga, de Rougemont and Spender illustrates the transnational discourse on Europe in the years immediately following the Second World War. These writers were themselves translated into multiple languages: Jaspers' many books and pamphlets were quickly presented to English, French, Italian and Spanish readers; De Rougemont wrote in French and was translated into German and English; while Madariaga wrote in Spanish, English and French, and was published in German and Italian as well. In terms of other languages, they were all translated into Swedish, for example, and all except Spender into Dutch.[44] We can see that many of their publications on the European issue were disseminated in several of these languages, such as Jaspers' *The European Spirit*, Madariaga's *Victors, Beware*, de Rougemont's *Freedoms We May Lose*, and Spender's *European Witness*.

Moreover, they fervently exchanged ideas with one another as well as with other intellectuals at congresses. With the exception of Madariaga, the other three met at the congress organised by Julien Benda in Geneva in 1946 to discuss the European spirit. Madariaga was one of the chairmen of the Congress of Europe in The Hague in 1948, in which de Rougemont also took part, and both were central figures in the newly established

European Movement. When the movement launched a cultural committee, it was chaired by Madariaga. In The Hague in 1948, plans were made for a European Centre for Culture, with de Rougemont leading the way. They all belonged to an organisation named the Congress for Cultural Freedom, initiated in Berlin in 1950 with activities throughout the 1950s and until 1967, when it collapsed after it was revealed that its financial support from American foundations had originated from the CIA. De Rougemont knew about this and Jaspers had at least some information, but no misgivings: 'Truth also needs propaganda', he is quoted as saying.[45] Jaspers and Madariaga became two of the honorary chairmen, with Denis de Rougemont serving as president of its executive committee and Stephen Spender the editor (with Irving Kristol) of its main journal *The Encounter*.[46] All four published in the organisation's five journals in English, French, German, Italian and Spanish. It is clear that these men had become interconnected within the same transnational network. Moreover, this community shared some fundamental traits of political thinking. The Congress of Cultural Freedom was an organisation with an explicit anti-communist bias, though its magazines were equally characterised by their criticism of McCarthyism; Peter Coleman concludes that they mainly represented the non-communist left, including liberals and social democrats with the views of the British Labour and French Socialist parties. One of the main ideas of the organisation was that Europe's unification would be the best way to counter communism.[47]

When a range of prominent intellectuals met for the congress L'esprit européen in Geneva in 1946, Julien Benda framed the discussion by insisting on the divisions of Europe. Certainly, although the differences within Europe were also underscored by the other speakers, the divisions among the nationalities were essential when considering the European spirit, which he also acclaimed. Benda was unclear how to depict the duality between a unified European spirit and a diversity of nations.[48] When he had called for a united Europe in the 1930s, it had taken the form of a French nation.[49] For the participants of the congress, it became clear that the nations would somehow have to acquiesce to a common European spirit. It was one of the main themes not only of the congress, but also of the Europeanist project and of the discourse on European unity for years to come.

As we have seen, the pre-Second World War concept of Europe evoked crisis, decline and nihilism, often alluding to a weakened position for Europe, a lack of capabilities, and general dismay at declining morals and Christianity. However, it also included progress and civilisation, together with a general Eurocentric attitude of rightfully dominating the world because of European superiority. This was the backdrop against which Jaspers, Madariaga, de Rougemont and Spender considered Europe and nationalism in the early post-war years. In turning to some of their key texts, the first step is to illustrate their concept of Europe.

During his journey in the British-occupied zone of Germany in the summer and autumn of 1945, Stephen Spender meditated on the 'corpse towns' that had emerged as a result of the deliberate efforts of civilisation and of cooperation between the victorious nations. The organic life of the old cities, with architecture and life forms that fused past and present, that connected the present with the Middle Ages, had been killed. A city such as Cologne had been like a waiting room for its inhabitants while they were journeying through their time on Earth. Now it was all ruins. In these dead cities, the 'citizens go on existing with a base mechanical kind of life like that of insects ... The destruction of the city itself, with all its past as well as its present, is like a reproach to the people who go on living there. The sermons in the stones of Germany preach nihilism'.[50] Thus, Spender described not only the destruction of Europe but also the common representation of the war as a nihilism that was intimately related to civilisation. First, it was a climax of technological development and cooperation that destroyed these cities and, in the end, brought the atomic bomb to the world. To this was added the nihilistic regimes of fascism, especially Hitler's, and the war that resulted in the severing of European civilisation.[51]

De Rougemont emphasised that Western civilisation tends towards technocracy and science, both of which are problematic in their own ways. Technocracy entails the danger of confusing means with ends, as it tends to 'overlook the final ends of the human venture' and aligns us with nihilism, which can be illustrated by the threat of the atomic bomb. Overall, progress was wholly negative when it came to the wars of the first half of the twentieth century, which killed more people than ever before; however, progress also ensured a level of material well-being previously unknown. On one hand, there was an ever-increasing number of inventions that could be applied to achieve social ends; on the other, there was the emerging production and refinement of atomic bombs. Thus, de Rougement conceded that the idea of progress was contradictory, and added that it was Europe that originated it: 'Let it be admitted that Europe, in forming it, "infected" the whole world; the world will never recover'. Typically for de Rougemont, he added European responsibility to the European quest: 'Europe, being responsible for the idea of Progress, is also responsible for correcting it aright'.[52]

Madariaga criticised the subjection of man to machine: 'men degenerate to the status and function of pegs in a huge kind of factory that tends to supersede the State and Society itself'. Quantitative considerations dictate societal life, including organisations that have been set up to coordinate on the international level. Democracy tends to be reduced to a market fair, a vulgar thing, humiliating candidates and promising material benefits that turn elections into auctions. Moreover, this development brings a threat of moral decline and even destruction.[53] Finally, Jaspers declared his mistrust in modern civilisation with its science, technology, and idea of progress, all of which he included when defining Europe. It was the time, he claimed, to look for a new European consciousness: after years of desperate yearning through nihilism, it was time to evoke new creativity, and to set out in a new direction.[54]

Clearly, the experiences of war and the development of weapons caused these writers to deliver a critique of progress, conceptualising it as nihilism. For them, Europe was seriously wounded and could never be the same as it had been before the two world wars. All four gave history a prominent place when they traced the decline of Europe in the twentieth century and described the contemporary situation. In this, they treated Europe's demise and ultimate downfall as the outcome of a lack of unity, with internal divisions between the nations and the loss of shared beliefs and principles. Madariaga viewed the first half of the twentieth century as unstable, in sharp contrast to the relative stability of the nineteenth century. He mentioned not only that century-long period of relative peace within Europe, but also the general increase in wealth, the trust in reason and liberty as guiding principles, and the belief in the idea of progress: 'On the whole, the men of 1900 could look forward with confidence to an era of ever-ascending progress under the guidance of reason in a world of liberty'.[55] De Rougemont described how Europe had dominated the world for centuries through its culture, trade and weapons, with its machinery and capital. The previous thirty years and the two world wars had left Europe compromised and weakened by the pressure of America and Russia (typically, they vacillated between using the official name 'the Soviet Union' and Russia, the latter indicating a threat and otherness predating communist rule), dispossessed of its powers, demoralised and emptied of dreams, divided and lost. Yet, until the last war, the name of Europe had still radiated across the globe. Now, Europeans were in shock, ruined, and living in the shadows of the two great powers.[56] For Spender, Europe was at the end of a long period of dominating the world. It had been corrupted by both war and fascism, ruined and divided. It had become small and weak, and had reached a decisive turning point, facing the possibility of meeting the end of its existence. At this juncture, Europe had to learn from the past and understand its history, to revive some past values and completely transform others.[57] Jaspers stated that there was something to keep and to protect in Europe, not least a historical mind that offered the possibility of learning from the past. However, the European mind would need to face its contemporary context, look towards the future, and represent itself in the present course of events. Europe had become small, while the new masters of the world now came from America and Asia. With the potential of China, and the energy and growing strength of the United States and Russia, Europe was stuck between two politically superior powers. Europe was shrinking and losing self-confidence, which caused 'waning, suffering and humiliation'. He concluded that Europe had to accept its loss of world power and find new ways to define itself, adding that there was a chance to accomplish this in the present situation; it was still possible to set Europe on a course that would lead to new greatness.[58]

In their reflections, Europe of the early post-war years stands out as characterised by dismay and decline. De Rougemont noted that the idea of progress had migrated from Europe, its birthplace, to America and Russia. Spender, like Madariaga, stressed that the machine had enslaved men to the degree that they had become trained to support the needs of machinery, leading to overwhelming feelings of helplessness. The clearest result of the machine age was the atomic bomb; with this in mind, Spender warned that machinery could destroy civilisation and kill us all through its capacity for annihilation. He was utterly clear on the responsibility this bestowed on Europe. The evils that happened to Europe were chosen by the Europeans. They were responsible for the methods and for inventing the devices of mechanised society. Therefore, they also had the responsibility for mitigating its outcome.[59] De Rougemont also warned of the threat of total destruction, and added that the atomic bomb was linked to the notion of totalitarian dictatorship.[60] Jaspers – who later wrote the most extensive philosophical tract on the atomic bomb[61] – argued that Europe had a particular responsibility, and was guilty of many shameful acts: 'What Europe has brought forth, European spirit itself must overcome'. As Europe was the origin and inventor of science and technology, which have the capacity for great destruction, Europe also had the responsibility to set itself on a new future course. Moreover, as Europe had spread Janus-faced science and technology throughout the world, its present task would be to expand European humanism and the European idea of freedom.[62] Apparently, these writers shared the idea of European responsibility.

It is against the background of a European catastrophe that these four writers depicted the European spirit as a force for salvation, and even specified that intellectuals were the ones who should represent this spirit, stressing themselves as a force going beyond nationalistic endeavours. At the 1946 congress in Geneva, de Rougemont declared that the mind was the only thing left to hope for, and Spender professed that when material achievements and institutions could no longer be relied on, then the mind would have to be called upon; a spiritual rebirth was needed.[63]

So, we may ask, where did they find the European spirit? De Rougemont stated that while the bourgeoisie had resigned itself to decadence and the working class was inching towards communism, the European spirit, which could span the continent, was left to the intellectuals, who were most inclined to think independently. In 1946, he also included the farmers as free thinkers, but later dropped them, seeing only the intellectuals as capable of restoring or reinventing the common principles of thinking and acting.[64] Spender agreed, saying that the artists and thinkers had kept the idea of freedom alive through the dark years that Europe had undergone. He turned to the 'spiritual values' of seeking the truth, loving the beautiful, and longing for human fraternity, all represented in culture, in architecture and art, in literature, and by brilliant minds.[65] He gave the intellectuals a central role in reintegrating Germany, and wrote of their duty to seek out and encourage their German colleagues. He believed that intellectuals of various nationalities should work together to encourage and demonstrate international understanding through joint conferences, exhibitions and concerts, leading to the spiritual rebirth of Europe. It would not come down to establishing new organisations, but rather to changing the minds of individuals. If elite prophets could envision where Europe was and what steps it needed to take, then many others would follow.[66] Madariaga seemed to agree on the special place of the intellectuals when he identified the main characteristic of the European individual as the desire to know and to practise Socratic doubt as a method to expand knowledge.[67]

Above all, they praised the individual. In accordance with thinkers such as Alexis de Tocqueville and John Stuart Mill from the preceding century, Madariaga, Jaspers and Spender called for exceptional individuals. Madariaga echoed Mill in claiming that such individuals were 'the salt of the earth', and he repeated much of Ortega y Gassett's criticism of mass society and mass movements from the interbellum period.[68] Jaspers said that, on the one hand, each individual is potential unto himself, neither solely material nor part of a machine; on the other, he assigned importance to the greatness of a few exceptional individuals.[69] De Rougemont regarded self-realisation as a basic individual freedom.[70] He viewed the individual through the lens of his philosophical conviction of personalism when conforming to a shared quest for Europe and the wider circle of Western civilisation, which included identifying the individual as an autonomous and freely acting person. From this, he developed the idea of the European as a man who aims for consciousness and meaning in life going beyond mere production and consumption; as someone who seeks the truth, is sceptical, and practises critical thinking and civic morality.[71]

Their praise of the individual arose from the idea of human nature and social life as complicated and not reducible to economic terms. Utilitarianism reduced 'spontaneous forms of social nature' and every inequality to a matter of income, and deprived society of differences that were the very flavour of its many constituent communities.[72] Modern man must be aware, using his senses to experience his world and be more spiritually alive. The triumph of life is to be found in culture.[73] This group was thus far from the economic utilitarianism and materialism that we associate with individualism today, and they called for cultivation of the spirit to be the task of intellectuals. Today, some would find that elitist, while others – including myself – would view it as a call for current intellectuals to take stronger stands in public debate.

Towards Unity without Nationalism

In the early post-Second World War period, the burning question of national sovereignty and its limits was evoked in the frequent calls for a world authority, and in the intense discourse on European unification. With the nation state assumed to be of ongoing relevance to the world order, and nationalism seen as evoking the possibility of states launching wars on their neighbours, sovereignty was a key issue. Madariaga solved the problem by asserting that no nation could be absolutely sovereign, as it would have to voluntarily engage in various foreign relations. Jaspers mistrusted the ability of sovereign nations to find a working political balance, and concluded that, in a coming world order, all nations would need to give up some of their sovereignty in exchange for negotiated decisions on shared issues. Nations would need to accept being subjects under international law, and abide by it when attempting to make changes. They would need to protect the rights of minorities and uphold the rule of law. For a new world order, this implied that no culture should rule others, and that 'people [should] set one another free and engage in mutual concern for one another'.[74]

The distinction between nationalism and nations was crucial to this group of thinkers. Spender condemned the former as outdated, based on its record of violence and political aggression. Still, there could be greatness and a sense of true glory when people came together and expressed national culture.[75] De Rougemont conceived of nationalism as coinciding with total war and anarchical individualism – both European inventions. Moreover, total war was the outcome of nationalism in conjunction with centralist states, propaganda, and industrial technology. However, he found that Europe had also devised pacifism, federalism and a communal spirit.[76] Madariaga argued that it was impossible to erase nations or their cultures, as Germany had attempted to do in previous years.[77] They implored Europeans to make a choice, to move away from nationalism. The way to do this was to unify Europe.

Spender believed that the world was on the brink, and that nations would have to make a choice between two diverging directions. They could continue with destruction and hatred, represented by the bombed-out towns of Germany, or opt for cooperation. The choice was either a 'new chaos' or a 'new pattern of unity'. At the time, Spender argued, civilisation 'may recreate everything or destroy everything'. The contemporary situation demanded worldwide unity, 'with consent of all nations', in which peace was more important than national interests, and priority was given to 'the whole human interest in front of the existing power-and-wealth interests'.[78]

More specifically, the issue of unity concerned Europe. Spender observed the hatred against the Germans, that they were no longer considered human beings, but seen as reprehensible. Still, he contended that there was no German problem but only a European one. France felt disgraced, as did Germany. Not only had many Germans failed when being tried, but so had many French – and the higher in society, the more people were compromised. France had its aftershocks following 'five years of war, bitterness and corruption'. Spender called for Europe to form a unity based on sympathy for other nationalities, a unity in which the people and nations accepted their responsibility for the whole continent. Only through cooperation among France, Germany, and the rest of Europe would it be possible to repair the damage. Europe's unification was presented as the only sensible way forward.[79]

De Rougemont considered nationalism to be a romantic disease that had vanished from Europe, relating it to fascism, imperialism and the totalitarian spirit. At one point, he differentiated between bad and good notions of the nation. One referred to absolute sovereignty demarcated by well-defined borders, defended by armies that always ended up in wars, while the other described 'centres of radiance and . . . communities of peoples allied, by their traditions or by their ideals – in other words, by destiny or by choice'. Categorically, he wanted to maintain the nation state. The problem emerged when nation states became the supreme forces in the international order, because states tended to destroy cultural uniqueness. De Rougemont doubted that representatives of nation states would be able to lead international affairs. In general, he saw salvation in what he defined as a European virtue, which is the quest for a balance between extremes. This European quest opposes both the totalitarian state and unrepentant individualism. Europe should therefore not eliminate nation states altogether, but instead endeavour to balance them by creating a federation, while respecting the diversity of the continent. As a federation, the countries would be able to demonstrate a new degree of confidence, opening themselves to one another, weakening borders and the requirement for visas, and opening Europe to the rest of the world.[80]

De Rougemont, like Spender, observed a contemporary political ambivalence: 'The disunity of European nations has reached the height of absurdity; and their move towards union grows at the same time'. Europe was in crisis, and faced two options: the first was to unite and the second to disappear into the catacombs of history. The continent was fractured, other powers were taking over, and a definitive decline was a real possibility for Europe unless it discovered its vocation. He found this in the movement towards uniting Europe: 'In saving itself by federation ... it can offer the world the recipe and the most fruitful transcendence of the national framework'.[81] This could only happen if the Europeans realised that they belonged to one common nation and the same culture, and managed to revitalise the European spirit. This did not imply that they should subjugate national differences, argued de Rougemont; instead, the federation would act as a device guarding against anarchy while still guaranteeing diversity.[82]

In sum, Jaspers, Spender and de Rougemont emphasised the need to overcome the disunity of the European nations. When asked what would come out of this kind of unity, they answered European cooperation and a political federation. Madariaga shared this conviction, but believed that unification would come whether or not it was wanted; rather, the European nations would need to choose how the unification should be designed. At the end of the war in Europe, he stated that Germany had tried to create a new Europe in which the nations were subjugated to the Nazis. Their project had failed because it was impossible to erase Europe's national feelings and consciousness; but even so, the Nazis had played a role in the longer process of European unification. Although their reign was a nightmare, it contributed to fostering a spirit of unity: 'The spirit of unity is in the air of our epoch'. Madariaga drew parallels to the centralised states that were formed centuries ago, when increasing communication and exchange made regions increasingly interdependent and the monarchs built the centralised power of nations. He stressed the ongoing process towards European unification and defined it as the birth of the European nation.[83]

We can see a distinct split between nations and nationalism. The claim that there could be such a thing as good national culture recalled the idea of the 'spring of nations' in 1848, as advocated by the Italian leader of Young Europe, Giuseppe Mazzini. Young Europe included national movements freeing people from the yokes of the old regimes of European states, and promoted the creation of a European federation of the people. However, a hundred years later, pleas for European unity coincided with the renunciation of nationalism. Moreover, it is also possible to see the difference between Madariaga, who argued that unity was a sign of the times, and the other three thinkers, who stressed that unification was a matter of choice. This can be interpreted, using Isaiah Berlin's distinction, as a difference between facts and values. For Madariaga, the coming unity was presented as a matter of fact, while for the other three it was a matter of value.[84]

With Madariaga stressing the unity of Europe and hailing the dawn of a European nation, we have now arrived at another question for those who advocated European unification post-Second World War. How do a shared European spirit, conscience and culture come together with national cultures? After the first reactions to this question, and to the notions of a Europe without nationalism as well as European unification, further support was needed. Madariaga offered a more extensive discussion of this. He contended that the existing nations would not dissolve in a unified Europe, but would continue to exist: 'Nations, big or small, are facts of nature, and it is not in our power to destroy them'. All nations, even small ones, should be appreciated for their cultures. With a Herderian approach, Madariaga insisted that it is through local national cultures that 'universal culture reaches the consciousness of most men' and that this 'is the only way in which they can assimilate it'. For Madariaga just as for Herder, universalism is only reachable through the national cultures. Moreover, in his mind, the European nation was something different from most European nations. It would not be founded on a shared language but, like Switzerland, would have to be 'built over several languages'. Its main enemy would not come from outside, but rather from the risk of wars between fellow European nations. A permanent European peace would be achieved through establishing a European commonwealth and by implementing European standards. Everything came down to the European spirit, as practical arrangements and institutions 'will avail nothing if the spirit is not there'. However, the old spirit dies hard, and new habits have to be fostered by wise statesmanship: 'What is needed is the habit of thinking and feeling in European terms'. Concretely, he asked for a European board to examine practical issues that extended across borders and had a truly European character. He offered a few examples, such as rail and air transportation as well as physical and moral health. The idea was to create a board that would consider the issues 'only from the standpoint of a nation called Europe'.[85]

Moving into the 1950s, Madariaga dwelt on the question of how a European spirit could be combined with national cultures. He further developed his conception of Europe and its spirit, emphasising more than before the material interconnectedness of Europe, conceived as a single physical entity. He contrasted this interconnectedness to the essential lack of moral solidarity between the European peoples and nations, by which he meant that Europe was not 'one consciousness' as, for example, Italy was. It was necessary to reconsider national histories as parts of European history, to appreciate the works of Dante, Shakespeare and Goethe as works of European art. Europeans would need to understand and appreciate one another, including all their cultural differences. These differences caused tension, but instead of prompting warlike fantasies, they should be kept in perspective.

The tension between different cultures and nations could 'be integrated into the common life of Europe, which they ought to quicken and stimulate'. In Madariaga's view, such life and strife belonged to Europe.[86]

Madariaga's intention in the book *Portrait of Europe* is to reveal the unity behind the variety of European nations. Although one can identify the purported national characteristics of the peoples of Europe, such as the slow Swede or aesthetic Italian, they are all Europeans. Although the continent has many beloved and distinct cities, the unity of their underlying style and configuration leaves a lasting impression. Madariaga referred to Montesquieu's claim as to the European physical environment's optimal temperature, conferred by the Gulf Stream and other geographical conditions: 'Unity comes from the relatively short limits of climate and the configuration within which the life of Europe has to flow'. Similarly, Europe's inhabitants are a mixed lot, so no nation can declare itself a pure race; instead, this mixture 'is perhaps the true cause of European unity'. On this basis, Madariaga declared the national types to have specific historical flair and spirits of their own: Europe is rich in national characters, and they 'are the true components of the European spirit'.[87] In conclusion, it is Madariaga who propagated the idea of diversity in unity. For him, the cause of Europe's wars was not national diversity, which was not a necessary evil Europe had to live with. Instead, diversity was sharply distinguished from nationalism and was the very essence of a shared European culture. Madariaga was the one of the four thinkers who promoted cultural diversity, making it the definitive feature of the cultural and spiritual unity of Europe.

Karl Jaspers, Salvador Madariaga, Denis de Rougemont, and Stephen Spender took part in the transnational discourse and intellectual exchange among writers, critics and scholars concerning Europe's future. Beginning with the Geneva congress L'esprit européen, they were primarily addressing the dreadful consequences of Europe's ill-fated politics. A Europe in ruins conflicted with the European spirit and its possibilities. In the years that followed, they adapted their values to the new situation that had gradually begun to constitute the post-war order. Examining their standpoints on European issues in the early post-war years, we can see that they were struggling to come to terms with the entanglement of nations, nation states and Europeanness. They depicted Europe as a continent in crisis because of nationalism. Their critique concerned fundamental aspects of European growth and expansion, such as the idea of progress and technological development without limits. We should not underestimate the experience of representing countries that had lost much of their influence in the world, nor the influence of the Cold War that squeezed Europe between the superpowers. Jaspers, Madariaga, de Rougemont and Spenders were strongly aligned with the liberal and economic ideologies of the West, stressing individual freedom.

These writers focused on the immediate context within Europe. This is to say that, in their concept of Europe, we find little about the colonies or about the future of the persistent ambitions to maintain the British or French empires. In their opinion, Europe had fallen apart during the First World War and became victim to nationalism because it lacked a common worldview or thought system, and this confusion had been amplified by the most recent war. The intellectuals had to undertake the task of awakening the European spirit and of making people aware of their shared European culture. Clearly, the crisis they acknowledged included the threat of a new war, this time with the possibility of the atomic bomb, as well as the threat of communists taking over Western Europe, either through Soviet troops or internal groups.

Nevertheless, the crisis could be interpreted as an opportunity to create a new Europe with a stronger sense of common culture and shared institutional bodies, which would stop internal nationalistic conflicts by limiting national sovereignty. This brings us back to European unification and how it was launched in these years.

Organising for Europe, Taking on a New World Mission

After the Second World War, some Europeanists were inclined to look to Switzerland as a model for the new Europe, where unity could transcend linguistic barriers in the name of common sense and intelligent progress.[88] Although the comparison was sometimes criticised, the message remained, that there was a need to limit absolute state sovereignty and hamper nationalism: 'A United States of Europe will be of necessity far more loosely knit, and the elements of exclusive nationalism will need to be guided into more fruitful channels if the experiment is ever to succeed'.[89] The Swiss capital of Zurich was the site of Winston Churchill's well-known and often-cited speech on the 'Tragedy of Europe', given on 22 September 1946, in his new role as leader of the Conservative opposition in the British Parliament. He explicitly asked for a United States of Europe, where France would take Germany by the hand, paying respect to Coudenhove-Kalergi and Aristide Briand as forerunners in substantiating the design, and then acknowledging the movement for unity in European countries.[90]

Churchill's speech in Zurich is often cited as the moment when serious discussions of and movements towards unification began. However, by then Europeanist organisations were already active. In Britain, Churchill founded the 'United European Movement' to campaign for the cause, but such groups had already been in existence during the war, as mentioned in the previous chapter. In France, the president of the National Assembly and former prime minister Édouard Herriot chaired the French Council for a United Europe, a group founded by Albert Camus, among others, in 1944. Similar organisations had begun to spring up in Belgium and the Netherlands, some with branches in most Western European countries. The European Parliamentary Union was founded on Coudenhove-Kalergi's initiative to provide a platform for parliamentarians of different nationalities, whereas the Economic League for European Cooperation was to promote cooperation in economic life, and the European Union of Federalists aimed for a federal Europe. In comparison with the organisations of the interwar period, these were less elitist in pursuit of a mass movement towards unification. Still, they directed their message towards politicians and were certainly, by no coincidence, chaired by people of prominence, mostly former ministers or prime ministers. While the ambition was to attract people across political divides, some organisations attracted more conservatives and others more liberals. In addition, the Christian Democrat Party had its 'Nouvelles Equipes Internationales', while the 'Movement for the Socialist States of Europe' appealed to the anti-Stalinist left.

No doubt, the call for European unity had considerable appeal; it was supported by broad public interest in rebuilding Europe along more peaceful lines with the purpose of facilitating life on the continent. The message was clear enough, but the design of its implementation less so. Obvious questions concerned the extent of the cooperation – or more bluntly, how much power the European bodies could claim and how much sovereignty the nation states would relinquish. Some urged a federal state while others wanted a looser union. The way forward would be to focus on attractive proposals, or at least on compromises that could be deemed acceptable from both standpoints. In all this, the concept of integration was critical, and we will return to this in the concluding section of this chapter.

The Congress of Europe in May 1948 presents us with a snapshot of the call for European unification. It was only one of many meetings and congresses held by Europeanist groups in those years, but it was the largest one and was framed as a way of building momentum and symbolically beginning a process towards unification: 'Isn't our ambition the highest? To build a world of peace, freedom, and social justice, and, in doing so, cement the first stones in making Europe!'[91] An organising committee was formed by most of the organisations mentioned above, but without the participation of the Movement for the United Socialist States of Europe. Former prime ministers and foreign secretaries as well as up-and-coming state leaders attended the unofficial gathering in The Hague. Both Winston Churchill and Harold Macmillan attended from the UK, Altiero Spinelli from Italy, Valéry

Giscard d'Estaing and François Mitterrand from France, Konrad Adenauer and Walter Hallstein (who was to become the first president of the European Commission) from the Bundesrepublik Germany, and Hendrik Brugmans from Belgium. Apart from these, there were many intellectuals and others interested in initiating European action and setting up committees, representatives from the industrial sector and trade unions, as well as people from diverse professions. Churchill told the congress that it 'may fairly claim to be the voice of Europe'.[92] Among the most notable in attendance were Richard Coudenhove-Kalergi, Salvador de Madariaga, Denis de Rougement, the French scholar Raymond Aron, the Polish writer Joseph H. Retinger, and the British philosopher and mathematician Bertrand Russell. The Dutch Parliament buildings were the venue of the congress, which was supported by the Dutch government. In his opening address, Winston Churchill recalled a unity to be found in 'the glorious treasures of literature, of romance, of ethics, of thought and toleration belonging to all, which is the true inheritance of Europe, the expression of its genius and honour', which goes beyond frontiers and barriers. By celebrating these resources, he suggested, Europe would erase its divisions.[93] At that time, only three years after the war in Europe had ended, the search for higher purposes and spiritual values was underway. Churchill called for 'the larger hope for humanity', and Coudenhove-Kalergi for 'the dignity of the human person', which he found in Greek individualism, and for 'generous help for those in need'. The Dutch socialist Hendrik Brugmans declared Europe to be 'a sense of freedom'.[94]

Churchill and his inaugural addresses invoked a European unity that contrasted with the contemporary threats of communism and the Iron Curtain posed by the Soviet Union and its allies, as well as with the wreckage of a devastating war. The desire was to learn from the mistakes after the First World War, 'when the slogan of the right of self-determination of the smaller nations was greatly in vogue in the whole of Europe', which if left unchecked, 'could only lead to the suicidal tendencies of military and economic autarky, which we have known indeed'.[95] It is not surprising that peace and a better standard of living were held up as objectives for a more united Europe, along with the security that comes with rule of law. We can recognise similarities to the interwar period, with reference to Ortega y Gasset, Huizinga and Rauschning, and themes such as nihilism, decline and crisis. Unification was seen as the one option that could rescue European civilisation.[96]

The event was widely recognised, being called 'a monumental moment for public opinion', according to an editorial in *The Times* on 10 May 1948.[97] In attendance were 250 journalists, reporting on the nearly 750 delegates from sixteen countries with various political views – conservative, liberal and socialist – including representatives of the Roman Catholic Church and trade unions. Half of the delegates came from France and Great Britain, and none came from the Central and East European countries behind the Iron Curtain. An additional forty observers came from ten countries, most from Central and Eastern Europe, but also four from the United States and two from Canada; there were no delegates from Spain (but four observers who lived in exile), and no Portuguese at all. The symbolism of the congress was obvious, especially when Churchill welcomed a large German delegation in his opening speech, given in a former occupied country and in the same town as the peace conferences that occurred between 1899 and 1907. The negotiations reportedly lasted until after midnight, taking dramatic turns, but in the end managing to overcome disputes. One witness reported to a British journal that 'indeed agreement was not reached without difficulty, without late sessions, and without considerable concessions being made'.[98] In the journal *Merkur*, Germans could read about 'contradictory conceptions that clashed several times', before common ground was finally attained.[99]

Looking at the list of inaugural speakers, we see only men, and few women spoke in committee sessions. In fact, under 4 per cent of the delegates and observers were women. Most of these came from political parties and Europeanist organisations, but some represented women's organisations. They did take part in certain discussions, especially bringing up issues related to displaced war refugees and youth education.[100] One of the very few to be heard in the cultural committee negotiations was Claire Saunier, who raised the issue of women being half of the European population in relation to youth education and the role of mothers – matters addressed in the final resolution.[101] In the final plenary session, and on behalf of the female delegates at the congress, she declared that they were not feminists, and stressed that women were part of the European family, together with their husbands and children.[102] Another delegate, Hilda Vermeij-Jonker, who was the first Dutch woman to present a dissertation in sociology and a leading socialist, raised the issue of displaced intellectuals, but she was seen as radical when demanding economic and social equality between the sexes.[103] Regardless, Europeanism mainly came together under the traditional view that a woman's place and role was in the family.

There were mentions of a 'United States of Europe', similar to the United States, a 'United Europe', and a 'European Union', and discussion of the extent and meaning of these notions. However, arguments for a European nation or a European state were rejected in the discussion, and another option was proposed: a federation of existing states that, although they differed in character, had in common that they were democracies and abided by the rule of law. A witness concluded that perhaps 'we have got to work out some new form of association which will neither conform to the patterns of previous Federations or Confederations – something [that] is suited to the special condition of Europe'.[104] In the end, the delegates sent a 'Message to Europeans' about the dangers of being divided: 'Alone, no one of our countries can hope seriously to defend its independence. Alone, no one of our countries can solve the economic problems of today'.[105] The delegates agreed on adopting resolutions that called for common political and economic action by transferring and merging some sovereignty from the independent states. Obviously, the understanding of European unification as creating something beyond historical and existing orders was already in the air.

The Congress of Europe had some immediate outcomes: one was the formation that autumn of the European Movement to gather all relevant groups, and another was to establish a European Centre for Culture in Geneva, led by de Rougemont. To some surprise, the declarations had more to offer than expected. Although he came to The Hague with low expectations, the conservative economist Arthur Salter concluded that the declarations had 'more substance in them than I should have thought possible in the circumstances'.[106] Perhaps the resolution with the most direct political bearing was the call for a European Assembly. Two years later, this resulted in the creation of the Council of Europe.[107] Moreover, the final resolutions addressed important issues in ways that foreshadowed later developments: the union would be open to all European democratic states and, perhaps most important, that 'the sole solution of the economic and political problems of Germany is its integration in a federated Europe'. We can see tensions familiar to us today in how the resolutions were worded then: independent states versus an energetic European political body, cultural unity versus diversity and national cultures, a European conscience versus the writing of national history and the educational systems of the states. The discussion of how to design the necessary institutions was also familiar, concerning, for example, what steps should be taken, and the speed at which it would be possible to realise European unity.

The participants had in mind a European unity beyond state borders. On the political committee, Countess Jean de Suzannet contended that the unification was fundamental to protecting 'our civilisation' and 'our moral and democratic values' with their freedoms and rights.[108] R.W.G. Mackay, a Labour MP who chaired a cross-party group of British parliamentarians in favour of European unity, eloquently asked the nation states to sacrifice some of their sovereignty and transfer it in favour of a 'larger sovereignty which can alone protect their diverse and distinctive customs and characteristics, and their national traditions'.[109] For Jo Josephy, chair of a Europeanist committee in Britain, it was important that there be an elected federal authority representing the European people, not the states, with the principle of one person one vote.[110] On the economic and social committee,

Arthur Salter took an approach that foreshadowed the strategy later used by the European Community and then the European Economic Community, by beginning with some financial and economic bodies to meet immediate challenges. These could gradually develop, 'acquiring by delegation of sovereignty and authority from the constituent members so much power as will, without any sudden break, enable international authorities to be constituted'.[111] Salter's personal history is telling. During and after the First World War he worked with Jean Monnet in the coordinating administration of the Allies, and during the Second World War he tried to convince the Allies to establish a supranational European government, again with Monnet.[112]

In the speeches and discussions in the cultural committee, the delegates disavowed nationalism but aligned themselves with the nations and peoples of Europe. They found unity in a legacy of cultural values grounded mainly in Christianity and humanism, as well as in a common belief in the inalienable rights of man. The role of Christianity was much debated on the cultural committee when the original draft of the resolution was criticised for not including it. We should remember that the congress included delegates from churches, the Holy See, and leaders of the emerging Christian Democratic parties, such as Adenauer and Robert Schuman, who used their Europeanness in defence of Western civilisation, embracing the notion of a Western Christianity of medieval origin that represented a higher spiritual community beyond materialism and nationalism, which juxtaposed fascism and communism.[113] Eventually, the accepted resolution referred to 'the common heritage of Christian and other spiritual and cultural values'.[114] The discussion illustrated how close the concept of Europe was to that of European exceptionalism – illustrated, for example, by the German delegate Christine Teusch's claim that human dignity and freedom were established in Europe by Christianity.[115] Indeed, the French professor of medieval philosophy Étienne Gilson was wary of letting Christianity define Europe, as it did not originate in Europe and was widespread outside Europe. Instead he turned to universalism: 'I think we should remember . . . that if there is a Western tradition of culture, its secret lies in its desire for universality, not in the desire to make the world believe that what is European is ipso jure universal, but on the contrary in the desire to affirm the world and to vigorously maintain that all that is universal is European ipso jure'.[116] It was possible for Europe and its culture to represent the interests of everyone in the world, and this could be a source of universality, but Gilson was careful not to confuse this with supremacy: 'We don't want to flatter ourselves with a European culture that would be superior to non-European cultures', but on the other hand, 'we have no intention of decreeing the universality of European culture'. Still, European culture became connected with universalism because in 'this desire for universalism, open to all to give and to receive, resides our only peculiarity'.[117]

Recently, research has confirmed that a certain relationship between the concept of Europe and colonialism prevailed during the period, influencing programmes for economic cooperation and negotiations on unification, even up to the Treaty of Rome. At the Congress of Europe in The Hague, there was no discussion of national independence for the European colonies. Instead, the close connections with Europe's 'overseas territories' were recognised as important reasons to unify, not least in order to maintain control of resources and economic development.[118] The renowned economist Arthur Salter saw Europe's colonies as opportunities for investment and a way to balance the power of the United States.[119] Furthermore, the call for unification came with Eurocentrism. Speakers such as the resistance fighter and Gaullist politician Raymond Triboulet proclaimed that Europe was a model for the rest of the world, so it was up to Europe to address the malaise that had caused the war and to find a way to overcome the crisis.[120] The congress adopted a 'Message to Europeans' that claimed a new global mission: namely, to set an example, establish world peace, and ensure individual rights and obligations. Europe was crucial for human dignity and freedom in the world, and a union would have to happen 'not only for the salvation of liberties we have won, but also for the extension of their benefits to all mankind. Europe's destiny and the world's peace depend on this union'.[121] Thus, by uniting itself, Europe would be taking on a new mission of civilising the world.

However, claims of European exceptionalism and superiority were not in the mind of every delegate. Bertrand Russell argued that the Europeans were not at all exceptional regarding freedom and tolerance. Quite the opposite: 'We have learned tolerance only with very great difficulty, whereas in other parts of the world – in China, India, among Mahometans – you find a much greater readiness for tolerance'. Russell encouraged the delegates to stop stressing the superiority of Europe in envisaging unity.[122] The Swiss delegate Ernest von Schenk, a leading member of the European Union of Federalists, told the cultural committee that if one looked at what European heritage had accomplished, it was nothing to be proud of, adding that Christianity could still be the basis for a new crusade and that the main issue would be to 'overcome militarism and totalitarianism in Europe'. Indeed, he cautioned the congress to take care when talking about Europe as representing humanitarian interests.[123]

In general, Europeanism entailed controversies concerning both European exceptionalism and supremacy. At the Congress of Europe, colonialism was not a focus of the discussions, mainly because the radical socialists were absent. Initially, some Europeanist leftists from Labour and the continental socialist and social democratic parties stood against what they considered to be Churchill's capitalist unification of Europe. Even before Churchill's Zurich speech, the economist André Philip, who also served briefly as the minister of finance in the French socialist government, took the initiative to gather anti-imperialistic and anti-Stalinist Europeanists in the Movement for the Socialist United States of Europe.[124] Historian Anne-Isabelle Richard has recognised this as the main group of Europeanists who supported decolonisation.[125] With its aim of uniting Europe to create a third power in world politics, the Movement for the Socialist United States of Europe called for meetings and conferences starting in 1946 until they also joined the European Movement several months after the Congress of Europe. Their conferences included representatives from the resistance movements, the European Union of Federalists, and colonial independence movements. Anti-colonialism and anti-imperialism were core themes, although the debates revealed a certain patronising sensibility vis-à-vis the colonies. The national independence of the colonies was frequently paired with the European need for their raw materials, the advances made by European civilisation that the colonies had yet to reach, and discussions of the 'primitive races of Africa' and feudal nations in the East. Anne-Isabelle Richard has concluded that joining the other Europeanist organisations was a sign that they prioritised European unification at the expense of anti-colonialism and their previous efforts to establish a socialist Europe.[126] Moreover, it confirmed the sense of European exceptionalism and a European prerogative in the world; it also confirmed the tensions within the European movement regarding imperialism, the independence of the colonies, and European supremacy.

European Unification and Integration

The fundamental distinction that developed in the early post-Second World War period meant that Europeanism encompassed both the conception of a European culture and that of European nations. As we have seen, this way of looking at Europe was made possible by opposing nationalism while maintaining confidence in the nation state. It became widespread among Europeanists and in reflecting on Europe's future. Nevertheless, this distinction was not enough to make European unity suitable for the post-war period, as Europeanists had to balance unity with national interests. The question of what this balance should be like remained.

As we saw in the previous section, decline and nihilism were concepts continuously referred to in discourses on European unity in order to gain an understanding of the political and economic situation. Colonialism and economic progress could be rescued by halting the decline. The Belgian socialist Paul-Henri Spaak wrote that Europe was threatened by decline and that it could only be salvaged by uniting.[127] At the Congress of Europe, inaugural speeches and committee discussions referred to the threat of nihilism and stressed that European civilisation was doomed if its self-destructive tendencies were not controlled.[128] It was in the context of crisis, decline and nihilism that the concept of integration entered the discourse. In due time, it would advance to become a central tenet of the political language of European unification, and would come to characterise the European unification of the post-war decades. In fact, during the initial introduction of the integration concept, it was already possible to discern the central place it would eventually inhabit.

In Germany, the theme of Europe was brought up by some influential professors who had been dismissed from their universities during the reign of the National Socialists and then been reinstalled. Among these academics, a United States of Europe that included both the Central and West European countries was declared as the only alternative to nihilism.[129] The economist Alfred Weber regarded nihilism as the fundamental reason behind the catastrophe, and considered it to be a European way of thinking and attitude that had since spread worldwide.[130] Of crucial importance to the post-war concept of European unity, Weber prescribed integration as the cure for nihilism.

Although Weber seemed to be the first person after the war to talk about integration, it was already being considered in the interwar intellectual debate. The idea of the economy as a means to tie the European countries together was already on the agenda by 1930, although the main postulated means was cooperation. However, economists soon used the concept of economic integration to depict the prerequisites for the European economy to connect its industries, concentrated in a few countries, with the vast areas that provided the raw materials.[131] Economists argued that with the establishment of new state borders, along with continuing interdependence and the need to trade across these borders, there was a great need for economic integration to address the situation.[132] In 1945, the integration concept was launched by Weber as an item on the agenda for rebuilding Europe and, in particular, for establishing a civilised order in Germany. The argument was that Germany would need raw materials from other countries for its industry, and that it would be in the best interest of other countries in Europe to sell raw materials to Germany.[133]

Alfred Weber should be seen as a representative of the resistance to Nazi unity who upheld the idea of European unity. From early in his career, he noted a cultural decline of the West. During the Weimar Republic, he publicly criticised antisemitism and fascism, not least the latter's celebration of expansionism and heroism. He condemned those who advocated nationalism, considered Europe to be organically culturally united, and served as the vice president of the European Cultural League, where intellectuals strove to establish 'a common European consciousness'. In a speech given in November 1932 entitled 'The Crisis of the European Man', he begged for a radical change of values to avoid militarism and war, and to provide the groundwork for a united Europe. Still living in Germany, he was not publicly outspoken after 1933, but he did invite former students to his home for political discussions in which he was frank enough about the Nazi regime to frighten them. During the war he belonged to a local resistance group and passed on news he picked up from British radio broadcasts to fellow resisters. At the age of 77, he entered politics following the downfall of the Nazi regime in Germany. By the spring of 1945, he had already begun to help the Americans to assemble regional authorities. He then produced several memoranda on economic recovery for the Allied authorities. He founded civil initiatives for a new democratic order, fought for political reform, and wrote articles demanding a new German character: German citizens had previously been characterised by their loyalty, lack of civil courage, and ruthlessness, but now they would be asked to commit to freedom, responsibility, humanity, and an ability to make good judgements. As one of the new deans, he made sure that no one formerly affiliated with the National Socialists could hold a position at the University of Heidelberg. He saw Germany's economic integration in Europe and European unification as the best means to overcome the devastating aftermath of nationalism. However, this was not enough: Europe had experienced its worst crisis ever and was still in danger of seeing integrated social life replaced with nihilism and chaos. The war was over but the threat of nihilism remained rooted in technological civilisation and bureaucratisation, which could only be cured by cultural revitalisation and the advent of a novel democratic citizenry.[134] Certainly, Weber wanted a new Germany and a new Europe, and this kind of conceptual framing placed him in company with other Europeanists who had also begun to talk about integration.

The dramatic decline of Europe was also a main theme for Barbara Ward, economist and journalist for *The Economist*. In her extensive 1948 article on a Western European Union, *The West at Bay*, she observed: 'It is either association or decadence'. When considering what was at stake economically, she observed the 'experiments in integration' in the branches of steel, electricity and transport – for example, a European transport commission that began to operate in 1945 with the purpose of pooling transport facilities in the chaos after the breakdown of Germany. From such examples she concluded that 'integration in certain fields of Western European activity was not as distant as is sometimes supposed'. Ward helped to apply the integration concept to technical cooperation, which promised to achieve 'the integration of . . . different branches on an international basis'. This would serve 'the purpose of widening the basis of Western European economy', to counter the decline by following the example of the United States with only one currency, no barriers to trade, and freedom of movement for both people and money within its borders.[135]

After the war, the concept of integration was applied with different meanings to different situations. The initial steps taken at the Congress of Europe in 1948 can serve as an example. At this event, 'European unity' was the key phrase, while the word 'integration' was only occasionally used. To begin with, the congress addressed the advantage of sharing resources. A suggestion was made in the morning session on the first day of political committee negotiations to alter the paragraph on the political resolution regarding the urgency of the European nations 'jointly exercis[ing] some part of the sovereign rights . . . so as to secure a common political and economic action for the integration and proper development of their common resources'.[136] This motion was passed and included in the English version of the congress's political resolution. In the afternoon session from the same day, the term 'integration' was mentioned in passing by three British delegates when discussing the need for an emergency council that 'should plan the subsequent stages of the political and economic integration of Europe'.[137] Clearly, they wanted to address a development that had already experienced coordination efforts, such as the American-controlled Organisation for European Economic Co-operation (OEEC, 1946), and the Economic Recovery Plan known best as the Marshall Plan (presented in June 1947 and established in April 1948), which at the time included sixteen countries for the purpose of economic recovery. Discussions took place between France and Italy regarding a customs union, the founding of the Benelux Customs Union, and the Brussels Treaty (which in March 1948 created the Western Union for Economic, Social and Cultural Collaboration and Collective Defence). However, the delegates also wanted to move on to further initiatives, envisaging a process of integration. In the session starting late on Sunday at 10.30 PM, the committee used the word 'integration' once again, now closely related to the issue of Germany. How could Germany's large production capacity be directed towards something other than military campaigns against its neighbours, and how could democratic development inside Germany be monitored and fostered? Some delegates, not least the German and French ones, reasoned that *'l'intégration de l'Allemagne dans la Fédération européenne est une necessité'* (the integration of Germany into the European Federation is a necessity), following the reasoning of Weber, who was cited by name.[138] In the English version of the final resolution, it was rephrased as 'the integration of Germany in a United or Federated Europe alone provides a solution to both the economic and political aspects of the

German problem'.[139] Obviously, the term 'integration' had a minor role in the political language of the Congress of Europe, underscored by the French version of the resolution, which used the word '*coordonner*' in one paragraph and omitted it altogether in the other. When used, integration connoted a rational economic order, a solution to the problem posed by Germany, and referred to a process leading towards European unity. Integration was not proposed as a goal, although it was presented along with many other similar suggestions. Weber, Ward, and the Congress of Europe saw integration not as a concept encompassing the lofty visions of unity, union and federation, but rather as something that addressed the practical questions and contested issues at hand.

Integration was a concept that meshed with the ambitions of political leaders hoping to find a path towards unification. It had reached the OEEC by October 1949, when the American director of Marshall Plan aid called for 'an integration of the Western European Economy' with 'the formation of a single market within which quantitative restriction on the movements of goods, monetary barriers to the flow of payments and, eventually, all tariffs are permanently swept away'.[140] Although not explicitly mentioned, the idea worked well for politicians who were ready to relinquish some of the sovereignty of their countries. Integration was a concept that suited such aims, but it did not dominate the rhetoric in the 1950s and had no significant place in the Treaty of Rome, which was signed in 1957. Yet, a description of the venture as 'European integration' was accepted, starting in the early 1950s.[141] The term found a place in political language, where it would eventually become emblematic, and was significantly illustrative of the post-war mindset. It signified practical issues and pragmatic solutions, while still upholding far-reaching visions. When Konrad Adenauer associated 'European integration' with the cooperation between the Christian Democratic parties of Western Europe and an extended understanding between France and Germany, he explained 'that this integration of Europe must be achieved if we want to rescue the Occidental culture and European Christianity'.[142] Robert Schuman talked about integration as a functional method that prioritised technical sectors without being at the centre of political controversies. Thus, he considered 'the coal and steel plan . . . a symbol of European political unity' that 'created an atmosphere in which integration can develop further'.[143] Another important aspect of the concept of integration was that it treated national particularism as a precondition, while still complying with the idea of keeping the European countries close to one another, both to prevent war and to overcome the obstacles facing the economy. Surprisingly, integration was seen as signifying the acceptance of nation states and even as a pledge to retain them, while it was also a way to remedy the conceived nihilism of an international order that set no limits on the nation states.

In a speech given by one of Germany's new leaders at the University of Bonn in 1951, the Christian Democrat Karl Arnold once again defined Hitler as 'a phenomenon of modern nihilism', with no sense of ethics, and whose only ideal was retaining power. Based on this and other previous failures of the German national project to bring peace and freedom to its citizens, Arnold declared that the classical notion of nation-state sovereignty was outdated; the time had come to acknowledge Europe as a fatherland, and to transfer the rights of state and interstate facilities to a European body. Declarations like Arnold's were also heard from politicians in Belgium, France, Italy and the Netherlands, and they were made in response to economic decline and political crisis. The idea was to give up national sovereignty in certain areas, such as defence and the economy, but not in others. Federalists went further and demanded a European political community, for example, when the Italian government of de Gasperi argued that the renunciation of national sovereignty should be followed by the creation of a European Assembly, or when Hendrik Brugmans suggested that a federal Europe could be a coherent alternative when nation states were 'becoming increasingly bureaucratic and centralised'.[144] But going this far was strongly rejected by the French leaders, and the focus turned to economic integration.[145] The history of the integration is well known, but it should be noted that it all took place against the background of perceived threats of decline, crisis and nihilism. Some of the leading politicians were outspoken, while others mentioned integration as one of the costs of internal progress and the price that Europe had to pay to prevent the recurring wars between Germany and France. It was also mentioned that Europe had lost its leading position in the world as a consequence of its divisions and conflicts, the new threat of communism in Eastern Europe, and nationalism in the colonies. However, this pessimistic background was countered by a new sense of optimism, hope, and a belief in European values.

In sum, the concept of integration advanced the political language so as to facilitate further advances of unification. Clearly, integration was more obscure a notion than that of a union or federation. It called for negotiation and would not be easily attained, once and for all. Europeanists married the concept of integration with the concept of European, which was crucial. The concept of integration emphasised the continuity with historical exchanges between states, organisations and people across European borders. It applied to sentiments of cultural unity as well as to national feelings, to the quest to establish shared standards and administrative measures, but also to the development of the nation state. Integration reinforced the closeness between the construction of the EC and the will to strengthen the nation state. Federal aspects were legitimated by national self-interest: Germany was not a threat to its neighbours, and small states found better conditions for their existence. The fear of decline was met with prospects of economic progress, and French hopes of regaining former glory intermingled with German efforts to re-enter Europe.[146] All of this was made possible by the distinction between nation and nationalism, the connected issue of sovereignty, and the concept of integration.

Simultaneously, the concept of European integration served to hide internal divisions between nations as well as aims that were not included, or were even contrary, to the Council of Europe's Declaration of Human Rights and to the values proclaimed in the Treaty of Rome. The approach to integration concealed the persistent colonialism and lingering ambitions to revive old imperialism or make Europe a world power. Throughout the 1950s, the overseas territories were mostly included in unification policies, as was the shameless assertion of cultural superiority.

In the context of unification, we find many international cooperation initiatives. Political parties established networks and set up international bureaus, some even reaching behind the Iron Curtain.[147] Hundreds of organisations were introduced as forums for cooperation in Western Europe. The United States formed some, including NATO, OECD, GATT, and the Bretton Woods bodies, which included non-governmental players such as the Ford Foundation. Others were set up for experts such as the Union for the Coordination of the Production and Transport of Electricity (UCPTE) beginning in 1951, and the European Conference of Ministers of Transport (ECMT) to coordinate transportation, formed in 1953 by sixteen countries and without supranational aspirations. With a transnational approach, recent research on the wide range of cooperation initiatives in Europe in the late 1940s and 1950s rejects the view that the EC was a unique venture, instead viewing it as one of many transnational ventures. A parallel technological Europeanisation took place with the standardisation and interconnection of networks.[148] It is worth noting that such cooperation would not infringe on national control. In the electricity sector, the aim was to create the Western European Pool.[149] Reflecting different notions of European unification, sixteen states founded the European Conference of Postal and Telecommunications Administrations (CEPT) in 1959, establishing an organisation independent of its members with the aim of establishing a supranational status. Such technological Europeanisation indicates the need to distance historical writing from the standard EC/EU approach, and to apply contextual dimensions and longer historical perspectives. Obviously, historian Kiran Klaus Patel's conclusion makes considerable sense, in that what made the EC stand out in contrast to other coordination enterprises was the way it held itself to a higher standard and represented a new option for Europe, not least by endorsing itself as a guarantor of peace and prosperity.[150]

These were the days of combining visions of European unity with the founding of European institutions. Pamphlets were distributed and appeals were published in newspapers and journals. There was the Stikker Plan and the Schuman Declaration. At the regional scale were the Benelux Union and the Nordic Council. There was the Council of Europe, the Organisation for European Economic Co-operation (OECD), and the Action Committee for the United States of Europe. While West European leaders were clearly in favour of unification, they remained divided and unclear as to what kind of unity they wanted. British politicians fostered hopes of being a third global superpower and, starting around 1950, made it clear that they wished to keep their full sovereignty, which put them on track for intergovernmental cooperation. The British media had signalled their wish to be separate from the rest of Europe since the late 1940s, associating the continent with wars and chaos, in contrast to the tolerance, civility and stability of Great Britain.[151] Instead, the French, German and Italian political leaders and parties generally thought it necessary to relinquish some of their sovereignty but differed as to which parts and how much to let go.

With the formation of the Council of Europe in 1949, which included most of the European states, one piece was finally in place, but it could not solve the immediate problems that demanded the relinquishment of sovereignty. However, a deep crisis in the coal and steel industry had begun, which led to the establishment of the more exclusive European Coal and Steel Community in the Paris Treaty of 1951 with its High Authority, which was a supranational executive mechanism, as well as the European Court of Justice. These proved to be the initial pieces that were needed. Meanwhile, the Benelux countries had already created a union, and de Gaspari's Italian government suggested the European Political Community. However, stumbling blocks were in the way. In Germany, formation of a European community was questioned, in fear that it might prevent reunification with its Eastern part; and the Soviet Union opposed a Western European Union, which they conceived as a military threat. The quest for a European Defence Community failed to pass the French National Assembly by a small margin in 1954, with the opposition afraid the French would not retain control of their military forces. Military co-operation emerged in its place, along with the Western European Union, but remained quite insignificant. The European Atomic Community was more successful. Behind all these efforts lay the history of Europe's crisis and decline, and the fear of a new wave of German nationalism, together with the potential economic and military opportunities presented by unification. As NATO came into being in 1955, the focus of European unity turned towards the economy. Germany strove for economic recovery, and its Western partners needed a strong German economy to push their own economies out of their trajectories of decline.[152] It is important to note that the focus on the economy had widespread appeal, as the Christian Democratic Italian prime minister de Gasperi noted in a speech: a European Union's 'ecclesiastical frontiers and frontiers of thought and culture raise no barriers, as may be seen at these international meetings where we find ourselves side by side with socialists, free thinkers, and – oddly enough – trade union representatives. Why? Because the necessity of obtaining an expanded market and the free circulation of labour, of overcoming economic frontiers, impels us all irresistibly'.[153] Indeed, the economic motivation offered a way forward.

In 1957, the six founding states signed the Treaty of Rome and formed the European Economic Community (EEC) with a common market, while in 1960, Austria, Great Britain, Portugal, Switzerland and the Scandinavian countries chose the more modest track of economic coordination with lower trade tariffs on certain products. At the time, sentiments were lukewarm in the European Free Trade Association (EFTA) countries towards European unification, but this would gradually change. The EEC developed into the European Community, and the European Union developed the integration project and attracted new members. The 1950s have been seen as a decisive period in European history, and this view is justifiable with regard to the launching of the EEC and EC, and subsequently the EU; finally, after dreaming of European unity for so long, something of that kind was about to materialise.

In this book and this chapter, the focus has been on the concept of Europe. Throughout the 1940s and 1950s, the idea of European cultural unity remained strong and was connected to the possibility of economic and political unification. The notions of European crisis, decline and nihilism were stressed, together with the view that Europe had lost its position as a world leader to the United States and the Soviet Union, while the concept of Europe and European ideas still embraced colonial sentiments and paternalistic attitudes towards overseas European subjects. The perceived threat of the Soviet Union coincided with a general fear of communism. America was the stronghold, though Europe was distinct from both superpowers. There was considerable fear of nationalism, and pressure to resolve the German question. The distinction between nation and nationalism, which supported retreating from the promise of nation-state sovereignty, also facilitated fusing demands for European unification with the concept of integration. If a country abstained from nationalism, it was then possible to focus on the development and welfare of one's own nation using European integration, allowing European unification to happen organically through nations coming together. As a result, visionary ideals were combined with practical action. Outspoken idealism was connected with pragmatism in practice. Importantly, the concept of Europe associated itself with both unity *and* borders within Europe.

Notes

1. See, e.g., Toynbee, *Civilization on Trial*; Meinecke, *Die deutsche Katastrophe*.
2. Cf. Ighe, 'Never Mind Patriarchy'.
3. Stråth, *Europe's Utopias of Peace*, 363.
4. Lipgens, *Documents on European Integration*.
5. Milward, *Rescue of the Nation-State*.
6. Forlenza, 'Politics of the Abendland', 261–86.
7. Benda, 'Conférence du 2 septembre', 5–9.
8. Spender, 'Conférence du 11 septembre', 267–69.
9. Benda, *L'esprit européen*, 162, 298, 347, 383.
10. Bernanos, 'Conférence du 12 septembre 1946', 351.
11. Benda, 'Conférence du 2 septembre', 36–38.
12. Flora, 'Conférence du 2 septembre', 39–45, 65.
13. Eliot, *Definition of Culture*, 120–22.
14. Ortega y Gasset, 'De Europa meditatio quaedam'; Ortega y Gasset, 'Gibt es ein europäisches Kulturbewusstsein?'; Gray, *The Imperative of Modernity*, 339–42; Berlanga, 'Europa hora cero'.
15. Hewitson, 'Inventing Europe', 65.
16. Rauschning, *Time of Delirium*, 355.
17. Jaspers, *Der philosophische Glaube*, 103.
18. Jaspers, *Europa der Gegenwart*, 38–40.
19. Ibid., 8–28.
20. Bess, *Realism, Utopia, Mushroom Cloud*, 4–21, quotation from 17.
21. Schmale, 'Before Self-Reflexivity'.
22. Reynold, *La Formation*.
23. Flora, 'Conférence du 2 septembre', 40.
24. Spender, 'Conférence du 11 septembre', 267–72, 289–90.
25. Ward, *The West at Bay*.
26. Ortega y Gasset, 'De Europa meditatio quaedam', quoted from Gray, *The Imperative of Modernity*, 339–41.
27. Madariaga, *Portrait of Europe*, 204.
28. Rougemont, *Man's Western Quest*.
29. Coudenhove-Kalergi, *Die europäische Nation*, 9–10, 145.
30. Rougemont, 'Conférence du 8 septembre', 172–97.
31. From Rougemont's quotations of Eliot: Rougemont, *Idea of Europe*, 429–31.
32. Aron, 'Old Nations, New Europe', 53.
33. Ortega y Gasset, 'Gibt es europäisches Kulturbewusstsein?'
34. From Rougemont's quotations of Ernst Jünger: Rougemont, *Idea of Europe*, 427–29.
35. From Rougemont's quotations of Jean-Paul Sartre: Rougemont, *Idea of Europe*, 433–34.
36. Madariaga, 'That European River'.
37. Eliade, 'Von der Unteilberheit Europas'.
38. Fornäs, *Signifying Europe*, 105.
39. Madariaga, *Victors, Beware*, 158–59.

40. Delanty, 'Europe and "Unity in Diversity"'.
41. Carr, *Jaspers as Intellectual Critic*, 71–72.
42. Dubreuil, 'Personalism of Denis Rougemont', 205.
43. Mannheim, *Sociology of Knowledge*, 276–320.
44. See WorldCat: www.worldcat.org. In, e.g. Swedish, we find Jaspers with his discussion of German guilt in 1947, Madariaga's six titles between 1938 and 1951, including one novel, literary criticism, and political writings, de Rougemont with his critique of fascism and communism in 1952, and Stephen Spender only in 1957 with his autobiography.
45. Saunders, *Who Paid the Piper?*, 92–97, 115–20, 142, 329, 394–95.
46. The other honorary chairs were Jacques Maritain, Reinhold Niebuhr and Bertrand Russell; the secretary-general was Nicolas Nabokov.
47. Coleman, *The Liberal Conspiracy*, 9, 31, 53, 95.
48. Llobera, 'Visions of Europe'.
49. Benda, *Discourse à la nation européenne*.
50. Spender, *European Witness*, 23–24.
51. Ibid., 94–97.
52. Rougemont, *Man's Western Quest*, 148–66, quotation from 166.
53. Madariaga, *Essays with a Purpose*, 12–15.
54. Jaspers, *Europa der Gegenwart*, 17–18, 35–36.
55. Madariaga, *Essays with a Purpose*, 3–5.
56. De Rougemont, 'Denis de Rougemont, 8 septembre 1946', 179–84.
57. Spender, 'Conférence du 11 septembre'.
58. Jaspers, *Europa der Gegenwart*, 1–56.
59. Spender, 'Conférence du 11 septembre', 271, 287–89.
60. Rougemont, *The Last Trump*, 128.
61. Jaspers, *Die Atombombe*.
62. Jaspers, *Europa der Gegenwart*, 34–36, 56.
63. Rougemont, 'Conférence du 8 septembre', 181–83; Spender, 'Conférence du 11 septembre', 269, 276.
64. Rougemont, 'Conférence du 8 septembre', 181–83; de Rougemont, 'Die Krankheit'.
65. Spender, 'Conférence du 11 septembre', 267–72, 279.
66. Ibid., 283–87.
67. Madariaga, *Portrait of Europe*, 17–25.
68. Madariaga, *Essays with a Purpose*, 12–15.
69. Jaspers, *Europa der Gegenwart*, 37. On Jaspers' view of greatness, see especially his extensive introduction, 'Über Grossheit', to Jaspers, *Die grossen Philosophen*.
70. Rougemont, *The Last Trump*, 90–91.
71. Rougemont, 'Conférence du 8 septembre', 185–93.
72. Madariaga, *Democracy versus Liberty?*, 4–13. The book is a translation of the second part of Madariaga's *De l'angoisse á la liberté* from 1954.
73. Spender, 'Conférence du 11 septembre', 279.
74. Jaspers, *Europa der Gegenwart*, 34–42, quotation from 38: 'Menschen sich gegenseitig freilassen und in gegenseitigen Betroffenheit aneinander teilnehmen'.
75. Spender, 'Conférence du 11 septembre', 279–81.
76. Rougemont, 'Conférence du 8 septembre'; Rougemont, 'Die Krankheit'.
77. Madariaga, *Victors, Beware*, 152–59.
78. Spender, *European Witness*, 93.
79. Spender, 'Conférence du 11 septembre', 281–82.
80. Rougemont, 'Conférence du 8 septembre', 189–92, 197; Rougemont, *The Last Trump*, 104–15, quotation from 110.
81. Rougemont, *Man's Western Quest*, 157, 177–79.

82. Rougemont, 'Die Krankheit'.
83. Madariaga, *Victors, Beware*, 152–59.
84. Berlin, *Sense of Reality*.
85. Madariaga, *Victors, Beware*, 152–59.
86. Madariaga, *Portrait of Europe*, 1–6.
87. Madariaga, *Portrait of Europe*, 9–16.
88. Madariaga, *Portrait of Europe*, 156. See also Madariaga, *The World's Design*.
89. Daniels, 'Europe and the Swiss System'.
90. Churchill, 'The Tragedy of Europe'.
91. *Congress of Europe*, 31: 'Notre ambition n'est-elle pas la plus haute? Construire un monde de paix, de liberté et de justice sociale, et, pour cela, cimenter les premiéres pierras en faisant l'Europe!'
92. Ibid., 8.
93. Ibid., 5.
94. Ibid., 11, 16.
95. Ibid., 5.
96. Ibid., 16.
97. Quoted from Walton, 'The Hague "Congress of Europe"'.
98. Roberts, 'Towards European Unity'.
99. Grewe, 'Europa-Kongress in Haag'.
100. E.g., Tory MP Lady Grant; see *Congress of Europe*, 215–16.
101. *Congress of Europe*, 334.
102. Ibid., 31.
103. Ibid., 203–4.
104. Roberts, 'Towards European Unity', 174–77.
105. *Europe Unites*, 94.
106. Quotation from Aster, *Power, Policy and Personality*, 524.
107. Guerrieri, 'From the Hague Congress'.
108. *Congress of Europe*, 87.
109. Ibid., 50–51. Regarding Mackay and the contestations within Labour on the European idea and the Congress of Europe, see Grantham, 'Labour and "Congress of Europe"'.
110. *Congress of Europe*, 74.
111. Ibid., 176.
112. Aster, *Power, Policy and Personality*, 501.
113. Forlenza, 'The Politics of the Abendland'.
114. *European Unites*, 88.
115. *Congress of Europe*, 397–98.
116. Ibid., 249–50: 'Je crois que nous devrions nous souvenir . . . que s'il y a une tradition occidentale de la culture, son secret réside dans sa volonte d'universalite, non pas dans la volonté do faire croire au mondo que ce qui est européen est universel de plein droit, mais au contraire dans la volonté d'affirmer su monde et de maintenir énergiquement que tout ce qui est universel est européen de plein droit'.
117. *Congress of Europe*, 401: 'Nous ne voulons pas nous flatter d'une culture européenne qui serait supérieure á des cultures non-européennes; nos no voulons pas inventar une culture qui seirat bonne parce qu'elle sera européenne. Nous voulons, au contraire, que notre culture soit europeenne parce qu'elle sera bonne. Nous n'avone aucunement l'intention de décréter l'universalité de la culture européenne, mais nous considérerons comme faisant partie de la culture de l'urope tout ce qui est universel et nous dirons que tout ce qui est universel est notre, et que, dans cette volonté d'universalisme, ouvert á tous pour donner et pour recevoir, réside notre seule particularité'.
118. Hansen and Jonsson, *Eurafrica*, 108–11.

119. *Congress of Europe*, 176.
120. Ibid., 361–64.
121. *Europe Unites*, 94.
122. *Congress of Europe*, 332–33.
123. Ibid., 336, 360, 402–3.
124. Grantham, 'British Labour and The Hague'.
125. Richard, 'The Limits of Solidarity'.
126. Ibid.
127. Schmale, 'Before Self-Reflexivity', 194–96.
128. *Congress of Europe*, 3–5.
129. Meinecke, *Die deutsche Katastrophe*, 161. See also Jaspers, *Europa der Gegenwart*.
130. Weber, *Abschied von der bisherigen Geschichte*, 13–14 (in English *Farewell to European History*). On Weber, see Heberle, 'In Memoriam: Alfred Weber'.
131. E.g., Herriot, *Europe*, 98.
132. Gaedicke and Eynern, *Die produktionswirtschaftliche Integration*. See also Machlup, *A History of Integration*, 4–6.
133. Weber, *Abschied von der bisherigen Geschichte*, 234–36.
134. Demm, 'Alfred Weber und die Nationalsozialisten', 223–31. Quotation from Loader, *Weber and Crisis of Culture*, 112, see also 61–63, 159–61.
135. Ward, *The West at Bay*, 186–95.
136. *Congress of Europe*, 73.
137. Ibid., 107.
138. Ibid., 112–26, quotation from 220.
139. *Europe Unites*, 38.
140. Stråth, *Europe's Utopias of Peace*, 353–54.
141. See, e.g., how it is used in the journal *Foreign Affairs* by Mansholt, 'Toward European Integration', or by Hallstein, 'Germany's Dual Aim'.
142. Adenauer, '14 September 1951'.
143. Schuman, 'France and Europe'.
144. Brugmans, *Towards a European Government*, 28; Gasperi, 'Extract from a Speech 1952'.
145. Hewitson, 'Europe and the Fate of the World', 47.
146. Bruneteau, 'The Construction of Europe'.
147. See, e.g., Kosnicki, 'The Soviet Bloc's Answer'.
148. Patel, 'Provincialising European Union'.
149. Lagendijk, 'Ideas, Individuals and Institutions'.
150. Patel, 'Provincialising European Union'.
151. Webster, 'From Nazi Legacy'.
152. For historians' perspectives on the European idea and the initial post-war integration, see Hewitson, 'Europe and the Fate of the World'; Pasture, *Imagining European Unity*, 165–84.
153. Gasperi, 'Extract from a Speech 1952', 199.

CHAPTER 9

Elevating European Awareness

Is Europe the same as the European Union (EU)? The question may appear naive, as we all know that substantial parts of the continent are not member states. We know the political history, that states successively joined 'the club' as it grew from six to twenty-eight members. Now, Britain has left, but perhaps more countries will join. The EU has certainly had a great impact on the rest of Europe. However, we are also aware that the Council of Europe has almost fifty members. Neither geographically nor politically is Europe interchangeable with the EU. Still, we often hear the terms used together, which can be very convenient. So, when did the EU become Europe? One answer is that it was there from the beginning of the economic community in the 1950s. The founding rhetoric took on the Europeanist claim to represent the future of Europe, as we saw at the Congress of Europe in 1948. Nine years later, the signatories of the Treaty of Rome attested to the claim of beginning a process in which others would follow, thereby representing Europe's unification and, in a sense, the essence of Europe. The treaty began by claiming to provide the 'foundation of an ever-closer union between the European peoples', not limiting itself to the then six member nations. The claim of the European Economic Community (EEC) to represent Europe included promises of 'eliminating the barriers which divide Europe' and improving the living standards and working conditions of its peoples. Only the final paragraph of the preamble's presentation of the basic principles of the treaty directed the reader's attention to the fact that some of Europe had been excluded, by 'calling upon the other peoples of Europe who share' the founding members' efforts. Moreover, the common bodies appointed

Notes for this section begin on page 295.

were the European Commission, the European Social Fund, the European Investment Bank, and the European Atomic Energy Community.[1] The new community and its institutions had dressed themselves up as Europe.

There is fundamentally more to the story, from the perspective of intellectual history. One major characteristic of post-World War Two Europe was the quest to revive the concept of Europe. However, the situation was always more complicated, with academic opinions split between unification or division, and between decline or hope of a new self-awareness. Defenders of unification claimed that the concept of Europe was synonymous with the integration that was underway. Along with this came the key theme of European awareness and the ambition to raise the consciousness of being European, which engaged intellectuals, not least historians, in the early decades of the post-war period. Beginning in the 1980s, another main theme emerged: European identity. It was nurtured within the European Commission's programmatic ambition to raise European consciousness, as well as because of a general interest in the concept of identity, reflected in politics and among intellectuals.

The concept of Europe was increasingly associated with unification as well as with borders within Europe, which had consequences regarding disputes about the meanings of Europe. What were the origins of European unity and its divisions? Was European awareness connected to its historical origins or focused on its future organisation? When did a European identity begin to emerge? Who was European? Just as the integration concept was a new contribution to the political language of post-war cooperation and unification, beginning around 1970 and gaining ground in the 1980s and 1990s, 'identity' had become interwoven with the political language. European identity became a key concept, just as European integration had previously. However, while integration was primarily associated with economic, legal and political affairs, identity was concerned with the conceptualisation of Europe as a community in the broader sense. It is perhaps no surprise, then, that the close ties between the EU agenda and the launching of European identity brought about controversies. The discourse on Europe's future was energised by visions of the future as well as by the concept of a European culture marked by its diversity.

Ambivalent Narrative: Unification or Division

Writing about the European idea in the 1960s, Denis de Rougemont highlighted the new interest of contemporary historians in a cultural unity that was much older than the Treaty of Rome. He illustrated this by citing historians from eleven different nationalities, all from countries west of the Iron

Curtain, and focused on the development of a Western culture, apparently based in Britain, France and Germany. Certainly, de Rougemont's historiography was intended to confirm the development of a European federation, presenting a teleological approach to history, and claiming that European civilisation should be based on Christian values, represent universalism, and be responsible for the future of humanity.[2] He stated that historians in Western Europe had answered the call for a historical narrative of the development of European unity rather than one emphasising the differences and disputes among nation states.[3] Recent research confirms this interest among post-war historians, and demonstrates the intensified activity that went into making Europe a theme in writing history.[4] However, the situation is more complex than that. It includes contrasting views between a concept of Europe that is limited to Western Europe and one that includes larger parts of the continent, and between the narrative of an emerging Europe, and one of a declining and disintegrating Europe.

De Rougemont silently neglected a range of historians who expressed pessimism about Europe's future and/or included Central European countries in their definition and discussion of the future of Europe. Exiled Polish historians Francis Dvornik, Oscar Halecki and Otto Forst de Battaglia recalled and elaborated on the concepts of Central Europe and East Central Europe as a territorial and cultural area that used to belong to Europe but was overtaken by the Soviet Union and the communists.[5] The emigrant historiographical literature reiterated Halecki and Dvornik's stressing of previous attempts at state building throughout history to embrace the multinational communities of the region. They were disillusioned by the region's nation states, with their weaknesses of aggressive tendencies, border disputes, and history of deportations and massacres. Some pleaded for a federation of states surrounding the Danube, recalling the Dual Monarchy of Austria-Hungary and its cultural heritage.[6] This literature was characterised by the intention to demonstrate alternatives to the polarisation between the Soviet Union and the United States with its consequences for Central Europe. The authors highlighted Yugoslavia and Romania's success in distancing themselves from the Soviet Union and the uprisings in East Germany, Poland, Hungary and Czechoslovakia, as illustrating a widespread desire for a neutral Central Europe. They mentioned propositions from the British Labour leader Denis Healey to make Central Europe into a nuclear-free zone, and from Khrushchev and Churchill about a neutral Germany. A neutral zone between the East and the West – perhaps also encompassing the Nordic countries, the Baltic states, and the Balkans – was conceived as an essential way for Central Europe to oppose the rule of the Soviet Union.[7]

Historians who avoided the narrative of European unity could nevertheless draw attention to European awareness. Oscar Halecki, living in exile in the United States, sided with American scholars who spoke in terms of an Atlantic community to indicate the end of Europe's position of leadership as the stronghold of Western civilisation. The Second World War, Halecki concluded, definitely brought 'the passing from the European to the Atlantic Age', which implied that Europe and European civilisation could no longer be considered global models, and that we had arrived at 'the end of European history'. Furthermore, while Europe had previously been a unique community with an awareness of unity that transcended national and political differences, it had now ceased to exist: 'It is disintegrating right before our eyes', leaving contemporary historians to mark 'the un-making of Europe'.[8] The conclusion was logical. Halecki's Europe embraced the nations of Central Europe, the Baltic states, and the Balkans, which generally included the nations west of Russia (Ukraine and Belarus would also be classified as European nations if they 'should get free from Soviet Russia').[9] In Britain, Geoffrey Barraclough stated that history writing had new premises, as Europe's historical importance belonged to the past. Europe was politically insignificant in a global age, while some of its heritage could live on, such as an awareness of 'the worth of human dignity and the importance of the human individual'. He added that 'we must not expect the same implicit acceptance of these values as in the past'.[10] In Austria, the cultural historian Friedrich Heer argued that more attention must be paid to Eastern Europe, especially by Western intellectuals and elites. Through teaching and research, universities would need to engage in elevating awareness and knowledge of East European nations and languages. Heer – the same scholar who had pleaded for a German Europe during the war – now attested to a long history of unity with the West as he focused on the cultural traditions and expressions of cultural unity from Croatia to Poland, clearly emphasising the role of Western Christianity. Like Halecki and Barraclough, Heer found elements of Western culture in Russia, though they were not enough to overcome what he saw as the basic conflict between East and West: 'the unavoidable opposition between Greek and Latin spirit and genius'. Instead, he (vaguely) hoped to change the relationship, permitting new forms of productive exchange.[11]

In Chapter 8, we examined the post-1945 notion of a European heritage of cultural unity that could go beyond national differences. This perspective grew in popularity with the Council of Europe's attempts to nurture the consciousness of belonging to Europe and of being Europeans. In the 1950s, these attempts largely emphasised the writing of history, including sponsoring conferences with the aim of rewriting history textbooks, establishing courses on the idea of Europe, and promoting studies of integration. The Council of Europe initiated discussions with historians, for example, at the European Round Table in Rome in 1953 and in

Strasbourg in 1955, in which historians played key roles. These meetings brought historians together with high-ranking politicians such as Alcide de Gasperi and Robert Schuman, as well as other scholars from various disciplines in order to scrutinise the background of European unity. The Council of Europe appointed Denis de Rougemont as chair, the young British historian Max Beloff as secretary, and Arnold Toynbee as an additional discussant. Among the government-appointed delegates was the only female participant, the Irish historian Síle Ní Chinnéide.[12] Afterwards, Beloff summed up the discussions in *Europe and the Europeans* (1957), with lengthy presentations about European history and upcoming tasks. At the time, Beloff leaned towards liberalism and shared some of the enthusiasm regarding European integration, something that would change later in his career. Yet, he wanted to draw his own conclusions and distanced himself from the federalist convictions of de Rougemont, instead pleading for a kind of integration that could preserve the nation states, certain jointly conducted affairs, and common bodies. Moreover, his view of the historical background differed from the teleological approach represented by de Rougemont. He did not agree that the historical European unity had ended or been severely damaged by the two world wars. He attested only to a historical unity following cultural exchanges, and cited many examples of Europe's political and religious divisions from the Middle Ages up to the present. For Beloff, political unification after 1945 was a substantially new concept, as it was impossible for the states to return to their pre-war conditions. In addition, he made a general statement at the round-table discussions stressing not only the need to coexist with Christianity but also 'the presence of sizable groups of adherents of non-Christian faiths to all of whom toleration must be granted'. He continued to assert that the contrast of politics with religions, literature, art, architecture and music had never ceased at national borders. The national schools of painting represented a major development. Within the different national literatures, there was a European pattern. About European literature, Beloff wrote 'this European sense of the pity and the dignity, and the tragedy of the personal human adventure resisted all the challenges of time'.[13] In architecture, the central traditions commingled with many regional varieties. Beloff stressed 'common trade-routes of European sensibility' and 'a capacity for mutual understanding' crossing national borders. He also said that 'many Europeans today are unaware that these common elements in their culture are more fundamental than the national differences, and do not appreciate the originality of this common culture'.[14] He ended up agreeing that it was necessary to increase awareness of a European culture.

Therefore, in the first decades following the Second World War, some historians began to take a new interest in European history, emphasising

European unity in one way or another. This coincided with the drive to advance European awareness and the consciousness of being European. It is typical that the French author of a three-volume work on Europe's history would state his understanding of the politicians' struggle to unify Europe, in addition urging them to care 'for the pupils of their countries learning European history'.[15] A federalist school began to develop in the 1970s, which investigated the historiography of European integration. Walter Lipgens, a founding member of this school, had a degree of respect throughout Western Europe, and especially among Italian historians. The school's focus was on the crisis of the nation state and on the federalist movement's promotion of the teleological approach. Federalist historiography upheld a political outlook, which came as no surprise – Lipgens saw the decline of Christianity as a driving force of the European crisis, and wanted any unification to come hand in hand with a redefinition of values that would create a roadmap for academic research. In this tradition, 'federation is written into the destiny of the Europeans, and the role of scholars is to disclose the true path of history'.[16]

The recurring topic of European awareness also entailed discussion of the weak European consciousness. On the one hand, the EEC had achieved economic success and attracted other countries to join its ranks; on the other, critics were quick to point out that the six founding states had little sense of community among themselves. The French sociologist Raymond Aron warned of the disintegration of European culture caused by the influences of mass consumption and American culture, exemplified by cinema and music, and by the trend of students and researchers preferring to visit universities in the United States rather than those in Germany, Great Britain or France. He saw a waning awareness of European cultural unity, with, for example, the decreasing exchange of cinema and literature between France and Spain. Coupled with a lack of political will to create a European state, he concluded that 'Europe will have to settle for continued economic growth', clearly seeing the EEC as the essence of Europe, with which the other West European nations would cooperate in one way or another.[17] In the late 1970s, he published articles and a book entitled *In Defence of Decadent Europe* that continued the lamentations about European culture in decline, hedonistic lifestyles, and the loss of traditional authorities, resulting in the disintegration of values such as tolerance and critical thinking. With less of a sense of European civilisation, socialists and peace activists were unaware of the imminent threats posed by Marxism, communism and the Soviet Union. Based on this, he believed it was crucial for Europe to rely on NATO, the United States, and nuclear weapons for defence. In the late 1970s, this meant arming the borders of Eastern Europe with Pershing II missiles.[18] Apparently, the communist countries were excluded from Europe, and a conservative-leaning intellectual such as Aron found appeal in the idea of European unification but was pessimistic about it in the face of perceived disintegration.

Europe beyond the Iron Curtain: The Central European Perspective

After 1968, when Soviet and Warsaw Pact troops had crushed all major rebellion and protest in Czechoslovakia's Prague Spring, very few in Western Europe considered the possibility of demolishing the wall between Europe's capitalist West and the communist East. This was when Central European intellectuals advocated the concept of Europe in hopes of a new order. Expelled from Charles University during the repression of the Hušak regime in the 1970s, the philosopher Jan Patočka held private seminars with other dissidents, in which he laid out a concept of Europe that accepted neither being divided into nation states nor the existence of a divide between East and West through the middle of Europe. Patočka identified a common European trait in a technological civilisation that had taken over the world; it had presented 'substitutes where the original is needed' and 'alienated humans from themselves, depriving them of dwelling in the world, submerging them in the everyday alternative which is not so much toil as boredom'. Humans were 'destroyed externally and impoverished internally'; deprived of themselves, 'they are identified with their roles, standing and falling with them'. Taking a position similar to those of José Ortega y Gasset and Karl Jaspers, his criticism of some European accomplishments was countered by a defence of the relevance of others. This very same civilisation provided opportunities 'more than any other constellation: a life without violence and with far-reaching equality of opportunity'. Never before in history had humankind been so equipped with 'the means to struggle with external misery, with lack and want, which this civilisation offers'.[19] Patočka energised his concept of Europe with hope that emerged from existing possibilities.

Like Václav Havel, the most famous member of his seminars, Patočka was a spokesman for the Charta 77 declaration, together with Jiří Hájek, who served as foreign minister during the Prague Spring. According to Patočka, the Charta called for citizenship rights and political freedom, emphasising the need to establish a moral foundation for society and an active citizenry.[20] Its originators were severely harassed by the police, leading to the death of Patočka in March 1977. Havel adopted the distinction between a life in truth and a life in lies from Patočka, and the subtitle of his most famous essay, 'The Power of the Powerless', paid tribute to the late philosopher: 'In Memory of Jan Patočka'.

In his essay 'Politics and Conscience', Václav Havel echoed Patočka when he identified Europe as the place where the rationalistic spirit of modern science and the universalising trend of modern civilisation had originated, emphasising technological achievements while neglecting real-world experiences, empathy and common sense, and 'relegating personal conscience and consciousness to the bathroom'. With this civilisation came impersonal power and management techniques that originated in Western Europe and were often forced on the rest of the world. This tendency was embraced and further developed in communist Eastern Europe. Most of all, Havel concluded, the totalitarian regimes in communist Eastern Europe represented 'a convex mirror [reflecting] the inevitable consequences of rationalism, . . . of its own deep tendencies, . . . an ominous product of its own expansion'. Consequently, he issued a warning to contemporary civilisation, and regarded the deployment of nuclear missiles by the United States and Soviet Union in Central Europe as a disastrous consequence of the rationalistic spirit. Worried about the future, he noted the hope of 'Europe soon to turn into a free community of independent countries in which no great power would have its armies and its rockets', and to convert itself 'into a continent of peace'.[21]

Among 1980s dissidents, definitions of Europe alluded to both political tasks and cultural heritage. To undermine bloc politics, Hungarian novelist György Konrád called for European emancipation, independence, and a new self-consciousness based on neutrality. This would set the stage for a large European Union including East Central Europe, with the further mission to integrate the world, defend human rights and the value of each individual, and ensure that humankind would avoid wars and ecological disasters in order to survive. Culturally, he identified a long collective memory emanating from and including European literature: in reading the shared classics, a dialogue between people of different ages and parts of the continent emerged. He likened Europe to a lively library in which authors, dead and alive, walked among the readers.[22] As for the association of the concept of Europe with the East–West divide and the nuclear arms race, so typical of the 1980s, Havel elaborated on a vision of another European future in his acceptance speech when awarded the Erasmus Prize in 1986. He alluded to Patočka when he returned to the idea of a free and peaceful pan-European community, urging both governments and people to press forward to realise it. He contrasted the troublesome and threatening rationalist spirit of science with the common spiritual heritage stemming from antiquity and traditional Judeo–Christian principles that had shaped Europe for the better. The concluding words of his speech were: 'There exists but one Europe, a Europe [that] may be divided politically but is not divided – indeed, it is spiritually indivisible'.[23]

In the 1980s, intellectuals east of the Iron Curtain entertained a concept of Central Europe that allowed a self-understanding in contrast to the area's communist regimes, and offered another example of the elevation of European awareness. All those engaged in upholding this concept refused to accept that the area's true character was connected to the Soviet Union. In a key 1984 essay, 'The Tragedy of Central Europe', the exiled Czech novelist Milan Kundera related the concept of Central Europe to a strong desire to get away from the Soviet Union. Like others, he expanded on a Russian anti-Western tradition traceable to the old Byzantium, a tradition kept alive and thriving under Soviet communism. Central Europe had been abducted and politically defined by the East, while remaining culturally at home with and longing to return to the West.[24] Moreover, these intellectuals expanded on the concept of Central Europe to identify specific characteristics of the area.

The playwright Václav Havel, writing in a unique blend of seriousness, humour and irony, stated that Central Europeans feel that taking themselves too seriously appears foolish, but that they understand that it is important to take risks to make one's life worth living.[25] Czesław Miłosz, the Polish author and Nobel Prize winner, identified irony and the presence of history as elements of the attitude of certain Central European intellectuals, extending beyond their linguistic and national groupings. They had developed a conviction that true citizenship demanded a political and social life free from the state and church: 'Central Europe is an act of faith, a project . . . a utopia'.[26]

Likewise, the Hungarian author György Konrád connected Central Europe with a worldview that went beyond nationalism: 'Being a Central European does not mean having a nationality but rather an outlook on the world'. He talked about the dream of Central Europe, referring to both the vanished Austria-Hungary and a yet-to-exist community beyond the divisions of Europe. This community would be held together by a civil spirit surpassing national egotism; it would tolerate minorities and eschew the military blocs of the Cold War. This worldview encompassed a range of positive attributes: the power to manage contradictions; aesthetic sensitivity to the complexity of contexts; a strategy of understanding when meeting enemies; and acknowledgement of and solidarity with the individuality of every person. Although Central Europe did not yet exist, it was an ideal worth fighting for.[27]

However, the Serbian author Danilo Kiš disputed the existence of any such Central European community. He confessed to recognising some common culture in Central Europe – legends, poems and dramas from the Middle Ages and the Renaissance – but argued that differences between the national cultures trumped the resemblances. National cultures had developed despite Austria and the Habsburg rule, primarily in regional opposition to Vienna and the influence of France and West European thought, representing national antagonisms overruling mutual understanding. Kiš mentioned Croatian intellectuals around the year 1900 who conceived of Vienna as the target of their political reaction, and disliked modern artists, Sigmund Freud, and everything else associated with the Austrian capital. In addition, he recognised Serbian culture as influenced by Russia and its mythology.[28] In this way, Kiš reconfirmed the previous national and religious differences from the Austrian Empire, and entertained doubts about the possibility of transcending national borders. Still, he recognised a kind of antiauthoritarianism particular to Central Europe, associating it with Karl Popper's vision of the open society, and believing that it emerged from Central Europeans.[29]

In the quest for Central European uniqueness, nostalgia was never far away, with dreams of the Habsburg Double Monarchy and the lost *fin-de-siècle* culture of Budapest, Prague and Vienna. For instance, Konrád praised the coexistence of nationalities in Kakania, while Kiš commented on the interest in Central Europe as simply a longing for a Europe undivided between East and West.[30] By contrast, the Slovak Milan Simečka noted the dark sides of Central Europe. In the Central European closet were secrets and mysteries that might not be explained simply by Russian influence and domination. Recalling the interbellum authoritarian regimes, he hinted that even at the end of the Second World War, national interests were worth more than democratic freedoms.[31]

A recurring theme was that the Jewish population had contributed to the high culture of the Central European metropolises of the 1900s, giving Central European culture a cosmopolitan and integrating character.[32] Kiš saw a substantial Jewish contribution to Central European culture; it brought culture, colour and music, and was its dynamic force. However, as the Jewish population was almost gone, he concluded that Central Europe as a historical and cultural phenomenon belonged to the past.[33]

Culture emerged as a theme in the discussion, and several writers resorted to belles-lettres as a way of exposing the uniqueness of Central Europe. Hungarian historian István Fried noted the development of a more political and patriotic sense of responsibility in nineteenth-century Central Europe, compared with Western Europe. Hungarian literary scholar Csaba G. Kiss claimed that Central European literature was able to express the weakness of small nations under the threat of powerful states, in addition to exposing national coexistence amid linguistic and cultural diversity. For Kiss, this was one aspect of the cultural melting pot that he and several others considered to be the defining feature of Central Europe.[34] Kundera added another Central European feature – namely, the expectation that authors and philosophers should speak out on political issues and represent unassailable moral values, citing examples from the post-war revolts in

Budapest, Prague and Warsaw that appeared in novels, poetry, and literary magazines, on stage, in movies, and in cabarets, as well as in historical writing and philosophical debates.[35]

Turning to Identity

With the fall of communism in 1989–91, the theme of European identity became salient. Its emergence was by no means sudden, but well prepared. We find it in the early post-World War Two period in relation to common values – for example, regarding whether to consider undemocratic Portugal and Spain as countries with European values, and 'the establishment of a European identity within the Atlantic Alliance'.[36] In the early 1970s, the concept of European identity gained currency in political contexts. In 1969, a speaker in the British Parliament mentioned European identity in conjunction with European states' contributions to NATO, but soon the notion became connected to the issue of a common identity, as opposed to national identities. In the Dutch Parliament, European identity became associated with issues of second-language learning in schools and withstanding the pressure of American popular culture. Swedish members of parliament agreed with the idea of a European identity, and discussed whether this entailed alignment with the European Community and NATO, or whether they could continue to remain neutral.[37]

The discourse of European identity extended several discourses that preceded the fall of communism, some with roots in the nineteenth and twentieth centuries. Havel and Konrád represented one case, associating Central European freedom with a shared European sense of unity and a common destiny. Another case was the relationship between Russia and Europe, posited as central during the perestroika of the 1980s. Mikhail Gorbachev argued strongly that Russia had a place in the 'house of Europe', while others both inside and outside of Russia stressed important differences between the two areas.[38] The relationship between several European countries and Europe as a whole represented a similar issue when it came to Member States, accession states, and other bordering states.

The ideas surrounding European identity were developed and emphasised within the EC/EU discourse beginning in 1973 when a declaration stated that economic integration of the nine members should go hand in hand with an evolving European identity. In a shaky global economic order and amid an oil price crisis, the declaration was launched with the objective of strengthening EC unity in relation to the world. In presenting a hierarchical order, its friendly European neighbours were of top priority, while China and Latin America came last. Initially, the EC regarded European identity as a consequence of economic integration, and used the concept to support measures for economic transformation.[39] An emphasis on identity in relation to a shared European culture took hold during the 1980s, and the European Commission discussed proposals supporting 'European consciousness'. The lack of a European identity was seen as the only piece of the puzzle that was missing in the attempt to forge an integrated Europe. European identity was considered necessary to ensuring citizen loyalty to the EU, as well as giving it badly needed legitimacy.[40] Among intellectuals, it was often believed that Europe was turning towards a common consciousness during the post-war decades. References were made to the ebbing conflict between French and German national chauvinism, specifically, and of such chauvinism throughout Europe more generally in the face of the US–Soviet threat, increasing exchanges of various kinds, and expanding tourism. Interestingly, these intellectuals included some from the political left who had criticised the EU's capitalism, colonialism, and what could at times be construed as the continuation of a National Socialist mindset. For instance, the French sociologist Edgar Morin wanted Europe to become aware of such weaknesses: 'Frailty, your name is Europe'. Now Morin and other leftists could discuss Europe in terms of its destined unity and history of humanism and civilisation.[41]

The European Commission's promotion of a common European identity in the 1980s and 1990s resulted in a wide range of policy documents, efforts to use cultural measures to forge a deeper sense of belonging to a shared community among member state populations, and various ways of visualising a common European sentiment. This included the introduction of the Euro, the flag and anthem, European citizenship and the associated passport, exchange programmes for students, subsidies for teaching 'The History of the Construction of Europe', and so on. The commission encouraged concepts such as a shared 'European culture' and 'European heritage' that could foster a common 'European consciousness' and 'European identity'. The emphasis was on strengthening the EU's legitimacy in a period when it faced criticism for its seemingly exclusive focus on economic and legal issues. Indeed, European integration had until then only been pursued as a technical issue, and the commission was widely looked upon as a committee of technocrats. Moreover, according to a then widespread neoliberal critique, Western Europe was suffering from 'Euro-sclerosis'. The commission therefore sought ways to speed up economic integration, based on the idea that further integration could only win support if citizens began to feel European – if people continued to identify only as German, Italian or British, it would be impossible to build a European society. National politicians needed to demonstrate loyalty to a community beyond the nation state, and citizens needed to be imbued with a feeling, sense and consciousness of being European, all with the explicit aim of building a 'European identity'.[42]

In the EU process, identity policies were Janus faced. On the one hand, they were intended to encourage and contribute to a shared European identity; on the other, the commission emphasised that its aim was not to eradicate national cultures and identities – on the contrary, it introduced other measures to increase the significance of cultural borders, viewing them as crucial to Europe and European thought. The EU stressed the role of regions and in some cases strengthened the status of minority languages. This was also seen in the definition of European identity. An important theme of the EU's identity policies was 'handling difference', which was often signalled by the expression 'unity in diversity'. This expression, in combination with 'European identity', saw increased usage in EU discourse. 'Unity in diversity' became a key slogan, indicating that Europe was flourishing thanks to its diversity, its avoidance of national chauvinism, and despite its history of warfare between neighbouring countries. It had one common history with shared values that supported its cultural variety. The idea was that Europe enjoyed cultural diversity within the framework of a common identity or civilisation. This is how it was possible for the EU to rhetorically affirm cultural borders and claim to solve what Edgar Morin called 'the Gordian knot of European identity'.[43]

In fact, a wave of significant identity making had swept through Europe in the second half of the nineteenth century, after the completion of a system of national identities in the first half of the century. Europe would afterwards be presented as a continent of homogeneous nation states, and the borders on the map seemed to be clearly demarcated. In the 1980s, it was clear that globalisation, migration processes, and minority movements had launched a second wave of identity making. New emphasis was placed on national identities and other cultural identities following the fall of communism, the emergence of the European Union, regionalisation, and a renewed focus on local government. Identity politics emerged as a distinguishing characteristic of our time.[44] In 1992, sociologist Sven Papcke stated that identity 'is a catchword of our age, and one may observe something like a scramble for identity all over Europe at the moment'.[45]

The turn towards identities took place in the fields of history, philosophy and social science, coupled with an interest in the North American discussion between liberals and communitarians about what it means to belong to a society, with political implications for the definition of citizenship rights. The public discussion also encompassed whether Russia and Turkey were European states. In the countries outside the EC, issues of how countries could become member states were high up on the agenda. Whether or not to belong was a main public concern in these countries. In Sweden, it was common for Swedes to regard their country as geographically separated from 'the continent'. In Portugal, José Saramago presented his novel *A Jangada de Pedra* (1986), in which the Iberian Peninsula drifted away from the

European continent into the Atlantic. With this fantasy, Saramago illustrated that Europe was incomplete without the Iberian nations. In a commentary, he stated that 'there will be no new Europe unless we abolish, not so much selfish nationalism, which is often nothing more than a defensive reflex, but the preconceptions of the domination or subordination of cultures'.[46]

Around 1990, a widespread notion confirmed the radical historical changes taking place: 'History has become mobilized: it is accelerating, even overheating', Jürgen Habermas stated in 1992.[47] The debates regarding European identity played out against the backdrop of the fall of communism in Central Europe – what Jacques Derrida called the earthquakes of Central and Eastern Europe in 1990, adding that they took place under the banner of 'perestroika, democratization, reunion, reunification, entry into the market economy, [and] access to political and economic liberalisms'.[48] The process was paradoxical: while borders were opening with the dismantling of Soviet dominance in the Baltic region and Central Europe, Europe gained a range of new nation states, all with their own borders. In Central Europe, the changes were mostly peaceful, although many feared the violent suppression of protests, while the Balkans saw the break-up of Yugoslavia, with its accompanying war. Both hope and fear accompanied the process. The period saw the creation and re-creation of nations, emphasising cultural borders and Europe as a continent defined by many national borders. In the same period, the integration of Western Europe expanded to include Greece, Spain and Portugal in 1985, and Austria and the Scandinavian countries (apart from Norway) applied for membership and entered in 1995. The establishment of the Maastricht Treaty in 1991 entailed the integration of politics, law and economies, which eventually led to the EC becoming the European Union. Indeed, unification and the issue of borders were both in the air. There seemed to be good reasons to seek a European identity that could transcend cultural borders and hold a multicultural Europe (or EU) together.

By focusing on European identity, we can examine the main issues and contestations facing Europe in the 1990s and 2000s. In this period, European identity was a key concept, and the historian Bo Stråth even remarked that an 'obsession with the concept of European identity is readily identifiable'.[49] Transnational events orchestrated the debate, such as Gianni Vattimo's symposium on the cultural identity of Europe, held in Turin on 20 May 1990 with, among others, Jacques Derrida, Agnes Heller, José Saramago, Fernando Savater and Vittoria Strada. A vast range of conferences and actions took place throughout the 1990s on the topic of identity and related themes such as diversity and unity, borders, and frontiers. The simultaneous publication of articles on 23 May 2003 by Derrida, Habermas, Savater, Vattimo, Umberto Eco and Adolf Muschg, all demanding stronger European unity after the Iraq War, is just one example.

Many intellectuals recognised the need to develop a European identity that could serve as a common basis for the European institutions that were desperately trying to gain legitimacy as they were gaining more power. When focusing on the need for a common political identity, some intellectuals referred to values. One example was the Italian philosopher Furio Cerutti, who defined European identity as the awareness that implementing the 'values of freedom, peace, equality and solidarity' required a common European polity.[50] Sven Papcke reiterated the long-established notion of the individual free will as a European invention that comprised 'the ideas of personality, democracy, tolerance, social justice, liberty, human rights'.[51] British public historian Timothy Garton Ash related European identity to a new narrative centred on the goals of European societies, mentioning 'freedom, peace, law, prosperity, diversity, and solidarity'.[52] Often, things became more problematic, as it was no simple task to settle on what should be considered common European traits. Some continued to argue that Christianity represented a shared heritage, while others noted that Islam, which had existed in Europe for twelve centuries, had played an important role in Europe's political, intellectual and cultural history.[53] Obviously, European identity was and is a controversial concept with different connotations, and it can be defined in various ways. The superficially simple question of what characterises Europe and Europeans turns out to be highly complex, making European identity a controversial concept. In the next section, I will examine the discourse on European identity mainly among historians and philosophers in the early 1990s, asking two key questions: (1) What historical era would they consider to be the origin of Europe? The answers range from Antiquity and the Middle Ages, the Renaissance, the Enlightenment, and the French Revolution, to 1945 and post-war European integration; and (2) How should Europe and/or the EU develop? At the heart of the debates regarding European identity have been questions about historical origins and future development, whose answers are crucial to defining Europe. In addition, the proponents turned to the concept of Europe when addressing the development of the EU, citing objectives and directives and claiming to define the future of the European Union. In this new century, this became even more urgent, as demonstrated in the following sections.

Looking for a Definition: A New Beginning, a Long History, and Modernity

The solemnity of the events that took place in 1989 in Central Europe, the process of German unification, and the turbulence of the Soviet Union had a great impact on the concept of Europe as discussed by intellectuals in the early 1990s. Derrida's speech given during the symposium in Turin became widely recognised, with shortened versions of it published in leading newspapers in France, Germany, Italy and Spain. It began by claiming that we were living through a time of great change in Europe, when something as yet unknown was being created. It was a time of possibilities and dangers, when Europe and its identity were being created, but had not yet fully taken shape. To start, he suggested that European identity was still only a name without a face, which meant that it elicited both fear and hope as to its potential form. In Europe, 'the crimes of xenophobia, racism, anti-Semitism, religious or nationalist fanaticism, are being unleashed . . . but also . . . mixed in with the breath, with the respiration, with the very "spirit" of the promise'.[54] Expectations had undoubtedly changed with the fall of communism in Central Europe. A new Europe was possible, without the post-war divisions and nuclear threats, but with national freedom and hope of economic prosperity. In light of this, Derrida said that it might be irrelevant to invoke the notion of a European 'crisis' at such a moment; he claimed that Europeans were young, and that Europe, only just beginning to come into existence, faced the choice of either returning to a previous Europe or becoming something completely new.[55] However, a new cultural identity should neither be uniformly directed by a single authority nor have the implication of 'multiplying borders'. The responsible thing would be to invent something beyond these well-known and thoroughly experienced alternatives. Instead, Derrida asked for ethics and politics to promote a European identity based on the experience of going beyond the two opposing alternatives by turning the impossible into something possible. 'European cultural identity . . . must belong to this experience and experiment of the impossible'.[56] In this spirit, he concluded that a European identity should activate the notion of hospitality and tolerance, nurturing the ideas of critique, democracy, and international rights. Moreover, it should resist racism, nationalism and xenophobia.[57]

Derrida's speech from 1990 differs from other main contributions on European identity in not referring to the historical origin of this identity. Derrida saw the return to a former European culture as undesirable, and believed that establishing a European identity at odds with itself would be impossible, as the foundation of a culture or identity can never be associated with a single origin. An identity cannot exist independently, and always comprises differences. Europe should avoid pigeonholing itself in an identity that excludes other identities, and avoid obvious limitations and strict definitions.[58]

Consequentially, Derrida rejected the notion of a return to an earlier Europe, much cited in those days. He mentioned examples from French politics, but similar examples could be found throughout Europe, embodying the feeling of having finally overcome the Cold War division between Eastern and Western Europe. For Central Europeans, the juncture was about their return to Europe proper, whereas for Westerners it was about re-establishing a greater Europe. In both cases, the return of Europe implied that history had moved forward after forty-five years of stalemate – in short, this discourse saw 'a merry trend', as Peter Sloterdijk put it. Interest in this theme was displayed by the historian Hagen Schulze, who wrote a book entitled *Die Wiederkehr Europas* (The return of Europe), and by the novelist György Konrád, who called for Europe to refrain from 'being declared incapacitated'.[59] Sloterdijk, a philosopher from Karlsruhe, referred to the 'European vacuum of 1945–1989'. In 1945, Sloterdijk explained, Europe was liberated from the Nazis, but it was also conquered by the Soviet Union and the West. The Europeans carried with them this double experience over the next fifty years, developing 'vacuum ideologies' of nihilism, existentialism, consumerism, psychoanalysis and postmodernism. They were now poised to overcome these ideologies, and would then have to find their new role and 'learn anew the lines of their character in the world theatre'.[60]

For many, the return of Europe implied an identity that extended far back into history. Generally, the theme of identity emphasises issues related to who we are, where we come from, and where we are heading. Often, interest in identity coincides with engagement in culture and the past, but it is also a question of choice. As touched on in Chapter 2, research shows that the imagination and construction of historical narratives for communities, especially the invention of national traditions, are well-explored issues. In the debate that followed 1989, European identity was related to different origins, each with different implications for the definition of European identity.

Jacques Le Goff, the Annales School historian who specialised in the Middle Ages and its thinking, offered support from his own historical expertise in the Middle Ages when he claimed that the EU should create 'unity in diversity'. Typically, his definition of European identity invoked a long historical tradition, starting with Antiquity and the Middle Ages. He cited other interpretations according to which the duration of the tradition might be different, but it always went back a long way. From this historical vantage point, he argued that European identity had a kind of continuity from its earliest days, through modern times, and up to the present. Ancient Greece contributed the concepts of reason, science, freedom and the critical spirit. The heritage from the Roman Empire was Christianity and the dichotomy between the Latin West and the Greek East that characterised Christianity in the Early Middle Ages, and created a border within Europe. He identified the Catholic Church as the common denominator of Western Europe throughout the Middle Ages, bridging the divides between kingdoms, languages, and ethnic groups. Political unity was created by the Frankish Empire, which reached its zenith at the beginning of the ninth century, and its division established the boundary between France and Germany. Starting in the late Middle Ages, Le Goff identified two movements towards European identity. The first was the quest to defend Europe and exclude others. This often evolved into a passion for cleansing the area of 'others', illustrated by the treatment of heretics, Jews and homosexuals. The second movement was expansionistic, as in the Crusades, the commercial boom of Genoa and Venice, the reconquest of Spain, and overseas expansion. Le Goff concluded that there was an obvious *longue durée* of European identity based on the striving for unity and the preservation of diversity.[61]

The long history of European identity has appealed to many historians, such as Hagen Schulze at the Freie Universität in Berlin, who identified Roman traditions that contributed to shaping modern Europe.[62] One way to understand that long history was to point out a number of partially shared cultures. The Roman Empire affected certain parts of Europe more than others, Christian traditions became divided, the Italian Renaissance and French Enlightenment spread unevenly, and democracy and parliamentary institutions developed differently. Anthony D. Smith, a scholar of nationalism research at the London School of Economics, stressed that Europe 'revealed a gamut of overlapping and boundary-transcending political traditions and cultural heritages, which together make up what we may call the European experience and the European family of cultures'. Only by starting from this experience, Smith contended, would it be possible to find the 'legitimacy of a "European identity"'.[63]

Attempts to legitimise European integration by recalling long historical perspectives have corresponded to the views of a number of philosophers. Peter Koslowski, from Hanover, recalled the transnational Holy Roman Empire when he dubbed the European Union a 'renaissance' of the historical European idea of empire. He certainly recognised the democratic element of the EU and its member states, viewing them as modernising an older tradition, while there were several parallels to the traditional idea of empire, most importantly the limited sovereignty given to the EU.[64] Rémi Brague, from Paris, looked to Antiquity and the Middle Ages in developing a typical European identity, which he called an 'eccentric identity'. He stressed that, in Europe, every 'culture is acquired and never innate', meaning that Christianity was not of European origin, and that a European culture that developed from Greek and Roman origins was not unique, but rather a single branch of a larger tree.[65] Brague concluded that to be European was to accept the need to adopt knowledge from others, to accept oneself as barbaric, and to begin the learning process. He found specifically European culture in the creative learning of foreign culture in which new adaptations revise older ones – hence his claim that Europe had an eccentric identity.[66] Both Koslowski and Brague saw a connection between European identity and Catholicism. They gave talks on European identity at Katholische Forum Niedersachsen (1996), and Brague asserted the central place of Christianity in the future of Europe. Speeches made by Cardinal Joseph Ratzinger (the future Pope Benedict XVI) provided a further indication of the engagement of Catholic theology in European identity. He emphasised two cultures that characterised Europe: one was Christian and recognised the moral power of humanity, while the other was secular and nihilistic, believing in the powers bequeathed by technology and scientific rationality. The latter culture provided major opportunities, but also threatened the extinction of the human race. Ratzinger's conclusion was that European identity should be grounded in a culture that sustains eternal values and human dignity – meaning, Christian culture. He recognised that other religions also had potential, but argued that Christianity had brought eternal values and human dignity to Europe. He believed that without its Christian roots, Europe would be lost in nihilism.[67] According to Ratzinger, the basic tenet of European identity was the assertion of a culturalist definition that assumed an original identity that endured over the centuries without changing in any substantial way.

In the popular understanding of this long tradition of European identity, European history describes a linear progression from classical Greece to the Enlightenment. In a debate as to whether Turkey could become a member of the European Union, former French president Valéry Giscard d'Estaing declined that possibility by defining Europe on the basis of its ancient heritage and the creativity of the Renaissance. The elements were there from the beginning, but they required both time and space to evolve, leading to a homogeneous, contemporary European culture shared by both citizens and countries, thus excluding non-European countries such as Turkey.[68] By contrast, the previously mentioned scholars, who took account of a long tradition when discussing the return of Europe and defining a historical origin of European identity, often included a critique of the tradition. Thus, Le Goff dissociated himself from the imperial idea and tradition. Smith warned against the development of a political unification that would require the European identity to be culturally exclusive, even racist. Similarly Sloterdijk, who saw the imperial spirit of Rome transformed from epoch to epoch, with the 1991 Maastricht Treaty of the European Union as its latest outcome, took the contemporary opportunity to ask for the reconsideration of European identity through new eyes.[69] He believed that this identity should concentrate on inventing a new post- or trans-imperial principle that would combine states and unite them into a multinational federation.[70] Brague added to his thesis of European culture as successively adopted and revised, that what stood out as truly European was not its origin but the prospect of de-barbarising ourselves by learning what was hitherto unknown by our predecessors, and the objective of implementing universal truths in human history.[71]

Overall, this long historical approach to European identity either implicitly appealed to European integration or came together with straightforward suggestions of its future development. Koslowski pleaded for the EU to be a non-centralistic commonwealth of nations; that is, to avoid the model of the centralised modern nation state and only take on limited political ventures. Whereas the member states owed their legal power to the principle of one citizen–one vote, the EU held power based on its member states, which by necessity brought a democratic deficit to the union. Koslowski argued that this protected the smaller member states, and he also discussed the general role of the EU in protecting minorities.[72] Sloterdijk called for a political vision that went beyond the nation states but still included them, that eschewed the '*national-imperialismus*' of previous European history. It was his opinion that the EU should not copy the United States, but keep growing and become a federation of as many as twenty-six states (he wrote this before the enlargements in Central Europe), with leaders in Berlin, Brussels and Paris, noting the British opposition to binding the EU states more closely to one another. In this European vision, truth was necessary (to avoid nihilism), a good quality of life was required (to reduce human misery), and human beings' knowledge and understanding of their capacities for greatness and passion (despite despair) were essential. Most importantly, Europe should take no part in contempt: 'Europe's deepest thought is that one must resist contempt'.[73]

In contrast to the long historical approach, other scholars alluded to the modernity of European identity. Typically, the New York-based Hungarian philosopher Agnes Heller, who had presented at the Turin event together with Derrida, concluded that modernity had created Europe and that the culture of modernity had reached its zenith in the nineteenth century. This identity was future oriented and dynamic, which brought Europe a sense of rootlessness, despite the retrospectively invented traditions and cultural mythology of a long history. In its self-understanding, Europe represented indefinite progress marked by industrialisation, capitalism, and the statecraft of the nation state, together with a universal culture of humanity. This was complicated by the belief that 'modernity is no longer European', an idea that had spread throughout the world, and that 'barbarism . . . emerged as an outcome of European civilisation'. At this point, Europe now looked longingly backwards, its cities becoming museums. However, Heller saw the possibility of developing a new European culture, a new 'umbrella culture in whose framework, local, partial, and national cultures may thrive'. Heller viewed European identity as something in the making.[74] Overall, modernists were glad to allude to Benedict Anderson's thesis on the nation as an imagined community. Even Hagen Schulze, who referred to the long history of Europe when discussing its identity, still stated that Europe 'is an imagined community, thus it exists, when it exists, above all in the heads of the people'.[75]

A key contribution to the modernist approach to European identity was made by Jürgen Habermas in his 1992 article on Europe's future. In it, he criticised the EU for being a capitalist project driven by transnational bureaucratic elites, and warned that xenophobic nationalism could be mobilised against immigrants and asylum seekers alike. With increasing integration and looming EU enlargements, he saw the democratic necessity of a European citizenship that would correspond to a transnational political sphere beyond state boundaries.[76] This certainly implied that a common identity was being developed, a matter to which he returned when pleading for a European constitution as a crucial step in this direction. In 2001, he explicitly identified the potential of the European project as a force for justice, solidarity and human rights in international relations and the global economy. His often-cited definition of European identity emphasised the learning processes of the past and present. Europe had been able to manage social and political conflicts over values in its modern history. At present, a post-national democracy would need to respect the differences among national cultures. This would require a vision of integration that could offer more than just economic success, building citizens' awareness of Europe as their community.[77]

In the modernist understanding, European identity should be inclusive, open and self-reflexive; it was in the making, embedded in social achievements. Modernists related European identity to post-national identity, which is important to note. Drawing on Habermas, the French-American historian and political scientist Ariane Chebel d'Appollonia concluded that a European identity should be like a national identity and make use of notable realities and symbols from history, while still adapting to post-national politics: 'If a post-national Europe is to exist, it must be generally accepted that culturally different national communities can exist within the same political community'.[78] In a more theoretically based approach, the British sociologist Gerard Delanty assessed European identity to be 'trapped in racial myths of origin' and held ransom by nationalists with the possibility of future progressive transformation. In contrast with national identities, a European identity was not about cultural roots but 'an expression of multi-identification' that implied belonging to Europe as well as to one or more additional communities. It was of a fundamentally different character from national identities because of its cosmopolitanism and reflexivity, manifesting itself in post-national consciousness and openness to a self-critical dimension. In terms of a post-national identity, it referred 'to an identification with democratic or constitutional norms, and not with the state, territory, nation or cultural traditions'.[79]

Notably, both historical and modernist definitions imagined Europe as a place of progress without implying one-sided development, as they also emphasised the negative aspects of contemporary Europe. Still, they essentially supported belief in a European mission. In determining how to forge a union and states to create a new kind of federation that would transcend former ideas of being a world power, Europe might stand out as an example: 'Europe will become the seminar where people will learn to think beyond the Empire' (Sloterdijk).[80] Certainly, the concept of a European identity was closely related to the European Union and its further development. 'The European Union must become a visual and compelling identity. It needs myths as strong as those that sustain the individual nations of which it is composed. As Condorcet observed, "Citizens are not born; they are created through construction". *Homo Europeanus* is still waiting to be made' (d'Appollonia).[81]

Divided Europe

Beginning in the late 1960s, European identity would become increasingly associated with the development of the EU. However, this association became even more explicit starting in the late 1990s, when the EU and a range of former communist countries prepared for their new memberships, discussion regarding a European Constitution began, and the euro and the Charter of Fundamental Rights were introduced. This discussion included pleas for a 'core Europe' that would be tasked with more rapid integration than the rest of Europe was prepared for. In the first years of the 2000s, the world was rocked by an altered, more threatening situation stemming from 9/11, the 'War on Terror', and the US-led invasion of Iraq. In May 2000, German minister of foreign affairs Joschka Fischer delivered a now well-known political speech on the general direction of the EU, and identified its two main challenges to be eastward enlargement and the union's capacity to act with so many member states.[82] One year later, French prime minister Lionel Jospin suggested EU-wide social solidarity and stronger rights for all EU citizens. He viewed support of the EU's diversity of cultures as essential in order to sustain a common identity, move toward a 'federation of nation states', and give Europe a distinct voice in the world with a common defence and foreign policy.[83] British prime minister Tony Blair likewise advocated a strong Europe, but was cautious even about mentioning a common identity. Instead, he spoke at length about the fundamental British identity that could not be damaged by EU enlargement or by British commitments to the union.[84] These speeches illustrated several points, one of them centred on whether the EU should build a strong Europe and realise dreams of being a major world power, or accept its weakness and settle for a more modest future. Sociologist Göran Therborn effectively described this latter role as follows: 'The best Europeans can hope for is to constitute a nice, decent periphery of the world, with little power but some good ideas'.[85] Another point concerned the relationship between the European and national identities, a topic discussed throughout Europe and was certainly at the top of the political agenda in Britain.[86] The concept of European identity was largely related to general political developments in the EU and its member states. As a consequence, it was possible to hear voices of both dissent and support regarding the existence and importance of this identity.

One reason for dissent was simply the belief that the nation state should be the main site for the construction of cultural identity. Rainer Lepsius, a sociologist from Mannheim, argued that no common European cultural identity was emerging, despite the initiatives of the European Commission, because cultural objects and norms to identify with would stay at the nation-state level. No matter what the commission did, Europe would be composed of a collection of identities with different values.[87] In the same vein, British anthropologist Chris Shore and Swedish political scientist Peo Hansen interpreted the striving for European identity as an attempt to create a 'European people', despite the lack of a 'European demos' and despite the gap between the project's elites and the ordinary citizens.[88]

Another critical approach considered the practical issues of integration: 'It is doubtful if this [i.e. European identity] will do to ensure a smooth process of ongoing European integration and successfully address the challenges of the ongoing European societies', according to Dirk Jacobs and Robert Maier.[89] Author Joscha Schmierer from Frankfurt issued a warning about negating European identity's 'composite character', which could lead to dangerous policies of exclusion.[90] The very discussion of European identity represented an approach that concealed existing problems. Rather than real understanding, we had 'a cacophony of synchronous monologues', according to the historian Lutz Niethammer.[91]

A more radical view was suspicious of the very concept of identity. In an interview, Jean Baudrillard explained that identity 'is where one takes refuge when there is nothing else left to do. . . . When one truly exists because there is strength and glory, at base, there is no need for identity. Identity is a weak value, a refuge value somehow. Today it is on this that Europe is built'.[92] Besides Baudrillard, identity was also notably dismissed by Étienne Balibar, who approved of European identity as a modernist construct in several articles, very much akin to the policies of the European Union. However, he argued that such a fictional identity served the purpose of excluding and limiting democracy in Europe, and stated that leaders seemed to be avoiding the political issues associated with the concept of European identity. He discussed mechanisms that excluded people from the rights of citizenship, and others that included people in the economy and workforce, resulting in a kind of apartheid system. He concluded that extended and expanded citizenship rights were inconsistent with the establishment of European identity. Balibar dismissed the notion of European identity, emphasising the lack of fixed borders throughout Europe. Neither Europe nor its neighbours had borders that were historically or culturally continuous. He argued that Europe was a border in itself, containing layer upon layer of different borders, sharing histories and cultures with much of the rest of the world.[93] In this discourse, Balibar made a distinction by relating European identity to the establishment of exclusionary characteristics.

Some critics stressed the risk of essentialising Europe by relating it to identity, as Bo Stråth argued. Social responsibility might serve as an alternative for integrating the citizens of Europe, fostering an understanding of Europe's cultural borders as open and in flux, continuously being created and recreated. Stråth viewed the concept of Europe as something that should stress openness, but the concept of European identity 'necessarily contains a demarcation from the non-European', with the great risk of making the transitional situation of migrants permanent, which would present 'a fiction of peace and concord as well as strength and power'.[94] Or, as Talal Asad put it, when addressing the exclusion of Muslims from historical narratives and the contemporary debate, 'the discourse of European identity is a symptom of anxieties about non-Europeans'.[95] Likewise, the Italian cultural historian Luisa Passerini wanted past forms of European identity to be critically reviewed and reworked to combat Eurocentrism and dissolve the pretence of Europe serving as a universal civilisation. Passerini hoped to find 'a common ground for exchange with all of those who want neither to be assimilated nor to remain alien to European culture'. Such a common ground would hold 'the abandonment of the European identity's internal and external hierarchies . . . between centre and periphery, between East and West, between the Mediterranean and the North . . . or the hierarchical contrasts between Europe and Asia or between Europe and America'.[96]

Indeed, many contributions to the discourse on European identity have been caught up in the race to legitimise the European idea of unification.[97] Some were strident, like Zygmunt Bauman's call for Europe to accept its moral imperative to unite humanity: Europe had a duty to go global with its mission to defend and disseminate the values of rationality, fairness, democracy and freedom.[98] For others, impending political events and processes led them to consider European identity. In 2003, Habermas coordinated a group of prominent intellectuals to initiate debate about the core of Europe, by publishing articles in renowned European newspapers. The notion of a core Europe implied that certain member states should proceed with integration more quickly than others. The intellectuals launched this debate in response to the divisions that had emerged in Europe following the US decision to invade Iraq without UN support, leaving international institutions behind. Several arguments addressed what the changing international scene demanded from Europe. It ought to have a common voice in foreign affairs and a common military force (Fernando Savater in *La País*). Europe should take political responsibility by acting through the institutions of international law, and set a precedent for 'governance beyond the nation-state' (Habermas and Derrida collaborated on an article published in *Frankfurter Allgemeine Zeitung* and *La Libération*). The authors stressed the dissimilarities between Europe and the United States. Europe had relationships with Africa and Asia as well as interests in the Balkan and Arab worlds that differed from those of the United States, whose interest had shifted to the Pacific (Umberto Eco in *La Republica*). Europeans enjoyed a high standard of living and a well-developed social safety net (Habermas and Derrida). Europeans had higher expectations of their public institutions, holding on to the kernel of socialism that made them more supportive of the state (Gianni Vattimo in *La Stampa*). These articles advocated a new level of integration with 'an effective federal body' (Adolf Muschg in *Neue Zürischer Zeitung*) and with a political order 'able to bestow on Europe the dignity and significance it deserves in world politics' (Vattimo). As a prerequisite for taking such steps, the 'citizens of one nation must regard the citizens of another nation as fundamentally "one of us"' (Habermas and Derrida). The group thus embraced the concept of European identity, which would be unlike the nations' claim to have an original belonging and 'can only exist as a unity of "cultures"' (Vattimo). Still, European identity related to shared memories and experiences, expressing a common destiny (Muschg). It existed in legacies from Antiquity and the French Revolution, from modern science, capitalism and secularisation, and was found in Roman law and ideas of justice, setting it apart from, for example, American identity (Eco). This common identity encompassed the experience of communicating conflicts through stable institutions, recognising differences, building the welfare state, limiting the sovereignty of the nation state within the EU, and acting for the common European good and not as individual nation states (Habermas and Derrida). The need for a future-oriented European identity was clear; one that was capable of keeping Europe together in the contemporary world. The suggestions made were necessary 'in order to safeguard subsequent conquests, such as the welfare state, a secular sense of the political order, and civil rights for all' (Savater).[99]

Habermas et al. faced criticism for questioning the transatlantic link and attempting to identify how Europe and the United States diverged rather than what they had in common. European cooperation with the world's hegemonic power was emphasised as fundamental to its foreign affairs, as was the exclusion of Russia and Turkey from the European legacy and identity. Critics argued that the welfare regimes of Europe were on the defensive and that many Europeans saw no benefit in a greater Europe, but had experienced deterioration in their living standards.[100] In addition, the idea of proclaiming a European identity as a policy guideline from above was criticised, stressing that intellectuals should give up the identity game, which had quickly become an enemy game, just as had the creation of national identities.[101]

The notion of a core Europe was criticised by Central Europeans who saw it as a way to divide Europe, despite the unification process. The Hungarian novelist Péter Esterházy noted the accusation by Western Europeans that the new Central European member states would constitute a disruptive factor that should be left outside the core group. Polish author Andrzej Stasiuk sarcastically contended that the Habermas group was preparing the EU for the entrance of the barbarians, recalling a West European view of the people of Central Europe. Likewise, the Polish writer Adam Krzemiński maliciously accused 'the great minds of the West' of being blind to the other Europe of Poles and Hungarians: 'They never belonged to Europe's inner circle, say the Lords of the Rings. They will first have to humbly wait outside, wearing the penitential robes of their poverty, until the doors are opened for them'. Krzemiński stressed that the Central Europeans were already in Europe and would 'take their seats and enjoy equal rights at the Round Table of the Union'. Habermas et al. saw their countries as the main forces behind the European spirit.[102] These assessments of the arguments of Habermas et al. concerned aspects of the concept of Europe addressed in previous chapters – for instance, the notion that some nations were further along in the civilising process and thus higher in the 'pecking order' of Western Europe. In addition, they represented a critique of the European idea that shifted attention from the institutions of the EU to the peripheries and local communities.

At this point, the conception of European identity had somewhat stabilised regarding the idea of unification and the EU, in the sense that the debates about integration were energised and played out via European identity. But that was not the whole picture. It is possible to find presentations of another Europe that avoided talking about European identity when making their case.

Europe viewed from the periphery was a theme throughout the period, beginning in the late 1980s and continuing to the present. In 1988, José Saramago penned his critique of the Eurocentrism evident within Europe itself. The Portuguese novelist saw the existence of one Europe at the centre and another on the periphery, which revealed itself in how the 'rich countries of Europe, who revel in the narcissistic view that wealth makes them culturally superior, regard the rest of Europe as something vague, diffuse, a trifle exotic and something picturesque'. He observed that Europe should be a moral entity that regarded cultures as different and equal, not as superior or inferior, where there was agreement between Europe and the peripheral cultures that each needed the other. He stated that 'there will be no new Europe unless we abolish not so much selfish nationalism, which is often nothing more than a defensive reflex, but the preconceptions of the domination or subordination of cultures'.[103]

In 2000, Andrzej Stasiuk wrote about the Central European experience, describing it as living 'between the East, which never existed, and the West, which exists all too much' amid the economic unification, NATO, and 'a thousand years of culture and civilization'. He compared it to going swimming or being on a ship, exposed to the wind and the currents, seeing the weather change and 'only thinking about the now and the future', because all that comes to mind when thinking of the past is that it would have been better to stay at home.[104] Both the Portuguese author Saramago and the Polish author Stasiuk saw Europe in terms of centre and periphery.

In an essay from 2004, the German author Iris Radisch wrote that authors such as Stasiuk gave literary voice to a European periphery that was trying to justify itself to the centres of the West. She noted the peripheral European love of the local community, '*die kleine Heimat*', which, in Central Europe, was combined with the critique of Western Europe as a role model, and with a diffuse and fragile nationalism. Radisch focused on authors who represented a 'poetic of the local community', practised in the communist period as an expression of love for small communities and a hatred of the regimes, which had now begun to find new expression under the pressure of a unification driven by the centres. In citing Stasiuk, she noted that geography rather than history represented Europe in the former communist countries. This is where she found the real soul of Europe that could raise the standard of spiritual regionalism against the forces of the global economy. From one's own geography it was possible to find one's proper history 'in the small things ... on the compost heaps and dunghills of the present'. History, she said, quoting Olga Tokarczuk, who many years later was awarded the Nobel Prize in Literature, 'is only what I see for myself'. Radisch gave expression to the historical mental border between Central/Eastern Europe and the West, connecting this to the romantic critique of an estranged modernity. Against economic globalisation, she raised the standard of spiritual regionalism, which might connect people with their small communities. Although Radisch mentioned the poetic of small communities as a way to understand some of the nationalist feelings that had fractured Yugoslavia, she saw regional communities and small societies as the future of Europe, as the location of Europe's soul.[105] Thus, for the periphery, the conception of European identity was unattractive because of its adherence to strength and to an integration driven by the main countries of Western Europe.

Notes

1. 'Treaty Establishing the European Economic Community', 1957.
2. De Rougemont, *The Idea of Europe*.
3. De Rougemont, *The Idea of Europe*, see especially 409. He draws on a number of works, most importantly Reynold, *La Formation de l'Europe*; Curcio, *Europa: Storia di un'idea*; Gollwitzer, *Europabild und Europagedanke*; Corral, *The Rape of Europe*.
4. Ifversen, 'Myth and History', 82. In this section I am in debt to Iversen's article for pointing out the works of Barraclough, Halecki and Beloff.
5. Quotation from Wagner, 'Foreword', XI.
6. Wagner, 'Introduction'; Chaszer, 'Place of East Central Europe'; Miksche, 'Danubian Federation'; Tassonyi, 'Central European Federation'.
7. See the following contributions in Wagner, *Toward a New Central Europe*: Wagner, 'Introduction'; Padànyi-Gulyás and Gallus, 'Signs of the Times'; Padànyi-Gulyás, 'Toward a Constructive Ideology'; Chaszer; 'Neutralized Zone in Central Europe'. See also Varsányi, *Quest for a New Central Europe*, with contributions from a symposium organised by Studies for a New Central Europe.
8. Halecki, *Limits and Divisions*, 7–21, 46–61.
9. Ibid., 137.
10. Barraclough, *History in a Changing World*, 218–20.
11. Heer, 'Osteuropa in Europa'.
12. Beloff, *Europe and the Europeans*, vii–viii. On Chinneide, see Smith, 'A Manly Study?', 188–98.
13. Beloff, *Europe and the Europeans*, 114, 123–24, 143, 151–54, quotations from 124 and 143.
14. Ibid., 79–80, 107.
15. Berl, 'Europa und die Geschichte'.
16. Pasquinucci, 'Political Commitment and Academic Research', 67.
17. Aron, 'Old Nations, New Europe'.
18. Aron, *In Defence of Decadent Europe*; Aron, 'My Defence of Decadent Europe'.
19. Patočka, *Heretical Essays*, 95–119, quotations from 118–19.
20. Patočka, 'Was dürfen wir erwarten'.
21. Havel, 'Politics and Conscience', 142, 146; Havel, 'An Anatomy of Reticence', 179, 192.
22. Konrád, *Från Europas navel*, 72, 90–98, 111–16.
23. Havel, 'Acceptance Speech'.
24. Kundera, 'Tragedy of Central Europe'.
25. Havel, 'An Anatomy of Reticence', 9–12. On irony as a Central European characteristic, see also Czarny, 'Imaginary-Real Lives', 279; Ionesco, 'The Austro-Hungarian Empire'; Rohlik and Kinyon, 'The Right of Self-Determination', 9.
26. Miłosz, 'Central European Attitudes', 105.
27. Konrád, 'Is the Dream Still Alive?', 109–18.
28. Kiš, 'Variations on Central Europe', 1–9.

29. Ibid.
30. Konrád, *Från Europas navel*, 118–19; Kiš, 'Variations on Central Europe'.
31. Simečka, 'Another Civilization?', 179. See also Zagajewski, 'A High Wall', 27–37.
32. Kundera, 'Tragedy of Central Europe'; Vajda, 'Was ist jüdisch in Mitteleuropa?', 12–15.
33. Kiš, 'Variations on Central Europe', 6–9.
34. Fried, 'Besonderheiten der Anfänge', 364; Miłosz, 'Central European Attitudes'; Kiss, 'Central European Writers', 125–30.
35. Kundera, 'Tragedy of Central Europe'.
36. Search on Google Books, 9 September 2020; 'Fifth NATO Parliamentarians' Conference 1959', 23.
37. Andrén and Ejnatten, 'European Unity and the Nation State'.
38. Neumann, *Russia and the Idea*, 160–79.
39. Stråth, 'A European Identity'.
40. Shore, *Building Europe*, 15–65; Stråth, 'A European Identity'.
41. Morin, *Europa denken*, 140–63, quotation from 154; Olsson and Svenning, *Tillhör Sverige Europa?*
42. Shore, *Building Europe*; Hansen, *Europeans Only?*; Fornäs, *Signifying Europe*.
43. Hansen, *Europeans Only?*, 51–71; Delanty, 'Europe and the Idea'; Lähdesmäki and Wagener, 'Discourses on Governing Diversity'; Morin, *Europa denken*, 168–69.
44. On identity politics, see, e.g., Meyer, *Identitätspolitik*.
45. Papcke, 'Who Needs European Identity?', 69.
46. Saramago, 'A Country Adrift'. See also Lough, 'National Identity and Historiography'.
47. Habermas, 'Citizenship and National Identity'.
48. Derrida, *The Other Heading*, 19.
49. Stråth, 'Preface', 11.
50. Cerutti, 'Towards the Political Identity'.
51. Papcke, 'Who Needs European Identity?', 72.
52. Ash, 'Europe's True Stories'.
53. Grinell, 'Ilm al-Hududiyya'.
54. Derrida, *The Other Heading*, 5–6.
55. Ibid., 42–45.
56. Ibid., 31–32, 45.
57. Ibid., 56–58.
58. Ibid., 25–26.
59. Konrád, *Från Europas navel*, 49.
60. Sloterdijk, *Falls Europa erwacht*, 12–26.
61. Le Goff, *Das alte Europa*.
62. Schulze, 'Die Identität Europas'.
63. Smith, 'National Identity'.
64. Koslowski, 'Vaterland Europa'.
65. Brague, *Eccentric Culture*, quotation from 122.
66. Brague, 'Sohnland Europa'.
67. Ratzinger, 'Europa in der Kris'; Ratzinger, 'Gemeinsame Identität'. See also Robbers, *Staat und Kirche*; Müller-Graff and Schneider, *Kirchen und Religionsgemeinschaften*.
68. d'Estaing, 'Pour ou Contre l'Adhésion'.
69. Sloterdijk, *Falls Europa erwacht*, 24, 33–37.
70. Ibid., 48–49.
71. Brague, 'Sohnland Europa', 37–40.
72. Koslowski, 'Vaterland Europa'.

73. Sloterdijk, *Falls Europa erwacht*, 50–58, quotation from 58: 'Europas tiefster Gedanke ist, dass man der Verachtung widerstehen muss'.
74. Heller, 'Europe: An Epilogue?', 21, 25.
75. Schulze, 'Die Identität Europas', 23: 'Es ist eine imagined community, besteht also, wenn es besteht, vor allem in den Köpfen der Menschen'.
76. Habermas, 'Citizenship and National Identity'.
77. Habermas, 'Braucht Europa eine Verfassung?'
78. d'Appollonia, 'European Nationalism', 189.
79. Delanty, *Inventing Europe*, 163; Delanty, *Citizenship in a Global Age*, 115–16; Delanty, 'Models of European Identity'.
80. Sloterdijk, *Falls Europa erwacht*, 48.
81. d'Appollonia, 'European Nationalism', 190.
82. Fischer, 'From Confederacy to Federation'.
83. Jospin, 'An Enlarged Europe'.
84. Blair, 'Tony Blair's Britain Speech'.
85. Quoted from Passerini, 'The Last Identification', 65.
86. Spiering, *History of British Euroscepticism*.
87. Lepsius, 'Bildet sich eine kulturelle Identität?'
88. Shore, *Building Europe*; Hansen, *Europeans Only?*
89. Jacobs and Maier, 'European Identity'.
90. Niethammer, 'A European Identity'.
91. Ibid., 111.
92. Sassatelli, 'Interview with Jean Baudrillard'.
93. Balibar, 'Europe as Borderland'.
94. Stråth, 'A European Identity'.
95. Asad, 'Muslims and European Identity'.
96. Passerini, 'The Last Identification', 64.
97. E.g., the speech by Kocka, 'Wege zur politischen Identität Europas'.
98. Bauman, *Europe: An Unfinished Adventure*.
99. The six original articles were gathered with further contributions from the debate in Levy, Pensky and Torpey, *Old Europe, New Europe*.
100. See Garton Ash and Ralph Dahrendorf, Matthias Greffrath, Hans-Ulrich Wehler and Joachim Starbatty in Levy et al., *Old Europe, New Europe*.
101. Müller, 'European Intellectuals'.
102. See Péter Esterházy, Andrzej Stasiuk and Adam Krzemiński in Levy et al., *Old Europe, New Europe*, quotations from 147, 151.
103. Saramago, 'A Country Adrift'.
104. Stasiuk, 'Logbuch', 141.
105. Radisch, *Die Seele Europas*, 18.

Conclusion

This book's chapters have explored the main dimensions of the concept of Europe, all of which emphasise Europe as a unity, but one marked by borders and divisions. In certain respects, Europe is obviously a unifying concept that has made it possible to think beyond divisions and transcend borders. Europe has been associated with pleadings for a political unity that could undo the legacy of war, and with pledges to uphold a common culture. As a unifying concept, it can be associated with idealism, at times with humankind's higher goals, but also with the pragmatism of putting social organisation into practice.

The chapters have also offered much evidence that the concept of Europe is associated with hierarchies, exclusion and borders, confirming historical differences and stressing current divisions. From certain perspectives, Europe can be seen as a dividing concept, highlighting political borders and cultural differences. This is related to differences between regions and nations within Europe, however geographically defined, and there is a long history of associating these differences with hierarchies. For instance, in Victor Hugo's imagined European Parliament, French would be spoken: 'The United States of Europe speaking German would mean a delay of three hundred years. A delay, that is to say, a step backward'.[1] In the economic crises of the 2010s, we heard arguments that the countries of Southern Europe were less well organised, and that their people worked too little in comparison with those in Northern Europe.

From the early 1800s until the present, the concept of Europe has appealed to different visions. Romantics and conservatives, market-oriented

---

Notes for this section begin on page 307.

liberals and revolutionary socialists have all articulated political visions of European unity. So too have experts who turned to technical measures for unification. Some wanted to restore Europe to its previous glory or reacted to a perceived decline, while others looked for a Europe entering a new stage of development. Europe has been associated with threats and with hopes, with superiority and inferiority. Sometimes, the visions represented idealistic dreams and sometimes mere exercises of the will. As a unifying and dividing concept, Europe is contested and an object of disputes.

New Interpretations of Old Themes: Notes on the Debate of the 2010s

As previous chapters have demonstrated, there has been no consensus regarding the definitions of European civilisation, European culture, the European spirit, European integration or European identity. Whatever definition was applied to Europe, it was contested, and contemporary debate continues this pattern. Despite the considerable talk about European unity and disunity in recent decades, a common definition remains out of reach.

Notably, with the introduction of the euro and the enlargement of the European Union (EU) to encompass the Baltic States and Central Europe, some books have presented extremely hopeful views of the future of Europe and the EU – for example: Jeremy Rifken's *The European Dream: How Europe's Vision of the Future Is Quietly Eclipsing the American Dream* (2004) and Mark Leonard's *Why Europe Will Run the 21st Century* (2005). By the 2010s, economic crises brought back the key theme from the first half of the twentieth century regarding Europe's general decline and weakened position in global competition. Titles from this period instead centred on the crises facing Europe, including keywords such as 'death', 'deadlock', 'decline' and 'doomed'.[2] In the aftermath of the financial crisis, much of the discussion concerned the malaise facing Europe, including both the way the union worked and the standards of the continent in general. Such a dramatic turn in the debate on Europe had not been seen in decades, possibly not since the aftermath of the Second World War. Remarkably, the book titles from this time made no distinction between Europe and the EU, using the terms interchangeably. Let us take a closer look at the arguments behind these titles.

Much of this literature addresses the theme of European decline – falling birth rates, technological inferiority to the United States and China, economic policy misconduct, and a widespread culture based on consuming beyond one's means were all topics that garnered attention.[3] According to *The*

Decline and Fall of Europe (2012) by Francesco Bongiovanni, several aspects fed into the decline, including many laws and decrees emanating from the elites and bureaucrats in Brussels.[4] He noted the widespread exploitation of the system in Europe, allowing values such as egoism and hedonism to take root, especially in Southern Europe; however Britain, Ireland and France were part of this culture too, mortgaging the future of their children and grandchildren in exchange for current pleasures.[5] Bongiovanni concluded that growth was no longer part of the culture, and that Europeans had settled for mediocrity: 'It is a crisis of the entire European model, construct and philosophy of life'. However, he hoped that the crisis would serve as a wake-up call.[6] David Marsh, a writer with expertise in European monetary affairs, predicted in 2012 that Europe would likely lose its position on the world stage. The EU's negligence in establishing the euro and shortcomings in handling the crisis gave him little hope for the future, unless the EU could radically transform itself into a political union.[7] David Marquand – a former British MP, an EU official, and the principal of Mansfield College, Oxford – called for a European federation in a world where the West had begun to shrink in importance.[8]

These responses to the crisis are representative in that few of the critics wanted to give up on European integration. Early in this heated discussion, Fernando Savater expressed the widely held opinion that 'European countries have no alternative to sticking together in many essential social, cultural and economic respects', but were deficient in their ability to aspire to the more ambitious goals that the crisis required: 'They lack significant joint projects and shared democratic values and convictions'.[9] However, the debate continued with plenty of suggestions regarding common projects and grand visions for the future of integration.

Some rejected this notion of decline, maintaining that Europe was doing fine and that things were much better than they appeared, in both Europe and the EU.[10] They noted the use of soft power to resolve disputes peacefully through extended negotiations, and that European laws mostly concerned international trade. They said that the EU was no more elitist than its member states and was more transparent, with relatively efficient institutions and a limited number of bureaucrats. The remarkable amount of public support for the union and the euro, even during the crisis, was also cited as an argument in favour of the EU. The defenders stressed that the EU had achieved much worth protecting.[11] However, some considered the union inefficient, and many argued that it should be reformed, made more flexible, and have its decision-making processes sped up in the interest of more clearly defined leadership and greater democratic participation.[12] Political scientist Jan Zielonka suggested that European integration should develop in a new direction. Noting that the growing interdependence between member states 'no longer generates integration but instead prompts disintegration', he warned of the impending dissolution of the union. In alignment with Alan Milward, Zielonka stated that post-war integration had rescued and strengthened the nation states of Europe. However, he pointed out that with local government, regions, large cities, and transnational NGOs acting in networks beyond the nation states and on the European stage to implement their own agendas, integration was a factor that could affect the member states' varying levels of support for the EU. To deal with this, integration should embark on a new vision that would exchange the one-size-fits-all model for one of plurality and hybridity: 'Integration recognizing local conditions and rejecting rigid hierarchical blueprints may prove more effective in coping with problems of complex interdependence'. This, he argued, would lead to a revival of integration.[13]

Disputes continued regarding the division between the economically successful Northern countries, with Germany at their core, and the less successful Southern countries.[14] The growing gap caused many public intellectuals to dispute current economic policies and favour a European politics emphasising social responsibility, often coupled with proposals for a federal EU. The Berlin sociologist Claus Offe saw the divide between the centre and periphery as widened by neoliberal politics and social injustices. He wanted Europe/the EU to refocus on 'improving social justice through social security redistribution across Member States and social classes'.[15] For the Ljubljana philosopher Slavoj Žižek, Europe was a necessary alternative to American-driven global capitalism and Chinese authoritarianism, but it would have to be redefined beyond technocratic pragmatism and selected aspects of its heritage. Srećko Horvat, a philosopher from Zagreb, wanted to refine the European idea to align more with an economic path going beyond neoliberal austerity.[16] Luis Moreno, a Spanish social scientist, found a way out of the crisis by politically unifying and defending the welfare state model as an alternative to economic globalisation.[17] The political philosopher Sami Naïr proposed common European social policies to address the inequalities created by globalisation and national interests, which would require a European federation and a common consciousness and identity.[18] The Munich sociologist Ulrich Beck warned that the present discontent arising from the widening gap between the powerless masses and the mighty elites would diminish people's expectations of freedom and equity. He proposed a social contract for Europe that would define integration as a project for social welfare and democracy, healing the division and gaining legitimacy for the EU.[19] The literature offers us a range of voices critical of the EU that simultaneously continue to argue in favour of integration, suggesting a perspective of strong European awareness.

In the early 2010s, the catchphrase 'European identity' decreased in usage, though it was still used in several contexts – for example, in political programmes for integration (e.g. when the European Parliament sought to create a European identity), when advocating for solutions to European crises, and when analysing contemporary Europe.[20] Descriptive inquiries were often interspersed with normative proclamations in a way that made it difficult to distinguish one from the other. This dynamic was common in European Commission research initiatives that centred on European identity.[21] In the debate on identity, it was possible to find a common basis that incorporated a long heritage of shared European values such as rationalism and democracy, a basis that did not rely on group loyalty to any one political regime.[22] Others saw European identity as a necessary phenomenon that had actually arrived along with peace and freedom: a common identity was already in place, and all that remained was for it to acquire greater substance to become fully established in the collective consciousness. This was the standpoint of public intellectual Umberto Eco, who, during the European debt crisis in 2012, said that the current European identity remained shallow but was in the process of growing deeper, step by step. Eco was confident that 'we're now all culturally European' and that 'we will remain a federation'.[23]

Calls for a 'two-speed' process persisted, with the euro-zone countries integrating at a faster pace than the rest, perhaps under a single government.[24] Even British voices in favour of the EU, such as the Liberal Party leader David Owen, who argued for a 'two-speed' Europe, preferred that Britain stay outside the core group that was moving forward at a quicker pace.[25] Among Britain's hardcore EU critics, nationalism was salient. The writer and conservative MP Daniel Hannan compared the EU to the communist system, speaking of European *apparatchiks* and the gap between what was officially said and the actual truth, likening himself to a dissident in the former Eastern Europe. He believed that Britain's main reason to leave the EU was so that it could continue to build on its nationalism, leading to progress and entrepreneurship, and offering a refuge from totalitarian ideologies.[26] Of course, national sentiments were on the rise in places besides Britain. For Václav Klaus, former president of the Czech Republic, the parallels between European governance and the centralised communist system were remarkable, and he warned that the further development of integration might erase the nation state. He instead insisted on preserving the EU as collaboration among sovereign countries.[27]

The refugee crisis in 2015 and the Brexit referendum in 2016 contributed to the discourse of crisis, and intensified arguments about the disintegration of the EU. Still, developments were by no means one-dimensional, as European integration was simultaneously accelerating and being called into question. In previous chapters we mentioned 'the border paradox' of European integration, which is relevant here and indicates that some borders between member states were weakening, while legal, economic and political integration persisted. On the other hand, certain older cultural borders continue to emphasise regional autonomy and minority rights. Other cultural borders have followed the migration of people who have brought religious and linguistic multiculturalism to Europe. As a result, the cultural borders of Europe have become more accentuated than before. The refugee crisis fuelled nationalist sentiments throughout Europe, leading to the establishment of border controls and rhetoric about defending national values; it also forced the member states to take collective action, strengthening integration in the affected policy areas. During the Brexit process following the referendum, opinions and political actions regarding Britain's departure from the EU became increasingly entrenched in the UK, and especially in England, while support for the EU grew within the union. The reasons for Brexit were certainly complex, but historians have stressed it as a mainly English phenomenon, undergirded by a 'strange sense of imaginary oppression' tangled up with nationalism and fantasies of a British empire.[28] The campaign for Brexit increased scepticism towards European integration, which had been expressed in the 1950s and continued following British admission to the EU. The mentality of British scepticism towards integration insinuated that Britain was a strong country, while the EU was strongly connected to Europe, which was regarded as a threat to Britain. Memories of German bombing and plans to invade Britain during the Second World War contributed to British concerns and were recounted as European attacks. British Eurosceptics conceived their country as an island separated from Europe by the Channel, with EU membership serving as a bridge by which (Eastern) Europeans could invade their country.[29] When viewed in this light, Europe was the same as the EU, and both were repudiated.

The responses to the second round of crisis were similar to those from the first half of the decade, contending that the EU was an elite project largely driven by the core countries, leaving those on the periphery behind. The proposed solutions included calls for social justice and utilising European social rights to overcome divisions. Proposals to both centralise and further regionalise were made, in attempts to move past the nation state; the options ranged from embracing a United States of Europe as a fully fledged federation, to further democratisation and the development of a transnational republic. These suggestions were often combined with observations that the crisis had infused more of a sense of European consciousness among its citizens.[30]

So, Where Do We Stand?

Assessing the development of European awareness during the 2010s, one could initially consider the unification concept to be in eclipse; upon closer examination, however, the concept can instead be regarded as reaching a new zenith, with the idea of European unification characterising the concept of Europe more than ever before. Here, I will reinforce this argument by making a few brief observations regarding the debates surrounding the concept of Europe. Considering the sentiments stirred up by the chain of crises in the 2010s and early 2020s, we can say that they have two sides. On the one hand, some believed that the sense of cooperation within the EU was threatened by these crises, while on the other, there were indications of increasing concern about European society. Even in 2012, Ulrich Beck concluded that the crisis had 'torn Europe apart but brought Europeans closer [together]'. Looking at the European community, he saw a renewed European consciousness as a common thread addressed in newspapers, in local discussions, and around dinner tables. In a noteworthy book about the consequences of the refugee crisis, the social scientist Ivan Krastev took a more radical stand: the prerequisites for democracy in the nation states had changed, and a revolt against the liberal elites had taken hold, leading to doubts regarding 'Europe's political, economic and social model'. Pessimistically, Krastev predicted the disintegration of Europe. The refugee crisis had bolstered national identity and solidarity, altering the dynamics of European integration and deepening the chasm between Brussels and the member states of Central and Eastern Europe. He found hope in the European public's increased confidence in the EU, and prescribed more compromise and conciliation as the key elements of integration. Even Krastev could observe a European awareness in the midst of crisis. His observation illustrates the close association of the concept of Europe with unification. In contemporary Europe, the EU and the various European integration measures constitute the concept of Europe, establishing its boundaries and prerequisites.

To make a fair assessment of the concept of Europe, both what is said and the act of its being said must be observed and considered. According to the performative perspective, identity is not an attribute that defines a community and moves it forward; rather, it is actively performed, for example, through defining an identity.[31] This is similar to the concept of Europe, which is performed by applying it and imprinting it with meaning. We must therefore ask why the concept of Europe has been used. In the nineteenth century, claiming the existence of European cultural unity was a way to ascertain it. On closer inspection, one can see that the concept of Europe includes performative aspects. Beethoven's cantata 'The Glorious Moment', Opus 136, does not simply describe Europe as something that exists, but also as something in the making, even remaking itself. The performative aspect of the European idea became increasingly prominent over the course of the century; so did its normative dimension and its connection to the new way of understanding and narrating society, accompanied by changes in how the concepts of history, progress and development were understood. Previous eras had explored multiple histories and developments, but in the 1800s these concepts had begun to appear as so-called collective singulars. Europe had begun to be framed by and connected to *the* development, *the* progress, and *the* history.[32] By the end of the 1840s, the Swedish novelist Carl Johan Almqvist connected 'the European spirit' and demands for liberation from the old society. He articulated the upheavals of this period in his call for individual freedom. Almqvist believed that 'the European future is standing by us all in the entrance hall, and it wants to come in'.[33] Europe represented *the* future.

However, acts of unity often also include aspects of hierarchies, divisions and borders. François Guizot's notion of European civilisation identified France as the most advanced country, while Thomas Buckle's notion stressed England's leading role. In another example, the concept of Central Europe could be used as a way to define a region within Europe in contradiction to Russia and Western Europe. In 'Mitteleuropa', Friedrich Naumann envisioned a region dominated by German culture and political interests. By contrast, Tomaš Masaryk's Central Europe was a region of Hungarians and Slavic nations bordering on Germany and Russia. Moreover, throughout the nineteenth and twentieth centuries, visions of European unity repeatedly stressed Europe's cultural borders with Russia and the United States, and notions of a European world mission and European superiority were recurrent. Recent debates on European identity address divisions and hierarchies between Southern and Northern Europe, between Western 'core' member states and Central European countries.

Beginning in the late twentieth century, it was alleged that European identity could promote the quest for further integration, certainly in the EU discourse striving to construct legitimacy, but also by public intellectuals. European identity was supposed to shift attention away from national sentiments and allegiances, as reflected in the EU's ambition to manifest European identity and 'unity in diversity' and as conveyed by public intellectuals articulating a European duality that both creates unity and protects diversity. However, it is uncertain what characteristics can be attributed to European identity in upcoming discussions about the future of Europe. It is important that these characteristics continue to relate to democracy, rule of law, individual rights and the welfare state. However, we also know that the concepts of Europe and European identity play an important role in xenophobic and Islamophobic political programmes to defend Europe against perceived threats. In fact, the concept of European identity might also contribute to discourses that question the welfare state or promote national homogenisation. Neoliberal economic policies have defined Europe in significant ways since the 1980s, and although they have recently been called into question, they maintain a strong grip on Europe. Anti-immigrant and anti-Muslim discourses are prominent in the context of increasingly integrated EU responses to the crises of the 2010s. We can conclude that the various values and implications of European identity are also contested, as is the concept of Europe. There are good reasons to be aware of the competing political implications of references to European identity and to understand the discourse of European identity as a controversial space.

It is vital to acknowledge that an important performative component of definitions of Europe is to conceal some of Europe's exclusions and heritage. Many cases can be found in which Europe is described as a homogeneous Christian continent, which tends to omit the Muslim elements of European history and their presence in contemporary Europe. This is problematic, given the history of south-east and south-west Europe, the fact that Christianity and Islam share common roots, and the vital role of Arabic intellectual culture in medieval Europe.[34] We have also seen modern Europe as defined by the Enlightenment, which promotes secularism, individual freedom, rational thinking, and science. However, it is well known that modern European history includes colonialism and brutality towards both non-Europeans and Europeans. This is not something that has necessarily been hidden in the definitions of European identity. For example, Luisa Passerini, Jürgen Habermas and Gerard Delanty emphasise that an up-to-date consideration of the concept of Europe must include contemplation of the dark aspects of its modern incarnation. Yet, in the quest to unify Europe, such facets of the common identity tend to be subordinated.

Europe's history since 1800 is obviously connected to national histories, languages and identities. This book has presented a narrative of the intellectual discourses of the concept of Europe, illustrating a history entangled with the concept of the nation. This narrative emphasised major shifts around 1800, the two world wars, and the dismantling of the Iron Curtain, as well as responses to changing international relations, the development of the nation state, and demands for democracy and citizen rights. We see the contours of a narrative in which nationality and European unification may be aligned. However, it is also a narrative in which unification and nationalism are in sharp contrast to each other, with the latter stressing national independence, exclusive sovereignty, and strict borders.

It is plausible to argue that nationalist sentiments are appealing in contemporary Europe, and that a European integration in which the EU offers a stage for its many nationalities offers these nationalities room to grow rather than snuffing them out. We should not be surprised, because an 'ever ongoing integration' implies the persistence of nation states, without which there would be nothing to integrate. In addition, many observations suggest that national and European sentiments do not contradict each other but are instead complementary. Edgar Morin and Mauro Ceruti have argued that we have, and should have, the right to develop a wide range of identities that encompass beliefs, political views, and relationships among local, national and European identities. They see – and I agree – that a belief in pure identities is brutalising, contributing to the European barbarism we see perpetrated against minorities, against colonial populations, and in situations where ethnic cleansing has occurred over the past century. They conclude that only a European political project offers us the possibility of resisting the brutality of nationalism, and they insist that there is no essential conflict between European identities and national ones.[35] However, our examinations of the concept of Europe and of the discourse of European identity show that a European project can be realised alongside multiple political visions. It is not enough simply to define the contemporary project of European integration if the aim is to avoid what Morin and Ceruti consider 'European barbarism'. European nationalism could also treat minorities and people defined as others in barbaric ways.

Certainly, the original ideas of establishing peace, stopping fascism, and resisting communism persist in the official presentation of the EU, which refers to a dark history of colonisation and the trauma of wartime. In the present, the overarching idea of the EU is one in which common European problems can only be solved together through further integration.[36] At its best, this idea incorporates ideals of tolerance, equality, and human rights. However, we know that considerations of a unified Europe and pleas for political unification have found support from both ends of the political spectrum, and that during the post-war period, integration was championed by conservatives, liberals and socialists – in both politics and intellectual life. We also know that integration has been, and continues to be, hotly debated and criticised. The European project, as such, is no guarantee that brutality, for example, towards refugees, will be avoided. The various means, measures, treaties, laws, and institutional bodies that together contribute to forming the EU are also an arena for contestations about differing visions, where pragmatism confronts economic interests and struggles for power.

Notes

1. Hugo, 'Letter to D'Alton Shee'.
2. Bongiovanni, *The Decline and Fall*; Gillingham, *The EU: An Obituary*; Laqueur, *The Last Days of Europe*; Lacqueur, *After the Fall*; Marsh, *Europe's Deadlock*; Murray, *Strange Death of Europe*; Simms and Zeeb, *Europa am Abgrund*.

3. Moyo, *How the West Was Lost*, 87–89.
4. Bongiovanni, *The Decline and Fall*, 39–40.
5. Ibid., 124–43.
6. Ibid., 206, 219, 278, quotation from 292.
7. Marsh, *Europe's Deadlock*, 117–20.
8. Marquand, *End of the West*.
9. Savater, 'EU Needs to Stand Up'.
10. Kundnani and Leonard, 'Think Again: European Decline'.
11. See, e.g., the political scientist McCormick, *Why Europe Matters*, 19–26, 146–82.
12. Giddens, *Turbulent and Mighty Continent*; McCormick, *Why Europe Matters*, 146–82; Piris, *The Future of Europe*, 146: Weidenfeld, *Europa: Eine Strategie*.
13. Zielonka, *Is the EU Doomed?*, 93.
14. Marsh, *Europe's Deadlock*, 18–26; Manolo Monereo (Podemos MP), *Por Europa y contra el systema euro*, 63.
15. Offe, *Europe Entrapped*, 122.
16. Žižek and Horvat, *What Does Europe Want?*, 56, 89–91.
17. Moreno, *Europa sin estados*, 14–16.
18. Naïr, *El desengaño europeo*.
19. Beck, *German Europe*, 12, 70–77.
20. 'We Need to Invest'; Darnstädt, Schult and Zuber, 'How to Forge'; Venet et al., *European Identity through Space*.
21. European Commission, 'Development of European Identity'.
22. Green, *The European Identity*.
23. Eco, 'It's Culture'.
24. Piris, *The Future of Europe*, 147.
25. Owen, *Europe Restructured*, 301–34.
26. Hannan, *A Doomed Marriage*, ix–x, 20, 73, 110–11.
27. Klaus, *Europe*.
28. O'Toole, *Heroic Failure*, xvi–xvii, 1–3. See also Dorling and Tomlinson, *Rule Britannia*.
29. Spiering, *History of British Euroscepticism*.
30. Fazi, *The Battle for Europe*; Guérot, *Warum Europa eine Republik*; Guérot, *Europa erneuern!*; Krastev, *After Europe*; Roll, *Wir sind Europa!*; Simms and Zeeb, *Europa am Abgrund*; Wirtén, *Är vi framme snart?*
31. Kuus, 'Ubiquitous Identities'. 'Performative approaches do not treat identity as an attribute or a property of the subject – something that subjects such as individuals or states express. It conceives subjectivity explicitly in processual terms, not as a source but as an effect of identity claims. Identity then is not something that states, groups or individuals have, but something that groups and individuals do'.
32. Koschorke, *Hegel und wir*, 82–92.
33. Almqvist, *Det europeiska missnöjets grunder*, 26.
34. Grinell, 'Ilm al-Huddiyya'.
35. Morin and Ceruti, *Nuestra Europa*.
36. Ighe, 'Never Mind Patriarchy'; Lähdesmäki, 'Narrative and Intertextuality'.

Bibliography

'I. Paneuropakongress'. *Zeitschrift Pan-Europa* 3(13–14) (1926), 53–54.
Abercromby, Helen. 'The Harvest (September 1914)', in Charles F. Forshaw (ed.), *One Hundred of the Best Poems on the European War: By Women Poets of the Empire* (London: Elliot Stock, 1916), 14–16.
Adamovsky, Ezequiel. 'Euro-Orientalism and the Making of the Concept of Eastern Europe in France, 1810–1880'. *The Journal of Modern History* 77(3) (2005), 591–628.
Adamthwaite, Anthony P. *Grandeur and Misery: France's Bid for Power in Europe, 1914–1940.* London: Arnold, 1995.
Adenauer, Konrad. '14 September 1951. "Deutschland und der Friede in Europa": Ansprache vor den Nouvelles Equipes Internationales in Bad Ems', in Hans-Peter Schwartz (ed.), *Konrad Adenauer Reden 1917–1967: Eine Auswahl* (Stuttgart: Deutsche Verlags-Anstalt, 1975), 230.
Adler, Moritz. *Der Krieg, die Congressidee und die allgemeine Wehrpflicht im Lichte det Aufklärung und Humanität unserer Zeit allen Freunden des Fortschritts gewidmet/ von einem Freunde der Wahrheit.* Prague: Steinhauser, 1868.
Agnelli, Ardiono. *La genesi dell'idea di Mitteleuropa.* Milan: Giuffrè, 1971.
Agnelli, Giovanni, and Attilio Caiati. *Federazione Europea o Lega delle Nazioni?* Turin: Bocca, 1918.
Agorio, Adolfo. *La Sombre de Europa: Trasformación de los sentimientos y de las ideas.* Montevideo: Claudio García, 1917.
Ahnlund, Claes. *Diktare i krig: K.G. Ossiannilsson, Bertil Malmberg och Ture Nerman från debuten till 1920.* Hedemora: Gidlunds förlag, 2007.
Alcalde, Ángel. 'The Transnational Consensus: Fascism and Nazism in Current Research'. *Contemporary European History* 29(2) (2020), 243–52.
Allen, Emory Adams. *History of Civilization.* Cincinnati: Central Publishing House, 1889–91.
Allmendinger et al. *Soft Spaces in Europe: Renegotiating Governance, Boundaries and Borders.* London: Routledge, 2018.
Almqvist, Carl Jonas Love. 'Det europeiska missnöjets grunder' [The reasons for the European discontent], in *Törnrosens bok* III (Stockholm: Albert Bonniers förlag, 1847), 5–153.

Altamira, Rafael. *Historia de España y de la civilización Español*, I–IV. Barcelona: Juan Gili, 1900.
Amberley, John Russell. 'Can War Be Avoided?' *Fortnightly Review*, vol. 15. London: Chapman and Hall, 1871.
Amyne, Richard, and John Pinder. *Federal Union: The Pioneers: A History of Federal Union*. London: Macmillan, 1990.
Anastasiadou, Irene. *Constructing Iron Europe: Transnationalism and Railways in the Interbellum*. Amsterdam: Amsterdam University Press, 2011.
Anderson, Benedict. *Imagined Communities*. London: Verso, 1983.
Anderson, Perry. *The New Old World*. London: Verso, 2009.
Andrén, Mats. *Att frambringa det uthärdliga: Studier kring gränser, nationalism och individualism I Centraleuropa* (The Discourse about Central Europe). Hedemora: Gidlunds förlag, 2001.
——. *Den europeiska blicken och det lokala självstyrets värden*. Hedemora: Gidlunds förlag, 2007.
——. 'Entanglements: Cultural Borders in Visions of European Unification'. *European Review* 28(3) (2020), 416–24.
——. 'Europe of Nations, Europe without Nationalism'. *History of European Ideas* 46(1) (2020), 13–24.
——. 'Local Government and Local Citizens: Beginnings in the 1830s', in Mats Andrén (ed.), *Local Citizenship* (Gothenburg: University of Gothenburg, 2007), 17–31.
——. 'Robinson Crusoe och ekonomerna, eller Den ekonomiska människan', in Claes Ekenstam and Per Magnus Johansson (eds), *Människobilder: Tio idéhistoriska studier* (Hedemora: Gidlunds förlag, 2007), 84–106.
——. 'The Controversial Concept of European Identity', in Mats Andrén, Thomas Lindkvist, Ingmar Söhrman and Katharina Vajta (eds), *Cultural Borders of Europe: Narratives, Concepts and Practices in the Present and the Past* (New York: Berghahn Books, 2017), 159–69.
Andrén, Mats, and Joris van Ejnatten. 'European Unity and the Nation State', in Pasi Ihalainen and Antero Holmila (eds), *Nationalism and Internationalism Intertwined: A European History of Concepts beyond Nation States: Concepts beyond Nation States* (New York: Berghahn Books, 2022), 223–46.
Andrén, Mats, Thomas Lindkvist, Ingmar Söhrman and Katharina Vajta (eds). *Cultural Borders of Europe: Narratives, Concepts and Practices in the Present and the Past* (New York: Berghahn Books, 2017).
Andrén, Mats, and Ingmar Söhrman. 'Introduction', in Mats Andrén, Thomas Lindkvist, Ingmar Söhrman and Katharina Vajta (eds), *Cultural Identities and National Borders* (Gothenburg: CERGU, University of Gothenburg, 2009), 9–14.
Andrén, Mats, and Ingmar Söhrman. 'Introduction', in Mats Andrén, Thomas Lindkvist, Ingmar Söhrman and Katharina Vajta (eds), *Cultural Borders of Europe: Narratives, Concepts and Practices in the Present and the Past* (New York: Berghahn Books, 2017), 1–17.
Andrews, John. *The Present Relations on War and Politics between France and Great Britain*. London: George Robinson, 1806.
Andrian-Werburg, Victor von. *Österreich und dessen Zukunft*. Hamburg: Hoffmann und Campe, 1841.
Angell, Norman. 'Introduction', in Edward Krehbiel, *Nationalism, War and Society: A Study of Nationalism and its Concomitant, War, in their Relation to Civilization; and of the Fundamentals and the Progress of the Opposition to War* (New York: Macmillan Company, 1916), xiii–xxxv.
——. *The Peace Treaty and the Economic Chaos of Europe*. London: The Swarthmore Press, 1920.
——. *The Political Conditions of Allied Success: A Plea for the Protective Union of the Democracies*. New York: G.P. Putnam, 1918.
——. *War Aims: The Need for a Parliament of the Allies*. London: Headley, 1917.

Anonymous. 'Der Wille zum Frieden'. *Neues Frauenleben: organ der freiheitlichen frauen in Österreich* 16(12) (1914), 261–68.
Anonymous. *Europa: wird es republikanisch oder kosakisch? Eine auf die Memoiren Napoleon's, das Testament Peter des Grossen and viele andere gewichtsvolle Documente gestützte Abhandlung über die usnerem Welttheil drohenden Gefahren und die Mittel zu deren Abwendung als Vorlage für einen europäischen Kongress*. Leipzig: E.P. Kasprowicz, 1866.
Anonymous. 'Iceland and Denmark: A Protest'. *The New Europe* 6(84) (1918), 135.
Anonymous. Article in *Illustriertes Familien-journal: zur unterhaltung und Belehrung*. 1862.
Anonymous. 'In ernster Zeit'. *Neues Frauenleben: organ der freiheitlichen Frauen in Österreich* 16(12) (1914), 266–67.
Anonymous. 'Keep to the Left!' *The New Europe* 6(69) (1918), 8.
Anonymous. 'Lord Robert Cecil and the Rome Congress'. *The New Europe* 6(85) (1918), 163–64.
Anonymous. 'The Triumph of Russian Autocracy'. *The Eclectic Magazine*, 1844.
Anonymous. 'The Very Stuff of Triumph'. *The New Europe* 6(91) (1918), 295.
Appleton, Nathan. *Europe and America in 1870*. New York: Printed for the author, 1870.
Armitage, David. *Foundations of Modern International Thought*. Cambridge: Cambridge University Press, 2013.
———. 'The International Turn in Intellectual History', in Darrin M. McMahon and Samuel Moyn (eds), *Rethinking European Intellectual History* (Oxford: Oxford University Press, 2014), 232–52.
'Arms and The Men'. *The Times* [London], 2 September 1914, 4. Retrieved 9 November 2017 from *The Times Digital Archive*.
Arndt, Christian Gottlieb von. *Über den Ursprung und die verschiedenartige Verwandschaft der europäischen Sprachen: Nach Anleitung des russischen Allgemeinen vergleichenden Wörterbuchs*. Frankfurt am Main: H.L. Brönner, 1818.
Arnold, Günter, Kurt Kloocke and Ernest A. Menze. 'Herders Reception and Influence', in Hans Adler and Wulf Köpke (eds), *A Companion to the Works of Johann Gottfried Herder* (New York: Camden House, 2009), 391–420.
Aron, Raymond. *In Defence of Decadent Europe*. New Brunswick, NJ: Transaction Publishers, 1979.
———. 'My Defence of Our Decadent Europe', *Encounter* (September 1977), 7–50.
———. 'My Defence of Our Decadent Europe', *Encounter* (October 1977), 11–33.
———. 'Old Nations, New Europe'. *Daedalus* 93(1) (1964), 43–66.
Asad, Talal. 'Muslims and European Identity: Can Europe Represent Islam?', in Anthony Pagden (ed.), *The Idea of Europe: From Antiquity to the European Union* (Cambridge: Cambridge University Press, 2002), 209–27.
Ash, Timothy Garton. 'Europe's True Stories'. *Prospect* 131 (February 2007).
Aster, Sidney. *Power, Policy and Personality: The Life and Times of Lord Salter, 1881–1975*. No place of publication, 2015.
Attlee, C.R. 'The Peace We Are Striving For', in Attlee et al., *Labour's Aims in War and Peace* (London: Lincolns-Prager, 1940), 106.
Balibar, Étienne. 'Europe as Borderland'. *Environment and Planning D: Society and Space* 27(2) (2009), 190–215.
———. 'World Borders, Political Borders'. PMLA 116(1) (2002), 71–78.
Balmes, Jaime Luciano. *European Civilization: Protestantism and Catholicity Compared*. London: Burns & Lambert, 1845.
Barraclough, Geoffrey. *History in a Changing World*. Oxford: Basil Blackwell, 1955.
Barrès, Maurice. *The Faith of France: Studies in Spiritual Differences and Unity*. Boston, MA: Houghton Mifflin, 1918.
Barrow, John. *An Auto-Biographical Memoir of Sir John Barrow*. London: J. Murray, 1847.

Bartlett, Robert. *The Making of Europe: Conquest, Colonization and Cultural Change 950–1350*. London: Penguin Books, 1994.
Battaglia, Roger. *Ein Zoll- und Wirtschaftsbündnis zwischen Österreich-Ungarn und Deutschland (Geschichte – Konstruktion – Einwendungen)*. Vienna: Wilhelm Braumüller, 1917.
Bauman, Zygmunt. *Europe: An Unfinished Adventure*. Cambridge: Polity, 2004.
Beattie, Owen, and John Geiger. *Frozen in Time: The Fate of the Franklin Expedition*. Vancouver: Greystone Books, 2016.
Beck, Ulrich. *German Europe*. Cambridge: Polity Press, 2013.
Beck, Ulrich, and Edgar Grande. *Das kosmopolitische Europa: Gesellschaft und Politik in der Zweiten Modernität*. Frankfurt am Main: Suhrkamp Verlag, 2004.
Beecher, Jonathan. *Victor Considerant and the Rise and Fall of the French Romantic Socialism*. Berkeley: University of California Press, 2001.
Beethoven, Ludwig van, and Alois Weissenbach. 'The Glorious Moment, Opus 136, Choral Fantasy', English translation by Keith Anderson. Retrieved 22 October 2020 https://www.naxos.com/sharedfiles/PDF/8.572783_sungtext.pdf.
Belloc, Hilaire. *A General Sketch of the European War*. London: Nelson, 1915.
———. *The Crisis of Our Civilization*. London: Cassel and Company, 1937.
Beloff, Max. *Europe and the Europeans: An International Discussion*. London: Chatto & Windus, 1957.
———. *The Intellectual in Politics and Other Essays*. London: Weidenfeld & Nicolson, 1970.
Benda, Julien. *Discourse à la nation européenne*. Paris: Gallimard, 1933.
———. 'Julien Benda: Conférence du 2 septembre', in Benda (ed.), *L'esprit européen* (Neuchatel: Èditions de la Baconniére, 1947), 5–38.
———. 'Future of the Small Nations and the Idea of Federation'. New York: Czechoslovak Information Service, 1942.
Benes, Vojta. 'The Mission of Small States' [1941], in Lipgens (ed.), *Documents on European Integration*, Vol. 2 (Berlin: Walter de Gruyter, 1986), 373–74.
Benhabib, Seyla. *The Claims of Culture: Equality and Diversity in the Global Era*. Princeton, NJ: Princeton University Press, 2002.
Benson, Robert Hugh. *Lord of the World*. New York: Dodd, Mead & Company, 1907.
Berger, Stefan, and Caner Tekin. 'Introduction: Towards a "Europeanized" European History', in Stefan Berger and Caner Tekin (eds), *History and Belonging: Representation of the Past in Contemporary European* (New York: Berghahn Books, 2018), 1–20.
Bergfalk, Per Erik. *Om Svenska Städernas Författning och Förvaltning*. Uppsala: Leffler och Sebell, 1838.
Bergson, Henri. 'The Vital Energies of France', in *The New York Times Current History of the European War: Vol. 1, No. 1. What Men of Letters Say* (New York: The New York Times Company, 1914), 152–53.
Berl, Emmanuel. 'Europa und die Geschichte: Plädoyer für ein neues lehrbuch'. *Merkur* 20(2) (1966), 66–74.
Berlanga, José Luis Villacañas. 'Europa hora cero: meditación Europea de Ortega'. *ÁGORA: Papeles de Filosofía* 24(2) (2005), 177–98.
Berlin, Isaiah. *The Sense of Reality: Studies in Ideas and Their History*. Princeton, NJ: Princeton University Press, 1966.
Bernal, Martin. *Black Athena: The Afroasiatic Roots of Classical Civilization*. London: Free Association Books, 1987.
Bernanos, George. 'George Bernanos: Conférence du 12 septembre 1946', in Julien Benda (ed.), *L'esprit européen* (Neuchatel: Èditions de la Baconniére, 1947), 328–62.
Bess, Michael. *Realism, Utopia, and the Mushroom Cloud: Four Activist Intellectuals and Their Strategies for Peace, 1945–1989*. Chicago: University of Chicago Press, 1993.
Billig, Michael. *Banal Nationalism*. London: Sage Publications, 1995.

Björnstjerna, Magnus. *Grunder för Representationens möjliga ombyggnad och förenkling*. Stockholm: no publisher, 1839.
Blair, Tony. 'Tony Blair's Britain Speech' [2000]. Retrieved 11 April 2022 from https://www.theguardian.com/uk/2000/mar/28/britishidentity.tonyblair.
Blum, Antoinette. 'A European Dialogue: Romain Rolland and Charles Baudouin'. *The European Legacy: Towards New Paradigms* 1(1) (1996), 250–56.
Blum, Oscar. *Trümmerfeld Europa*. Leipzig: Franz Schneider Verlag, 1924.
Bluntschli, Johann Caspar. 'Die Organisation der Europäischen Statenvereins', in *Gesammelte kleine Schriften II* (Nördlingen: Verlag der C.H. Beck'schen Buchhandlung, 1879).
——. *Politik als Wissenschaft*. Stuttgart: J.G. Cotta, 1876.
Bödy, Paul. *Joseph Eötvös and the Modernization of Hungary 1840–1870: A Study of Ideas of Individuality and Social Pluralism in Modern Politics*. Philadelphia, PA: American Philosophical Society, 1972.
Boehm, Max Hildebert. *Europa irredenta: Eine Einführung in das Nationalitätenproblen der Gegenwart*. Berlin: Verlag von Reimar Hobbing, 1923.
Boleski, Andrzej. 'Die Einheit Mitteleuropas als kulturtpolitisches Ziel'. *Poelen: Wochenschrift für polnische Interessen* 2(54) (1916), 35–40.
Bongiovanni, Francesco M. *The Decline and Fall of Europe*. New York: Palgrave Macmillan, 2012.
Bonn, Moritz Julius. *Die Krisis der europäischen Demokratie*. Karlsruhe: Verlag G. Braun, 1925.
Bosc, L. *Zollalliancen und Zollunionen*. Berlin: E. Staude, 1907.
Bosco, Andrea. *The Federal Idea: The History of Federalism from Enlightenment to 1945*. London: Lothian Foundation Press, 1991.
Bowden, Brett. *The Empire of Civilization: The Evolution of an Imperial Idea*. Chicago: Chicago University Press, 2009.
Boyce, Robert. 'British Capitalism and the Idea of European Unity between the Wars', in Peter M.R. Stirk (ed.), *European Unity in Context: The Interwar Period* (London: Pinter Publishers, 1989), 65–83.
Brague, Rémi. *Eccentric Culture: A Theory of Western Civilization*. South Bend, IN: St. Augustine's Press, (1992) 2002.
——. 'Sohnland Europa', in Peter Kosolowski and Brague (eds), *Vaterland Europa: Europäische und nationale Identität im Konflikt* (Vienna: Passagen Verlag, 1997), 21–40.
Brechtefeld, Jörg. *Mitteleuropa and German Politics: 1848 to the Present*. Basingstoke: Macmillan, 1971.
Brender, Reinhold. *Collaboration in Frankreich im Zweiten Weltkrieg: Marcel Déat und das Rassemblement national Populaire*. Munich: R. Oldenbourg Verlag, 1992.
Briand, Aristide. 'Organisation eines europäischen Bundessystems', *Zeitschrift Pan-Europa* 6(6–7) (1930), 186–201.
Briffault, Robert. *Breakdown: The Collapse of Traditional Civilization*. London: Victor Gollancz, 1935.
——. *Europa: The Days of Ignorance*. New York: Charles Scribner's Sons, 1935.
——. *The Decline and Fall of the British Empire*. New York: Simon & Schuster, 1938.
Brooks, Sydney. 'The New Europe'. *North American Review* 200(708) (1914), 663–72.
Bruck, Carl von. *Die Aufgabe Österreichs*. Leipzig: O. Wigand, 1860.
Brugmans, Henri. *Towards a European Government*. Paris: The European Movement, 1953.
Bruneteau, Bernard. 'The Construction of Europe and the Concept of the Nation-State'. *Contemporary European History* 9(2) (2000), 245–60.
Buckle, Henry Thomas. *History of Civilization in England*, Volumes I–V. Leipzig: F.A. Brockhaus, 1865.
Buettner, Elisabeth. *Europe after Empire: Decolonization, Society, and Culture*. Cambridge: Cambridge University Press, 2016.

Bugge, Petter. 'The Use of the Middle: Mitteleuropa vs. Stredni Evropa'. *European Review of History / Revue europeenne d'histoire* 6(1) (1999), 15–35.
Burch, Ruth. 'On Nietzsche's Concept of "European Nihilism"'. *European Review* 22(2) (2014), 196–208.
Burckhardt, Jacob. *Civilization of the Renaissance in Italy*. Munich: C.H.Beck, 2018.
Burgess, Michael. *The British Tradition of Federalism*. London: Leicester University Press, 1995.
Burke, Edmund. *Reflections on the Revolution in France*. London: W.B. Clive, (1790) 1919.
Burke, Peter. 'Did Europe Exist before 1700?' *History of European Ideas* 1(1) (1980), 21–29.
Buschak, Willy. *Die Vereinigten Staaten von Europa sind unser Ziel: Arbeiterbewegung und Europa im Frühen 20. Jahrhundert*. Essen: Klartext, 2014.
Busek, Erhard. 'Metropole Wien', in Erhard Busek, Gerhard Wilflinger and György Konrad (eds), *Aufbruch nach Mitteleuropa: Rekonstruktion eines versunkenen Kontinents* (Vienna: Herold, 1986), 7–10.
Busek, Erhard, and Emil Brix. *Projekt Mitteleuropa*. Vienna: Ueberreuter, 1986.
Caffentzis, George C. 'On the Scottish Origin of "Civilization"', in Silvia Federici (ed.), *Enduring Western Civilization* (London: Praeger Publishers, 1995), 15–32.
Carls, Stephen D. *Louis Loucheur and the Shaping of Modern France, 1916–1931*. Baton Rouge: Louisiana State University Press, 1993.
Carlyle, Thomas. *Lectures on the History of Literature: or the Successive Periods of European Culture: Delivered in 1838*. London: Curven Cane, 1892.
Carpenter, Edward. *Civilisation: Its Cause and Cure and Other Essays*. London: Swan Sonnenschain & Co, 1891.
Carr, Godfrey Robert. *Karl Jaspers as an Intellectual Critic: The Political Dimension of his Thought*. Frankfurt am Main: Peter Lang, 1983.
Cattani, Paola. 'Europe as a Nation? Intellectuals and Debate on Europe in the Interwar Years'. *History of European Ideas* 43(6) (2017), 674–82.
Cerutti, Furio. 'Towards the Political Identity of the Europeans: An Introduction', in *A Soul for Europe Vol. 1, A Reader* (Leuven: Peeters, 2001), 1–31.
Chakrabarty, Dipesh. *Provincializing Europe: Postcolonial Thought and Historical Difference*. Princeton, NJ: Princeton University Press, 2008.
Chaszer, Edward. 'The Place of East Central Europe in Western Civilisation', in Francis Wagner (ed.), *Toward a New Central Europe: A Symposium on the Problems of the Danubian Nations* (Hamilton, ONT: Hunyadi MMK, 1970), 104–13.
——. 'The Possibility of a Neutralized Zone in Central Europe', in Francis Wagner (ed.), *Toward a New Central Europe: A Symposium on the Problems of the Danubian Nations* (Hamilton, ONT: Hunyadi MMK, 1970), 33–39.
Chiantera-Stutte, Patricia. 'Space, Großraum and Mitteleuropa in Some Debates of the Early Twentieth Century'. *European Journal of Social Theory* 11(2) (2008), 185–201.
Churchill, Winston. 'The Tragedy of Europe' [1946], in Brent F. Nelson and Alexander C.-G. Stubb (eds), *The European Union: Readings on the Theory and Practice of European Integration* (London: Lynne Rienner, 1994), 11–14.
Claeys, Gregory. '"Individualism", "Socialism", and "Social Science": Further Notes on a Process of Conceptual Formation, 1800–1850'. *Journal of the History of Ideas* 47(1) (1986), 81–93.
Clarke, Paul Barry (ed.). *Citizenship*. London: Pluto Press, 1994.
Clavin, Patricia. 'Introduction: Conceptualising Internationalism between the World Wars', in Daniel Laqua (ed.), *Internationalism Reconfigured: Transnational Ideas and Movements between the World Wars* (London: I.B. Tauris, 2011), 1–14.
Clout, Hugh. 'Albert Demangeon, 1872–1940: Pioneer of La Géographie Humaine'. *Scottish Geographical Journal* 119(1) (2003), 1–24.
Cobden, Richard. *Speeches on Questions of Public Policy, II*. London: Macmillan and Co., 1870.

———. *The Political Writings of Richard Cobden, I-II*. London: William Ridgeway, 1867.
———. *What Next and Next?* London: James Ridgeway, 1856.
Cohen, Max. 'Für deutsche Europapolitik'. *Sozialistische Monatshefte*, Bd. 36 (1930), 638–44.
———. 'Wege nach Kontinentaleuropa'. *Sozialistische Monatshefte*, Bd. 35 (1929), 478–82.
Cole, George Douglas Howard. *War Aims*. London: New Statesman and Nation, 1939.
Coleman, Peter. *The Liberal Conspiracy: The Congress for Cultural Freedom and the Struggle for the Mind of Postwar Europe*. London: Macmillan, 1989.
Congress of Europe. Strasbourg: Council of Europe Publishing, (1948) 1999.
Connolly, William E. *The Terms of Political Discourse*. Lexington, MA: Heath, 1974.
Conze, Vanessa. *Das Europa der Deutschen: Ideen von Europa in Deutschland zwischen Reichstradition und Westorientierung (1920–1970)*. Munich: R. Oldenbourg Verlag, 2005.
Cook, Edward Tyas. *Britain and the Small Nations: Her Principles and Her Policy*. London: Wyman and Sons, 1915.
Corral, Luiz Diez del. *The Rape of Europe*. London: Ruskin House, 1959.
Coudenhove-Kalergi, Rickard Nicolaus. 'Das Pan-Europa Program'. *Zeitschrift Pan-Europa* 1(1–2) (1924), 3–17.
———. *Die europäische Nation*. Stuttgart: Deutsche Verlags-Anstalt, 1953.
———. 'Drei Jahre Paneuropa'. *Zeitschrift Pan-Europa* 2(10) (1925), 21.
———. *Europa Erwacht!* Zurich: Pan-Europa Verlag, 1934.
———. 'Europäischer Pass: Vorschlag von R.N. Coudenhove-Kalergi'. *Zeitschrift Pan-Europa* 3(4) (1926), 24–26.
———. *Krise der Weltanschauung*. Vienna: Pan-Europa-Verlag, 1923.
———. 'Offener Brief an die französische Kammer'. *Zeitschrift Pan-Europa* 1(3) (1924), 20–23.
———. *Paneuropa*. Vienna: Paneuropa-Verlag, 1926.
———. 'Paneuropa: Hymne: Beethoven Das Lied an die Freude aus der IX. Symphonie'. *Zeitschrift Pan-Europa* 5(9) (1928), 23.
———. 'Paneuropa und der Völkerbund: Gesprochen auf dem Internationalen Weltfriedenkongress in Berlin'. *Zeitschrift Pan-Europa* 1(6) (1924), 20ff.
———. 'Paneuropa und Faszismus'. *Zeitschrift Pan-Europa* 9(5) (1933), 129–33.
———. *Paneuropa-Union*. Vienna: Paneuropa-Verlag, 1922.
———. 'Pazifismus'. *Zeitschrift Pan-Europa* 1(4–5) (1924), 15–17.
———. *Revolution durch Technik*. Vienna: Paneuropa-Verlag, (1922) 1932.Craig, Gordon A. *The Politics of the Unpolitical: German Writers and the Problem of Power, 1770–1871*. Oxford: Oxford University Press, 1995.
Crook, David Paul. *Darwinism, War and History: The Debate over the History of War from the 'Origin of Spicies' to the First World War*. Cambridge: Cambridge University Press, 1994.
Crotty, Raymond. *When Histories Collide: The Development and Impact of Individualistic Capitalism*. Boston, MA: Rowman & Littlefield, 2001.
Curcio, Carlo. *Europa: Storia di un'idea*. Florence: Vallecchi, 1958.
Czarny, Norbert. 'Imaginary-Real Lives: on Danilo Kiš'. *Cross Currents: A Yearbook of Central European Culture* 3 (1984), 279–84.
Dafinger, Johannes, and Dieter Pohl (eds). *A New Nationalist Europe under Hitler: Concepts of Europe and Transnational Networks in the National Socialist Sphere of Influence, 1933–1945*. London: Routledge, 2019.
Dahlstedt, Barbro Kvist, and Sten Dahlstedt (eds). *Nationell hängivenhet och europeisk klarhet: aspekter på den europeiska identiteten kring sekelskiftet 1900*. Stockholm: Brutus Östlings Bokförlag Symposion, 1999.
Dainotto, Roberto M. *Europe (in Theory)*. Durham, NC: Duke University Press, 2007.
Daitz, Werner. 'Das europäische Sittengesetz als Strukturgesetz der europäischen Grossraumwirtschaft'. *Nationalsozialistische Monatshefte: Zentrale politische und Kulturelle Zeitschrift der NSDAP* 146 (1942), 270–78.

Daniels, H.G. 'Europe and the Swiss System'. *The Contemporary Review* 171(1) (1947), 86–89.
Danilevsky, Nikolai. *Russland und Europa*. Osnabrück: Otto Zeller, (1895) 1965.
D'Appollonia, Ariane Chebel. 'European Nationalism and European Union', in Anthony Pagden (ed.), *The Idea of Europe: From Antiquity to the European Union* (Cambridge: Cambridge University Press, 2002), 171–90.
Darnstädt, Thomas, Christoph Schult und Helene Zuber. 'How to Forge a Common European Identity'. *Spiegel Online International*, 2 December 2011. Retrieved 11 April 2022 from https://www.spiegel.de/international/europe/citizens-of-the-eu-how-to-forge-a-common-european-identity-a-800775.html.
Davidson, Peter. *The Idea of North*. London: Reaktion Books, 2005.
Dawson, Christopher. *The Making of Europe: An Introduction to the History of European Unity*. New York: Meridian Books, (1932) 1956.
Defoe, Daniel. *The True-Born Englishman: A Satire*. Leeds: Alice Mann, (1701) 1836.
Degerman, Allan. *Vägar till fred: anteckningar rörande planer för världens återuppbyggnad efter kriget*. Stockholm: Informationsbyrån mellanfolkligt samarbete för fred, 1942.
De Gurowski, Adam G. *America and Europe*. New York: D. Appleton & Company, 1857.
——. *Russland und die Civilisation*. Leipzig: H. Hunger, 1840.
Delaisi, Francis. *Die Revolution der Europäischen Wirtschaft*. Stuttgart: Deutsche Verlags-Anstalt, (1942) 1943.
——. 'Europa als Wirtschaftseinheit'. *Zeitschrift Pan-Europa* 3(4) (1924), 6–10.
——. *Les Deux Europes*. Paris: Payot, 1929.
Delanty, Gerard. *Citizenship in a Global Age: Society, Culture, Politics*. Buckingham, UK: Open University Press, 2000.
—— 'Europe and the Idea of "Unity in Diversity"', in Rutger Lindahl (ed.), *Whither Europe? Borders, Boundaries and Frontiers in a Changing World* (Gothenburg: University of Gothenburg, 2003).
——. *European Heritage: A Critical Re-Interpretation*. London: Routledge, 2018.
——. *Inventing Europe: Idea, Identity, Reality*. Houndmills, UK: Palgrave Macmillan, 1995.
——. 'Legacies, Histories, and Ideas of Europe', in Ash Amin and Philip Lewis (eds), *European Union and Disunion: Reflections on European Identity* (London: The British Academy, 2017), 7–13.
——. 'Models of European Identity: Reconciling Universalism and Particularism'. *Perspectives on European Politics and Society* 3(3) (2009), 345–59.
Delanty, Gerard, and Chris Rumford. *Rethinking Europe: Social Theory and the Implications of Europeanization*. London: Routledge, 2005.
Demangeon, Albert. *America and the Race for World Domination*. New York: Garden City, 1921.
——. *Le déclin de L'Europe*. Paris: Payot, 1920.
Demm, Eberhard. 'Alfred Weber und die Nationalsozialisten'. *Zeitschrift für Geschichtswissenschaft* 47(3) (1990), 211–36.
D'Erbigny, M. *Essays on the Future Destinies of Europe*. London: Baldwin & Cradock, 1828.
Derrida, Jacques. *The Other Heading: Reflections on Today's Europe*. Bloomington: Indiana University Press, 1992.
D'Estaing, Valery Giscard. 'Pour ou Contre l'Adhésion de la Turquie á l'Union Européenne'. *Le Monde*, 8 November 2002.
Diezel, Gustav. *Die Frage der deutschen Zukunft: Zweifel und Lösungsversuche dem deutschen Volke*. Stuttgart: Verlag von K. Göpel, 1854.
——. *Russland, Deutschland und die östliche Frage*. Leipzig: Verlag von Karl Göpel, 1853.
Dix, Arthur. 'England und die Mitteleuropäische Verkehrseinheit', *Das Grössere Deutschland* 3 (1916), 73–76.
Djuric, G. 'The Southern Slavs and Italy: An Economic Study'. *The New Europe* 6(85) (1918), 156–62.

Donisthorpe, Wordsworth. *Individualism: A System of Politics*. London: Macmillan, 1889.
Dontsov, Dmytro. *Die ukrainische Staatsidee und der Krieg gegen Russland: Hrsg. von der Ukrainischen Zentralorganisation*. Berlin: C. Kroll, 1915.
Dorling, Danny, and Sally Tomlinson. *Rule Britannia: Brexit and the End of Empire*. London: Biteback, 2019.
D'Ors, Eugenio, et al. 'Manifesto of the Friends of a Moral Unity of Europe' [1914], in Romain Rolland, *Above the Battle* (London: George Allen & Unwin Ltd, 1916), 122–27.
Drace-Francis, Alex. 'A Provincial Imperialist and a *Curious Account of Wallachia*: Ignaz von Born'. *European History Quarterly* 36(1) (2006), 61–89.
———. *European Identity: A Historical Reader*. New York: Palgrave Macmillan, 2013.
Dresselhuys, H.-C., et al. 'Nederlandsche anti-oorlog raad' [1915], in Romain Rolland, *Above the Battle* (London: George Allen & Unwin Ltd, 1916), 131–35.
Droz, Jacques. *L'Europe Centrale*. Paris: Payot, 1960.
Dubreuil, Emmanuelle Hériard. 'The Personalism of Denis Rougemont: Spirituality and Politics in 1930s Europe'. PhD dissertation. Cambridge: St John's College, 2005.
Ducci, Annamaria. 'Europe and the Artistic Patrimony of the Interwar Period', in Mark Hewitson and D'Auria Matthew (eds), *Europe in Crisis: Intellectuals and the European Idea, 1917–1957*. New York: Berghahn Books, 2012.
Duhamel, Georges. *Mon Europe*. Paris: Flammarion, 1931.
Dumas, Alexander. *L'Étrangère: Comédie en cinq actes*. Paris: Calmann-Lévy, (1853) 1930.
Dykman, Klaas.'How International was the Secreteriat of the League of Nations?' *The International History Review* 37(4) (2015), 721–44.
Eckardt, Julius. *Die baltischen Provinzen Russlands: Politische und culturgeschichtliche Aufsätze*. Leipzig: Duncker & Humblot, 1869.
Eco, Umberto. 'It's Culture, not War, that Cements European Identity'. *The Guardian*, 26 January 2012. Retrieved 12 April 2020 from http://www.guardian.co.uk/world/2012/jan/26/umberto-eco-culture-war-europa.
Einstein, Albert, and Georg Friedrich Nicolai. 'Manifesto to the Europeans'. Retrieved 15 November 2020 from https://realprogressinenglish.blogspot.com/2014/04/einsteins-manifesto-for-united-europe.html.
Eliade, Mircea. 'Von der Unteilberheit Europas'. *Merkur* 6(12) (1952), 101–10.
Eliot, Thomas Stearns. *Notes towards the Definition of Culture*. London: Faber and Faber, (1946) 1948.
Elliott, J.H. 'A Europe of Composite Monarchies', *Past & Present* 137 (Nov. 1992), 48–71.
Eötvös, Joseph. *Die Reform in Ungarn*. Leipzig: Köhler, 1846.
Erasmus. *The Praise of Folly and Other Writings*. New York: W.W. Norton & Company [1510, 1517] 1989.
Ernst, Johann. *Reden des Kaisers: Ansprachen, Predigten und Trinksprüche Wilhelms II*. Munich: Deutschen Taschenbuchverlag, 1966.
Erste, Louis. 'Legal Effects of the Yalta Agreement'. *Cross Currents: A Yearbook of Central European Culture* 2 (1983), 55–70.
'Et nyt Europa'. Editorial. *Det ny Europa: Internationalt Tidsskrift* 1(1) (1918), 2.
Europa als Lebenskampfgemeinschaft: Europäische Vorlesungen gehalten auf einem europäischen Studenten- und Frontkämpfertreffen, veranstaltet von der Reichsstudentenführung. Berlin: Akademische Kulturaustausch, 1942.
European Commission. 'The Development of European Identity: Unfinished Business'. 2012. Retrieved 4 December 2020 from file:///C:/Users/xanmat/AppData/Local/Temp/175214213_9680.pdf.
Europe Unites: The Hague Congress and After. London: Hollis & Carter, 1949.
Evans, Richard J. *The Pursuit of Power: Europa 1815–1914*. London: Penguin, 2016.

Evola, Julius. 'Über die geistigen voraussetzungen einer europäischen Einheit'. *Zeitschrift Pan-Europa* 8(10) (1932), 301–11.
Falchi, Federica. 'Democracy and the Rights of Women in the Thinking of Giuseppe Mazzini'. *Modern Italy* 17(1) (2012), 15–30. Fazi, Thomas. *The Battle for Europe: How an Elite Hijacked a Continent and How we Can Take it Back*. London: Plutopress, 1914.
Fazlhashemi, Mohammed. *Exemplets makt: Föreställningar om Europa/Väst i Iran 1850–1980*. Stockholm: Symposium, 1999.
Febvre, Lucien. 'Civilization: Evolution of a Word and a Group of Ideas', in Peter Burke (ed.), *A New Kind of History from the Writings of Febvre* (London: Routledge & Kegan Paul, 1973), 219–57.
Ferrero, Guglielmo. *Europe's Fateful Hour*. New York: Dodd, Mead and Company, 1918.
———. *Who Wanted the European War?* Oxford: The Clarendon Press, (1914) 1915.
Ferrer y Suberana, Jose. 'La nacionalidad', *La civilización: revista religiosa, filosofica, politíca y literaria de Barcelona*, t.ii (Barcelona: Brusi, 1841), 61–75.
Fichte, Johann Gottlieb. *Reden an die deutsche Nation*. Leipzig: Fikentscher, 1808.
'Fifth NATO Parliamentarians' Conference 1959'. Washington, DC: United States Government Printing Office, 1960.
Fischer, Fritz. 'Weltpolitik, Weltmachtstreben und deutsche Kriegsziele', in *Historische Zeitschrift* 199(1) (1964), 265–346.
Fischer, Johann Ludwig. *Über die Zukunft der europäischen Kultur*. Munich: Drei Masken Verlag, 1929.
Fischer, Joschka. 'From Confederacy to Federation: Thoughts on the Finality of European Integration' [2000]. Retrieved 26 August 2020 from https://www.cvce.eu/content/publication/2005/1/14/4cd02fa7-d9d0-4cd2-91c9-2746a3297773/publishable_en.pdf.
Fischer, Jürgen. *Oriens – Occidens – Europa: Begriff und Gedanke 'Europa' in der späten Antike und im frühen Mittelalter*. Wiesbaden: Franz Steiner Verlag, 1957.
Flammarion, Camille. *Omega: The Last Days of the World*. Lincoln: University of Nebraska Press, (1894) 1999.
Flora, Francesco. 'Francesco Flora: Conférence du 2 septembre', in Julien Benda (ed.), *L'esprit européen* (Neuchatel: Éditions de la Baconniére, 1947), 38–66.
Forlenza, Rosario. 'The Politics of the Abendland: Christian Democracy and the Idea of Europe after the Second World War'. *Contemporary European History* 26(2) (2017), 261–86.
Fornäs, Johan. *Signifying Europe*. Bristol: Intellect, 2012.
Forsell, Carl. *Anteckningar i anledning av en Resa till England i slutet av sommaren år 1834*. Stockholm: Hörberg, 1835.
———. *Om kommunal-nämnder*. Stockholm: no publisher, 1843.
———. *Om småbarnskolor*. Stockholm: no publisher, 1837.
———. *Plan till en på Actier grundad Transport-inrättning emellan Stockholm och Göteborg, medelst tvenne ångbåtar, en på Mälaren och en på Venern, samt Forvagnar (till hvilkas inrättande ett bidrag av Statsmakten blifver att påräkna) emellan Ångbåtarnes ömsesidiga landningsställen*. Stockholm: Elméns och Granbergs tryckeri, 1820.
———. *Underrättelse om de i America nyligen stiftade Temperance-societies, jemte Förslag till dylikas eller så kallade Måttlighets och Sedlighets Föreningars inrättande i Fäderneslandet*. Stockholm: no publisher, 1830.
———. *Utkast till handbok för småbarnskolor*. Stockholm: no publisher, 1841.
Frantz, Constantin. *Unsere Politik*. Berlin: Schneider, 1851.
Fried, Alfred. *Der Kaiser und der Weltfrieden*. Berlin: Maritima Verlagsges, 1910.
———. *Europäische Wiederherstellung*. Zurich: Art. Institut Orell Füssli, 1915.
———. *Pan-Amerika: Entwicklung, Umfang u. Bedeutung der pan-amerikanischen Bewegung (1820–1910)*. Zurich: Art. Institute Orell Füssli, 1910.
———. *The Restoration of Europe*. New York: The Macmillan Company, 1916.

Fried, Ferdinand. *Das Ende der Kapitalismus*. Jena: Eugen Diederichs, 1931.
——. *Das soziale Revolution: Verwandlung von Wirtschaft und Gesellschaft*. Leipzig: Wilhelm Goldmann, 1943.
Fried, Istvàn. 'Einige Besonderheiten der Anfänge der Romantik in Mittel- und Osteuropa', in Lászlo Szikly et al. (eds), *Aufklärung und Nationen im Osten Europas* (Budapest: Corvina, 1983), 333–72.
Fröbel, Julius. *Briefe über die Wiener Oktober-Revolution*. Frankfurt am Main: Verlag von Joh. Valentin Meidinger, 1849.
——. 'Denkschrift des Herrn von der Pfordten 7.7.1849', in *Kleine politische Schriften I* (Stuttgart: Gottaschen Buchhandlung, [1855] 1866), 5–13.
——. *Die deutsche Auswanderung und ihre culturhistorische Bedeutung*. Leipzig: Franz Wagner, 1858.
——. 'Die europäischen Ereignisse und die Weltpolitik', in *Kleine politische Schriften I* (Stuttgart: Gottaschen Buchhandlung, [1855] 1866), 50–56.
——. 'Die Österreichische Politik and ihre Wendungen' in *Kleine politische Schriften II* (Stuttgart: Gottaschen Buchhandlung, [1865] 1866), 355–413.
——. 'Die Zukunft Europa's vom Standpunkte des Flüchtlings' [1852], in *Kleine politische Schriften I* (Stuttgart: Gottaschen Buchhandlung, 1866), 1–12.
——. *Wien, Deutschland und Europa*. Vienna: Joseph Reck und Sohn, 1848.
Frommelt, Reinhard. *Paneuropa oder Mitteleuropa: Einigungsbestrebungen im Kalkül deutscher Wirtschaft und Politik 1925–1933*. Stuttgart: Deutsche Verlags-Anstalt, 1977.
Gaedicke, Herbert, and Gert Eynern. *Die produktionswirtschaftliche Integration Europas: eine Untersuchung Über die Aussenhandelsverflechtung der europäischen Länder*. Berlin: Junker und Dünnhaupt, 1933.
Gaertner, Gustav Friedrich. *Ueber die Provinzial-Rechte: Sendschreiben*. Berlin: Dunker und Humblot, 1837.
Ganilh, Charles. *An Inquiry into the Various Systems of Political Economy; their Advantages and Disadvantages; and the Theory most Favourable to the Increase of National Health* (trans. from French). London: Henry Colburn, 1812.
Garver, Bruce M. 'Masaryk and Czech Politics, 1906–1914', in Stanley B. Winters (ed.), *Masaryk, T.G. (1850–1937): Volume I: Thinker and Politician* (Basingstoke, UK: Macmillan, 1990) 245–50.
——. *The Young Czech Party 1874–1901 and the Emergence of a Multiparty System*. New Haven, CT: Yale University Press, 1978.
Gasperi, Alcide de. 'Extract from a Speech to the Italian Chamber by the Prime Minister, Signor Alcide De Gasperi, 22 October 1952', in Denise Folliot (ed.), *Documents of International Affairs 1952* (London: Oxford University Press, 1953), 197–202.
Geijer, Erik Gustaf. 'Litteratur-Bladet 1838–39', in *Samlade skrifter: Åttonde delen* (Stockholm: Norstedt, 1928), 225–30.
Gellner, Ernst. *Encounters with Nationalism*. Oxford: Blackwell, 1994.
——. *Nations and Nationalism*. Oxford: Blackwell, 1983.
Giddens, Anthony. *Turbulent and Mighty Continent: What Future for Europe?* Cambridge: Polity Press, 2014.
Gillingham, John R. *The EU: An Obituary*. London: Verso, 2016.
Gingerich, Stephen D. 'European Frenzy: European and Spanish Universality in Maria Zambrano'. *The New Centennial Review* 8(3) (2009), 189–214.
Goebbels, Joseph. 'The New Europe' [1942], in Walter Lipgens (ed.), *Documents on the History of European Integration*, vol. 1 (Berlin: Walter de Gruyter, 1985), 107–8.
GoGwilt, Chris. 'True West: The Changing Idea of the West from the 1880s to the 1920s', in Silvia Federici (ed.), *Enduring Western Civilization: The Construction of the Concept of Western Civilization and Its 'Others'* (Westport, CT: Praeger, 1995), 37–62.

Gollwitzer, Heinz. *Europabild und Europagedanke: Beiträge zur deutschen Geistesgeschichte des 18. und 19. Jahrhunderts*. Munich: C.H. Beck, 1951.
Gosewinkel, Dieter (ed.). *Anti-liberal Europe: A Neglected Story of Europeanization*. New York: Berghahn Books, 2015.
Gossman, Lionel. 'The Idea of Europe'. *Common Knowledge* 16(2) (2010), 198–222.
Göttingisches Taschenbuch zum Nuzsen und Vergnügen für das Jahr 1802. Göttingen: Heinrich Dieterich, 1802.
Gowing, Richard. *Richard Cobden*. London: Cassel Company, 1885.
Graham, Stephen. *Europe – Whither Bound? (Que Vadis Europa?): Being Letters of Travel from the Capitals of Europe in the year 1921*. London: Thornton Butterworth, 1921.
Grantham, John T. 'British Labour and the Hague "Congress of Europe": National Sovereignty Defended'. *The Historical Journal* 24(2) (1981), 443–52.
Gray, Rockwell. *The Imperative of Modernity: An Intellectual Biography of José Ortega y Gasset*. Berkeley: University of California Press, 1978.
Green, Stephen. *The European Identity: Historical Roots and Cultural Realities We Cannot Deny*. London: House Curiosities, 2015.
Grewe, Wilhelm G. 'Europa-Kongress in Haag'. *Merkur* 2(9) (1948): 446–53.
Gribble, Francis. 'The War Aims of Luxemburg'. *The New Europe* 6(83) (1918), 110–13.
Grinell, Klas. 'Ilm al-Hududiyya: Un-Inheriting Eurocentricity', in Mats Andrén et al. (eds), *Cultural Borders of Europe: Narratives, Concepts and Practices in the Present and the Past* (New York: Berghahn Books, 2017), 54–68.
Grucza, Monika. 'Bedrohtes Europa: Studien zum Europagedanken bei Alfons Paquet, André Suarès und Romain Rolland in der Periode zwischen 1890 und 1914'. Dissertation. Gießen: Justus-Liebig-Universtität, 2008.
Grużewski, Taduesz. 'Die koalition Mitteleuropas'. *Poelen: Wochenschrift für polnische Interessen* 2(59) (1916), 177–78.
Guénon, René. *The Crisis of the Modern World*. Hillsdale, NY: Sophia Perennis, (1927) 2001.
Guérot, Ulrike. *Europa erneuern! Eine realistische Vision für das 21. Jahrhundert*. Bielefeld: Transcript, 2019.
———. *Warum Europa eine Republik werden muss! Eine politische Utopie*. Bonn: Dietz, 2016.
Guerrieri, Sandro. 'From the Hague Congress to the Council of Europe: Hopes, Achievements and Disappointments in the Parliamentary Way to the European Integration (1948–51)'. *Parliaments, Estates and Representation* 34(2) (2014), 216–27.
Guizot, François. *The History of Civilization in Europe*. London: Cassell, (1828) 1911.
Gurevich, Aaron. *The Origins of European Individualism*. Oxford: Blackwell, 1995.
Gusejnova, Dina. 'Noble Continent? German-Speaking Nobles as Theorists of European Identity in the Interwar Period', in Mark Hewitson and D'Auria Matthew (eds), *Europe in Crisis: Intellectuals and the European Ideas, 1917–1957* (New York: Berghahn Books, 2012), 111–33.
Guyau, Jean Marie. *L'irréligion del'avenir: étude sociologique*. Paris: Félix Alcan, 1902.
Günther, Hans. *Kleine Rassenkunde Europas*. Munich: J.F. Lehmanns Verlag, 1925.
Habermas, Jürgen. 'Braucht Europa eine Verfassung?', in Habermas, *Zeit der Übergänge* (Frankfurt am Main: Suhrkamp, 2001), 104–28.
———. 'Citizenship and National Identity: Some Reflections on the Future of Europe', in Ronald Beiner (ed.), *Theorizing Citizenship* (Albany: State University of New York Press, 1992), 255–81.
Hale, John. *The Civilization of Europe in the Renaissance*. London: Harper Collins Publishers, 1993.
Halecki, Oscar. *Borderlands of Western Civilization: A History of East Central Europe*. New York: Ronald Press, 1952.
———. *The Limits and Divisions of European History*. London: Sheed & Ward, 1950.

Hall, Charles. *The Effects of Civilisation on the People in European States.* London: Charles Gilpin, (1805) 1850.
Hallstein, Walter. 'Germany's Dual Aim: Unity and Integration'. *Foreign Affairs* 31(1) (1952), 58–66.
Halperin, Sandra. *War and Social Change in Europe: The Great Transformation Revisited.* Cambridge: Cambridge University Press, 2004.
Hamann, Brigitte. *Bertha von Suttner: A Life for Peace.* Syracuse, NY: Syracuse University Press, 1996.
Hannaford, Ivan. *Race: The History of an Idea in the West.* Baltimore, MD: Johns Hopkins University Press, 1996.
Hannan, Daniel. *A Doomed Marriage: Britain and Europe.* London: Notting Hill Editions, 2012.
Hansen, Peo. *Europeans Only? Essays on Identity Politics and the European Union.* Umeå: Umeå University, 2000.
Hansen, Peo, and Stefan Jonsson. *Eurafrica: The Untold History of European Integration and Colonialism.* London: Bloomsbury, 2014.
Harskamp, Anton van, and Albert W. Musschenga (eds). *The Many Faces of Individualism.* Leuven: Peeters, 2001.
Hase, Johann Matthias. *Evropa.* Nürnberg: Homann, 1743.
Hathaway, Dona A., and Scott J. Shapiro. *The Internationalists: How a Radical Plan to Outlaw War Remade the World.* New York: Simon & Schuster, 2017.
Hauptmann, Gerhard. 'A Reply to Rolland', in *The New York Times Current History of the European War: Vol. 1, No. 1. What Men of Letters Say* (New York: The New York Times Company, 1914), 175–76.
———. 'Are We Barbarians?', in *The New York Times Current History of the European War: Vol. 1, No. 1. What Men of Letters Say* (New York: The New York Times Company, 1914), 178–79.
Havel, Václav. 'Acceptance Speech', 1986. Retrieved 25 June 2020 from https://erasmusprijs.org/en/laureates/vaclav-havel/acceptance-speech/.
———. 'An Anatomy of Reticence'. *Cross Currents: A Yearbook of Central European Culture* 5 (1986), 1–23.
———. 'Politics and Conscience', in Havel, *Living in Truth* (London: Faber and Faber, 1986), 136–57.
———. 'Power of the Powerless' [1983], in Havel, *Living in Truth* (London: Faber and Faber, 1986), 76–90.
Havlíček, Karel. *Politické Spisy II.* Prague: Laichter, 1901–1902.
Hay, Denys. *Europe: The Emergence of an Idea.* New York: Harper & Row, (1957) 1966.
Hazard, Paul. *The Crisis of the European Mind, 1680–1715.* New York: New York Review of Books, (1928) 2013.
Heater, Derek. *Citizenship: The Civic Ideal in World History, Politics and Education.* London: Longman, 1990.
———. *The Idea of European Unity.* Leicester: Leicester University Press, 1992.
Heber, Reginald. *Europe: Lines on the Present War.* London: J. Hatchard, 1809.
Heberle, Rudolf. 'In Memoriam: Alfred Weber 1868–1958'. *American Journal of Sociology* 64(2) (1958), 180–81.
Heer, Friedrich. 'Osteuropa in Europa'. *Merkur* 14(143) (1960), 53–68.
Heeren, Arnold Herrmann Ludwig. *Handbuch der Geschichte des Europäischen Staatensystems und seiner Colonien.* Göttingen: Johann Friedrich Römer, 1822.
Heerfordt, Christian Frederick. 'Introduction'. *A New Europe.* London: G. Allen & Unwin, 1925, 2–4.
———. Program für die skandinavische Initiative (1926).

——. Eine Hinwendung an die hiesigen Ausserordentlichen Gesandten und bevollmächtigten Minister für Belgien, Deutschland, Finland, Frankreich, Grossbritannien, Italien, die Niederlande, Polen, die Schweiz, Spanien und die Tschechoslovakei (1926).

——. Adresse de l'Initiative Scandinave à monsieur Aristide Briand Ministre des Affaires étrangères de la France (1928).

——. Quelques Explications et Eclaircissements spécialement adressés a monsieur Aristide Briand Ministre des Affaires étrangères de la France (1928).

——. Esquisse d'un Projet Franco-Scandinave (1929).

Heffernan, Michael. *The Meanings of Europe: Geography and Geopolitics*. London: Arnold, 1998.

Hegel, Georg Wilhelm Friedrich. *Vorlesungen über die Philosophie der Geschichte*. Frankfurt am Main: Suhrkamp, (1840) 1986.

Heidegger, Martin. 'Europa und die deutsche Philosophie', in Hans-Helmuth Gander (ed.), *Europa und die Philosophie* (Frankfurt am Main: Vittorio Klosterman, [1936] 1993), 31–41.

——. *Nietzsche: Der Europäischer Nihilismus*. Frankfurt am Main: Vittorio Klostermann, 1986.

Heikkilä, Pauli. 'The Prons and Cons of Paneurope: Estonian Discussion on European Unification in the Interwar Period'. *Acta Historica Tallinnensia* 13 (2008), 68–91.

Heile, Wilhelm. *Nationalstaat und Völkerbund: Gedanken über Deutschlands europäische Sendung*. Halberstadt: H. Meyer's Buchdruckerei, 1926.

Heilner, Rickard. 'Europäische Zollunion'. *Zeitschrift Pan-Europa* 5(8) (1929), 11–21.

Heineman, Dannie H.. *Outline of a New Europe: Address Delivered at Cologne on November the 28th, 1930 and at Barcelona on December the 2nd, 1930*. Brussels: Vromant & Co., 1931.

Heine, Heinrich. *Deutschland: Ein Wintermärchen*. Stuttgat: Reclam, (1844) 1979.

Heller, Agnes. 'Europe: An Epilogue?', in Brian Nelson, David Roberts and Walter Veit (eds), *The Idea of Europe: Problems of National and Transnational Identity* (New York: Berg, 1992), 12–25.

Herder, Johann Gottfried. *Ideen zur Philosophie der Geschichte der Menschheit* I–II. Berlin: Aufbau-Verlag, (1791) 1965.

Herre, Paul. *Deutschland und die europäische Ordnung*. Berlin: Deutscher Verlag, 1941.

Herriot, Edouard. *Europe*. Paris: Les éditions Rieder, 1930.

Herrmann, Christian. 'Zum Europaproblem'. *Sozialistische Monatshefte*, Bd. 35 (1929), 1009–23.

Hewitson, Mark. 'Europe and the Fate of the World: Crisis and Integration in the Late 1940s and 1950s', in Hewitson and D'Auria (eds), *Europe in Crisis: Intellectuals and the European Idea 1917–1957* (New York: Berghahn Books, 2012), 35–61.

——. 'Inventing Europe and Reinventing the Nation-State in a New World Order', in Hewitson and D'Arioa (eds), *Europe in Crisis: Intellectuals and the European Idea 1917–1957* (New York: Berghahn Books, 2012), 63–81.

Heymann, Lida Gustava. *Erlebtes – Erschautes: Heymann – Memoiren: Deutsche Frauen kämpfen für Freiheit, Recht und Frieden 1850–1940*. Meisenheim am Glan: Anton Hain, 1972.

Hinsch, Werner. 'The River Elbe – International: A Historical Perspective'. *GeoJournal* 1(2) (1977), 45–48.

Hirschi, Caspar. *The Origins of Nationalism: An Alternative History from Ancient Rome to Early Modern Germany*. Cambridge: Cambridge University Press, 2012.

Hobhouse, Leonard. *Liberalism*. Kitchener, ONT: Batoche, (1911) 1999.

Hobsbawn, Eric. *Nations and Nationalism since 1780: Programme, Myth, Reality*. Cambridge: Cambridge University Press, 1986.

——. *The Age of Extremes: The Short Twentieth Century 1914–1989*. London: Abacus, 1994.

——. 'The Nation as Invented Tradition', in John Hutchinson and Anthony D. Smith (eds), *Nationalism* (Oxford: Oxford University Press, 1994), 76–82.

Hobsbawn, Eric, and Terence O. Ranger. *The Invention of Tradition*. Cambridge: Cambridge University Press, 1983.
Hobson, John A. *Democracy after the War*. G. Allen & Unwin, 1917.
———. *Imperialism: A Study*. London: James Nisbet & Co, 1902.
Hoffmann, Karl Friedrich Vollrath. *Europa und seine Bewohner: Ein Hand- und Lesebuch für alle Stände*. Leipzig: J. Scheible's Verlags-Expedition, 1836.
Höfken, Gustav. *Deutschlands Zoll- und Handelseinigung mit Hinblick auf die österreichische Zollreform und die Dresdener Conferenzen*. Regensburg, 1851.
Hofmannsthal, Hugo. 'Die Idee Europa' [1917], in *Gesammelte Werke: Reden und Aufsätze II 1914–1924* (Frankfurt am Main: Fischer Taschenbuch, 1979), 43–54.
———. *Gesammelte Werke: Reden und Aufsätze II, 1914–1924*. Frankfurt: Fischer, 1979.
Högselius, Per, Arne Kaijser and Erik van der Vleuten. *Europe's Infrastructure Transition: Economy, War, Nature*. Houndmills, UK: Palgrave Macmillan, 2016.
Hotz, Walter. 'Die Einheit Europas in der bildenden Kunst'. *Nationalsozialistische Monatshefte: Zentrale politische und Kulturelle Zeitschrift der NSDAP* 146 (1941), 289–301.
Hourani, Albert. *Islam in European Thought*. Cambridge: Cambridge University Press, 1991.
Huberman, Bronislaw. 'Mein Weg Zu Paneuropa'. *Zeitschrift Pan-Europa* 2(5) (1925), 22–26.
Hübner. *Die Zolleinigung und Industrie des Zollvereins Oesterreichs*. Berlin: Deckersche Geheime Ober-Hofbuchdruckerei, 1850.
Hugo, Victor. 'Letter to M. D'Alton Shee' [1870], in Pauö Meurice (ed.), *The Letters of Victor Hugo: From Exile, and after the Fall of the Empire* (Boston, MA: Houghton, Mifflin and Company, 1898), 235–38.
Huizinga, Johan. *I morgondagens skugga: en diagnos av vår tids kulturella onda* (Swedish translation of Dutch original: *In de Schauden van Morgen*). Stockholm: C.E. Fritzes, (1935) 1936.
Huntington, Samuel P. 'The Clash of Civilizations?' *Foreign Affairs* 72(3) (1993), 22–49.
Husserl, Edmund. *Die Krisis der europäischen Wissenschaften und die transzendentale Phänomenologie*. Haag: Martinus Nijhoff, (1935) 1979.
Hutchinson, John. *Modern Nationalism*. London: Fontana Press, 1994.
Hutchinson, John, and Anthony D. Smith (eds). *Nationalism*. Oxford: Oxford University Press, 1994.
Ifversen, Jan. 'Myth and History in European Post-War History Writing', in Spiering and Wintle (eds), *European Identity and the Second World War* (Houndmills, UK: Palgrave Macmillan, 2011), 75–91.
———. 'The Crisis of European Civilization after 1918', in Menno Spiering and Michael Wintle (eds), *Ideas of Europa since 1914: The Legacy of the First World War* (Houndmill, UK: Palgrave Macmillan, 2002), 14–31.
Ighe, Ann. 'Never Mind Patriarchy'. *European Review* 28(3) (2020), 365–77.
Ingram, Norman. *The Politics of Dissent: Pacifism in France 1919–1939*. Oxford: Clarendon Press, 2011.
'Introduktion til den danske læseverden!' Editorial, in *Det ny Europa: internationalt tidsskrift* 1(1) (1918), 1.
Ionesco, Eugéne. 'The Austro-Hungarian Empire: Forerunners of a Central European Confederation?' *Cross Currents: A Yearbook of Central European Culture* 4 (1985), 3–8.
Isambert, Gaston. 'Projet d'organisation politique d'une confederation européenne', in *Les États-Unis d'europe: congrés de sciences politiques de 1900* (Paris: société francoise d'imprimerie et de librairie, 1901), 137–55.
Israel, Jonathan. *A Revolution of the Mind: Radical Enlightenment and the Intellectual Origins of Modern Democracy*. Princeton, NJ: Princeton University Press, 2010.
Ivanka, Endré von (ed.). *Byzantinische Geschichtsschreiber*. Vienna: Fassbaender, 1954.

Jacobs, Dirk, and Robert Maier. 'European Identity: Construct, Fact and Fiction', in Marja Gastelaars and Arie de Ruijter (eds), *A United Europe: A Quest for a Multifaceted Identity* (Maastricht: Shaker, 1998), 13–34.

James, Henry. *The American*. London: Macmillan, 1877.

——. *The Europeans: A Sketch*. London: Macmillan, 1879.

Jaraush, Konrad S. *Out of Ashes: A New History of Europe in the 20th Century*. Princeton, NJ: Princeton University Press, 2015.

Jarosynska, Lotta Rydnicka. *Ett minnesrikt år*. Stockholm: Hugo Gebers förlag, 1925.

Jarret, Mark. *The Congress of Vienna and Its Legacy: War and Great Power Diplomacy after Napoleon*. London: I.B. Tauris, 2013.

Jaspers, Karl. *Der philosophische Glaube*. Munich: R. Piper, 1948.

——. *Die Atombombe und die Zukunft des Menschen: Politisches Bewusstsein unserer Zeit*. Munich: Piper, 1958.

——. *Die geistige Situation der Zeit*. Berlin: Sammlung Göschen, 1931.

——. *Die grossen Philosophen: Erster band*. Piper: Munich, 1957.

——. *Europa der Gegenwart*. Vienna: Amandus-Editon, 1947.

——. *The European Spirit*. London: SCM Press, 1948.

Joll, James. 'Europe: An Historian's View'. *History of European Ideas* 1(1) (1980), 7–19.

Jospin, Lionel. 'The Future of an Enlarged Europe' [2001]. Retrieved 26 August 2020 from https://www.cvce.eu/en/obj/address_given_by_lionel_jospin_on_the_future_of_an_enlarged_europe_paris_28_may_2001-en-642dc4c9-b224-4ea7-a77b-7e4d894b3077.html.

Jouvenel, Bertrand de. *Vers les Etats Unis d'Europe*. Paris: Valois, 1930.

Kaiser, Wolfram, and Johan Schot. *Writing the Rules for Europe: Experts, Cartels, and International Organizations*. Houndmills, UK: Palgrave Macmillan, 2014.

Källgren, Karolina Enquist. *María Zambrano's Ontology of Exile: Expressive Subjectivity*. Cham, Switzerland: Palgrave Macmillan, 2019.

——. 'Subjectivity from Exile: Place and Sign in the Works of María Zambrano'. PhD dissertation, University of Gothenburg, 2015.

Kann, Robert A. *Das Nationalitätenproblem der Habsburgmonarchie: Geschichte und Ideengehalt der nationalen Bestrebungen vom Vormärz bis zur Auflösung der Reiches im Jahre 1918, I–II*. Graz: Böhlau, 1964.

Kant, Immanuel. *Schriften zu Anthropologie, Geschichtsphilosophie, Politik und Pädagogik*. Darmstad: Suhrkamp Verlag, 1998.

——. 'Zum ewigen Frieden' [1795], in *Werkausgabe Band XI* (Frankfurt am Main: Suhrkamp, 1964), 191–251.

Karlsson, Klas-Göran. *Urkatastrofen: Första världskrigets plats i den moderna historien*. Stockholm: Atlantis, 2014.

Kautsky, Karl. *Die Befreiung der Nationen*. Stuttgart: J.H.W. Dietz, 1917.

——. *Die vereinigten Staaten Mitteleuropas*. Stuttgart: Dietz, 1916.

——. *Nationalstaat, Imperialistischer Staat und Staatenbund*. Nürnberg: Fränkischer Verlagsanstalt, 1915.

Kellersohn, Maurice. *Contre un cataclysme économique: que faire?* Paris: Stock, 1932.

Kerr, Philip. *Pacifism is Not Enough, nor Patriotism Either*. London: Oxford University Press, 1935.

Key, Ellen. 'Vart Fædreland Europa'. *Det ny Europa: Internationalt Tidsskrift* 1(2) (1918), 23–26.

Keynes, John Maynard. *The Economic Consequences of the Peace*. Mansfield Centre, CT: Martino Publishing, (1920) 2011.

Keyserling, Hermann Graf. *Das Spektrum Europas*. Heidelberg: Niels Kampmann Verlag, 1928.

Kipling, Rudyard. 'As They Tested Our Fathers', in *The New York Times Current History of the European War: Vol. 1, No. 1. What Men of Letters Say* (New York: The New York Times Company, 1914), 106.

Kirchhoff, Alfred. *Mensch und Erde: Skizzen von den Wechselbeziehungen zwischen beiden*. Leipzig: B.T. Teubner, 1901.
———. *Schulgeographie*. Halle a. S.: Buchhandlung des Waisenhauses, (1882) 1885.
Kiš, Danilo. 'Variations on the Theme of Central Europe'. *Cross Currents: A Yearbook of Central European Culture* 6 (1987), 1–14.
Kiss, Csaba G. 'Central European Writers about Central Europe: Introduction to the Non-existent Book of Readings', in George Schöpflin and Nancy Wood (eds), *In Search of Central Europe* (Cambridge: Polity Press, 1989), 125–36.
Klaein, Franz. *Die Kulturgemeinschaft der Völker nach dem Kriege*. Leipzig: S. Hirzel, 1915.
Klaus, Vaclav. *Europe: The Shattering of Illusions*. London: Bloomsbury Cintinuum, 2011.
Kleineibst, Richard. 'Die Entscheidung über Europa'. *Sozialistische Monatshefte*, Bd. 35 (1929), 273–77.
Kocka, Jürgen. 'Wege zur politischen Identität Europas: Europäische Öffentlichkeit und europäische Zivilgesellschaft'. On line Akademie, 2003. Retrieved 20 August 2020 from https://library.fes.de/pdf-files/akademie/online/50361.pdf.
Kolb, Annette. 'Briefe eines Deutsch-Französin', in *Internationale Rundschau: Erste Jahrgang* (Zurich: Orell Füssli, 1915), 160–65.
Konrád, György. *Från Europas navel*. Stockholm: Alba, 1990.
———. 'Is the Dream of Central Europe Still Alive?' *Cross Currents: A Yearbook of Central European Culture* 5 (1986), 109–21.
Kopp, Vilma. 'Die Frauen und Paneuropa'. *Zeitschrift Pan-Europa* 6(4) (1929), 12–16.
Koschorke, Albrecht. *Hegel und wir*. Berlin: Suhrkamp Verlag, 2015.
Koselleck, Reinhart. *Zeitschichten: Studien zur Historik*. Frankfurt am Main: Suhrkamp Verlag, 2000.
Koslowski, Peter. 'Vaterland Europa: über europäische und nationale Identität', in Peter Kosolowski and Rémi Brague (eds), *Vaterland Europa: Europäische und nationale Identität im Konflikt* (Vienna: Passagen Verlag, 1997), 43–70.
Kosnicki, Piotr H. 'The Soviet Bloc's Answer to European Integration: Catholic Anti-Germanism and the Polish Project of a "Catholic-Socialist" International'. *Contemporary European History* 24(1) (2015), 1–36.
Kramář, Karel. *Anmerkungen zur böhmischen Politik*. Vienna: E. Stülpnagel, 1906.
Kranold, Hermann. 'Nun erst recht Kontinentalpolitik!'. *Sozialistische Monatshefte*, Bd. 36 (1930), 845–54.
Krastev, Ivan. *After Europe*. Philadelphia: University of Pennsylvania Press, 2017.
Krause, Karl Christian Friedrich. 'Entwurf eines europäischen Staatenbundes als Grundlage des allgemeinen Friedens und als rechtlichen Mittels gegen jeden Angriff wider die innere und äussere Freiheit Europas, Maj 1814', in *Monatshefte der Comenius-Gesellschaft* (1899), 194–208.
Kretschmer, Konrad. *Historische Geographie von Mitteleuropa*. Munich: Oldenbourg, 1904.
Krüger, Peter. 'European Ideology and European Reality: European Unity and German Foreign Policy', in Peter M.R. Stirk (ed.), *European Unity in Context: The Interwar Period* (London: Pinter Publishers, 1989), 84–98.
Kühl, Joachim. *Föderationspläne im Donauraum und in Ostmitteleuropa*. Munich: R. Oldenbourg, 1958.
Kühnert, Herbert. 'Europaproblem'. *Sozialistische Monatshefte*, Bd. 36 (1930), 71–73.
Kundera, Milan. 'The Tragedy of Central Europe'. *New York Review of Books*, 26 April 1984, 33–38.
Kundnani, Hans, and Mark Leonard. 'Think Again: European Decline'. *European Council of Foreign Affairs*, 29 Apr 2013. Retrieved 4 December 2020 from http://ecfr.eu/content/entry/commentary_think_again_european_decline.

Kuus, Merje. 'Ubiquitous Identities and Elusive Subjects: Puzzles from Central Europe'. *Transactions of the Institute of British Geographers* 32(1) (2007), 90–101.
Laqua, Daniel (ed.). *Internationalism Reconfigured: Transnational Ideas and Movements between the World Wars*. London: I.B. Tauris, 2011.
———. 'Reconciliation and the Post-War Order: The Place of the *Deutsche Liga für Menschenrechte* in Interwar Pacifism', in Laqua (ed.), *Internationalism Reconfigured: Transnational Ideas and Movements between the World Wars* (London: I.B. Tauris, 2011), 209–38.
———. 'Transnational Intellectual Cooperation: The League of Nations, and the Problem of Order'. *Journal of Global History* 6(2) (2011), 223–47.
Lagarde, Paul. *Deutsche Schriften*. Göttingen: Becker & Eidner, 1920.
Lagendijk, Vincent. 'Ideas, Individuals and Institutions: Notion and Practices of a European Electricity System'. *Contemporary European History* 27(2) (2018), 202–30.
Lähdesmäki, Tuuli. 'Narrative and Intertextuality in the Making of a Shared European Memory'. *Journal of Contemporary European Studies* 25(1) (2017), 57–72.
Lähdesmäki, Tuuli, and Albin Wagener. 'Discourses on Governing Diversity in Europe: Critical Analysis of the White Paper on Intercultural Dialogue'. *International Journal of Intercultural Relations* 44 (January) (2015), 13–28.
Laing, Samuel. *Notes of a Traveller*. Philadelphia, PA: Carey and Hart, 1846.
Laqueur, Walter. *After the Fall: The End of the European Dream and the Decline of a Continent*. New York: Thomas Dunne Books, 2011.
———. *The Last Days of Europe: Epitaph for an Old Continent*. New York: Thomas Dunne Books, 2008.
Laski, Harold J. *Democracy in Crisis*. London: George Allen & Unwin, 1933.
Lauderdale, James Maitland. *An Inquiry into the Nature and Origin of Public Wealth: and the Means and Causes of its Increase*. Edinburgh: Arch, Constable and Co, 1804.
Le Goff, Jacques. *Das alte Europa und die Welt der Moderne*. Munich: Beck (1992) 1996.
Lehmann-Russbüldt, Otto. *Die Schöpfung der Vereinigten Staaten von Europa*. Berlin: Verlag Neues Vaterland, 1910.
Lemonnier, Charles. *Les Etats Unis d'Europe*. Paris: Librairie de la Bibliothèque Démocratique, 1872.
Lenin, Vladimir Iljitj. *The Imperialist War: The Struggle against Social-Chauvinism and Social-Pacifism 1914–1915*. London: Martin Lawrence, 1915.
Lenz, Fritz. 'Die Erblichkeit der geistigen Begabung'. In Fritz Lenz, *Grundrisse der Menschlichkeitslehre und Rassenhygiene*, vol. I. Munich: J.F. Lehmanns Verlag, 1921.
Leonhard, Jörn. 'Conceptual History: The Comparative Dimension', in Williband Steinmetz, Michael Freeden and Javier Fernández-Sebastián (eds), *Conceptual History in the European Space* (New York: Berghahn Books, 2017), 176–96.
Leppänen, Katarina. *Elin Wägner's Alarm Clock: Ecofeminist Theory in the Interwar Era*. New York: Lexington Books, 2007.
Lepsius, Rainer. 'Bildet sich eine kulturelle Identität in der Europäischen Union?' *Blätter für deutsche und internationale Politik* 8 (1997), 91–99.
Lepsius, Richard. *Das allgemeine linguistische Alphabet: Grundsätze der Übertragung fremde Schriftsysteme und bisher noch ungeschriebener Sprachen in europäischen Buchstaben*. Berlin: Verlag von Wilhelm Hertz, 1855.
Leroy-Beaulieu, Anatole. 1900. 'Les États-Unis D'Europe', in *La Revue des revues*, Paris.
———. 'Report General', in *Les États-Unis D'Europe: congrès de sciences politiques de 1900* (Paris: société francoise d'imprimerie et de libraire, 1901), 6–24.
Levy, Daniel, Max Pensky and John Torpey (eds). *Old Europe, New Europe, Core Europe: Transatlantic Relations after the Iraq War*. London: Verso, 2005.
Leyser, Karl J. 'Concepts of Europe in the Early and High Middle Ages'. *Past & Present* 137 (1992), 25–47.

Lindner, Theodor. *Geschichtsphilosophie: Einleitung zu einer Weltgeschichte seit der Völkerwanderung*. Stuttgart: Cotta, 1901.
Lipgens, Walter. *Die Anfänge der europäischen Einigungspolitik 1945–1950. Erster Teil 1945–1947*. Stuttgart: Ernst Klett, 1977.
——— (ed.). *Documents on the History of European Integration*, vol. 1–2. Berlin: Walter de Gruyter, 1986.
List, Friedrich. *Gesammelte Schriften II*. Stuttgart: Cotta, 1851.
List, Heinrich Theodor. *Deutschland und Mittel-Europa*. Berlin: Reimer, 1916.
Liszt, Franz von. *Ein Mitteleuropäischer Staatenverband als nächstes Ziel der deutschen auswärtigen Politik*. Leipzig: S. Hirzel, 1914.
Littré, Émile. *Études sur les barbares et le moyen âge*. Paris: Didier, 1867.
Llobera, Joseph R. 'Visions of Europe in the Dark Years: Julien Benda and José Ortega y Gasset'. *European Legacy* 1(7) (1996), 2084–93.
Loader, Colin. *Alfred Weber and the Crisis of Culture, 1890–1933*. New York: Palgrave, 2012.
Loch, Hermann. *Der mitteleuropäische Wirtschaftsbloch und das Schicksal Belgiens*. Leipzig S. Hirzel, 1914.
Longworth, Philip. *The Making of Eastern Europe*. Basingstoke, UK: Macmillan, 1992.
Lorimer, James. *The Institutions of the Law of Nations: A Treatise of the Jural Relations of Sepatate Political Communities*. Edinburgh: Blackwood, 1884.
Lough, Francis. 'National Identity and Historiography in José Saramago's *A Jangada de Pedra*'. *Journal of Iberian and Latin American Studies* 8(2) (2002), 153–63.
Loughlin, John. 'French Personalist and Federalist Movements in the Interwar Period', in Peter M.R. Stirk (ed.), *European Unity in Context: The Interwar Period* (London: Pinter Publishers, 1989), 188–200.
Louis, Paul. *Aspects politiques de la Guerre mondiale*. Paris: Librairie Félix Alcan, 1919.
———. *Le bouleversement mondial*. Paris: Librairie Félix Algan, 1920.
———. *L'Europe Nouvelle*. Paris: F. Alcan, 1915.
Löwith, Karl. 'European Nihilism: Reflections on the Spiritual and Historical Background of the European War' [1941], in *Martin Heidegger and European Nihilism* (New York: Colombia University Press, 1995), 192–208.
Maas, Walter. 'Briands Europainitiative'. *Sozialistische Monatshefte*, Bd. 36 (1930), 783–85.
Machlup, Fritz. *A History of Thought on Economic Integration*. New York: Columbia University Press, 1977.
MacLeod, Alexander. *European Life: Readings in the History of Western Civilisation*. Edinburgh: Andrew Elliot, 1863.
Madariaga, Salvador de. *Anarchy and Hierarchy*. London: George Allen & Unwin, 1937.
———. *De l'angoisse á la liberté: profession de foi d'un liberal revolutioonnaire*. Paris: Calmann-Lévy, 1954.
———. *Democracy versus Liberty? The Faith of a Liberal Heretic*. London: Pall Mall Press, 1958.
———. *Essays with a Purpose*. London: Hollis & Carter. 1954.
———. 'Europäischer Geist'. *Zeitschrift Pan-Europa* 2(10) (1934), 42–45.
———. *Portrait of Europe*. London: Hollis & Carter, 1952.
———. 'That European River, The Rhine'. *Virginia Quarterly Review* 32(2) (1956), 174–79.
———. *The World's Design*. Michigan: Allen & Unwin, 1938.
———. *Victors, Beware*. London: Jonathan Cape, 1946.
Malik, Kenan. *The Meaning of Race: Race, History and Culture in Western Society*. London: Macmillan, 1996.
Mamatey, Victor S. 'Masaryk and Wilson: A Contribution to the Study of their Relations', in Robert B. Pynsent (ed.), *T.G. Masaryk (1850–1937): Volume 2, Thinker and Critic* (London: Macmillan, 1989), 186–97.

Manela, Erez. *The Wilsonian Moment: Self-Determination and the International Origins of Anticolonial Nationalism*. Oxford: Oxford University Press, 2007.
Mann, Heinrich. *Sieben Jahre: Chronik der Gedanken und Vorgänge*. Berlin: Paul Zsolnay Verlag, 1929.
Mann, Thomas. 'Appell an die Vernunft', in *Achtung Europa! Aufsätze zur* Zeit (Stockholm: Bermann-Fischer Verlag, [1930] 1938), 80–91.
———. *Betrachtungen eines Unpolitischen*. Frankfurt am Main: Fischer, (1918) 2002.
Mannheim, Karl. *Essays on the Sociology of Knowledge*. London: Routledge, 1952.
Mansholt, Sicco. 'Toward European Integration: Beginnings in Agriculture'. *Foreign Affairs* 31(1) (1952), 106–13.
Marjanen, Jani. 'Transnational Conceptual History, Methodological Nationalism and Europe', in Williband Steinmetz, Michael Freeden and Javier Fernández-Sebastián (eds), *Conceptual History in the European Space* (New York: Berghahn Books, 2017), 139–74.
Marquand, David. *The End of the West: The Once and Future Europe*. Princeton, NJ: Princeton University Press, 2012.
Marsh, David. *Europe's Deadlock: How the Euro Crisis Could be Solved – and Why it Won't Happen*. New Haven, CT: Yale University Press, 2012.
Martin, Henri. *Russland und Europe*. Hannover: Karl Kümpler, (1866) 1869.
Martineau, Harriet. *Society in America I–III*. London: Saunders & Otley, 1837.
Martins, Oliveira. *Historia de la civilización Ibérica*. Madrid: Establecimiento Tipográfico de Fortanet, 1894.
Marvin, F.S. 'Preface', in *The Unity of Civilization: Essays Arranged and Edited* (London: Humphrey Milford, 1915), 3–4.
———. 'The Growth of Humanity', in *The Unity of Civilization: Essays Arranged and Edited* (London: Humphrey Milford, 1915), 301–15.
Masaryk, Tomáš. 'At the Eleventh Hour' [1915] in R.W. Seton-Watson, *Masaryk in England* (Cambridge: Cambridge University Press, 1943), 153–202.
———. *Česka Otázka: snahy tuzby národního obrození*. Prag: Knihtiskárna grafia, (1895) 1968.
———. *Das neue Europa: der slavische Standpunkt*. Berlin: C.A. Schwetschke, (1918) 1922.
———. 'Independent Bohemia' [1915], in R.W. Seton-Watson, *Masaryk in England* (Cambridge: Cambridge University Press, 1943), 116–34.
———. *Jan Hus: Naše obrození a naše reformace*. Prague: Knihtiskárna grafia, (1890) 1923.
———. 'Masaryk to Seton-Watson 3.5.1916', in R.W. Seton-Watson, *Masaryk in England* (Cambridge: Cambridge University Press, 1943), 86.
———. 'The Problem of Small Nations in the European Crises' [1915], in R.W. Seton-Watson, *Masaryk in England* (Cambridge: Cambridge University Press, 1943), 135–52.
———. *The Slavs Among the Nations*. London: Czech National Alliance in Great Britain, 1916.
Maschke, Erich. 'Die Verteidigung Europas'. *Nationalsozialistische Monatshefte: Zentrale politische und Kulturelle Zeitschrift der NSDAP* 146 (1942), 279–88.
Matlekovitz, Alexander. *Die Zollpolitik der oesterreichisch-ungarischen Monarchie von 1850 bis zu Gegenwart 1877*. Budapest: Franklin-Verein, 1877.
Mayreder, Rosa. 'Die Frau und die Internationalismus'. *Neues Frauenleben: organ der freiheitlichen Frauen in Österreich* 18(2) (1916), 25–32.
———. *Geschlecht und Cultur: Essays*. Jena: Eugen Diederichs, 1923.
Mazower, Mark. *Dark Continent: Europe's Twentieth Century*. London: Penguin Press, 1998.
———. *Hitler's Empire: How the Nazis Ruled Europe*. New York: Penguin: 2008.
Mazzini, André-Louis. *De l'Italie dans ses rapports avec la liberté et la civilisation moderne*. Leipzig: Brockhaus und Avenarius, 1847.
Mazzini, Guiseppe. *A Cosmopolitanism of Nations: Giuseppe Mazzini's Writings on Democracy, Nation Building, and International Relations*. Princeton, NJ: Princeton University Press, 2009.

——. 'Europe: Its Condition and Prospects' [1852], in *Essays: Selected from the Writings, Literary, Political and Religious of Joseph Mazzini* (London: Walter Scott, 1891), 261–98.
——. *Joseph Mazzini: His Life, Writings, and Political Principals*. New York: Hurd & Houghton, 1872.
——. *Selected Writings*. London: Lindsey Drummond Ltd, 1945.
——. 'The Holy Alliances of the Peoples' [1849], in *Life and Writings of Joseph Mazzini, Vol. V* (London: Smith, Elder, & Co., 1891), 265–82.
McCormick, John. *Why Europe Matters: The Case for the European Union*. Basingstoke, UK: Palgrave Macmillan, 2013.
McMahon, Darrin M. 'The Return of the History of Ideas?', in Darrin McMahon and Samuel Moyn (eds), *Rethinking European Intellectual History* (Oxford: Oxford University Press, 2014), 13–31.
Mehrmann, Karl. *Grossdeutschland: unsere Stellung in der Weltstaatengesellschaft*. Dresden: Das Grössere Deutschland, 1915.
Meinecke, Friedrich. *Die deutsche Katastrophe: Betrachtungen und Erinnerungen*. Zurich: Aero-Verlag, 1946.
'Memorandum of the German Majority Socialists', in Emily Green Balch, *Approaches to the Great Settlement* (New York: B.W. Huebsch, 1917), 174–75.
Metzidakis, Angelo. *Victor Hugo and the Idea of the United States of Europe*. Lincoln: University of Nebraska Press, 1994.
Meyer, Henry Cord. *Mitteleuropa in German Thought and Action, 1815–1945*. Haag: Springer, 1955.
Meyer, Thomas. *Identitätspolitik: Vom Missbrauch kultureller Unterschiede*. Frankfurt am Main: Suhrkamp, 2002.
Mick, Christopher. '1918: Endgame', in Jay Winter (ed.), *The Cambridge History of the First World War* (Cambridge: Cambridge University Press, 2014), 133–71.
Middelaar, Luuk van. *The Passage to Europe: How a Continent Became a Union*. New Haven, CT: Yale University Press, 2013.
Miettinen, Timo. 'The Particular Universal: Europe in Modern Philosophies of History', in Susanna Lindberg, Mika Ojakangas and Sergei Prozorov (eds), *Europe Beyond Universalism and Particularism* (New York: Palgrave Macmillan, 2014), 66–83.
Mikkeli, Heikki. *Europe as an Idea and an Identity*. Basingstoke: Palgrave Macmillan, 1998.
Miksche, F.O. 'Danubian Federation', in Wagner (ed.), *Toward a New Central Europe: A Symposium on the Problems of the Danubian Nations* (Hamilton, ONT: Hunyadi MMK, 1970), 138–45.
Mill, John Stuart. 'Tocqueville on Democracy in America I', in Gertrude Himmelfarb (ed.), *Essays on Politics and Culture* (New York: Doubleday, 1962), 173–213.
——. 'Tocqueville on Democracy in America II', in Gertrude Himmelfarb (ed.), *Essays on Politics and Culture* (New York: Doubleday, 1962), 214–67.
Miłosz, Czesław. 'Central European Attitudes'. *Cross Currents: A Yearbook of Central European Culture* 5 (1986), 101–8.
Milward, Alan. *The Rescue of the Nation-State*. London: Routledge, 1992.
Mishkova, Diana, and Balázs Trencsényi (eds). *European Regions and Boundaries: A Conceptual History*. New York: Berghahn Books, 2017.
Moering, Carl. *Entweder – oder*. Frankfurt am Main: F. Wilma, 1848.
——. *Sibyllinische Bücher aus Oesterreich I*. Hamburg: (no publisher), 1848.
Mogk, Walter. *Paul Rohrbach und das 'Grössere Deutschland': ethischer Imperialismus im Wilhelminischen Zeitalter*. Munich: W. Goldmann, 1972.
Mommsen, Wolfgang J. 'Die Mitteleuropaidee und die Mitteleuropaplanungen in deutschen Reich vor und während des ersten Weltkrieges', in Richard J. Plaschka et al. (eds),

Mitteleuropa-Konzeptionen in der ersten Hälfte des 20. Jahrhunderts (Vienna: Verlag der österreichischen Akademie der Wissenschaften, 1995), 3–24.

Monereo, Manolo. *Por Europa y contra el systema euro*. Barcelona: El Viejo Topo, 2014.

Monte, Hilda. *The Unity of Europe*. London: Victor Gollancz, 1943.

Montesquieu, Charles Secondat de. *Om lagarnas anda* [The spirit of the laws]. Cambridge: Cambridge University Press, (1757) 1989.

Montfrans, Manet von. '"Europe is the Country of the Spirit": Albert Camus and Europeanism in France, 1944–47', in Menno Spiering and Michael Wintle (ed.), *European Identity and the Second World War* (Houndmills: Palgrave Macmillan, 2011), 124–37.

——. 'Pacifism and the European Idea: War and Inner Conflict in the Work of Léon Werth', in Menno Spiering and Michael Wintle (eds), *Ideas of Europe since 1914: The Legacy of the First World War* (Houndmills: Palgrave Macmillan, 2002), 160–76.

Moravcsik, Andrew. *Choice of Europe: Social Purpose and State Power from Messina to Maastricht*. London: Routledge, 1998.

Moreno, Luis. *Europa sin estados: unión política en el (des)orden global*. Madrid: Catarata, 2014.

Morin, Edgar. *Europa denken*. Frankfurt am Main: Campus, (1987) 1988.

Morin, Edgar, and Mauro Ceruti. *Nuestra Europa: Qye podemos esperar? Que podemos hacer?* Barcelona: Pidós, 2013.

Moyo, Dambisa. *How the West Was Lost: Fifty Years of Economic Folly – And the Stark Choices Ahead*. London: Penguin Books, 2012.

Mühlstein, Hans. *Deutschlands Sendung*. Weimar: Gustav Kiepenheuer, 1914.

——. *Herrschaft der Weisen*. Leipzig: Der neue Geist, 1918.

Müller, Guido. 'France and Germany after the Great War: Businessmen, Intellectuals and Artists on Nongovernmental European Networks', in Jessica C.E. Gienow-Hecht and Frank Schumacher (eds), *Culture and International History* (New York: Berghahn Books, 2003), 97–110.

Müller, Jan-Werner. 'European Intellectuals Need to Quit Playing the Identity Game', *Politico*, 9 July 2003. Retrieved 4 September 2020 from https://www.politico.eu/article/europes-intellectuals-need-to-quit-playing-the-identity-game/.

——. 'On Conceptual History', in Darrin McMahon and Samuel Moyn (eds), *Rethinking European Intellectual History* (Oxford: Oxford University Press, 2014), 74–93.

Müller-Graff, Peter-Christian, and Heinrich Schneider (eds), *Kirchen und Religionsgemeinschaften in der Europäischen Union*. Baden-Baden: Nomos, 2003.

Murray, Alexander. *History of the European Languages*. Edinburgh: E. Constable & Co., 1823.

Murray, Douglas. *Strange Death of Europe: Immigration, Identity, Islam*. London: Bloomsbury, 2017.

Mussert, Anton. 'The Dutch State in the New Europe' [1942], in Walter Lipgens (ed.), *Documents on the History of European Integration*, vol. 1 (Berlin: Walter de Gruyter, 1985), 103–7.

Mussolini, Benito. 'Europäischer Völkerbund'. *Zeitschrift Pan-Europa* 10(2) (1934), 38–42.

Müller, Guido. *Europäische Gesellschaftsbeziehungen nach dem Ersten Weltkrieg: Das Deutsch-Französische Studienkomitee und der Europäische Kulturbund*. Munich: R. Oldenbourg Verlag, 2005.

Myrdal, Alva. 'När fredens nya värld planeras'. *Fred och Frihet* 16(6) (1942), 1–6.

Naïr, Sami. *El desengaño europeo*. Barcelona: Galaxia Gutenberg, 2014.

Naumann, Friedrich. 'Deutschland und Österreich' [1900], in *Werke 4: Schriften zum Parteiwesen und zum Mitteleuropaproblem* (Cologne: Westdeutsche Verlag, 1964), 400–441.

——. *Mitteleuropa* [1916], in *Werke 2: Politische Schriften* (Cologne: Westdeutsche Verlag, 1964), 485–767.

Nearing, Scott. *Where is Civilization Going?* New York: New Vanguard Press, 1927.

Neiburg, Michael S. *The Treaty of Versailles: A Concise History*. Oxford: Oxford University Press, 2017.

Neue Wandkarte von Europa, Afrikas' Nord Küsten and einem grossen Theile Asiens. Munich: J.B. Roost, 1857.
Neumann, Iver B. *Russia and the Idea of Europe: A Study in Identity and International Relations*. London: Routledge, 1996.
Neunsinger, Silke. 'Cross-over! Om komparationer, transferanalyser, histoire croisée och den metodologiska nationalismens problem'. *Historisk tidskrift* 130(1) (2010), 3–24.
Nicholls, David. 'Richard Cobden and the International Peace Congress Movement, 1848–1853'. *Journal of British Studies* 30(4) (1991), 351–76.
Nicolai, George Friedrich. *Die Biologie des Krieges: Betrachtungen eines Naturforschers den Deutschen zur Besinnung, Band I*. Zurich: Art. Institute Orell Füssli, 1917.
Niethammer, Lutz. 'A European Identity', in Stråth (ed.), *Europe and the Other and Europe as the Other* (Brussels: Peter Lang, 2000), 87–111.
Nietzsche, Friedrich. *Beyond Good or Evil*. New York: The Modern Library, (1885) 1917.
Nitti, Francesco. *Peaceless Europe*. London: Cassell and Company, 1922.
———. *The Wreck of Europe*. New York: Braunworth & Co, 1922.
Noe, Helga. *Die literarische Kritik am ersten Weltkrieg in det Zeitschrift 'Die weissen Blätter': René Schikele, Annette Kolb, Max Brod, Andreas Latzko, Leonhard Frank*. Konstanz: Maus, 1986.
Noser, V. 'Unrest in Bohemia'. *The New Europe* 6(86) (1918), 180–82.
Novalis. 'Die Christenheit oder Europa', in *Die Christenheit oder Europa und andere philosophische Schriften* (Cologne: Könemann, [1799] 1996), 23–43.
Novicow, Jacques. *Die Föderation Europas*. Berlin: Akademischer Verlag für sociale Wissenschaften, 1901.
O'Brien, Arctander. *Novalis: Signs of Revolution*. Durham, NC: Duke University Press, 1995.
Odijie, Michael. 'The Fear of "Yellow Peril" and the Emergence of European Federalist Movement'. *The International History Review* 40(2) (2018), 358–75.
Offe, Claus. *Europe Entrapped*. Cambridge: Polity Press, 2015.
Olsson, Jan, and Olle Svenning. *Tillhör Sverige Europa?* Stockholm: Författarförlaget, 1988.
Ortega y Gasset, José. 'De Europa meditatio quaedam' [1949], in *Obras completas*, vol. X (Madrid: Taurus, 2010), 75–135.
———. 'Gibt es ein europäisches Kulturbewusstsein?', in *Europäische Kultur und europäische Völker* (Stuttgart: Deutsche verlagsanstalt, 1954), 35–87.
———. 'La pedagogía social como programa politico', in *Obras Completas*, vol. I (Madrid: Revista del Occidente, 1946), 503–21.
———. *La rebelión de las masas*. Madrid: Revista de Occidente, (1930) 1931.
———. *The Revolt of the Masses*. New York: Norton & Company, (1930) 1993.
O'Toole, Fintan. *Heroic Failure: Brexit and the Politics of Pain*. London: Head of Zeus, 2018.
Owen, David. *Europe Restructured: The Eurozone Crises and its Aftermath*. York: Methuen, 2012.
Padànyi-Gulyás, Eugene. 'Toward a Constructive Ideology and Policy in a New Central Europe', in Wagner (ed.), *Toward a New Central Europe: A Symposium on the Problems of the Danubian Nations* (Hamilton, ONT: Hunyadi MMK, 1970), 25–32.
Padànyi-Gulyás, Eugene, and Alexander Gallus. 'Signs of the Times', in Wagner (ed.) *Toward a New Central Europe: A Symposium on the Problems of the Danubian Nations* (Hamilton, ONT: Hunyadi MMK, 1970), 13–24.
Pagden, Anthony. 'Europe: Conceptualizing a Continent', in Pagden (ed.), *The Idea of Europe: From Antiquity to the European Union* (Cambridge: Cambridge University Press, 2002), 33–54.
———. 'Introduction', in Pagden (ed.), *The Idea of Europe: From Antiquity to the European Union* (Cambridge: Cambridge University Press, 2002), 1–32.
Palacký, František. 'O poměru Čech i Rakouska k říší Německé', in *Radhost: sbírka spisuw drobných z oboru řeči a literatury, krásowdy, historie e politiky III*. Prague: Tempského, (1848) 1871.

———. 'Předmluwa ke wlastenskému čtenářstwu', in *Radhost: Sbirka spisůw drobných* I (Prague: Nákladem Bedřicha Tempského, 1837), 5–20.
Palmstierna, Erik. 'Europas förenta stater'. *Tiden* 7(10) (1915), 304–8.
———. *Orostid I, 1914–1915: Politiska dagboksanteckningar*. Stockholm: tidens förlag, 1951.
Pannwitz, Rudolf. *Die Krisis der europaeischen Kultur*. Nürnberg: Verlag Hans Carl, 1917.
Papcke, Sven. 'Who Needs European Identity?', in Brian Nelson, David Roberts and Walter Veit (eds), *The Idea of Europe: Problems of National and Transnational Identity* (New York: Berg, 1992), 61–74.
Pasquinucci, Daniele. 'Between Political Commitment and Academic Research: Federalist Perspectives', in Wolfram Kaiser and Antonio Varsori (eds), *European Union History: Themes and Debates* (Houndmills, UK: Palgrave Macmillan, 2010), 67–84.
Passerini, Luisa. 'From the Ironies of Identity to the Identities of Irony', in Pagden (ed.), *The Idea of Europe: From Antiquity to the European Union* (Cambridge: Cambridge University Press, 2002), 191–208.
———. *Love and the Idea of Europe*. New York: Berghahn Books, 2009.
———. 'The Last Identification: Why Some of Us Would Like to Call Ourselves Europeans and What We Mean by This', in Bo Stråth (ed.), *Europe and the Other and Europe as the Other* (Brussels: Peter Lang, 2000), 45–65.
———. *Women and Men in Love: European Identities in the Twentieth Century*. New York: Berghahn Books, 2009.
Pasture, Patrick. *Imagining European Unity since 1000 AD*. Houndmills, UK: Palgrave Macmillan, 2015.
Patel, Kiran Klaus. 'Provincialising European Union: Co-operation and Integration Europe in a Historical Perspective'. *Contemporary European History* 22(4) (2013), 649–73.
Patočka, Jan. 'European Culture' [1939], in Alex Drace-Francis (ed.), *European Identity: A Historical Reader* (New York: Palgrave Macmillan, 2013), 200–203.
———. *Heretical Essays in the Philosophy of History*. Chicago: Open Court, 1996.
———. 'Was dürfen wir von Charta 77 erwarten', in *Ausgewählte Schriften (5), Schriften zur tschechischen Kultur und Geschichte* (Stuttgart: Klett-Cotta, 1992), 315–24.
Pegg, Carl H.. *Evolution of the European Idea, 1914–1932*. Chapel Hill: University of North Carolina Press, 1983.
Pekař, Josef. 'Kdo založil Rakousko?' [1917], in *Na cestěk samostnatnosti* (Prague: Panorama, 1993), 35–39.
Penn, William. *An Essay towards the Present and Future Peace of Europe by the Establishment of an European Dyet, Parliament, or Estates*, Washington, DC: The American Peace Society, (1693) 1912.
Périer, Charles Francois du. *A Speculative Sketch on Europe* (translation from French by Monsieur Demouriez). London: J. Hatchard, 1798.
Perkins, James H. *Christian Civilisation: An Address Delivered Before the Athenian Society*. Cincinnati: A. Pugh. Print, 1840.
Perkins, Mary Ann. *Christendom and European Identity: The Legacy of a Grand Narrative since 1789*. Berlin: Walter de Gruyter, 2004.
Petty, William. 'A Treatise of Taxes and Contributions', in *The Economic Writings of William Petty* (Cambridge: The University Press, ([1662] 1899), 5–102.
Peus, Heinrich. 'Politik aus weite Sicht'. *Sozialistische Monatshefte*, Bd. 36 (1930), 644–49.
Peyré, Jean François Aimé. *Civilisation de l'Afrique centrale, . . . dont le but serait de substituer l'influence française à l'influence maure*. Paris: Delauney, 1832.
Pfordten, Ludwig von. 'Denkschrift des Herrn von der Pfordten 7.7.1849', quoted in Eduard Heller, *Mitteleuropas Vorkämpfer: Fürst Felix zu Schwarzenberg* (Vienna: Militärwissenschaftlicher Verlag 1933), 62–63.

Philippi, Ferdinand. *Geschichte der vereinigten Freistaaten von Nordamerika*. Dresden: P.G. Hilscher, 1826.
Philippovich, Eugen von. *Ein Wirtschafts- und Zollverband zwischen Deutschland und Österreich-Ungarn*. Leipzig: S. Hirzel, 1915.
Pickering, Charles. *The Races of Man and their Geographical Distribution*. London: H.G. Bohn, 1851.
Pieczewski, Andrzej. 'Joseph Retinger's Conception of and Contribution to the Early Process of European Integration'. *European Review of History – Revue européenne d'histoire* 17(4) (2010), 581–604.
Pinder, John, 'Federalism in Britain and Italy: Radicals and the English Liberal Tradition', in Peter M.R. Stirk (ed.), *European Unity in Context: The Interwar Period* (London: Pinter Publishers, 1989), 201–23.
———. 'Federal Union 1939–41', in Walter Lipgens (ed.), *Documents on the History of European Integration*, vol. 2 (Berlin: Walter de Gruyter, 1986), 26–34.
Piris, Jean Claude. *The Future of Europe: Towards a Two-Speed EU?* Cambridge: Cambridge University Press, 2012.
'Politiska nyheter'. *Dagens Nyheter*, 16 September 1870. Retrieved 20 November 2011 from http://arkivet.dn.se/arkivet/tidning/1870-09-16/1745/1?searchTerm=europas+f%c3%b6renta+stater.
Popovici, Aurel C. *Die Vereinigten Staaten von Gross-Österreich: Politische Studien zur Lösung der nationalen Fragen und staatsrechtlichen krisen in Österreich-Ungarn*. Leipzig: Verlag von B. Elischer Nachfolger, 1906.
Poschinger, Heinrich. *Preussen im Bundestag: 1851–1859; Documente der K. Preuß. Bundestags-Gesandtschaft*. Leipzig: Hirzel, 1965–69.
Prescott, Guillermo H. *Historia de la conquista del Perú: con observaciones preliminares sobre la civilización de los incas*. Madrid: Gaspar y Ruig, 1851.
Prettenthaler-Ziegerhofer, Anita. 'Richard Nikolaus Coudenhove-Kalergi, Founder of the Pan-European Union, and the Birth of a "New" Europe', in Mark Hewitson and D'Auria Matthew (eds), *Europe in Crisis: Intellectuals and the European Ideas, 1917–1957* (New York: Berghahn Books, 2012), 89–110.
Pumphrey, Stanley. *Indian Civilization: Lecture*. Philadelphia, PA: The Bible and Tract Distributing Society, 1877.
Pütz, Wilhelm. *Manual of Modern Geography and History*. New York: D. Appleton & Company, 1851.
Quartara, Giorgio. *Gli Stati Uniti d'europé e del Mundo*. Turin: Bocca, 1930.
Quisling, Vidkun. 'Norway and the Germanic Task in Europe' [1942], in Walter Lipgens, *Documents on the History of European Integration*, vol. 1 (Berlin: Walter de Gruyter, 1985), 98–102.
Qvanten, Emil van. *Fennomani och skandinavism*. Stockholm: Z. Häggström, 1855.
Qvarnström, Sofi. *Motståndets berättelser: Elin Wägner, Anna Lenah Elgström, Marika Stiernsted och första världskriget*. Hedemora: Gidlunds, 2009.
Radisch, Iris. *Die Seele Europas und die kleine Heimat: Zwei Texte*. Wieser: Klagenfurt, 2005.
Rakovski, M. 'Transylvania and Macedonia'. *The New Europe* 6(73) (1918), 255–57.
Ransmayr, Christoph. *Im blinden Winkel: Nachrichten aus Mitteleuropa*. Innsbruck: Wagner, 1985.
Rappard, William E. *The Crisis of Democracy*. Chicago: The University of Chicago Press, 1938.
Ratzinger, Joseph. 'Europa in der Krise der Kulturen', in Mercello Pera and Joseph Ratzinger, *Ohne Wurzeln: der Relativismus und die Krise der Europäischen Kultur* (Augsburg: Sankt Ulrich Verlag, 2005), 62–84.
———. 'Gemeinsame Identität und gemeinsames Willen: Chancen und Gefahren für Europa' [2001], in Ratzinger, *Werten in Zeiten des Umbruchs: Die Herausforderungen der Zukunft bestehen* (Breisgau: Herder, 2005), 89–97.

Rauschning, Hermann. *Die Revolution des Nihilismus*. Zurich: Europa-Verlag, 1938.
——. *Time of Delirium*. New York: D. Appleton-Century Company, 1946.
Reden, Friedrich Wilhelm von. *Ost-Europa: Kampf-Gebiet und Sieges-Preis in geschichtlich-statischer Darstellung*. Frankfurt and Main: K.T. Völcker, 1854.
Reijnen, Carlos, and Marleen Rensen. 'Introduction: European Encounters and Intellectual Exchange and Rethinking of Europe 1914–1945'. *European Studies* 32 (2014), 13–30.
Renan, Ernest. 'Open Letter to David Strauss' [1870], in Alex Drace-Francis (ed.), *European Identity: A Historical Reader* (New York: Palgrave Macmillan, 2013), 141–42.
Renner, Karl. *Der Selbstbestimmungsrecht der Nationen in besonderer Anwendung auf Oesterreich*. Leipzig: F. Deuticke, 1918.
——. *Oesterreichs Erneuerung*. Vienna: I. Brand & Co, 1916.
Report of the International Congress of Women: The Hague – The Netherlands, April 28th to May 1st, 1915. [Chicago]: Women's Peace Party, [1915?].
Reuter, Gabriele. 'The German Religion of Duty', in *The New York Times Current History of the European War: Vol. 1, No. 1. What Men of Letters Say* (New York: The New York Times Company, 1914), 170–73.
Réveillère. *L'europe Uni*. Paris: Berger Levraut, 1896.
Reynold, Gonzague de. *La Formation de l'Europe*. Paris: Plon, 1953.
Richard, Anne-Isabelle. 'Huizinga, Intellectual Cooperation and the Spirit of Europe, 1933–1945', in Mark Hewitson and Matthew D'Auria (eds), *Europe in Crisis: Intellectuals and the European Idea, 1917–1957* (New York: Berghahn Books, 2012), 243–56.
——. 'The Limits of Solidarity: Europeanism, Anti-Colonialism and Socialism at the Congress of the Peoples of Europe, Asia and Africa in Puteaux, 1948'. *European Review of History – Revue européenne d'histoire* 21(4) (2014), 519–37.
——. 'In Search of a Suitable Europe: Paneuropa in the Netherlands in the Interwar Period'. *European Studies* 32 (2014), 247–69.
Rider, Jacques Le. 'Mitteleuropa, Zentraleuropa, Mittelosteuropa: A Mental Map of Central Europe'. *European Journal of Social Theory* 11(2) (2008), 155–69.
Ridley, Francis A. *Unite or Perish: The United Socialist States of Europe*. London: Independent Labour Party, 1944.
Ridley, Francis A., and Bob Edwards. *The United Socialist States of Europe*. National Labour Party, 1944.
Riemeck, Renate. *Mitteleuropa*. Frankfurt am Main: Fischer Verlag, 1983.
Rietbergen, Peter. *Europe: A Cultural History*. London: Routledge, 1998.
Riou, Gaston. *L'Europe: Ma patrie*. Paris: Valois, 1928.
Ritter, Albert (Winterstetten). *Berlin-Bagdad: neue Ziele mitteleuropäischer Politik*. Munich: J.F. Lehmann. 1914.
——. *Nordkap-Bagdad: das politische Programm des Krieges*. Frankfurt am Main: Neuer frankfurter Verlag, 1914.
Robbers, Gerhard (ed.). *Staat und Kirche in der Europäischen Union*. Baden-Baden: Nomos, 1995.
Roberts, Wilfried. 'Towards European Unity'. *The Contemporary Review* 176(July) (1948), 8–10.
Robertson, William. *The History of the Reign of Emperor Charles V*. London: W. and W. Strahan, 1769.
Roobol, Wim. 'Aristide Briand's Plan: The Seed of European Unification', in Menno Spiering and Michael Wintle (eds), *Ideas of Europe since 1914: The Legacy of the First World War* (New York: Palgrave, 2002), 32–46.
Roca y Cornet, Juaquin. 'Bentham: Escuela utilitaria', *La civilización: revista religiosa, filosofica, política y literaria de Barcelona*, t.ii. Barcelona: Brusi, 1842.
——. 'La civilización'. *La civilización: revista religiosa, filosofica, política y literaria de Barcelona*. Barcelona: Brusi, 1841.

Rodrígues Pridall, Fernando. *Influencia del cristianismo en la civilisación Europeano*. Dissertation. Madrid : Universidad Central, 1854.

Rohan, Karl Anton Prinz. *Schicksalsstunde Europas: Erkenntnisse und Bekentnisse, Wirklichkeiten und Möglichkeiten*. Graz: Leykam, 1937.

Rohlik, Josef, and Susan FitzGibbon Kinyon. 'The Right of Self-Determination and Central-Europe'. *Cross Currents: A Yearbook of Central European Culture* 4 (1985), 9–38.

Rohrbach, Paul. *Der Krieg und die deutsche Politik*. Dresden: Verlag Das Grössere Deutschland, 1914.

Roll, Evelyn. *Wir sind Europa! Eine Streitschrift gegen den Nationalismus*. Berlin: Ullstein, 1916.

Rolland, Romain. *Above the Battle*. London: George Allen & Unwin Ltd, 1916.

Roth, Philip. *The Hotel Years: Wanderings in Europe Between the Wars*. London: Granta, 2015.

Rotteck, Carl von. *Europe: Vorlesungen and der Universität zu Berlin gehalten*. Ed. by H.A. Daniel. Berlin: G. Reimer, (1824) 1863.

Rougemont, Denis de. 'Denis de Rougemont: Conférence du 8 septembre', in Benda (ed.), *L'esprit européen: Rencontres internationales de Genève* (Neuchâtel, 1946), 172–97.

———. *Man's Western Quest: The Principles of Civilization*. New York: Harper, 1947.

———. *The Last Trump*. New York: Doubleday, 1947.

———. 'Die Krankheit der europäischen Kultur'. *Der Monat* 3(32) (1951), 116–23.

———. *Freedoms We May Lose*. Paris: Congress for Cultural freedom, 1960.

———. *The Idea of Europe*. New York: Macmillan, 1964.

Rubicon. 'The Czechs and Austria'. *The New Europe* 6(70) (1918), 144–49.

Rumpler, Helmut, and Jan Paul Niedrekorn (eds). *Der Zweibund 1879: das deutsch-österreichisch-ungarische Bündnis und die europäische Diplomatie*. Vienna: Verlag der Österreichischen Akademie der Wissenschaften, 1996.

Said, Edward W. *Orientalism*. New York: Pantheon, 1978.

Saint-Simon, Henri. *Selected Writings on Science, Industry and Social Organization*. London: Croom Helm, 1975.

Salewski, Michael. 'Ideas of the National Socialist Government and Party', in Walter Lipgens (ed.), *Documents on the History of European Integration*, vol. 1 (Berlin: Walter de Gruyter, 1985), 37–54.

Salisbury, Robert Cecil. 'English Politics and Parties'. *Bentley's Quarterly Review* 1(1) (1859), 1–32.

———. 'Europeisk Federation'. *Dagens Nyheter*, 12 November 1897. Retrieved 5 November 2020 from http://arkivet.dn.se/arkivet/tidning/1897-11-12/9996A/3?searchTerm=europeisk+federation.

Salter, Arthur. *The United States of Europe and Other Papers*. London: George Allen & Unwin, 1933.

Saramago, Jose. 'A Country Adrift'. *The Times Literary Supplement* (9 December 1988), 1370.

Sassatelli, Monica. 'An Interview with Jean Baudrillard: Europe, Globalization and the Destiny of Culture'. *European Journal of Social Theory* 5(4) (2002), 521–30.

Saunders, Frances Stoner. *Who Paid the Piper? The CIA and the Cultural Cold War*. London: Granta Books, 1999.

Savater, Fernando. 'EU Needs to Stand Up to the Nationalists', in *The Guardian*, 5 January 2011. Retrieved 16 September 2020 from https://www.theguardian.com/commentisfree/2011/jan/05/eu-nationalists.

Scadding, Henry. *English Civilization Undemonstrative: The Address to the St. George's Society*. Toronto: Rowsell & Hutchinson, 1860.

Scheidler, Karl Hermann. *Die Lebensfrage der europäische Zivilisation und die Bedeutung der Fellenbergischen Bildungsanstalten und zy Hofwyhl für ihre befriedigendste Lösung*. Jena: Bransche Buchhandlung, 1839.

Schiller, Friedrich. 'Was heisst und zu welchem Ende studiert man Universalgeschichte' [1789], in *Sämtlicher Werke*, Zehnte Band. Berlin: A. Weichert, 1902.

Schipper, Frank. *Driving Europe: Building Europe on Roads in the Twentieth Century*. Amsterdam: Aksant Academic Publishers, 2008.

Schlegel A.W. 'Ueber Litteratur, Kunst und Geist des Zeitalters: Einige Vorlesungen in Berlin, zu Ende des J. 1802', in *Europa*, Zweiter Band (Frankfurt am Main: Friedrich Wilmans, 1803), 95–152.

Schlögel, Karl. 'Europe and the Culture of Borders: Rethinking Borders after 1989', in Manfred Hildermeier (ed.), *Historical Concepts between Western and Eastern Europe* (New York: Berghahn Books, 2007), 73–84.

Schlözer, August Ludwig. *Geschichte der Deutschen in Siebenbürgen*. Göttingen: Vandenhok & Ruprechtschem Verlage, 1795.

Schmale, Wolfgang. 'Before Self-Reflexivity: Imperialism and Colonialism in the Early Discourses of European Integration', in Menno Spiering and Michael Wintle (eds), *European Identity and the Second World War* (Houndmills, UK: Palgrave Macmillan, 2011), 186–201.

Schmidt, Paul Ferdinand. 'Das Herz Europas'. *Sozialistische Monatshefte*, Bd. 36 (1930), 145–47.

Schmiedt-Phiseldeck, Konrad George von. *Europa und Amerika, oder die künftigen Verhälltnisse der civilisierten Welt*. Copenhagen: Friederich Brummer, 1820.

——. *Der europäische Bund*. Copenhagen: Friederich Brummer, 1821.

——. *Die Politik nach den Grundsätzen der Heiligen Allianz*. Copenhagen: Friderich Brummer, 1822.

——. *Politiken* (Swedish transl.). Stockholm: Zacharias Häggström, 1822.

Schön, Johann. *Allgemeine Geschichte und Statistik der europäischen Civilization*. Leipzig: Verlag der J.C. Hinnrichsschen, 1833.

Schonfield, Ernest. 'Heinrich Mann's Political Essays of the 1920s and Early 1930s', in Mark Hewitson and Matthew D'Auria (eds), *Europe in Crisis: Intellectuals and the European Idea, 1917–1957* (New York: Berghahn Books, 2012), 257–70.

Schuchardt, Ottomar. *Der mitteleuropäische Bund*. Dresden: Zahn & Jaensch, 1913.

——. *Die deutsche Politik der Zukunft*, T. I–IV. Dresden: Zahn & Jaensch, 1900–1904.

——. *Umrisse einer Staatsverfassung für das mittlere Europa: eine Ergänzung der Politik der Zukunft*. Dresden: v. Zahn & Jaensch, 1905.

Schultz, Hans-Dietrich, and Wolfgang Natter. 'Imagining Mitteleuropa: Conceptualisations of "Its" Space in and Outside German Geography'. *European Review of History – Revue europeenne d'histoire* 10(2) (2003), 273–92.

Schulz, August. 'Die Verbreitung der holophilen Phanerogamen in Mitteleuropa nördlich der Alpen', in *Forschungen zur deutschen Landes- und Volkskunde im: Auftrage der Centralkommission für wissenschaftliche Landeskunde von Deutschland*, Bd. 13 (Stuttgart: J. Engelhorn, 1901), 269–360.

——. 'Entwicklungsgeschichte der phanerogamen Pflanzdecke Mitteleuropas nördlich der Alpen', in *Forschungen zur deutschen Landes- und Volkskunde: im Auftrage der Centralkommission für wissenschaftliche Landeskunde von Deutschland*, Bd. 11 (Stuttgart: J. Engelhorn, 1899), 229–447.

Schulze, Hagen. 'Die Identität Europas und die Wiederkehr der Antike', in *ZEI Discussion Paper* C34 1999 (Bonn: Rheinische Friedrich Wilhelms-Universität Bonn, 2001). Retrieved 3 December 2020 from http://aei.pitt.edu/310/1/dp_c34_schulze.pdf?origin=publication_detail.

Schulze, Winfried, and Gerd Helm. 'Conrad George Friedrich Elias von Schmied-Phiseldeck', in Heinz Durchhardt et al. (eds), *Europa-Historiker: ein biografisches Handbuch* (Göttingen: Vandenhoeck & Ruprecht, 2006), 107–28.

Schuman, Robert. 'France and Europe'. *Foreign Affairs* 31(3) (1953), 349–60.

Schütz, Friedrich. 'Franz Palacky', *Die Gartenlaube: illustriertes Familienblatt*. Leipzig: Keil-Verlag, 1876.
Schweitzer, Albert. *Civilization and Ethics*. London: Adam & Charles Black, 1923.
Secord, James A. 'Knowledge in Transit'. *ISIS* 95(4) (2004), 654–72.
Seipel, Ignaz. *Nation und Staat*. Vienna: W. Barumüller, 1916.
Semmig, Hermann. *Geschichte der französischen Literatur im Mittelalter nebst ihre Beziehungen im Gegenwart*. Leipzig: Otto Wigand, 1862.
Seton-Watson, Hugh. *The Decline of Imperial Russia 1855–1914*. London: Methuen, 1952.
Seton-Watson, Robert William. *Masaryk in England*. Cambridge: Cambridge University Press, 1943.
———. 'The Musings of a Slavophile'. *The New Europe* 6(73) (1918), 248–49.
Sforza, Carlo. *Europe and Europeans: A Study in Historical Psychology and International Politics*. Indianapolis, IN: Bobbs-Merrill Co, 1936.
Shanahan, Daniel. *Toward a Genealogy of Individualism*. Amherst: University of Massachusetts Press, 1992.
Shaw, Desmond. 'Nationalitet og Internationalisme'. *Det ny Europa: Internationalt Tidsskrift* 1(2) (1918), 27–31.
Shore, Chris. *Building Europe: The Cultural Politics of European Integration*. London: Routledge, 2000.
Šimečka, Milan. 'Another Civilization? An Other Civilization', in George Schöpflin and Nancy Wood (eds), *In Search of Central Europe* (Cambridge: Polity Press, 1989), 157–62.
Simmel, George. 'Der Krieg und die geistigen Entscheidungen' [1917], in Alex Drace-Francis (ed.), *European Identity: A Historical Reader* (New York: Palgrave Macmillan, 2013), 168–69.
———. 'Die beiden Formen des Individualismus', in Rüdiger Kramme (ed.), *Gesamtausgabe 7: Aufsätze und Abhandlungen 1901–1908* (Frankfurt am Main: Suhrkamp, [1901] 1995), 49–56.
Simms, Brendan, and Benjamin Zeeb. *Europa am Abgrund: Plädoyer für die Vereinigten Staaten von Europé*. Munich: C.H. Beck, 2016.
Simpson, M.C.M. (ed.). *Correspondence & Conversations of Alexis de Tocqueville with Nassau William Senior from 1834 to 1859*. London: H.S. King and Co., 1872.
Sked, Alan. *The Decline and Fall of the Habsburg Empire 1815–1918*. London: Longman, 1989.
Sloterdijk, Peter. *Falls Europa erwacht: Gedanken zum Programm einer Weltmacht am Ende des Zeitalter ihrer politischen Absence*. Frankfurt am Main: Suhrkamp Verlag, 1994.
Smith, Adam. *An Inquiry into the Nature and Causes of the Wealth of Nations* I. Oxford: Oxford University Press, (1776) 1976.
Smith, Andrew, Simon Mollan and Kevin D. Tennent (eds). *The Impact of the First World War on International Business*. New York: Routledge, 2016.
Smith, Anthony D. *Ethnic Origins of Nationalism*. Oxford: Blackwell, 1986.
———. 'National Identity and the Idea of European Unity'. *International Affairs* 68(1) (1992), 55–76.
———. *Nations and Nationalism in a Global Era*. Cambridge: Polity Press, 1995.
Smith, Nadia C. 'A "Manly Study"? Irish Women Historians as Public Intellectuals, 1868–1949'. Dissertation. Boston: Boston College, 2003.
Sohlmann, August. *Det unga Finland: en kulturhistorisk betraktelse*. Stockholm, Thimgren, 1855.
Sombart, Werner. *Händler und Helden: patriotische Besinnungen*. Munich: Duncker und Humblot, 1915.
Sörgel, Herman. *Mittelmeer-Senkung. Sahara Bewässerung (Panropa-Projekt)* Leipzig: J.M. Gebhardt's Verlag, 1929.
Spann, Othmar. *Der wahre Staat: Vorlesungen über Abbruch und Neubau der Gesellschaft*. Vienna: Verlag von Quelle und Meyer in Leipzig, 1920.

Spaventa, Bertrando. *La filosofia Italiana nelle sue ralazioni con la filosofia Europea*. Bari: Gius. Laterza & Figli, (1862) 1908.
Spencer, Herbert. 'The Development of Political Institutions'. *The Popular Science Monthly* (January 1881), 289–302.
Spender, Stephen. *European Witness*. London: Hamish Hamilton, 1946.
——. 'Stephen Spender: Conférence du 11 septembre 1946', in Benda (ed.), *L'esprit européen: Rencontres internationales de Genève* (Neuchâtel, 1946), 267–91.
Spengler, Oswald. *Der Untergang des Abendlandes: Umrisse einer Morphologie der Weltgeschichte*. Munich: Oskar Beck, (1918) 1919.
Spiering, Menno. *A Cultural History of British Euroscepticism*. London: Palgrave, 2015.
——. 'Engineering Europe: The European Idea in Interbellum Literature, The Case of Pan-ropa', in Menno Spiering and Michael Wintle (eds), *Ideas of Europe since 1914: The Legacy of the First World War* (Palgrave Macmillan, 2002), 177–99.
Spinelli, Altiero, and Ernesto Rossi. *The Ventotene Manifesto*. Ventotene: The Altiero Spinelli Institute for Federalist Studies, 1941.
Staël, Germaine de. *Germany*. Boston, MA: Houghton Mifflin & Company, (1810) 1859.
Starr, William Thomas. *Romain Rolland and a World at War*. Evanston, IL: Northwest University Press, 1956.
Stasiuk, Andrzej. 'Logbuch', in Juri Andruchowytsch and Andrzej Stasiuk, *Mein Europa* (Frankfurt am Main: Suhrkamp, [2000] 2004), 75–145.
Stead, William Thomas. *The United States of Europe on the Eve of the Parliament of Peace*. London: Review of Reviews Office, 1899.
Stehr, Hermann. 'Der Krieg bricht los', *Neue Rundschau* 25(7) (1914), 5–8.
Stein, Karl von. *Freiherr vom Stein: Briefe und amtliche Schriften* II/I. Stuttgart: Kohlhammer, 1959.
Stein, Lorenz von. *Oesterreich und der Frieden*. Vienna: Wilhelm Braumüller, 1856.
Stein, Robert. *Die Vereinigten Staaten von Europa*. Berlin: Wilhelm Süsselrott, 1908.
Stenographischer Bericht über die Verhandlungen der deutschen constituierenden Nationalversammlung II. Frankfurt am Main, 1848–49.
Stern, Jacques. *Mitteleuropa: von Leibniz bis Naumann über List und Frantz, Planck und Lagarde*. Stuttgart: Deutsche Verlagsanstalt, 1917.
Stevenson, David. 'The First World War and European Integration'. *The International History Review* 34(4) (2012), 841–63.
Stirk, Peter M.R. 'Introduction: Crisis and Continuity in Interwar Europe', in Peter M.R. Stirk (ed.), *European Unity in Context: The Interwar Period* (London: Pinter Publishers, 1989), 1–22.
Stolper, Gustav. *Das Mitteleuropäische Wirtschaftsproblem*. Vienna: F. Deiticke, 1917.
——. *This Age of Fable: The Political and Economic World We Live In*. New York: Reynal & Hitchcock, 1941.
——. *Wir und Deutschland*. Vienna: F. Deuticke, 1917.
Stössinger, Felix. 'Kontinentalpolitik als Beginn der Neuzeit'. *Sozialistische Monatshefte*, Bd. 36 (1930), 455–61.
Strahlenberg, Philipp Johann von. *Das nord- und ostliche Theil von Europa und Asia*. Stockholm, 1730.
Stråth, Bo. 'A European Identity: To the Historical Limits of a Concept'. *European Journal of Social Theory* 5(4) (2002), 387–401.
——. *Europe's Utopias of Peace: 1815, 1919, 1951*. London: Bloomsbury, 2016.
——. 'Preface', in Stråth (ed.), *Europe and the Other and Europe as the Other* (Brussels: Peter Lang, 2000), 11–12.
Streit, Clarence Krishman. *Union Now: A Proposal for a Federal Union of the Democracies of the North Atlantic*. London: Harpers and Brothers, 1938.

Stülpnagen, F. von, and J.C. Bär. *Karte von Europa und den Mittelländischen Meer*. Gothia: A. Petermann, 1871.
Suchtelen, Nico van. *Europas forenede stater: forelæsning om et Europæisk statsforbund*. København: V. Pios Boghandel, 1916.
———. *Europe United: A Lecture on the European Federation*. Unknown publisher, 1915.
Sully, Maximilian de Béthune du. *Sully's Grand Design of Henry IV*. London: Sweet & Maxwell, (1640) 1921.
Suttner, Bertha von. *Memoirs of Bertha von Suttner: Records of an Eventful Life II*. Boston, MA: Ginn & Company, 1910.
Svedelius, Vilhelm Erik. *Studier i Sveriges statskunskap*, vol. 1. Uppsala: Schultz, 1875.
Svennungsson, Jayne. 'Christian Europe: Borders and Boundaries of a Mythological Conception', in Susanna Lindberg, Mika Ojakangas and Sergei Prozorov (eds), *Europe beyond Universalism and Particularism* (Houndmills, UK: Palgrave Macmillan, 2014), 120–34.
Swart, Koenraad W. '"Individualism" in the Mid-Nineteenth Century (1826–1860)'. *Journal of the History of Ideas* 23(1) (1962), 77–90.
Swensson, Gunnar S. 'Den parlamentariska diskussionen kring den kommmunala självstyrelsen i Sverige 1817–1862'. Dissertation. Gothenburg: Göteborgs högskola, 1939.
Sziklay, László. 'Die Anfänge des "nationalen Erwachsen", der Aufklärung und der Romantik in Mittel- und Osteuropa', in László Sziklay (ed.), *Aufklärung und Nationen im Osten Europas* (Budapest: Corvina, 1983), 15–49.
Talbot, Édouard. *Europa den Europäern*. Zurich: F. Schultheiss, 1869.
Talmor, Ezra. 'Reflections on the Rise and Development of the Idea of Europe'. *History of European Ideas* 1(1) (1980), 63–66.
Tapa, Eugenio de. *Historia de la civilizacion Española desde la invasion de los Árabes hasta la Época presente*. Madrid: Imprenta de Yenes, 1840.
Tassonyi, Gyula. 'Central European Federation Including Switzerland', in Wagner (ed.), *Toward a New Central Europe: A Symposium on the Problems of the Danubian Nations* (Hamilton, ONT: Hunyadi MMK, 1970), 223–27.
Taylor, Charles. *Sources of the Self*. Cambridge: Cambridge University Press, 1989.
'The First Phase'. *The Times* [London], 2 September 1914, 9. Retrieved 11 September 2017 from *The Times Digital Archive*.
Theiner, Peter. *Sozialer Liberalismus und deutsche Weltpolitik: Friedrich Naumann im wilhelminischen Deutschland (1860–1919)*. Baden-Baden: Nomos Verlagsgesellschaft.
Thompson, Martyn M. 'Ideas of Europe during the French Revolution and Napoleonic Wars'. *Journal of the History of Ideas* 55(1) (1994), 37–58.
Thun, Leo. *Über den gegenwärtigen Stand der böhmischen Literatur und ihre Bedeutung*. Prague: Kronberger u. Řiwnac, 1842.
Tilly, Charles. *Coercion, Capital, and European States, AD 990–1992*. Cambridge: Cambridge University Press, 1992.
Tocqueville, Alexis de. *De la démocratie en Amérique*. Paris: Libraire de C. Gosselin, 1835–1840.
Todorov, Tzvetan. *The Morals of History*. Minneapolis: University of Minnesota Press, 1995.
Tooze, Adam. *The Deluge: The Great War, America and the Remaking of the Global Order, 1916–1931*. New York: Penguin Books, 2014.
Topelius, Zacharias. *Boken om vårt land: Dagbok för lägsta läroverken i Finland*. Helsinki: (no publisher), 1905.
Toynbee, Arnold. *Civilization on Trial*. London: Oxford University Press, 1948.
———. *Nationality and the War*. London: J.M. Dent & Sons, 1915.
———. *The New Europe: Some Essays in Reconstruction*, London: J.M. Dent & Sons, 1915.
'Treaty Establishing the European Economic Community', 1957. Retrieved on 9 July 2020 from https://www.cvce.eu/obj/treaty_establishing_the_european_economic_community_rome_25_march_1957-en-cca6ba28-0bf3-4ce6-8a76-6b0b3252696e.html.

Treitschke, Heinrich. *Politics*. London: Constable and Company, (1897) 1916.
Tronchon, Henri. *La Fortune Intellectuelle de Herder en France. La Préparation*. Paris: F. Rieder et Cie, 1920.
Tuchman, Barbara. *The Proud Tower: A Portrait of the World before the War, 1890–1914*. New York: The Macmillan Company, 1966.
Tyrrell, Alexander. 'Making the Millennium: The Mid-Nineteenth Century Peace Movement'. *The Historical Journal* 21(1) (1978), 75–95.
Ule, Willi. 'Niederschlag und Abfluss in Mitteleuropa', in *Forschungen zur deutschen Landes- und Volkskunde: im Auftrage der Centralkommission für wissenschaftliche Landeskunde von Deutschland*, Bd. 14 (Stuttgart: J. Engelhorn, 1903), 435–516.
Unamuno, Miguel de. 'Some Arbitrary Reflections upon Europeanization', in *Essays and Soliloquies* (New York: Alfred A. Knopf, [1902] 1925), 52–76.
———. 'Spanish Individualism', in *Essays and Soliloquies* (New York: Alfred A. Knopf, [1902] 1925), 48–51.
Urbinati, 'Mazzini and the Making of the Republican Ideology', *Journal of Modern Italian Studies* 17(2): 183–204.
Vajda, Mihaly. 'Was ist jüdisch in Mitteleuropa – wer ist Jude in Mitteleuropa?', in Heino Berg and Peter Burmeister (eds), *Mitteleuropa und die deutsche Frage* (Bremen: Edition Temmen, 1990), 12–20.
Valentin, Hugo. 'Sweden and the Åland Islands'. *The New Europe* 6(71) (1918), 184–88.
Valéry, Paul. 'Crisis of the Mind' [1919], in *History and Politics* (London: Routledge, 1963), 23–36.
———. 'European Man' [1922], in Alex Drace-Francis (ed.), *European Identity: A Historical Reader* (New York: Palgrave Macmillan, 2013), 183–87.
Varsányi, Julius. *Quest for a New Central Europe: A Symposium*. Adelaide: Australian Carpathian Federation, 1976.
Vegesack, Siegfried von. 'Der Frieden in 100 Jahren', in Arthur Brehmer (ed.), *Die Welt in hundert Jahren* (Berlin: Verlagsanstalt Buntdruck, 1910), 48–59.
———. *Der Kampf um die Vermeidung des Weltkrieges Band II*. Zurich: Art. Institut Orell Füssli, 1917.
———. 'Stimmen brausen'. *Zeitschrift Pan-Europa* 2(11–12) (1925), 33–34.
Venet, Christophe, et al. *European Identity through Space: Space Activities and Programmes as a Tool to Invigorate the European Identity*. Vienna: Springer, 2013.
Venning, Mary-Anne. *A Geographical Present: Being Descriptions of the Principal Countries of the World*. New York: William Burgess, 1829.
Verdery, Katherine. *National Ideology under Socialism: Identity and Cultural Politics in Ceausescu's Romania*. Berkeley: University of California Press, 1991.
Verga, Marcello. 'European Civilization and the "Emulation of the Nations": Histories of Europe from the Enlightenment to Guizot'. *History of European Ideas* 34(4) (2008), 353–60.
Vermeiren, Jan. 'Notions of Solidarity and Integration in Times of War: The Idea of Europe, 1914–18'. *European Review of History – Revue européenne d'histoire* 24(6) (2017), 874–88.
———. 'Imperium Europaeum: Rudolf Pannwitz and the German Idea of Europe', in Mark Hewitson and D'Auria Matthew (eds), *Europe in Crisis: Intellectuals and the European Ideas, 1917–1957* (New York: Berghahn Books, 2012), 135–54.
———. *The First World War and German National Identity: The Dual Alliance at War*. Cambridge: Cambridge University Press, 2016.
Vogt, Nicolaus. *System des Gleichgewichts und der Gerechtighkeit*. Frankfurt am Main: Andreschichen Buchhandlung, 1802.
Waechter, Max. 'For United Europe: Not Against US', *The New York Times*, 20 September 1908. Retrieved 5 November 2020 from https://www.nytimes.com/1908/09/20/archives/for-united-europe-not-to-oppose-us-sir-max-waechter-in-berlin-to.html?searchResultPosition=4.

———. 'How to Prevent War: The United States of Europe', *The Glasgow Herald*, 15 February 1914.
Waern-Bugge, Elisabeth. *Grundvalen för världens framtid*. Stockholm: Fredens förlag, 1942.
Wägner, Elin. *Från Seine, Rhen och Ruhr: små historier från Europa*. Stockholm: Albert Bonniers förlag, 1923.
———. 'Hvad säga kvinnorna?' *Idun* 27(43) (1914), 683–84.
———. *Väckarklocka*. Stockhlom: Bonnier, 1941.
Wagner, Francis S. 'Foreword', in Wagner (ed.), *Toward a New Central Europe: A Symposium on the Problems of the Danubian Nations* (Hamilton, ONT: Hunyadi MMK, 1970), XI–XII.
———. 'Introduction to the History of Central Europe', in Wagner (ed.), *Toward a New Central Europe: A Symposium on the Problems of the Danubian Nations* (Hamilton, ONT: Hunyadi MMK, 1970), 1–10.
Walicki, Andrzej. 'Russia, Poland and France in the Paris Lectures of Mickiewicz', in Bengt Jangfeldt et al. (eds), *We and They: National Identity as a Theme in Slavic Cultures* (Copenhagen: Rosenkilde & Bagger, 1984).
———. *The Slavophile Controversy: History of a Conservative Utopia in Nineteenth-Century Russian Thought*. Oxford: Clarendon, 1975.
Walton, Clarence C. 'The Hague "Congress of Europe": A Case Study of Public Opinion'. *The Western Political Quarterly* 12(3) (1959), 738–52.
Ward, Barbara. *The West at Bay*. Allen & Unwin: London, 1948.
Webb, Beatrice, and Sidney Webb. *The Decay of Capitalist Civilisation*. London: George Allen & Unwin, 1923.
Weber, Alfred. *Abshied von der bisherigen Geschichte: Überwindung des Nihilismus*. Bern: Verlag A. Francke AG, 1946.
———. *Farewell to European History, or the Conquest of Nihilism*. New Haven, CT: Yale University Press, 1948.
Webster, Wendy. 'From Nazi Legacy to Cold War: British Perceptions of European Identity, 1945–54', in Menno Spiering and Michael Wintle (eds), *European Identity and the Second World War* (Houndmills, UK: Palgrave Macmillan, 2011), 92–110.
Weidenfeld, Werner. *Europa: Eine Strategie*. Munich: Kösel, 2014.
Weiland, C.F. *Europa*. Weimar: Verlage des geogr. Instituts, 1838.
Weir, Archibald. *The Historical Basis of Modern Europe (1760–1815): An Introductory Study to the General History of Europe in the Nineteenth Century*. London: Swan Sonneschein, 1889.
Wells, H.G. *After Democarcy: Addresses and Papers on the Present World Situation*. London: Watts & Co, 1932.
———. *The New World Order: Whether It Is Attainable, How It Can Be Attained, and What Sort of World a World of Peace Will Have To Be*. London: Secker & Warburg, 1940.
———. *The Salvaging of Civilization*. London: Cassel and Company, 1921.
———. *What Is Coming? A European Forecast*. New York: Macmillan, 1917.
'We Need to Invest in a European Identity'. *Euobserver*, 13 March 2012. Retrieved 11 April 2022 from https://euobserver.com/eu-political/115759.
Werner, Michael, and Benedicte Zimmermann. 'Beyond Comparison: Histoire Croisée and the Challenge of Reflexivity'. *History and Theory* 45(1) (2006), 30–50.
Wettstein, George. *Europas Einigungskrieg: Seine Ursachen und seine Resultate: objektiver Ausblick eines Neutralen*. Zurich: Lohbauer, 1914.
Whyte, A.F. 'The Versailles Mustard Seed'. *The New Europe* 6(72) (1918), 195–96.
Wilde, Oscar. *The Soul of Man under Socialism*. London, (1891) 1990.
———. *Vera or the Nihilists*. London: Methuen & Co., (1882) 1927.
Wilkinson, James D. *The Intellectual Resistance in Europe*. Cambridge, MA: Harvard University Press, 1981.

Wilson, Woodrow. 'The Ideals of Democracy', in Dickinson G. Lowes (ed.), *Liberty, Peace and Justice* (Boston, MA: Houghton Mifflin Company, 1918), 115–23.
Winter, Jay. *Sites of Memory, Sites of Mourning: The Great War in European Cultural History*. Cambridge: Cambridge University Press, 1995.
Wintle, Michael. *The Image of Europe: Visualizing Europe in Cartography and Iconography Throughout the Ages*. Cambridge: Cambridge University Press, 2009.
Wirtén, Per. *Är vi framme snart? Drömmen om Europas förenta stater*. Stockholm: Albert Bonnier, 2017.
Wolf, Julius. *Das Deutsche Reich und der Weltmarkt*. Jena: Gustav Fischer, 1901.
——. 'Europäische Sanierung durch den europäischen Zusammanschluss? Mitteleuropa und Paneuropa'. *Zeitschrift Pan-Europa* 6(4) (1929), 6–11.
——. *Materialien betreffend einer mitteleuropäischen Wirtschaftsverein (Verein zur Förderung der gemeinsamen wirtschaftlichen Interessen der mitteleuropäischen Staaten)*. Berlin: George Reimer, 1903.
Wolf, Larry. *Inventing Eastern Europe: The Map of Civilization on the Mind of the Enlightenment*. Stanford, CA: Stanford University Press, 1994.
Wolff, Elisabetta Cassina. 'Apolitía in Julius Evola as Reaction to Nihilism'. *European Review* 22(2) (2014), 258–73.
Wollstonecraft, Mary. *A Vindication of the Rights of Women*. London: Verso, (1792) 2019.
Woodbridge, William Channing. *A System of Universal Geography: On the Principles of Comparison and Classification*. Hartford, CT: Oliver D. Cooke & Co., 1827.
——. *School Atlas to Accompany Woodbridge's Rudiments of Geography*. Hartford, CT: Oliver D. Cooke & Co., 1829.
Woolf, Stuart. 'The Construction of a European World-View in the Revolutionary-Napoleonic Years', *Past & Present* 137 (1992), 72–101.
Woytinsky, Wladimir. *Die Vereinigten Staaten von Europa*. Berlin: Dietz, 1926.
——. *Tatsachen und Zahlen Europas*. Vienna: Paneuropa Verlag, 1930.
Würtenberg, Thomas. 'Legitimität, Legalität', in *Geschichtliche Grundbegriffe* (Stuttgart: Clett Kotka, 1982), 685–712.
Wyrwa, Ulrich. 'Richard Nikolaus Graf Coudenhove-Kalergi (1894–1972) und die Paneuropa-Bewegung in den zwnziger Jahren'. *Historische Zeitschrift* 283 (2006), 103–22.
Yapp, M.E. 'The Cultural and Political Construction of Europe'. *Past & Present* 137 (1992), 134–55.
Zagajewski, Adam. 'A High Wall'. *Cross Currents: A Yearbook of Central European Culture* 6 (1987), 15–43.
Zeitschrift Pan-Europa, Vienna: Pan-Europa Verlag, 1924–1934.
Zielonka, Jan. *Is the EU Doomed?* Cambridge: Polity Press, 2014.
Zimmern, Alfred. *The New International Outlook*. Buffalo, NY: University of Buffalo, 1926.
Zimmern, Alfred E. *Europe in Convalescence*. London: Mills & Boon, 1922.
Žižek, Slavoj, and Srećko Horvat. *What Does Europe Want? The Union and its Discontents*. London: Istrosbooks, 2013.
Zöllner, Erich. 'Der Österreichbegriff', in Richard G. Plaschka, Gerald Stourzh and Jan Paul Niederkorn (eds), *Was heisst Österreich? Inhalt und Umfang des Österreichsbegriff vom 10. Jahrhunderts bis Heute* (Vienna: Archiv für österreichische Geschichte, 1995), 65–87.
Zweig, Stefan. 'Der europäische Gedanken in seiner historischen Entwicklung', in *Zeit und Welt: Gesammelte Aufsätze unf Vorträge 1904–1904* (Stockholm: Bermann-Fischer Verlag, [1931] 1946), 302–27.
——. *Messages from a Lost World: Europe on the Brink*. London: Pushkin Press, 2016.
——. *The Struggle with the Daemon*. London: Pushkin Press, (1925) 2012.

Index

Abercromby, Helen, 136
activism, 149, 192–93
Adenauer, Konrad, 206, 211, 253, 259
Africa: Asia and, 79, 94, 148; colonialism in, 255–56; Eurafrican project, 198–99; Europe and, 205; racism against, 255; trade with, 31
Agorio, Adolfo, 149
Almqvist, Carl Johan, 100, 305
America. *See* United States
Amery, Leo, 206
Anderson, Perry, 40–41, 191
Andrian-Werburg, Victor von, 69
Angell, Norman, 142, 170, 197
anti-colonialism, 160
anti-modernism, 185
d'Appollonia, Ariane Chebel, 288
Ariosto, Ludivico, 19
aristocracy, 26, 155
Arnold, Karl, 260
Aron, Raymond, 233–73–274, 273
art, 246–47
Asad, Talal, 291
Ash, Timothy Garton, 282
Asia: Africa and, 79, 94, 148; Australia and, 39; colonialism in, 31; Great Britain and, 103n79; history of, 82; Mongols in, 205; Montesquieu on, 80; North America and, 240–41; Russia and, 58–59, 62, 69; Said on, 81; scholarship on, 75n65; society in, 123; Turkey and, 48; United States and, 12, 179; West, 58

Asquith, H.H., 149
Atlee, Clement, 213
atomic science, 229–30, 239, 241
Attila the Hun, 60
Augsburg, Anita, 209
Australia, 39
Austria: as empire, 68; Germany and, 63–67, 134–35, 144, 215; government in, 206; Habsburg Empire and, 151; Hungary and, 59, 70; Prussia and, 22. *See also* Great War
Austria and its Future (Andrian-Werburg), 69
Axis Powers. *See* World War II

Bach, Johann Sebastian, 145
Bakunin, Mikhail, 40
Balibar, Étienne, 46, 290–91
Balmes, Jaime Luciano, 91–92
Baltic states, 59–62, 66–67
barbarism, 307
Barbusse, Henri, 192
Barduzzi, Carlo Enrico, 199

Barraclough, Geoffrey, 271
Barthélemy, Joseph, 217
Bartlett, Robert, 105
Baudrillard, Jean, 290
Bauman, Zygmunt, 291
Beck, Ulrich, 104–5, 301, 304
Beethoven, Ludwig van, 24, 304–5
Belgium, 2–3, 71–72
Belloc, Hilaire, 138, 173
Beloff, Max, 272
Benda, Julien, 2, 10, 179–81, 229–30, 237–38
Benedict XVI (pope), 286
Beneš, Edvard, 174, 206
Benson, Robert Hugh, 39
Bentham, Jeremy, 117
Bergfalk, Pehr Erik, 119
Bergson, Henri, 138
Berlin, Isaiah, 245
Bernal, Martin, 84
Bernanos, Georges, 230
Bismarck, Otto von, 56, 66, 234
Black Athena (Bernal), 84
Blair, Tony, 289–90
Bluntschli, Johann Caspar, 33–34, 40–41, 57
Boehm, Max Hildebert, 168
Bolshevik Revolution, 191, 204
Bonaparte, Napoleon, 1–2, 19–20, 23–24
Bongiovanni, Francesco, 299–300
books, 115–20, 189–95
Brague, Rémi, 285–86
Breakdown (Briffault), 172
Brexit, 302–3
Briand, Aristide, 143, 166, 196–98; government of, 210; Heerfordt and, 203; Herriot and, 206; legacy of, 215, 217, 248; socialism and, 211
Briffault, Robert, 172, 189–90
Bruck, Carl von, 63
Brüggemann, Karl, 121
Brugmans, Hendrik, 250, 260
Buckle, Thomas, 71, 90, 305
Burckhardt, Jacob, 40, 118, 122–23
Burke, Peter, 19, 85
Byzantine Empire, 79–80

Camus, Albert, 176, 217, 249
capitalism, 121–22, 142–43, 150–51

Carnegie Endowment for International Peace, 192–93
Carpenter, Edward, 97–99
cartography. *See* maps
Catholicism, 21, 57, 91–93
Cattani, Paola, 180
Central Europe: borders for, 62–67; communism in, 2; Eastern Europe and, 293, 304; EU and, 275; nationalism in, 11–12, 75n80; politics in, 13; Slavic people in, 63–65, 128n15; Southern Europe and, 9; Soviet Union and, 274–78; World War II and, 218–19
Central Powers, 150, 152, 155–57. *See also* Great War
Ceruti, Mauro, 307
Cerutti, Furio, 282
Chaadayev, Pyotr Yakovlevich, 113
Chakrabarty, Dipesh, 9, 78
Chamberlain, Austen, 166
Charlemagne, 19, 79
China, 123, 199, 207, 231, 240–41, 278–79, 299–300
Chinnéide, Síle Ní, 272
Choice for Europe (Moravcsik), 7
Die Christenheit oder Europa (Novalis), 17–18
Christianity: Catholicism and, 57; citizenship and, 30; culture of, 4, 39, 232; in Enlightenment, 18; in Europe, 17, 91–93, 253, 286; Islam and, 79, 282; in modernity, 204; moral values from, 230, 275; nationalism and, 22, 189–90; Novalis on, 20–21; politics of, 79; Reformation, 55, 57, 91–92, 122, 145, 189; in Russia, 24; in Turkey, 28–29; unity in, 46, 89
Churchill, Winston, 213, 219, 248–51, 255
citizenship, 10–11, 30, 106–10, 118–19, 289–90
civilisation: atomic science for, 239; Chakrabarty on, 78; concepts of, 93–97; crisis of, 171–76; in Europe, 287–88, 299–303; in Great War, 98–99; history of, 89–90, 101n42, 117; militarism and, 141–42; modernity in, 137, 172–75; nationalism and, 88;

Ortega y Gasset on, 232–33; philosophy of, 85–90; revolution and, 97–100
Civilization (Carpenter), 97–98
Civilization of the Renaissance in Italy (Burckhardt), 122–23
Clavin, Patricia, 194–95
Cobden, Richard, 60–61, 81–82, 95–96
cognitive fragmentation, 195
Cold War, 247–48, 276, 284. *See also* Soviet Union
Coleman, Peter, 238
colonialism: in Africa, 255–56; anti-colonialism, 160; in Asia, 31; concepts of, 20; East India Company and, 103n79; by Europe, 54, 143–44, 198; in Latin America, 28; in North America, 79; by Spain, 93
commerce. *See* trade
commercialisation, 138–39
communism, 2, 13, 219, 241–42, 294
Concert of Europe, 34
Congress of Europe, 249–58
Congress of Vienna, 23–27, 37, 126, 153
Congress System, 186, 197
Constant, Victor, 26
Constantinople, 21
cooperation. *See* unity
Coudenhove-Kalergi, Richard von: leadership of, 174–75, 204, 216, 218–19; legacy of, 233, 248–49; on unification, 204–11, 250
Council of Europe, 261–63, 271–72
COVID-19 pandemic, 6
Crémieux, Albert, 192
Crimean War, 94, 96–97, 135
The Criterion (Eliot), 192
Curtis, Lionel, 218
Czech Republic, 55–56, 110, 149, 155, 274–75

Dafoe, Daniel, 50
Dainotto, Robert M., 4, 9, 18, 95
Danilevsky, Nikolaj, 61
D'Appollonia, Ariane Chebel, 3, 5
Darwin, Charles, 71
Dawson, Christopher, 193
Déat, Marcel, 217
Decadent Movement, 177

The Decline and Fall of Europe (Bongiovanni), 299–300
The Decline and Fall of the British Empire (Gibbons), 172
Defoe, Daniel, 115–16
De la démocratie en Amérique (Tocqueville), 117–19
Delaisi, Francis, 171, 217
Delanty, Gerard, 5, 8, 104–5, 288–89, 306
De l'esprit des lois (Montesquieu), 116
Demangeon, Albert, 170–71
Democracy in America (Tocqueville), 30
Denmark, 55, 135
D'Erbigny, Michel, 60
Derrida, Jacques, 281, 283–84, 292
Deutschland (Heine), 115
Diezel, Gustav, 61, 92
diversity, 3, 33–34, 72–73, 234, 236
Dr. Faustus (Mann, T.), 185
Donisthorpe, Wordsworth, 72
Donne, John, 19
Dual Monarchy, 152
Ducci, Annamaria, 200
Du contrat social (Rousseau), 116
Duhamel, Georges, 179
Dumas, Alexandre, 83
Dvornik, Francis, 270
Dykmann, Klaas, 200

Eastern Europe: Central Europe and, 293, 304; history of, 75n65; Middle East and, 235; migration from, 166–67; to Russia, 156; Southern Europe and, 198; Soviet Union in, 281; totalitarianism in, 275; Western Europe and, 1, 11, 57–62, 67
East India Company, 103n79
EC. *See* European Community
Eckardt, Julius, 59
Eco, Umberto, 292, 302
economics, 35, 92–93, 116–18, 176, 195–99, 243, 294
education, 140
Egypt, 81, 84
Einstein, Albert, 140–41, 142
Elbe Navigation Act (1821), 26
Eliade, Mircea, 235
Eliot, T.S., 192, 230, 233
England. *See* Great Britain

Enlightenment, 84–85; Christianity in, 18; concepts after, 72–73; democracy and, 7; philosophy of, 18, 51, 52; religion after, 175; revolution after, 22–23, 53, 55; technology after, 185; trade during, 19
Erasmus, 18–19
d'Estaing, Giscard, 250
Esterházy, Péter, 293
Estonia, 1
Le États Unis d'Europe (journal), 37, 39–40
EU. *See* European Union
eugenics, 84, 216
Eurafrican project, 198–99
Eurocentrism, 80–81, 86, 200, 204, 291
Europa (Briffault), 189–90
Europa und Amerika (Schmidt-Phiseldeck), 27
Europe. *See specific topics*
Europe (Crémieux), 192
Europe (in Theory) (Dainotto), 9
European awareness, 268–69, 304–7
European Centre for Culture in Geneva, 252
European Commission, 236, 302
European Community (EC), 2, 6–7, 11, 13, 253, 260–61, 280–81. *See also* European Union
European Conference of Ministers of Transport, 261
European Conference of Postal and Telecommunications Administrations, 261
European Cultural League, 257
The European Dream (Rifken), 299
European Economic Community, 2, 6–7, 13, 253, 263, 268, 273, 278–79. *See also* European Union
European Free Trade Association, 263
Europeanisation: of community, 104–6; concepts in, 106–10, 167–68; in culture, 115–20, 128n3; modernity and, 110–15; philosophy of, 120–23; standards in, 123–27; after World War II, 248–55
European reason, 181–86
The European Spirit (Jasper), 237
European Union (EU): alliances in, 38; Brexit to, 302–3; Central Europe and, 275; China and, 231; citizenship and, 10–11, 289–90; community with, 3; concepts of, 32, 105, 251–52; culture of, 285–87; EC and, 261, 263, 278–79, 281; goals of, 305–7; history of, 28–29, 227–28; identity and, 299–303; institutionalism from, 8; membership, 293; narratives, 9; nationalism and, 306–7; organisation of, 228–29, 282; philosophy of, 219, 268–69; policy of, 6; politics in, 302; process, 279–80; rhetoric, 235
European Witness (Spender), 237
L'Europe Nouvelle (Louis), 153–57
Evola, Julius, 172–73, 180, 184, 210
Existenzphilosophie, 231

fascism, 172–73, 176, 184, 215, 216–17
Febvre, Lucien, 88
Federalist Movement, 217–18
feminism, 107, 173–74
Ferguson, Adam, 51
Ferrero, Guglielmo, 135–38
Fichte, Johann Gottlieb, 54–55, 121
Finland, 60–61, 97, 161
Fischer, Johann Ludwig, 181–82
Fischer, Joschka, 289
Flammarion, Camille, 39
Flora, Francesco, 230, 232
Foreign Affairs (Angell), 197
Forlenza, Rosario, 229
Forsell, Carl, 114
Forst de Battaglia, Otto, 270
Fourier, Charles, 117
France: Briand and, 196–97; community in, 108–9; Duke of Sully in, 22; as empire, 68; French revolution, 49, 53, 55, 85, 106–8, 154; Germany and, 32–34, 38, 72, 135, 139, 198, 285; Great Britain and, 27, 35, 78, 90, 93–94, 115, 213; hegemony of, 111; leadership from, 19–20; military of, 51; revolution in, 22–24, 49, 53, 55, 85, 106–8, 154; Russia and, 70–71; Spain and, 18–19, 49–50, 59; United States and, 22–23
Franco, Francisco, 176
Franco-Prussian war, 32–33
Frankfurt Parliament, 62–63
Frankfurt School, 172
Franz Ferdinand, 69–70

Frederick II (king), 95
Frederick the Great (king), 22
Freedoms We May Lose (de Rougemont), 237
free trade, 29, 123–24, 126
French Declaration on the Rights of Man and the Citizen, 106–7
French revolution, 49, 53, 55, 85, 106–8, 154
Freud, Sigmund, 178, 277
Fried, Alfred, 35–36, 37–38, 195
Fried, Ferdinand, 172
Fried, István, 277
Fröbel, Julius, 26, 63

Galton, Francis, 84
Ganilh, Charles, 117
de Gasperi, Alcide, 260, 262–63, 272
Geijer, Erik Gustaf, 119
Genghis Khan, 60
geography, 43, 47–48, 102n43
Germany: Austria and, 63–67, 134–35, 144, 215; borders for, 234–35; conflict with, 70–71; culture of, 12, 64; Denmark and, 55; diplomacy with, 143; to Europe, 78; France and, 32–34, 38, 72, 135, 139, 198, 285; Great Britain and, 20, 121, 139; Greece and, 84; Guizot on, 121; Habsburg Empire and, 48, 63–70, 147; hegemony of, 111; imperialism by, 143–48; intellectual approach in, 183, 242; Italy and, 48; language in, 110; leadership of, 36, 48–49, 54–55, 145; migration and, 53, 111–12; Mitteleuropa to, 151–52, 155–56, 163n61, 216; nationalism in, 26, 200–201, 207; Nazis in, 176, 184–85; nihilism in, 239; North Atlantic Treaty Organization and, 262–63; Ottoman Empire and, 47–48; Pan-German League, 55; peace in, 186n3; philosophy in, 87, 98–99; Prussia and, 108, 114–15, 153; religion in, 253; reputation of, 136–38; revolution to, 154; Russia and, 39, 62–63, 96–97, 115, 133, 149; Scandinavia and, 193; socialism in, 196; sovereignty to, 51–52, 218–19; Spain and, 113–14; to spender, 244; United States and, 138; West Germany, 206; after World War II, 252, 256–61. *See also* Great War

Gibbons, Edward, 51, 172
Gilson, Étienne, 253–54
globalization, 289–95
Der Glorreiche Augenblick (Weissenbach), 24
God, 20, 100, 175, 183–84
Goebbels, Joseph, 216
Goethe, Johann Wolfgang von, 121, 140, 175
Gorbachev, Mikhail, 278
government, 105–10, 114, 119–20, 206, 210, 260, 262
Graham, Stephen, 168
Grande, Edgar, 104–5
Great Britain: Asia and, 103n79; borders in, 72; Brexit, 302–3; commercialisation in, 138–39; as empire, 68; Englightenment in, 85; Europe and, 135; France and, 27, 35, 78, 90, 93–94, 115, 213; Germany and, 20, 121, 139; Gibbons on, 172; Habsburg Empire and, 155–56; hegemony of, 111; Ireland and, 161; leadership of, 32–34, 59; Municipal Corporation Act in, 108; Russia and, 143; Salisbury for, 37; self-rule in, 2–3; Sweden and, 114; unification for, 262; United States and, 120–21, 289–90
Great Depression, 176
Great War: civilisation in, 98–99; culture after, 166–68, 186n3; diplomacy after, 168–69; Europe in, 133–39; fascism after, 176, 215; Habsburg Empire before, 68; institutionalism and, 54; modernity after, 184; nationalism and, 1–2, 143–48, 180–81; nationality and, 148–52; politics before, 40; self-determination after, 250; society during, 152–59; sovereignty after, 169–70; to Spain, 140; Treaty of Rome related to, 228; Treaty of Versailles after, 165, 195; unity in, 139–43; Wilson in, 159–62; World War II and, 12, 212
Greece, 18, 27–28, 80, 81, 84, 126
Greenland, 2
Grucza, Monika, 38
Guénon, René, 173, 181
Guglielmo, Ferrero, 10–11

Guizot, François, 89–94, 117, 121, 305
Gusejnova, Dina, 180, 210

Habermas, Jürgen, 281, 288, 291–93, 306
Habsburg Empire: Austria and, 151; collapse of, 191; diplomacy with, 154; Germany and, 48, 63–70, 147; Great Britain and, 155–56; before Great War, 68; imperialism to, 158–59; legacy of, 276–77; Poland and, 149; Spain and, 18–19
Halecki, Oscar, 270–71
Hannan, Daniel, 302
Hansen, Peo, 290
Hardenberg, Friedrich von, 10
Hase, Johann Matthias, 47
Havel, Václav, 274–76, 278
Havlíček, Karel, 65
Hazard, Paul, 50
Healey, Denis, 270
Heer, Friedrich, 271
Heerfordt, C.F., 203
Hegel, Georg Wilhelm Friedrich, 52, 185, 231
hegemony, 111
Heidegger, Martin, 182, 185
Heile, Wilhelm, 174, 203
Heine, Heinrich, 115
Heineman, Dannie, 198
Heller, Agnes, 10, 287–88
Henry IV (king), 22
Herder, Johann Gottfried, 53, 55, 80, 122, 246; influence of, 87–88, 116; legacy of, 63; for unity, 85
heroism, 115–16, 175
Herre, Paul, 216
Herriot, Édouard, 195–96, 206, 249
Hiller, Kurt, 210, 211
Histoire générale de la civilisation en Europe (Guizot), 117
historical determinism, 146–47
The History of Civilization in Europe (Guizot), 89–90
Hitler, Adolf, 180, 184–85, 216, 236, 260
Hobbes, Thomas, 122
Hobhouse, Leonard, 122
Hobsbawm, Eric, 139
Hobson, John, 149–50

Höfken, Gustav, 63–64
Hofmannsthal, Hugo von, 141, 180, 201
Hofwyhl (institute), 96
Horvat, Srećko, 301
Huberman, Bronislaw, 194
Hugo, Victor, 36–37, 125, 209
Huizinga, Johann, 176–78, 180–81
humanism, 55
humanity, 183–84
Hungary, 59, 66, 70, 110, 112, 146–47
Huntington, Samuel P., 47
Husserl, Edmund, 182

Iceland, 79–80, 157
The Idea of Europe (Pagden), 5
Ideen zur Philosophie der Geschichte der Menschheit (Herder), 116
identity, 10–13, 278–83, 289–95, 299–303, 308n31
ideology, 184, 190, 202, 215–17
Ifversen, Jan, 185
Imagining European Unity (Pasture), 5–6
immigration, 3–4
imperialism, 143–50, 158–59
India, 199
individualism, 120–23
institutionalism, 8, 12–13, 54, 96
integration, 13, 255–64
International Committee of Women for Permanent Peace, 149
International Congress of Women in The Hague (1915), 149
internationalism, 150–51, 170
international law, 33, 47
International Peace Bureau, 193
International Postal Union, 124, 126
International Railway Bureau, 126
Inventing Europe (Delanty), 5
Iraq War, 281, 289–90, 292
Ireland, 72, 161
Iron Curtain. *See* Soviet Union
Isambert, Gaston, 35, 40
Islam, 28, 54–55, 79, 81, 95, 282, 305–6
isolationism, 218
Italy: fascism in, 172–73; Germany and, 48; government in, 260, 262; Islam in, 95; politics in, 215; Renaissance, 47, 57, 285; reputation of, 47, 50; Spain and, 21; unification for, 263

Jacobs, Dirk, 290
James, Henry, 83
A Jangada de Pedra (Saramago), 280–81
Japan, 123, 170–71, 199
Jarret, Mark, 25–26
Jaspers, Karl, 184, 230–31, 236–43, 245, 247–48, 265n44, 274
Jews, 277, 285
Joint Peace Council, 193
Joll, James, 127
Josephy, Jo, 252
Jünger, Ernst, 234
jurisdictional independence, 47

Kaiser, Wolfram, 124, 127
Kant, Immanuel, 36–37, 40, 107, 122, 145, 209
Kautsky, Karl, 147–48, 150–51
Key, Ellen, 60
Keynes, John Maynard, 169, 197
Keyserling, Hermann Graf von, 193
Kierkegaard, Søren, 185
Kipling, Rudyard, 85, 137–38
Kireyevsky, Ivan, 112–13
Kiš, Danilo, 276–77
Kiss, Csaba G., 277
Klaus, Václav, 302
Kolb, Annette, 141
Komensky, Jan Amos, 209
Konrád, György, 275–76, 278, 284
Kopp, Vilma, 207
Koslowski, Peter, 285–87
Das kosmopolitische Europa (Beck and Grande), 104–5
Kossuth, Lajos, 64
Kramář, Karel, 155
Krastev, Ivan, 304
Krause, Karl, 23, 31, 33, 36
Kreisky, Bruno, 211
Kristol, Irving, 238
Krzemiński, Adam, 293
Kundera, Milan, 276, 277–78

Lagarde, Paul, 56, 66
language: borders with, 73; culture and, 3, 66–67; diversity, 33–34; in Europe, 55; in Germany, 110; history of, 108–9; in nationalism, 68, 86; Palacký on, 64–65; religion and, 78, 81; unity with, 53–54

Latin America, 28, 278–79
League of Nations, 142, 158–59, 174, 192; Congress System in, 197; failure of, 199–200, 207, 210, 213
Le Goff, Jacques, 284–85, 286
Leibniz, Gottfried, 71
Lemonnier, Charles, 32, 40
Lenk, Timur, 60
Leonard, Mark, 299
Lepsius, Rainer, 290
Leroy-Beaulieu, Anatole, 35, 40
liberty, 57
Lipgens, Walter, 228–29, 273
List, Friedrich, 114–15
Liszt, Franz von, 144–46
Lithuania, 59, 80, 157, 160–61, 167, 208
Locarno Pact (1925), 166, 201
Locke, John, 122
Lorimer, James, 33–34
Louis, Paul, 153–54, 158, 170
Löwith, Karl, 185
Lukács, Georg, 208, 211, 229
Luther, Martin, 145, 189

Mackay, R.W.G., 252
Macmillan, Harold, 249–50
Macpherson, James, 111
Madariaga, Salvador de, 10, 207, 233–43, 245–48, 265n44
Maier, Robert, 290
Mann, Heinrich, 206, 211
Mann, Thomas, 176–78, 183, 185, 206, 212
Mannheim, Karl, 237
maps, 43, 47–48, 66–67, 102n43
Marquand, David, 300
Marsh, David, 300
Marshall Plan, 258–59
Martel, Charles, 79
Martin, Henri, 57, 60
Martineau, Harriet, 30, 82–83
Marvin, F.S., 140
Marx, Karl, 117, 185
Marxism, 172, 182, 214–15
Masaryk, Tomáš, 2, 10, 55–56, 155–57, 218–19, 305
materialism, 243
Mayreder, Rosa, 139, 173–74
Mayrisch, Émile, 195–96, 202

Mazzini, Giuseppe, 26, 32, 40–41, 52–53, 125, 209, 245
Meisel, Hilde, 213–15
Mercator, Gerardus, 47
Mickiewicz, Adam, 111
Middle Ages, 122–23, 284–85
Middle East, 111, 235
Mignolo, Walter, 9
migration, 31, 53, 66, 111–12, 166–67
militarism, 141–42
military, 41, 51, 115, 135–36, 157, 273–74, 276
Mill, John Stuart, 117–18, 178, 242
Miłosz, Czesław, 276
Milward, Alan, 6–7, 229, 301
Mitteleuropa, 62–67, 134–35, 143–48, 151–52, 155–56, 163n61, 207, 216. See also Central Europe
Mitteleuropa (Naumann), 145–47, 305
Mitterand, François, 250
modernity: anti-modernism, 185; Christianity in, 204; in civilisation, 137, 172–75; in Europe, 78, 104, 152–59; European awareness in, 304–7; Europeanisation and, 110–15; after Great War, 184; history and, 179–80, 282–89; philosophy in, 242–43; psychology in, 177–78; trains and, 123–27
Mongols, 112, 205
Monnet, Jean, 213, 253
Monnier, Charles, 32, 38, 40
Monte, Hilda, 213–14
Montesquieu, Charles Louis, 49, 57–58, 80, 116, 247
moral values, 176–81, 230, 275
Moravcsik, Andrew, 7
Moreno, Luis, 301
Morin, Edgar, 10, 279, 307
Morris, William, 98
Mühlstein, Hans, 145, 153
Müller, Guido, 203–4
multiculturalism, 56–57
multilateral cooperation, 106
multinationalism, 70
Municipal Corporation Act, 108
Murray, Alexander, 86
Muschg, Adolf, 292
Mussert, Anton, 216

Mussolini, Benito, 180, 184, 209–10
Myrdal, Alva, 218

Napoleonic Wars, 19–20, 23–27, 36
The Nation (Keynes), 197
nationalism: borders and, 49–52; in Central Europe, 11–12, 75n80; Christianity and, 22, 189–90; civilisation and, 88; communism and, 294; concepts of, 53–57; culture in, 53, 73, 194; diplomacy and, 178–79; EU and, 306–7; in Europe, 39, 236–43; federation and, 31–36; in Germany, 26, 200–201, 207; Great War and, 1–2, 143–48, 180–81; history of, 56; in Hungary, 110; intellectual approach to, 194–95; language in, 68, 86; Mann, T., on, 212; multinationalism, 70; in Napoleonic Wars, 23–24; nationality, 134, 148–52; Palacký for, 69; politics of, 2–3, 139; to Slavic people, 151, 159; sovereignty and, 200; third world, 231; unity and, 3–6, 227–29, 243–48; World War I and, 1–2
National Socialism, 172, 184–85, 202. See also Germany
Native Americans, 82, 93
natural borders, 114–15
Naumann, Friedrich, 135, 145–47, 152, 201, 305
Nazis, 176, 184; concepts from, 216; eugenics to, 216; in Europe, 214, 217; history of, 202; Hitler and, 184–85; Soviet Union and, 284; unification and, 245, 256–57; after World War II, 219
neoliberalism, 306
Netherlands, 36, 72
Neuropa, 216–17
The New Europe (Heerfordt), 203
The New Europe (Louis), 155–57, 159
Newton, Isaac, 71
The New York Times Current History of the European War, 137–38
Nicholas II (tsar), 38
Niethammer, Lutz, 290
Nietzsche, Friedrich, 98–99, 175, 193–94, 201–2, 209
nihilism, 181–86, 229–30, 239, 260
Nitti, Francesco, 172, 196
nobility, 24–25, 59–60

North America, 33, 61, 79, 82, 93, 117–18, 240–41
North Atlantic Treaty Organization, 262–63, 273–74, 278
Northern Europe, 9, 11, 57–62, 114, 120
Novalis, 17–21, 24, 40, 86, 125
Novicow, Jacques, 71, 125

Odijie, Michael, 199
Offe, Claus, 301
Opus 136 (Beethoven), 304–5
Organisation for European Economic Co-operation, 258–59, 262
Orientalism (Said), 81
Ortega y Gasset, José, 2, 10, 113–14, 176–82, 230–34, 242, 274
Oscar II (king), 66
Ottoman Empire, 29, 47–48, 52–53, 81–82, 94–95, 125–26, 135
Owen, Robert, 120–21, 302

pacifism, 144, 179
Pagden, Anthony, 5
Palacký, František, 55, 64–65, 69, 110
pan-Americanism, 35–36
Pan-American Union, 204
Pan-Europa (Pan-European League), 190
pan-Europeanism, 37–38, 191–95, 204–11
Pan-European League, 190, 217
Pan-European Union, 203
Pan-German League, 55
pan-Slavism, 61
Papcke, Sven, 282
Paris Peace Conference (1919), 169
Paris Treaty (1951), 262
Passerini, Luisa, 291, 306
Pasture, Patrick, 5–6
Patel, Kiran Klaus, 261
Patents, Copyrights and Trade Marks Bureau, 126
Patočka, Jan, 11, 179, 182, 274
Pekař, Josef, 151–52
Penn, William, 22, 33, 36
Pfordten, Ludwig von, 63
Philip, André, 255
Philippovich, Eugen von, 145
Pius II (pope), 21
Podebrad, George von, 21
Poland, 148–49, 160–61, 204

political borders, 86–87, 298
political integration, 71–72
'Politics and Conscience' (Havel), 275
Popper, Karl, 277
Portrait of Europe (de Madariaga), 233, 247
Portugal, 89, 204, 278, 280–81
positivism, 183–84
Prettenthaler-Ziegerhofer, Anita, 211
propaganda, 37–38, 101n24, 150–51
Protestants. *See* Christianity
Proudhon, Pierre-Joseph, 40, 117
Prussia, 22, 64, 67, 108, 114–15, 153
Pusta, C.R., 208

Quartara, Marquis Giorgio, 215
Quisling, Vidkun, 216
Qvanten, Emil von, 97

race, 83–85, 101n24, 107
racism, 204–5, 255
Radisch, Iris, 294–95
Ramsen, Marleen, 192
Ranke, Leopold von, 40
Rappard, William E., 176
Rathenau, Walther, 145, 196
rationalism, 55, 111, 181–86, 201–2
Ratzinger, Joseph (pope), 286
Rauschning, Hermann, 184–85, 230
reason, 181–86
recruitment, military, 135–36
reform, 113–14, 145–46
Reformation, 55, 57, 91–92, 122, 145, 189
Reijnen, Carlos, 192
religion, 12, 20, 48, 78–81, 91–93, 100, 175, 253. *See also specific religions*
Renaissance, 47, 57, 285
Renan, Ernest, 32–33
Renner, Karl, 70, 211
Restoration, 120
Rethinking Europe (Rumford and Delanty), 104–5
Retinger, Joseph, 218
Reuter, Gabriele, 140
Revolt of the Masses (Ortega y Gasset), 176–79, 181
The Revolution of Nihilism (Rauschning), 184
de Reynold, Gonzague, 232
Richard, Anne-Isabelle, 181, 255

Rifken, Jeremy, 299
Ritter, Albert, 145
Rivarol, Antoine de, 51
Robertson, William, 51
Robinson Crusoe (Defoe), 115–16, 123
Rohan, Karl Anton, 201–4, 216
Rohrbach, Paul, 137, 147
Rolland, Romain, 141, 192
Romanticism, 53
Rome, 18, 41, 57, 72, 79, 81
Rossi, Ernesto, 217
Roth, Joseph, 166–67
de Rougemont, Denis, 10, 237–45, 247–48, 252, 269–70, 272
Rousseau, Jean-Jacques, 53, 85–86, 111, 116, 122
Rumford, Chris, 104–5
Russell, Bertrand, 250, 254, 265
Russia: Asia and, 58–59, 62, 69; Bolshevik Revolution, 191; Christianity in, 24; Czech Republic and, 55; diplomacy with, 99, 103n90; Eastern Europe to, 156; as empire, 68; Europe and, 205; Finland and, 161; France and, 70–71; Germany and, 39, 62–63, 96–97, 115, 133, 149; Great Britain and, 143; imperialism to, 149; to Martin, 60; Mongols in, 112; Nicholas II, for, 38; Ottoman Empire and, 52–53; Portugal and, 89; Scandinavia to, 60–61; Soviet Union, 10–11, 13; Turkey and, 4, 22, 35, 293; unity to, 60; Western Europe and, 112–13
Russia and Europe (Danilevsky), 61

Said, Edward, 9, 81
Saint-Simon, Henri, 23, 31–32, 36, 38–40, 54, 120
St. Pierre, Abbé, 22, 209
Salisbury, Lord, 37, 70
Salter, Arthur, 213, 253, 254
Saramago, José, 10, 280–81, 293–94
Sartre, Jean-Paul, 234
Saunier, Claire, 251
Savater, Fernando, 292, 300
Scandinavia, 9, 60–61, 193
Scheidler, Karl Hermann, 96
Schenk, Ernest von, 254
Schikele, René, 141
Schiller, Friedrich, 36–37
Schlegel, August Wilhelm, 2, 18, 40, 49, 58
Schlögel, Karl, 105
Schmidt-Phiseldeck, George von, 10, 27–30, 33, 41, 82, 110, 123–25
Schmierer, Joscha, 290
Schmitt, Carl, 201
Schönerer, George, 151
Schot, Johan, 124, 127
Schuchardt, Ottomar, 66
Schulze, Hagen, 284–85, 288
Schuman, Robert, 253, 259, 272
Schweitzer, Albert, 173
science: atomic, 229–30, 239, 241; conflict in, 99–100; in Czech Republic, 110; knowledge from, 90; philosophy and, 71–72, 113–14; race in, 84; scholarship on, 80; scientists, 142–43
scientific rationalism, 201–2
Scotland, 72, 88
Seipel, Ignaz, 70, 152, 206
self-determination, 151–52, 154–61, 165, 250
Senior, Nassau William, 118
Sforza, Carlo, 191–92
Shakespeare, William, 140
Shore, Chris, 290
Simečka, Milan, 277
Simmel, Georg, 121, 179
slavery, 107
Slavic people, 59–61, 63–66, 112–13, 128n15, 146–49, 151, 157–59
Sloterdijk, Peter, 284, 287
Smith, Adam, 116–17, 122
Smith, Anthony D., 285
social contract theory, 116
social democrats, 150–52
socialism, 117–18; Briand and, 211; capitalism and, 121–22, 142–43; in Europe, 249–50; in Europeanisation, 255; in Germany, 196; Marxism and, 182, 214–15; National Socialism, 172, 184–85, 202; philosophy of, 213–14
social reform, 145–46
Society in America (Martineau), 30
sociology, 290
Sombart, Werner, 138–39

Somson, Geert, 195
Sörgel, Herman, 199
South America, 192
Southern Europe, 9, 11, 57–62, 95, 120, 198
Soviet Union: Central Europe and, 274–78; collapse of, 306; communism in, 13, 219; diplomacy with, 261; in Eastern Europe, 281; Eurocentrism and, 204; Europe and, 250, 270, 282–83; Nazis and, 284; North Atlantic Treaty Organization and, 273–74; Stalin for, 237; United States and, 10–11, 240, 263–64
Spaak, Paul-Henri, 256
Spain: Catholicism in, 91–93; colonialism by, 93; France and, 18–19, 49–50, 59; Franco and, 176; Germany and, 113–14; Great War to, 140; Habsburg Empire and, 18–19; Islam in, 54–55; Italy and, 21; Portugal and, 278, 280–81; self-rule in, 2–3
Spann, Othmar, 168–69
Spaventa, Bertrando, 94
Spencer, Herbert, 71–72
Spender, Stephen, 11, 237–44, 247–48
Spengler, Oswald, 62, 210
Spinelli, Altiero, 217, 249–50
The Spirit of Europe, 229–35
Staël, Anne Louis Germaine de, 2, 10, 49, 51–52
Stalin, Joseph, 237, 255
Starobinski, Jean, 229–30
Stasiuk, Andrzej, 293–94
Stead, William Thomas, 124–26
Stehr, Hermann, 136
Stein, Karl von, 109–10
Stein, Lorenz von, 52–53, 58–59, 126
Stevenson, David, 145
Stolper, Gustav, 133, 152
Stråth, Bo, 3, 281, 291
Streit, Clarence K., 213
Stresemann, Gustav, 166, 196, 206
Sully, Duke of, 22
Suttner, Bertha von, 10–11, 37–39, 71
Suzannet, Jean de, 252
Sweden, 1, 60–61, 66, 97, 114, 118–19, 136
Switzerland, 71, 248–49

Talmor, Ezra, 46
tariffs, 171
Tatars, 60, 97
technology, 124, 126, 184–85
telegraphs, 124, 126
Therborn, Göran, 290
third world nationalism, 231
Thomas, Albert, 198–99
Tilly, Charles, 56
Tocqueville, Alexis de, 30, 117–20, 178, 242
Tokarczuk, Olga, 294
Topelius, Zacharias, 60
totalitarianism, 229–30, 241, 275
Toynbee, Arnold, 149, 153–54, 213, 219, 272
trade, 19, 29–31, 41, 95–96, 123–26, 171, 256–57
'The Tragedy of Central Europe' (Kundera), 276
trains, 123–27
Treaty of Rome (1957), 228, 254, 259, 263
Treaty of Utrecht, 24
Treaty of Versailles, 165, 195
Treitschke, Heinrich, 71
Triboulet, Raymond, 254
Turkey, 28–29, 48, 80–82, 126, 286; Constantinople and, 21; Russia and, 4, 22, 35, 293

Unamuno, Miguel de, 121
unification: concepts of, 304; Coudenhove-Kalergi on, 204–11, 250; economics of, 294; for Great Britain, 262; for Italy, 263; Nazis and, 245, 256–57; politics of, 123–27, 269–74. *See also* unity
Union for the Coordination of the Production and Transport of Electricity, 261
United Kingdom. *See* Great Britain
United States: Asia and, 12, 179; China and, 299–300; concepts of, 30; Europe and, 29, 31, 84, 205, 270–71, 292–93; exile from, 26; France and, 22–23; Germany and, 138; Great Britain and, 120–21, 289–90; in Iraq War, 281, 289–90, 292; Japan and, 170–71; Marshall Plan, 258–59; military, 273–74;

revolution in, 28; society in, 82–83; South America and, 192; sovereignty of, 158; Soviet Union and, 10–11, 240, 263–64

unity: borders and, 68–72; in Christianity, 46, 89; concepts of, 5, 11, 46–47; in crisis, 168–71; in culture, 18, 21, 24–25, 42n18; in democracy, 143; diversity and, 3, 72–73; economics in, 35; in Europe, 195–99; in Great War, 139–43; history of, 30, 298–99; integration and, 255–64; with language, 53–54; after Napoleonic Wars, 24–26; nationalism and, 3–6, 227–29, 243–48; for peace, 36–40; politics of, 22–23, 78; to Russia, 60; to Schmidt-Phiseldeck, 110; scholarship on, 207; standards for, 123–27; World War II and, 12, 212–19

The Unity of Europe (Meisel), 214–15

utilitarianism, 243

Valéry, Paul, 171, 175–76, 179–81, 201

Vattimo, Gianni, 281, 292

Ventotene Manifesto, 217

Vermeij-Jonker, Hilda, 251

Vermeiren, Jan, 134

Victors, Beware (Madariaga), 237

Vienna Congress, 23–26, 37

Viênot, Pierre, 202, 204

violence, 44n98, 182–83

Waechter, Max, 142

Die Waffen Nieder (Suttner), 38

Wägner, Elin, 11, 167, 169, 174

Ward, Barbara, 232, 257–59

The Wealth of Nations (Smith, Adam), 116–17

Webb, Beatrice, 173

Webb, Sidney, 173

Weber, Alfred, 256–59

Weber, Max, 172

Weimar Republic, 256–57

Weiss, Louise, 231

Weissenbach, Alois, 24

Wells, H.G., 2, 142, 144, 148–50, 174, 212

West Asia, 58

Western Europe, 1, 9, 11, 57–62, 67, 111–13, 167

West Germany, 206

Westphalian Peace Treaty, 20

Why Europe Will Run the 21st Century (Leonard), 299

Die Wiederkehr Europas (Schulze), 284

Wilde, Oscar, 122, 183

Wilkinson, James D., 217–18

Wilson, Woodrow, 158–62

Wolf, Julius, 207

Wollstonecraft, Mary, 107

women, 107, 141–42, 149, 173–74

Women's International League for Peace, 193

World War I. *See* Great War

World War II: Axis Powers after, 228; Central Europe and, 218–19; culture in, 1; Europe and, 190, 233, 269; Europeanisation after, 248–55; Germany after, 252, 256–61; Great War and, 12, 212; history and, 105, 270–73; identity after, 13; Nazis after, 219; Ortega y Gasset after, 234; scholarship on, 7; unity and, 12, 212–19

Woytinsky, Vladimir, 211

Wyrwa, Ulrich, 210–11

xenophobia, 305–6

Yugoslavia, 159, 281, 294–95

Zambrano, Maria, 182–83

Zielonka, Jan, 300–301

Žižek, Slavoj, 301

Zum ewigen Frieden (Kant), 36

Zweig, Stefan, 139, 193–94

www.ingramcontent.com/pod-product-compliance
Lightning Source LLC
Chambersburg PA
CBHW071331080526
44587CB00017B/2799